M000307823

The Light of Discovery

The Evangelical Theological Society Monograph Series

David W. Baker, Editor

VOLUME 4

Did Jesus Teach Salvation By Works?
The Role of Works in Salvation in the Synoptic Gospels

—Alan P. Stanley

VOLUME 5

Has God Said?
Scripture, the Word of God, and the
Crisis of Theological Authority

—John Douglas Morrison

VOLUME 6

The Light of Discovery:
Studies in Honor of Edwin M. Yamauchi

—John D. Wineland, editor

"In the light of past discoveries one may expect that future archaeological finds will continue to support the biblical traditions against radical reconstructions. Such finds will no doubt further illuminate the background of both the Old Testament and the New, making clear what has been obscure."

—Edwin M. Yamauchi
The Stones and the Scriptures (164–65)

Dr. Yamauchi and several of his doctoral students. Special Session honoring Dr. Edwin Yamauchi at the Annual Meeting of the Near East Archaeological Society, Valley Forge, Pennsylvania, November 2005. From left to right: John DeFelice, John Wineland, Edwin Yamauchi, Carl Smith, Jerry Pattengale, Steve Stannish, Robert Smith, and Adam Chambers.

The Light of Discovery

*Studies in Honor of
Edwin M. Yamauchi*

EDITED BY
JOHN D. WINELAND

Pickwick *Publications*

An imprint of *Wipf and Stock Publishers*
199 West 8th Avenue • Eugene OR 97401

THE LIGHT OF DISCOVERY
Studies in Honor of Edwin M. Yamauchi

The Evangelical Theological Society Monograph Series 6

Copyright © 2007 John D. Wineland. All rights reserved. Except for brief quotations in critical publications or reviews, no part of this book may be reproduced in any manner without prior written permission from the publisher. Write: Permissions, Wipf & Stock, 199 W. 8th Ave., Eugene, OR 97401.

ISBN 10: 1-55635-045-7
ISBN 13: 978-1-55635-045-0

Cataloging-in-Publication data:

The light of discovery : studies in honor of Edwin M. Yamauchi / edited by John D. Wineland.

Eugene, Ore.: Pickwick Publications, 2007
The Evangelical Theological Society Monograph Series 6

xliv + 294 p. ; 23 cm.

ISBN 10: 1-55635-045-7
ISBN 13: 978-1-55635-045-0

1. Church history—Primitive and early church, ca. 30–600. 2. Judaism—History—Post-exilic period 586 B.C.–210 A.D. 3. Gnosticism. 4. Bible—Manuscripts. 5. Van Kampen Collection. 6. Egypt—Religion. I. Yamauchi, Edwin M. II. Wineland, John D. III. Title. IV. Series.

DS56 L75 2007

Manufactured in the U.S.A.

Table of Contents

List of Contributors

Chapter Contributors

Kenneth R. Calvert
  Associate Professor of History
  Hillsdale College, Hillsdale, Michigan

Scott Carroll
  Professor of History
  Cornerstone University, Grand Rapids, Michigan

John F. DeFelice
  Assistant Professor of History
  University of Maine, Presque Isle, Presque Island, Maine

Darlene L. Brooks Hedstrom
  Assistant Professor of History
  Wittenberg University, Springfield, Ohio

Daniel Hoffman
  Associate Professor of History
  Lee University, Cleveland, Tennessee

Lester Ness
  Foreign Affairs Office, Southwest Forestry Institute
  Kunming, Yunnan Province, PR China

Jerry Pattengale
  Assistant Vice President
  Indiana Wesleyan University, Marion Campus

Steven M. Stannish
  Assistant Professor of History
  State University of New York, Potsdam, Potsdam, New York

Carl B. Smith II
  Associate Professor of History and Religion
  Palm Beach Atlantic University, West Palm Beach, Florida

Robert W. Smith
  Professor of Bible
  Roanoke Bible College, Elizabeth City, North Carolina

List of Contributors

Foreword

Paul L. Maier
   The Russell H. Seibert Professor of Ancient History
   Western Michigan University, Kalamazoo, Michigan

Copy Editor

Connie Wineland
   Instructor of English
   Ohio University, Southern Campus

Editor

John D. Wineland
   Professor of History and Archaeology
   Kentucky Christian University, Grayson, Kentucky

Foreword

Paul L. Maier

❄A JAPANESE Buddhist, born in Hawaii, moves to Ohio and becomes an internationally-known historian and one of the most influential Christian scholars of our time. What are the odds? No publisher on earth would buy such a plot, but welcome to the world of Edwin M. Yamauchi!

Beyond all debate, this unique individual is a great gift both to the discipline of history as well as to Christianity itself. Although this volume of essays in his honor was written by those he impacted most— his own doctoral students at Miami University—his vast scholarship has served the cause of historical truth throughout the world.

In our age of specialization, we often bewail the passing of "the Renaissance Man"—the multi-talented individual gifted with a variety of skills—yet here is one of them. "Dr. Y," as his students affectionately call him, has worked with 22 languages, dug archaeologically, taught brilliantly, read voraciously, researched meticulously, and published endlessly. He is a rare combination of professor, author, ancient historian, classicist, biblical scholar, linguist, exegete, archaeologist, and evangelical Christian apologist.

What sets the Yamauchi publications apart, however, is not only their quantity but especially their crucial *quality*. No one in the academic world today can better sniff out sensationalism in place of sense, excesses beyond the evidence, and speculation instead of scholarship. Whatever historical or theological fad might come along—and *so* many have!— one brilliant article by Yamauchi supplies the evidence to skewer any bloated pretensions against the cause of truth. Yet the methodology in these battles in behalf of authentic history were never hot, strident, or vindictive. Rather, through crystal logic and hard, potent evidence, he coolly disposed of errant theories in so genteel a manner that their exponents sometimes praised him without knowing that they had actually been mortally wounded!

One of Ed Yamauchi's greatest contributions was utterly to dismantle the still-popular claim that Christianity drew from antecedent Gnosticism, rather than the factual opposite. Other crucial services of his in the cause of truth include stripping away the caricatures of Christ that have cluttered literature over the past fifty years: Jesus the Passover Plotter, the Mushroom Cultist, the Master Magician, the Happy Husband, the Senescent Savior, the Rustic Redeemer, and so on.

Many are the other targets that have received the full Yamauchi treatment: arbitrary presumptions and dated conclusions from the higher critics, false claims about the relationship of the Dead Sea Scrolls to Christianity, annual parades of misinformation from the so-called Jesus Seminar, pathetic attempts by biblical "minimalists" to deny archaeological evidence supporting Scripture, sloppy historical methodology in general, the excessive Afrocentrism in Martin Bernal's *Black Athena*, and others. In case after case, Dr. Yamauchi demonstrated how unwarranted theory far outran any supporting evidence.

Edwin Yamauchi, however, was by no means an oracle captive to Christian ultra-conservatism or fundamentalism. When it comes to errors, exaggerations, and overstatements from those on the religious right, he has proved himself an equal-opportunity agonist for the truth, opposing, for example, the far-fetched claims and misidentifications of the prophecy specialists, ranging from Hal Lindsey to the *Left Behind* series. Balance, then, was and is a great attribute of Yamauchi scholarship, as Kenneth Calvert will show in his insightful biography on the pages to follow.

Professor Yamauchi, however, was far more than a critic of arbitrary excesses in ancient studies. Our knowledge of the biblical world of antiquity is all the richer for the massive scholarship published in his cavalcade of books and articles listed elsewhere in this volume. As time went on, his interests seemed to verge eastward, culminating in his 578-page book, *Persia and the Bible*. Now the role of Orientalist was added to his many other attainments.

By our very roles as ancient historians, both Dr. Yamauchi and I have had the opportunity to relate biblical documents to their many secular contexts in ancient history, and we've been surprised at how admirably evidence from secular history correlates with material in the Old and New Testaments. This is not always the case, certainly, but with such frequency that our colleagues in secular ancient history seem to have a much higher regard for the reliability of information in the biblical documents than do many critical theologians! This paradox was well noted by the English scholar, Geza Vermes, who styled the latter as "sawing off the very branches on which they are sitting." Across the years, then, I've always found in Yamauchi works a treasure-trove of these correlations, which also serve dramatically to extend our knowledge of the biblical world.

We all have our Yamauchi stories. Mine is one of utter astonishment at the man's production and erudition. Hardly a season went by, it seemed, that I did not receive an inscribed packet of publications from his restless pen. When Ed invited me to contribute several articles to a huge reference work he was editing, I did my best and mailed him the results. In ever so gracious a manner, however, he added some very significant material to the text in each case and supplied more titles to the bibliographies—so meticulous he was with his copious reference tools. Clearly, the man is not simply a scholar: he is instead a scholar's scholar.

His doctoral students will report a man so in love with languages—as well as efficiency—that en route to conquering another new tongue, he regularly brought word cards along to Miami basketball games so that he could thumb through them during half-time! Attending grand opera in Cincinnati, he always eschews any glance at the English translation projected above the stage in order to keep his Italian in fresh trim. Blessed with a very gracious wife in his beloved Kimi, Ed gladly lets her supervise the social activities in his surcharged schedule for which otherwise he might not have spared the time.

Perhaps the best measure of a professor's success is to gauge the worth of his students, particularly the many doctoral candidates Dr. Yamauchi has seen through to their Ph.D.'s. The rest of this book lets readers judge for themselves, and they will not be disappointed. The articles that follow—all of them carefully researched and written in a manner to engage both a professional and lay readership—will testify to their master's prowess in passing on his research secrets so that all might enjoy *The Light of Discovery*. This collection is ambitious in terms of time—from ancient Egypt to Late Antiquity—and wide-ranging in topic—from astrology and Gnosticism to the Van Kampen Collection in Orlando.

Just so. These disciple-historian authors are merely reflecting the universal interests of their master. All of us, then, extend profound admiration and congratulations to a great, world-class scholar on the occasion of his retirement, but with the sure knowledge that we will read much more in the future from one of the most gifted pens of our time.

Preface

✼I RECEIVED an email message in the fall of 2004 announcing that Dr. Yamauchi would complete his full time teaching duties at the end of the 2004-2005 academic year. I knew that this was an end of an era. Edwin Yamauchi attracted many graduate students to Miami University during his teaching career. These students were drawn to Dr. Yamauchi because of his scholarship and faith. He was a demanding mentor, but each of us knew that he wanted us to succeed. This volume is a labor of love by eleven of his Ph.D. students whom he guided, encouraged, and challenged. He was and is our model of how to bring scholarship and faith together.

I first came to know Dr. Yamauchi, as many others have, through his writings. I was working on both a Master of Arts in Ancient Near Eastern Studies, and a Master of Divinity at Cincinnati Christian Seminary. Through the encouragement of Dr. Reuben Bullard, I became keenly interested in ancient history and field archaeology in the Middle East. As I studied, I read Dr. Yamauchi's books *The Stones and Scriptures* and *Archaeology and the Bible*. His books were clear, and yet contained a depth of scholarship and insight that challenged my thinking. When I helped Dr. Bullard plan and lead a study tour to Turkey and Greece in the summer of 1983, Dr. Yamauchi's book *New Testament Cities in Western Asia Minor* was invaluable for me as I prepared the guidebook for our trip. As I studied New Testament history, his book *Harper's World of the New Testament* became a valuable resource. It seemed that in every area which I studied I was enriched by Dr. Yamauchi's insights.

I eventually went to Oxford, Ohio in 1983 to serve as the campus minister at the Christian Student Fellowship while I was still a seminary student. I soon discovered that Dr. Yamauchi taught in the Department of History at Miami University. It then became my dream to study with him. I first met him during a visit to the history department at Miami, and when he learned of my interest in archaeology and the Bible he invited me to travel with him to the Wheaton Archaeology Conference at Wheaton College.

When I became a graduate student at Miami University in 1986, I found that I was not alone in my experience; many students had come to Miami because of Dr. Yamauchi. Most came to study ancient history with him, but others came to study other periods of history as well. All of these students were drawn to Oxford, Ohio by the writings and influence of this one man. As I began my studies at Miami, I remember vividly Dr. Yamauchi calling me into his office in Irvin Hall. I was nervous, and somewhat intimidated. He told me that although the History Department at Miami University only required Ph.D. students to study two foreign languages (both modern), he however, required his ancient history doctoral students to study at least four ancient languages in addition to the History Department language requirement. It became clear to me that students would not be able to cut any corners with Dr. Yamauchi, and in the end we all benefited from his high expectations. Yamauchi students always knew that he wanted us to succeed, but that he would not allow us to bypass any requirements. We knew that he would be demanding, but always fair and encouraging.

After the news of Dr. Yamauchi's upcoming retirement was announced, much discussion began to take place via email. This correspondence reunited several former classmates, while also bringing some of his students together who had never met. My tenure in Oxford was extended because of my work with the campus ministry. Consequently, I have had the opportunity to know many of Dr. Yamauchi's students. During the fall of 2004 I attempted to contact as many of his doctoral students as I could find. I invited them to contribute to a volume to honor our mentor. I contacted Wipf and Stock Publishers, and they graciously agreed to publish the volume. Then I arranged for a special day of papers at the Annual Meeting of the Near East Archaeological Society (NEAS) near Valley Forge, Pennsylvania in November of 2005. NEAS holds its annual meeting with the Evangelical Theological Society (ETS) each year. Dr. Yamauchi is a long time member of both of these organizations, so I knew that he would be in attendance. Seven of his doctoral students, Jerry Pattengale, John DeFelice, Robert W. Smith, Daniel Hoffman, Carl Smith, Steve Stannish, and I, also attended the conference. This was a special time to publicly honor our mentor, and to further pave the way for the publication of this volume.

The variety of essays in this festschrift is a testament to the depth and breadth of Dr. Yamauchi's interests and knowledge that he instilled and inspired in his students. Eleven of his Ph.D. students have contributed to this volume. The chapters deal with topics including Egyptology, Early Church History, Gnosticism, Archaeology, Early Judaism, and the study of the Van Kampen collection of ancient manuscripts.

I must acknowledge the work of the ten contributors, and thank them for their patience and willingness to work with me to make this volume possible. I also need to thank the editors and staff at Wipf and Stock Publishers, especially Jim Tedrick. I must also take this opportunity to thank my wife, Connie Wineland, who served diligently as a copy editor. She has read and reread, corrected and suggested many alterations which have greatly improved the quality of this volume. I would also like to thank Paul Maier, the Russell H. Seibert Professor of Ancient History at Western Michigan University, Kalamazoo, Michigan, for his willingness to write the foreword to this volume.

Finally, this book is dedicated to Dr. Edwin M. Yamauchi who has trained and inspired us, challenged and at times chided us, but who always led us down the path of scholarship and deep faith in Christ. This volume is dedicated to you and your example which each of us keeps at the front of our minds as we teach our students. We hope that you will accept this volume as a modest attempt to honor you, our mentor, our *Doktor Vater*.

John D. Wineland, Editor

The Essence of a Mentor

A Tribute to Dr. Edwin Yamauchi

Jerry Pattengale
Shriver Center, Miami University of Ohio,
May 29, 2005

❀DR. YAMAUCHI,

I stand here today as someone who has survived your driving, but one who has also witnessed your insatiable drive to please God. As someone who has graduated from your demanding courses, but also one whose life course is better for doing so.

Dr. Yamauchi, you have researched many ancient buildings that once cast shadows on their communities.

But my dear mentor, no shadow lasts longer than that of a legend.

You have learned many languages.

But my dear mentor, in every language is a word for humility.

Your books cover a wide range of subjects in numerous translations.

And my dear mentor, at some level they all tie to your life thesis that a first-century carpenter reigns supreme now and forever more.

Dr. Yamauchi, you have lectured in cities throughout this nation.

And my dear mentor, our dear mentor, you saw each one as a city on a hill where your light should shine, and it did so ever brightly from an assortment of public candlesticks for all to see in order that your heavenly Father in Heaven be glorified.

Your life's journey has already taken you many miles.

And my dear mentor, our dear mentor, Grace and Mercy have always been your passengers.

Your daily schedule and to-do lists have filled thousands of computer punched cards.

And our dear mentor, your church has held regular priority among those punched cards.

Dr. Yamauchi, your life's mantra has been to consider the primary sources as your primary starting point.

And our dear mentor, your life's mission is all about a source primary to the very fabric of life, the very thread that ties us to a hope of eternity.

Kimi, precious Kimi, you know this man well. He is MENSA, he is prolific. He is a steward. And I think you'd agree that he's also *sui generic*, or in local Oxford English, a rare bird. A funny man.

I've sat with him at ballgames while he flipped language cards at intermissions and timeouts. I've been in a crowd of 1200 when he shot students in the front row with an upside down laser pen. I've caught a glimpse of his studious mowing patterns.

One humid August day as his assistant we sat in his un-air-conditioned office and he offered me the latest drink, a Cherry Coke. I was rather excited until he reached into his desk drawer for a warm can. And yes, I've seen him laugh deep and long at some of our answers, and in my case, probably looking for a lobotomy scar. He once told a student who forgot the meaning of the Coptic word "Pae-ee" that he could get it if he just thought of the word it sounded like in Akkadian. And I will never forget him telling the Coptic meaning of "ought-oh," "I'm pregnant."

And Kimi, Brian, and Hurako, Dr. Yamauchi constantly taught us the value of critical inquiry, and always with an eye to the maxim in I Cor. 13, that ". . . *now we see through the glass darkly but then we shall see face to face.*" The key is, we do see enough to know the truth.

I can not help thinking someday many years from now that he will indeed stand face to face with his Creator. Imagine with me those first moments when the glass will be removed and he will stand face to face with a Glory that his brilliant but finite mind will understand more fully. Face to face with the love of his life. Face to face with an image that escaped the Jesus Seminar. It will be an ultimate *Veritas Forum*.

He will one day stand **Face to face** with a God he had exhausted himself to understand by design not default.

Face to face with a God he followed from Hawaii to Brandeis and beyond.

Face to face with the obvious thesis of every single lecture and forty years of Sunday School lessons.

Face to face with his daily punch card purpose!

Kimi, one day he will stand face to face with the primary source, and the books on the ping pong table will all make ultimate sense.

Our mentor will stand Face to face with the One who witnessed his silent contribution to a ridiculed Galilean attacked by Gnostics and disinterested Relativists. I can only imagine what joy it must be to have exhausted one's life and energies for the utmost cause, then to come face to face with the reality of truth.

And God will say on that day, "Ed, my dear Ed, well done my good and faithful servant." And I imagine God will pause, look deep into our mentor's eyes, then smile. In 22 languages God will say, "Very well done."

You, my mentor, are a true testimony that it is not one's duration but donation in life that matters. You have been blessed on both accounts.

Our dear mentor, we have been truly blessed.

Dr. Yamauchi, you have inspired us to be whole people, to live wholesome lives for holy causes higher than ourselves.

In whatever language, my toast is to say, "I love you." And our toast, "We love you."

I hesitate to end on a personal note, and now with some nervousness hope it's appropriate. Dr. Yamauchi, I don't believe you know that at 16 I not only had graduated from high school, but was without a home. My dad had long since abandoned his eight children. It was embarrassing, and so I chose not to discuss it. How was I to know that years later when I came to Miami for cognitive development and vocational training, that I'd also find a fatherly mentor who would embrace me for the next 20 years.

Sir, your touch and time are my life's treasures.

I have also learned that Dr. Yamauchi is not a hugger. Dr. Yamauchi, consider yourself hugged.

Abbreviations

AHR	American Historical Review
Arch	Archaeology
BA	Biblical Archaeologist
BAR	Biblical Archaeology Review
BETS	Bulletin of the Evangelical Theological Society
BSac	Bibliotheca Sacra
CSR	Christian Scholar's Review
CT	Christianity Today
FH	Fides et Historia
JAOS	Journal of the American Oriental Society
JASA	Journal of the American Scientific Affiliation
JECS	Journal of Early Christian Studies
JETS	Journal of the Evangelical Theological Studies
JLH	Journal of Library History
NEASB	Near East Archaeological Society Bulletin
SecCent	Second Century
Them	Themelios
TSFB	Theological Students Fellowship Bulletin
TynBul	Tyndale Bulletin
WTJ	Westminster Theological Journal

Publications of Edwin M. Yamauchi

A. Books

1. *Composition and Corroboration in Classical and Biblical Studies.* (An International Library of Philosophy and Theology.) Philadelphia: Presbyterian and Reformed Pub., 1966.

2. *Greece and Babylon: Early Contacts between the Aegean and the Near East.* Baker Studies in Biblical Archaeology. Grand Rapids: Baker, 1967.

3. *Mandaic Incantation Texts.* American Oriental Series. New Haven: American Oriental Society, 1967. Reprinted, Piscataway, NJ: Gorgias Press, 2005.

4. *Gnostic Ethics and Mandaean Origins.* Harvard Theological Studies. Cambridge: Harvard University Press, 1970.

    a. British Edition: London: Oxford University Press, 1970.

    b. Reprint Edition: Piscataway, NJ: Gorgias Press, 2004.

5. *The Stones and the Scriptures.* Evangelical Perspectives. Philadelphia: Lippincott, 1972.

    a. British Edition: London: Inter-Varsity Press, 1973.

    b. Spanish Edition: Las Excavaciones y las Escrituras, tr. Francisco Liévano. El Paso: Casa Bautista, 1977.

    c. Reprint Edition: Grand Rapids: Baker, 1981.

6. *Pre-Christian Gnosticism.* London: Tyndale, 1973.

    a. U.S. Edition: Grand Rapids: Eerdmans, 1973.

    b. Second Edition: Grand Rapids: Baker, 1983.

    c. Reprint Edition: Eugene: Wipf & Stock, 2003.

7. With D. J. Wiseman. *Archaeology and the Bible.* Contemporary Evangelical Perspectives. Grand Rapids: Zondervan, 1979.

    a. British Edition: London/Glasgow: Pickering & Inglis, 1980.

    b. Japanese Edition: *Seisho to Kokogaku.* Tokyo: Inochi no Kotoba, 1985.

8. *The Archaeology of New Testament Cities in Western Asia Minor.* Grand Rapids: Baker, 1980.

    a. British Edition: London: Pickering & Inglis, 1980.

    b. *New Testament Cities in Western Asia Minor.* Grand Rapids: Baker, 1987.

    c. Reprint Edition: Eugene, OR: Wipf & Stock, 2003.

9. *The Scriptures and Archaeology.* Bueermann-Champion Lectures. Portland: Western Conservative Baptist Seminary, 1980.

10. *The World of the First Christians.* Tring: Lion, 1981.

    a. British Paperback Edition: Tring: Lion, 1982.

    b. Canadian Edition: Toronto: Fitzhenry & Whiteside, 1981.

    c. Australian Edition: Sutherland: Albatross, 1981.

    d. U.S. Edition: *Harper's World of the New Testament.* San Francisco: Harper & Row, 1981.

    e. Norwegian Edition: *De Forste Kristnes Verden*, tr. L. Gamlem. Oslo: Lunde, 1981.

    f. Swedish Edition: *De första Kristnas värld*, tr. J. Carlsson. Örebro: Svensk Bokförlaget Libris, 1981.

    g. German Edition: *Die Welt der ersten Christen*, tr. M. Drissen & T. Kriener. Wuppertal: Brockhaus, 1981.

    h. Dutch Edition: *De wereld van de eerste christenen*, tr. L. F. Stolk. The Hague: J. N. Voorhoeve, 1981.

    i. Finnish Edition: *Ensimmäisten kristittyjen masilma*, tr. M. Liljeqvist. Vantaa: Raamatun Tietokirja, 1983.

    j. Italian Edition: *Il mondo dei primi cristiani*, tr. G. Rinaldi. Torino: Claudiana, 1983.

    k. Croatian Edition: *Svijet Prvih Krs ̌c ́ana*, tr. I. Lovrec. Zagreb: Duhovna Stvarnost, 1985.

    l. Spanish Edition: *El mundo de los primeros cristianos*, tr. M. M. Lory. Mexico City: Trillas, 1985.

11. *Foes from the Northern Frontier.* Baker Studies in Biblical Archaeology. Grand Rapids: Baker, 1982. Reprint Edition: Eugene, OR: Wipf & Stock, 2003.

12. Co-edited with Jerry Vardaman. *Christos, Chronos, and Kairos* (Festschrift for Jack Finegan). Winona Lake, IN: Eisenbrauns, 1989.

13. *Persia and the Bible*. Grand Rapids: Baker, 1990; Paperback edition, 1997.

14. With R. Clouse and R. Pierard. *The Two Kingdoms: The Church and Culture throughout the Ages*. Chicago: Moody, 1993.

   a. *The Story of the Church*. Chicago: Moody, 2002.

   b. Portuguese Edition: *Dois Reinas*, tr. S. Klassen. São Paulo, Brazil: Editora Cultura Cristã, 2003.

15. Co-editor with G. Mattingly and A. Hoerth. *Peoples of the Old Testament World*. Grand Rapids: Baker, 1994.

   a. Recognized as one of the two "Best Popular Books on Archaeology," published in 1993–94 by the Biblical Archaeology Review.

   b. British Edition: Cambridge: Lutterworth, 1998.

   c. Paperback Edition: Grand Rapids: Baker, 1998.

16. Editor, *Africa and Africans in Antiquity*. East Lansing: Michigan State University Press, 2001.

17. *Africa and the Bible*. Grand Rapids: Baker, 2004.

   a. Received the *Christianity Today* Book Award for Biblical Studies in 2005.

   b. Paperback edition, 2006.

B. Chapters

1. "The Greek Words in Daniel in the Light of Greek Influence in the Near East." In *New Perspectives on the Old Testament*, ed. J. B. Payne, 170–200. Waco: Word Books, 1970.

2. "Cultic Prostitution—A Case Study in Cultural Diffusion." In *Orient and Occident* (Cyrus H. Gordon Festschrift), ed. H. Hoffner, 213–22. Alter Orient und Altes Testament. Kevelaer: Butzon und Bercker, 1973.

3. "The Archaeological Confirmation of Suspect Elements in the Classical and the Biblical Traditions." In *The Law and the Prophets* (O. T. Allis Festschrift), ed. J. Skilton et al., 54–70. Nutley, NJ: Presbyterian & Reformed Pub., 1974.

4. "Some Alleged Evidences for Pre-Christian Gnosticism." In *New Dimensions in New Testament Studies*, ed. R. N. Longenecker and M. Tenney, 46–70. Grand Rapids: Zondervan, 1975.

5. "Concord, Conflict, and Community." In *Evangelicals and Jews in Conversation on Scripture, Theology, and History*, ed. M. H. Tanenbaum, M. R. Wilson, and A. J. Rudin, 154–96. Grand Rapids: Baker, 1978.

6. "The Apocalypse of Adam, Mithraism and Pre-Christian Gnosticism." In *Études Mithriaques, Textes et Mémoires*, ed. J. Duchesne-Guillemin, 4:537–63. Acta Iranica. Teheran-Liège: Bibliothèque Pahlavi, 1978.

7. "Two Reformers Compared: Solon of Athens and Nehemiah of Jerusalem." In *The Bible World: Essays in Honor of Cyrus H. Gordon*, ed. G. Rendsburg, et al., 269–92. New York: Ktav, 1980.

8. "Jewish Gnosticism? The Prologue of John, Mandaean Parallels, and the Trimorphic Protennoia." In *Studies in Gnosticism and Hellenistic Religions* (Gilles Quispel Festschrift), ed. R. Van Den Broek and M. J. Vermaseren, 467–97. Leiden: Brill, 1981.

9. "Nehemiah, A Model Leader." In *A Spectrum of Thought: Essays in Honor of Dennis F. Kinlaw*, ed. Michael L. Peterson, 171–80. Wilmore, KY: Francis Asbury, 1982.

10. "Ramsay's Views on Archaeology in Asia Minor Reviewed." In *The New Testament Student and His Field*, ed. J. H. Skilton and C. A. Ladley, 27–40. Phillipsburg, NJ: Presbyterian & Reformed Pub., 1982.

11. "Babylon." In *Major Cities of the Biblical World*, ed. R. K. Harrison, 32–48. Nashville: Thomas Nelson, 1985.

12. "Postbiblical Traditions about Ezra and Nehemiah." In *A Tribute to Gleason Archer*, ed. W. Kaiser and R. Youngblood, 167–76. Chicago: Moody, 1986.

13. "Magic or Miracle? Demons, Diseases and Exorcisms." In *The Miracles of Jesus*, ed. D. Wenham and C. Blomberg, 89–183. (Gospel Perspectives VI.) Sheffield: JSOT Press, 1986.

    13a. "Magia o Miracolo? Malattie, Demoni ed Esorcismi," J. Terino, tr. *Studi di Teologia* 11 (1988) 53–144.

14. "Ezra, Nehemiah." In *The Expositor's Bible Commentary*, ed. F. E. Gaebelein, 4:563–771. Grand Rapids: Zondervan, 1988. [A revised edition is forthcoming.]

15. "The Magi Episode." In *Christos, Chronos, and Kairos*, ed. J. Vardaman and E. Yamauchi, 15–39. Winona Lake, IN: Eisenbrauns, 1989.

16. "Archaeology and the Gospels: Discoveries and Publications of the Past Decade (1977–1987)." In *The Gospels Today*, ed. J. H. Skilton, 1–12. Philadelphia: Skilton, 1990.

17. "Persians." In *Peoples of the Old Testament*, ed. A. Hoerth, G. Mattingly and E. Yamauchi, 107–24. Grand Rapids: Baker, 1994.

18. "The Present Status of Old Testament Historiography." In *Faith, Tradition, and History: Old Testament Historiography in Its Near Eastern Context*, ed. D. Baker, J. Hoffmeier, and A. Millard, 1–36. Winona Lake, IN: Eisenbrauns, 1994.

19. "Jesus Outside the New Testament: What Is the Evidence?" In *Jesus Under Fire*, ed. M. J. Wilkins and J. P. Moreland, 207–29. Grand Rapids: Zondervan, 1995.

20. "Gnosticism and Early Christianity." In *Hellenization Revisited*, ed. W. Helleman, 29–61. Lanham, MD: University Press of America, 1994.

21. "The Archaeological Background of Daniel." In *Vital Old Testament Issues*, ed. Roy B. Zuck, 160–70. Grand Rapids: Kregel, 1996.

22. "Cambyses in Egypt." In *"Go to the Land I Will Show You": Studies in Honor of Dwight W. Young*, ed. Joseph Coleson and V. H. Matthews, 371–92.Winona Lake, IN: Eisenbrauns, 1996.

23. "The Issue of Pre-Christian Gnosticism Reviewed in the Light of the Nag Hammadi Texts." In *The Nag Hammadi Library after Fifty Years*, ed. John Turner and Anne McGuire, 72–88. Leiden: Brill, 1997.

24. "Greece and Babylon Revisited." In *To Understand the Scriptures: Essays in Honor of William H. Shea*, ed. in David Merling, 127–35. Berrien Springs, MI: Institute of Archaeology/Horn Archaeological Museum, 1997.

25. "Herodotus—Historian or Liar?" In *Crossing Boundaries and Linking Horizons: Studies in Honor of Michael C. Astour*, ed. G. D. Young, M. W. Chavalas, and R. E. Averbeck, 599–614. Bethesda, MD: CDL, 1997.

26. "Life, Death, and the Afterlife in the Ancient Near East." In *Life in the Face of Death: The Resurrection Message of the New Testament*, ed. by R. N. Longenecker, 21–50. Grand Rapids: Eerdmans, 1998.

27. "An Ancient Historian's View of Christianity." In *Professors Who Believe*, ed. Paul M. Anderson, 192–99. Downers Grove, IL: InterVarsity, 1998.

28. "The Romans and Meroe in Nubia." In *ItaliAfrica: Bridging Continents and Cultures*, ed. Sante Matteo, 38–46. Stony Brook, NY: Forum Italicum, 2001.

29. "The Eastern Jewish Diaspora under the Babylonians." In *Mesopotamia and the Bible*, ed. M. W. Chavalas and K. L. Younger Jr., 356–77. Grand Rapids: Baker Academic, 2002.

30. "Athletics in the Ancient Near East." In *Daily Life in the Ancient Near East*, ed. R. Averbeck, M. Chavalas, and D. Weisberg, 491–500. Bethesda: CDL, 2003.

31. "Exilic and Post-Exilic Period: Current Developments." In *Giving the Sense: Understanding and Using Old Testament Historical Texts* (Eugene H. Merrill Festschrift), ed. D. M. Howard Jr. and M. A. Grisanti, 201–14. Grand Rapids: Kregel, 2003.

32. "Homer and Archaeology: Minimalists and Maximalists in Classical Context." In *The Future of Biblical Archaeology*, ed. J. K. Hoffmeier and A. R. Millard, 69–90. Grand Rapids: Eerdmans, 2004.

33. "Elchasaites, Manichaeans and Mandaeans in the Light of the Cologne Mani Codex." In *Beyond the Jordan: Studies in Honor of W. Harold Mare*, ed. Glenn A. Carnagey Sr., 49–60. Eugene, OR: Wipf & Stock, 2005.

34. "Why the Ethiopian Eunuch Was Not from Ethiopia." In *Interpreting the New Testament Text: An Introduction to the Art and Science of Exegesis* (Harold W. Hoehner Festschrift), ed. B. Fanning and D. Bock. Wheaton: Crossway Books, forthcoming.

35. "Did Persian Zoroastrianism Influence Judaism." In *Illustrated Guide to Biblical Archaeology*, ed. Daniel Block. Nashville: Holman, forthcoming.

36. "Ezra, Nehemiah." In *Zondervan's Illustrated Bible Backgrounds Commentary*, ed. by John Walton. Grand Rapids: Zondervan, forthcoming.

37. "Akhenaten, Moses and Monotheism." In *Egypt and the Bible*, ed. Scott Carroll and Douglas Mohrman. Grand Rapids: Eerdmans, forthcoming.

C. Articles in Reference Works

1. "Descent of Ishtar." In *The Biblical World: A Dictionary of Biblical Archaeology*, edited by C. Pfeiffer, 196–200. Grand Rapids: Baker, 1966.

2. "Culture." In *Dictionary of Christian Ethics*, edited by C. F. H. Henry, 158–59. Grand Rapids: Baker, 1973.

3. "Gnosticism." In *The New International Dictionary of the Christian Church*, edited by J. D. Douglas, 416–18. Grand Rapids: Zondervan, 1974.

4. "Darius the Persian" (425), "Dead Sea Scrolls" (434–42), "Education" (493–97), "Machaerus" (1064), "Nabonidus" (1170–71), "Nebuzaradan" (1191), "Nergal-sharezer" (1198), "Palestine" (1259–73), "Patriarchal Age" (1287–91), "Rabsaris" (1437), "Rezin" (1468), "Solomon, Song of" (1608–10), "Tatnai" (1663), "Theudas" (1699), "Tammuz" (707). In *Wycliffe Bible Encyclopedia*, edited by C. F. Pfeiffer, H. F. Vos, and J. Rea. Chicago: Moody, 1975.

5. "Fertility Cults." In *The Pictorial Encyclopedia of the Bible*, edited by M. C. Tenney, 2:531–532. Grand Rapids: Zondervan, 1974.

6. "Hermetic Literature" (408), "Mandaeism" (563). In *Supplementary Volume, The Interpreter's Dictionary of the Bible*, edited by K. Crim. Nashville: Abingdon, 1976.

7. "The Religion of the Romans" (46–47), "Manichaeans" (48–49), "The Gnostics" (98–100). In *Handbook of Christian History*, edited by T. Dowley. Tring: Lion, 1977; Grand Rapids: Eerdmans, 1977.

8. "Archaeology and the New Testament." In *The Expositor's Bible Commentary*, edited by F. E. Gaebelein, 1:645–69. Grand Rapids: Zondervan, 1979.

9. "Agrapha" (69–71), "Apocryphal Gospels" (181–88), "Archaeology of Palestine and Syria" (270–82). In *The Internatonal Standard Bible Encyclopedia*, vol. I, edited by G. W. Bromiley. Rev. edition; Grand Rapids: Eerdmans, 1979.

10. "Prostitution." In *The Illustrated Bible Dictionary*, edited by N. Hillyer, 3:1289. Leicester: Inter-Varsity, 1980.

11. Forty entries discussing 75 Hebrew words in *Theological Wordbook of the Old Testament*, edited by R. L. Harris, G. L. Archer, and B. K. Waltke, 158, 261, 263–70, 274–76, 282, 284–86, 302–4, 310, 314–21, 332–33, 343–45, 349–51, 381, 401–3, 828–29. Chicago: Moody, 1981.

12. "The Gnostics" (110), "The Mandaeans" (110), "The Manichaeans" (113). In *The World's Religions*, edited by R. P. Beaver et al. Tring: Lion, 1982.

13. "Prostitution." In *New Bible Dictionary*, edited by J. Douglas and N. Hillyer, 988. Rev. edition. Leicester: Inter-Varsity, 1982.

14. "Aramaic" (38–41), "Archaeology in Israel and Jordan Since 1948" (60–66), "Bactria" (87–90), "Chaldea, Chaldeans" (123–25), "Cyrus" (145–46), "Darius" (149–53), "Ecbatana" (167–68), "Ekron" (173), "Etana" (187), "Evil-Merodach" (188), "Habiru" (223–24), "Jebusites" (256–57), "Joppa" (271–73), "Kassites" (276–78), "Marriage" (300–302), "Medes" (304–6), "Nabopolassar" (326–27), "Nebuchadnezzar" (332–34), "Nippur" (339–41), "Oaths" (343–44), "Pasargadae" (354–56), "Patara" (356–57), "Prostitution, Cultic" (369–71), "Qarqar" (375–77), "Qumran New Testament Fragments?" (379–81), "Shinar" (411), "Shishak" (412–13), "Solomon" (419–22), "Susa" (426–30), "Tell Arpachiyah" (438), "Tell Nagila" (442), "Tell Qasile" (442–43), "Tell Sheikh Ahmed el-'Areini" (443), "Tepe Gawra" (446–47), "Tepe Sialk" (447), "Tiglath-Pileser" (451–53), "Ummah" (461), "Urartu" (463–65), "Vultures, Stele of" (469–70), "Zarephath" (483), "Ziusudra" (485). In *The New International Dictionary of Biblical Archaeology*, edited by E. M. Blaiklock and R. K. Harrison. Grand Rapids: Zondervan, 1983.

15. "Jerusalem." In *Young's Bible Dictionary*, edited by G. Douglas Young, 333–40. Wheaton: Tyndale House, 1984.

16. "Notes on Ezra, Nehemiah, Esther." In *The NIV Study Bible*, edited by Kenneth Barker, 670–730. Grand Rapids: Zondervan, 1985.

17. "Logia" (152–54), "Meremoth" (324), "Nabonidus" (468–70), "Obelisk" (577–78), "Palace" (629–32), "Parbar" (662), "Perseus" (775–76), "Pyramid" (1060). In *The International Standard Bible Encyclopedia*, vol. III, edited by G. W. Bromiley. Grand Rapids: Eerdmans, 1986.

18. "Religions of the Biblical World: Persia." In *The International Standard Bible Encyclopedia*, edited by G. W. Bromiley, 4:123–29. Grand Rapids: Eerdmans, 1988.

19. "Gnosticism" (272–74), "History-of-Religions School" (308–9), "Zoroastrianism and Christianity" (735–36). In *New Dictionary of Christian Theology*, edited by S. B. Ferguson and D. F. Wright. Leicester: Inter-Varsity, 1988.

20. "Ignatius of Antioch" (35–38), "Justin Martyr," (39–42). In *Great Leaders of the Christian Church*, edited by J. D. Woodbridge. Chicago: Moody, 1988.

21. "Archaeology." In *Baker Encyclopedia of the Bible*, edited by W. A. Elwell, 1:148–56. Grand Rapids: Baker, 1988.

22. "Jews in the New Testament" (794–95), "Library" (879–91), and "Nineveh" (1024–25). In *Layman's Bible Dictionary*, edited by T. Butler. Nashville: Holman, 1991.

23. "Synagogue." In *Dictionary of Jesus and the Gospels*, edited by J. B. Green, S. McKnight, and I. H. Marshall, 781–84. Downers Grove, IL: InterVarsity, 1992.

24. "Ahasuerus" (1:105), "Assos" (1:503), "Astyages" (1:507–8),"Herodotus" (1:180–81), "Myra" (4:939–40), "Troas" (6:666–67), and "Tyrannos" (6:686). In *The Anchor Bible Dictionary*, edited by D. N. Freedman. Nashville: Abingdon, 1992.

25. "Archaeology and the Bible." In *The Oxford Companion to the Bible*, edited by B. M. Metzger and M. D. Coogan, 46–54. New York: Oxford University, 1993.

26. "Gnosticism" (350–54), "Hellenism" (383–88). In *Dictionary of Paul and His Letters*, edited by G. Hawthorne and R. Martin. Downers Grove, IL: InterVarsity, 1993.

27. "Pergamum Library." In *Encyclopedia of Library History*, edited by W. A. Wiegand and D. G. Davis, 491–92. New York: Garland, 1994.

28. "Nebuchadnezzar" (132–35), "Cyrus" (136–40), "Darius" (455–59), "Xerxes" (702–6). In *Leaders of the World*, vol. I, edited by A. Commire. Waterford, CT: Gale Research, 1994.

29. "Ezra and Nehemiah." In *Zondervan NIV Bible Commentary I: Old Testament*, edited by K. L. Barker and J. Kohlenberger III, 680–725. Grand Rapids: Zondervan, 1994.

30. "yᵉhûdî" (2:415–17), "yḥś" (2:437–39), "Cyrus" (4:493–95). In *New International Dictionary of Old Testament Theology & Exegesis*, edited by Willem A. VanGemeren. Grand Rapids: Zondervan, 1997.

31. "Herodotus" (528–29), "Josephus" (627–28). In *Encyclopedia of Historians and Historical Writing*, edited by Kelly Boyd. London & Chicago: Fitzroy Dearborn, 1999.

32. "Gnosticism" (414–18) and (with B. Chilton), "Synagogues" (1145–53). In *Dictionary of New Testament Backgrounds*, edited by C. A. Evans and S. E. Porter. Downers Grove, IL: InterVarsity, 2000.

33. "Achaemenian Dynasty" (I, 183–85), "Astyages" (I, 306), "Cyaxares" (II, 452), "Kassites" (II, 702–3), "Manichaeanism" (II, 759–60), "Zurvanism" (III, 1171–72). In *Encyclopedia of the Ancient World*, edited by J. Sienkewicz. Pasadena: Salem Press, 2002.

34. "Gnosticism" (406–10), "Synagogues" (1049–52). In *The IVP Dictionary of the New Testament*, edited by D. G. Reid. Downers Grove, IL: InterVarsity, 2004.

35. "Ezra and Nehemiah, Books of." In *Dictionary of the Old Testament: Historical Books*, edited by Bill T. Arnold and H. G. M. Williamson, 284–95. Downers Grove, IL: InterVarsity, 2005.

36. "Josephus." In *New Dictionary of Christian Apologetics*, edited by Campbell Campbell-Jack and Gavin J. McGrath, 373–74. Leicester: InterVarsity, 2006.

37. "World Religions of Ancient History," "Gnosticism." In *A History of World Civilizations from a Christian Perspective*, edited by Jerry Pattengale. Marion, IN: Triangle, forthcoming.

38. "Magic, Sorcery." In *The Encyclopedia of the Historical Jesus*, edited by Criag Evans. London: Routledge, forthcoming.

D. Articles in Journals

1. "Cultic Clues in Canticles?" *BETS* 4 (1961) 80–88.
2. "The Sapiential Septuagint." *BETS* 5 (1962) 109–15.
3. "Qumran and Colosse." *BSac* 121 (1964) 141–52.
4. "Tammuz and the Bible." *Journal of Biblical Literature* 81 (1965) 283–90.
5. "Abraham and Mesopotamia." *The Way* (June, 1965) 1–5.
6. "Joseph in Egypt." *The Way* (Sept., 1965) 28–36.
7. "Aramaic Magic Bowls." *JAOS* 85 (1965) 511–23.
8. "Do the Bible's Critics Use a Double Standard?" *CT* 10 (Nov. 19, 1965) 179–82.

    8a. Reprinted in: *Focus* 2 (1969) 21–27.

9. "The Daily Bread Motif in Antiquity." *WTJ* 28 (1966) 145–56.
10. "The Present Status of Mandaean Studies." *Journal of Near Eastern Studies* 25 (1966) 88–96.

Items:

HPB-Ohio
3860 La Reunion Pkwy.
Dallas, TX 75212
serviceohio@hpb.com

Qty	Title	Locator
1	The Light of Discovery: Studies ...	L01-1-60-003-001-36

Marketplace: AmazonMarketplaceUS
Order Number: 4039030
Ship Method: Standard
Customer Name: Connie Mullins
Order Date: 3/15/2019 11:15:52 AM
Marketplace Order #: 111-3306217-9028247
Email: 9zy3qvzklx52tl3@marketplace.amazon.com

If you have any questions or concerns regarding this order, please contact us at serviceohio@hpb.com

11. "Additional Notes on Tammuz." *Journal of Semitic Studies* 11 (1966) 10–15.

12. "Slaves of God." *BETS* 9 (1966) 31–49.

13. "The Teacher of Righteousness from Qumran and Jesus of Nazareth." *CT* 10 (May 13, 1966) 816–18.

    13a. Translated into Spanish as "Cristo y los Essenios." In *Quién es Cristo hoy?*, ed. J. S. Escobar, 35–48. Buenos Aires: Ediciones Certeza, 1970.

14. "Anthropomorphism in Ancient Religions." *BSac* 125 (1968) 29–44.

15. "A Mandaic Magic Bowl from the Yale Babylonian Collection." *Berytus* 17 (1967) 49–63.

16. "Stones, Scripts, and Scholars." *CT* 13 (Feb. 14, 1969) 432–34, 436–37.

17. "Anthropomorphism in Hellenism and in Judaism." *BSac* 127 (1970) 212–20.

18. "The Gnostics and History." *JETS* 14 (1971) 29–40.

19. "Historical Notes on the Trial and Crucifixion of Jesus Christ." *CT* 15 (Apr. 9, 1971) 6–11.

20. "Historical Notes on the (In)comparable Christ." *CT* 16 (Oct. 22, 1971) 7–11.

    20a. Revised and expanded as a pamphlet: *Jesus, Zoroaster, Buddha, Socrates, Muhammad.* Downers Grove, IL: InterVarsity, 1972.

    20b. Revised and reprinted as: *What's so Special about Jesus?* Richmond, BC: Digory Designs, 1999.

21. "Christianity and Cultural Differences." *CT* 16 (June 23, 1972) 5–8.

    21a. revised and reprinted as: "Go Ye Therefore and Insult All Nations." *Perspective Digest* 1.2 (1996) 14–21.

22. "How the Early Church Responded to Social Problems." *CT* 17 (Nov. 24, 1972) 6–8.

23. "Homer, History, and Archaeology." *NEASB* 3 (1973) 21–42.

24. "Immanuel Velikovsky's Catastrophic History." *JASA* 25 (1973) 134–39.

25. "Easter—Myth, Hallucination, or History?" *CT* 18 (March 15, 1974) 4–7; (March 29, 1974) 12–14, 16.

    25a. reprinted in *Impact* 21 (Feb.–March, 1997)

26. "Greek, Hebrew, Aramaic or Syriac?—A Critique of the Claims of G. M. Lamsa." *BSac* 131 (1974) 320–31.

27. "A Decade and a Half of Archaeology in Israel and in Jordan." *Journal of the American Academy of Religion* 42 (1974) 710–26.

28. "Problems of Radiocarbon Dating and of Cultural Diffusion in Pre History." *JASA* 27 (1975) 25–31.

29. "The Achaemenid Capitals." *NEASB* 8 (1976) 5–81.

30. "Meshech, Tubal, and Company." *JETS* 19 (1976) 239–47.

31. "Look at What They're Digging Up!" *Decision* 18 (Oct., 1977) 4–5.

32. "Critical Comments on the Search for Noah's Ark." *NEASB* 10 (1977) 5–27.

33. "The Greco-Roman World: A Bibliographical and Review Article." *JETS* 20 (1977) 157–64.

34. "The Word from Nag Hammadi." *CT* 13 (Jan. 13, 1978) 19–22.

35. "Is That an Ark on Ararat?" *Eternity* 28 (Feb. 1978) 27–32.

36. "Cultural Aspects of Marriage in the Ancient World." *BSac* 135 (1978) 241–52.

37. "Nehemiah: Master of Business Administration." *His* 39 (Jan. 1979) 8–10.

    37a. Reprinted: *Youth Leader* 36 (1979) 8–9.

    37b. Translated into Chinese: in *Ne Da Ren*, edited P. Chang and E. Poon, 71–76. Hong Kong: Christian Witness Press, 1985.

38. "Tells, Digs, and Buried Treasure." *Evangelical Newsletter* 6.7 (April 6, 1979) 4.

39. "Pre-Christian Gnosticism in the Nag Hammadi Texts?" *Church History* 48 (1979) 129–41.

40. "Documents from Old Testament Times." *WTJ* 41.1 (1978) 1–32.

41. "The Descent of Ishtar, the Fall of Sophia, and the Jewish Roots of Gnosticism." *TynBul* 29 (1978) 140–71.

42–44. "Archaeology and the Scriptures: Archaeology and the Patriarchs, From the Sojourn in Egypt to the United Monarchy, and The Divided Kingdoms." *The Seminary Journal* 25 (1974) 163–84, 185–213, 215–41.

45. "Recent Archaeological Work in the New Testament Cities of Western Anatolia." *NEASB* 13 (1979) 37–116.

46. "The Archaeological Background of Daniel." *BSac* 137.1 (1980) 3–16.

    46a. reprinted in *Vital Old Testament Issues*, edited by Roy B. Zuck, 160–70. Grand Rapids: Kregel, 1996.

47. "The Archaeological Background of Esther." *BSac* 137.2 (1980) 99–117.

48. "The Archaeological Background of Ezra." *BSac* 137.3 (1980) 195–211.

49. "The Reverse Order of Ezra/Nehemiah Reconsidered." *Them* 5.3 (1980) 7–13.

50. "Hermeneutical Issues in the Book of Daniel." *JETS* 23 (1980) 13–21.

51. "Was Nehemiah the Cupbearer a Eunuch?" *Zeitschrift für die alttestamentliche Wissenschaft* 92.1 (1980) 132–42.

52. "The Archaeological Background of Nehemiah." *BSac* 137.4 (1980) 291–309.

53. "Ancient Ecologies and the Biblical Perspective." *JASA* 32.4 (1980) 193–203.

54. "Josephus and the Scriptures." *FH* 13.1 (1980) 42–63.

55. "Josephus: First-Century War Correspondent." *Eternity* 32.4 (Apr. 1980) 35–39.

56. "Daniel and Contacts between the Aegean and the Near East before Alexander." *Evangelical Quarterly* 53.1 (1981) 37–47.

57. "Unearthing Ebla's Ancient Secrets." *CT* 25 (May 8, 1981) 18–21.

58. "The Crucifixion and Docetic Christology." *Concordia Theological Quarterly* 46.1 (1982) 1–20.

59. "The Scythians: Invading Hordes from the Russian Steppes." *BA* 46.2 (1983) 90–99.

60. "Magic in the Biblical World." *TynBul* 34 (1983) 169–200.

61. "The Proofs, Problems and Promises of Biblical Archaeology." *JASA* 36.3 (1984) 129–38.

    61a. reprinted in *The Evangelical Review of Theology* 9.2 (April, 1985) 117–38.

62. "Palaces in the Biblical Word." *NEASB* 23 (1984) 35–67.

63. "Pre-Christian Gnosticism, the New Testament and Nag Hammadi in Recent Debate." *Them* 10.1 (1984) 22–27.

64. "Sociology, Scripture and the Supernatural." *JETS* 27.2 (1984) 169–92.

65. "Obelisks and Pyramids." *NEASB* 24 (1985) 111–15.

66. "History and Hermeneutics." *Evangelical Journal* 5.2 (1987) 55–66.

67. "The Nag Hammadi Library." *JLH* 22 (1987) 425–41.

68. "Erasmus' Contributions to New Testament Scholarship." *FH* 19.3 (1987) 6–24.

69. "Gnosticism: Has Nag-Hammadi Changed Our View?" *Evangel: The British Evangelical Review* 8 (1990) 4–7.

70. "Christians and the Jewish Revolts against Rome." *FH* 23 (1991) 11–30.

71. "Mordecai, the Persepolis Tablets, and the Susa Excavations." *Vetus Testamentum* 42 (1992) 272–75.

72. "The Archaeology of Biblical Africa: Cyrene in Libya." *Archaeology in the Biblical World* 2 (1992) 6–18.

73. Interview with Timothy Jones, "Scrolls Hype." *CT* 37 (Oct. 4, 1993) 28–31.

74. "Metal Sources and Metallurgy in the Biblical World." *Perspectives on Science and Christian Faith* 45 (1993) 252–59.

75. "Hellenistic Bactria and Buddhism." *Humanitas* 18.3 (1995) 5–10.

76. "On the Road with Paul: The Ease and Dangers of Travel in the Ancient World." *Christian History* 14.3 (1995) 16–19.

77. "Cyrus H. Gordon and the Ubiquity of Magic in the Pre-Modern World." *BA* 59 (1996) 51–55.

78. "Afrocentric Biblical Interpretation." *JETS* 39 (1996) 397–409.

79. "Adaptation and Assimilation in Asia." *Stulos Theological Journal* 4.2 (1996) 103–26.

80. "'God and the Shah': Church and State in Sasanid Persia." *FH* 30 (1998) 80–99.

81. "Zarathustras laere og Det Gamle Testamente" [Danish: "Zoroaster's Teaching and the Old Testament"] *Tel* 4 (1999) 8–9.

82. "Martin Bernal's Black Athena Reviewed." *Journal of Ancient Civilizations* 14 (1999) 145–52.

83. "Attitudes Toward the Aged in Antiquity." *NEASB* 45 (200) 1–9.

84. "Mandaic Incantations: Lead Rolls and Magic Bowls." *Aram* 11 & 12 (1999–2000) 253–68.

85. "Banquets in the Biblical World." *Proceedings of the Eastern Great Lakes and Midwest Biblical Society* 22 (2002) 147–57.

86. "The Reconstruction of Jewish Communities during the Persian Empire." *The Journal of the Historical Society* 4 (2004) 1–25.

87. "Homer and Archaeology." *BAR* (forthcoming).

E. Reviews

1. W. Taylour, *The Mycenaeans. JAOS* 85 (1965) 415–18.

2. U. Cassuto, *The Documentary Hypothesis. JAOS* 85 (1965) 582–83.

3. R. Collin, *Evolution. JASA* 17 (1965) 123–24.

4. E. Speiser, *Genesis. JASA* 18 (1966) 57.

5. J. Myers, *I Chronicles and II Chronicles. Eternity* 17 (May, 1966) 44.

6. H. Schonfield, *The Passover Plot. Gordon Review* 10 (1967) 150–60.

   6a. Reprinted in *JASA* 21 (1969) 27–32.

   6b. Reprinted in *Christianity for the Tough-Minded*, ed. J. W. Montgomery, 261–71. Minneapolis: Bethany Fellowship, 1975.

7. C. Glock, *To Comfort and to Challenge. CT* ll (Sept. 15, 1967) 1206.

8. J. Myers, *Invitation to the Old Testament. Eternity* 19 (Jan., 1968) 45.

9. K. Kitchen, *Ancient Orient and Old Testament. JASA* 20 (1968) 94.

10. W. Albright, *Historical Analogy and Early Biblical Tradition. Arch* 22 (1969) 78, 80.

11. D. Kidner, *Genesis. Eternity* 20 (July, 1969) 47–48.

12. J. Bottéro et al., *The Near East. Arch* 22 (1969) 156.

13. E. Sollberger, *The Babylonian Legend of the Flood. Arch* 22 (1969) 156, 159.

14. A. Salonen, *Agricultura Mesopotamica nach sumerisch-akkadischen Quellen. AHR* 74 (1969) 1589.

15. O. Dalton, *The Treasure of the Oxus. JAOS* 90 (1970) 340–43.

16. W. McCullough, *Jewish and Mandaean Incantation Texts. Journal of Near Eastern Studies* 29 (1970) 141–44.

17. J. Finegan, *The Archaeology of the New Testament. CT* 14 (June 5, 1970) 31–32.

18. H. Camping, "The Biblical Calendar of History." *JASA* 22 (1970) 99–101.

19. J. Allegro, *The Sacred Mushroom and the Cross. Eternity* 22 (Nov., 1971) 54–55.

20. D. Freedman & J. Greenfield, edited, *New Directions in Biblical Archaeology. WTJ* 33 (1971) 199–202.

21. R. Longenecker, *The Christology of Early Jewish Christianity. CT* 15 (Aug. 27, 1971) 29.

22. H. Cohn, *The Trial and Death of Jesus. CT* 15 (Sept. 10, 1971) 22–23.

23. J. Isaac, *Jesus and Israel. CT* 15 (Sept. 24, 1971) 32–33.

24. J. Sanders, edited, *Near Eastern Archeology in the Twentieth Century. CT* 16 (Oct. 22, 1971) 26–27.

25. W. Wilson, *The Execution of Jesus.* CSR 1 (1971) 385–89.

26. D. Baly & A. Tushingham, *Atlas of the Biblical World. CT* 16 (March 17, 1972) 17–18.

27. E. Goodenough, *Jewish Symbols in the Greco-Roman Period XIII.* Arch 25 (1972) 318.

28. H. Orlinsky, *Understanding the Bible through History & Archaeology. The Review of Books and Religion* 2 (Jan., 1973) 10.

29. W. LaSor, *The Dead Sea Scrolls and the New Testament. CT* 17 (Sept. 28, 1973) 34–35.

30. "Archaeological Evidence for the Philistines," rev. of E. Hindson, *The Philistines and the Old Testament. WTJ* 35 (1973) 315–23.

31. "Biblical Backgrounds," rev. of J. Lewis, *Historical Backgrounds of Bible History. WTJ* 36 (1973) 82–89.

32. D. Courville, *The Exodus Problem and Its Ramifications. JASA* 25 (1973) 160–61.

33. J. Daniélou, *Gospel Message and Hellenistic Culture. CT* 18 (Apr. 12, 1974) 36, 38–40.

34. "A Secret Gospel of Jesus as 'Magus'?": rev. of M. Smith, *Clement of Alexandria* and *The Secret Gospel.* CSR 4 (1975) 238–51.

35. C. Andresen, *Einführung in die Christliche Archäologie.* AHR 80 (1975) 77–78.

36. "'Chariots' Is Just So Much Humbug," rev. of E. von Däniken, *Chariots of Gods?* and *Gods from Outer Space. Eternity* 25 (Jan., 1974) 34–35.

   36a. Reprinted in *The Christian Reader* 12 (June–Aug., 1974) 11–14.

37. M. Hengel, *Judaism and Hellenism*. *CT* 20 (Dec. 19, 1975) 321–22.

38. M. Avi-Yonah and I. Shatzman, eds., *Illustrated Encyclopedia of the Classical World*. *CT* 20 (June 4, 1976) 36.

39. G. Jeremias et al., eds., *Tradition und Glaube*. *WTJ* 39 (1976) 161–67.

40. E. Havelock, *Origins of Western Literacy*. *JLH* 13 (1978) 66–68.

41. E.-M. Laperrousaz, *Qoumrân: L'établissement Essénien des bords de la Mer Morte*. *AHR* 83 (1978) 135–36.

42. E. Lohse, *The New Testament Environment*. *Them* 4 (1978) 35–36.

43. J. M. Robinson, edited, *The Nag Hammadi Library in English*. *CT* 23 (Oct. 6, 1978) 36–40, 42–43.

44. E. Pagels, *The Gnostic Gospels*. *Eternity* 31 (Sept., 1980) 66–67, 69.

45. M. Magnusson, *Archaeology of the Bible*. *FH* 12 (1980) 150–52.

46. K. Kitchen, *The Bible in Its World*. *CSR* 10 (1980) 80–81.

47. S. Sandmel, *Philo of Alexandria*. *JETS* 23.3 (1980) 264–65.

48. R. Macuch, K. Rudolph & E. Segelberg, *Zur Sprache und Literatur der Mandäer*. *JAOS* 100 (1980) 79–82.

49. R. M. Grant, *Eusebius as Church Historian*. *AHR* 86 (1981) 1079–80.

50. P. Perkins, *The Gnostic Dialogue*. *CSR* 11 (1982) 171.

51. A. J. Heisserer, *Alexander the Great and the Greeks*. *JLH* 17.2 (1982) 193–95.

52. F. Reichmann, *The Sources of Western Literacy: The Middle Eastern Civilizations*. *JLH* 17.4 (1982) 479–81.

53. C. A. Raschke, *The Interruption of Eternity*. *JASA* 35.2 (1983) 111–12.

54. M. J. Gorman, *Abortion and the Early Church*. *Eternity* 34.6 (1983) 37–38.

55. E. P. Sanders, edited, *Jewish and Christian Self-Definition I: The Shaping of Christianity in the Second and Third Centuries*. *JETS* 26.2 (1983) 228–29.

56. E. Yarshater, edited, *The Cambridge History of Iran III: The Seleucid, Parthian and Sasanian Periods*. *AHR* 89 (1984) 1055–56.

57. G. Widengren, edited, *Der Mandäismus*. *JAOS* 105 (1985) 345–46.

58. C. H. Roberts and T. C. Skeat, *The Birth of the Codex*. *JLH* 20.2 (1985) 202–4.

59–60. John G. Gammie, *Daniel*; and W. Sibley Towner, *Daniel*. *TSFB* 9.1 (Sept.–Oct., 1985) 22, 24–25.

61. S. R. F. Price, *Rituals and Power: The Roman Imperial Cult in Asia Minor.* *AHR* 90 (1985) 1173.

62. R. Cameron, edited, *The Other Gospels.* *SecCent* 5.1 (1985–86) 49–51.

63. J. Baldwin, *Esther: An Introduction and Commentary.* *JETS* 28.4 (1985) 491.

64. & 65. R. E. Brown, *Recent Discoveries and the Biblical World*; and G. Báez-Camargo, *Archaeological Commentary on the Bible.* *CSR* 14.4 (1985) 375–78.

66. J. A. Davis, *Wisdom and Spirit.* *TSFB* 10 (Sept.–Oct., 1986) 33.

67. W. H. C. Frend, *The Rise of Christianity.* *CSR* 16.1 (1986) 66–70.

68. S. H. Ali Al-Khalifa and M. Rice, edited, *Bahrain through the Ages: The Archaeology.* *NEASB* 28 (1987) 78–83.

69. L. Bier, *Sarvistan: A Study in Early Iranian Architecture.* *NEASB* 28 (1987) 83–84.

70. P. A. Porter, *Metaphors and Monsters.* *JAOS* 107.3 (1987) 552–53.

71. C. Tuckett, *Nag Hammadi and the Gospel Tradition.* *Them* 13.2 (1988) 64–65.

72. A. K. Bowman, *Egypt after the Pharaohs: 322 BC—AD 642. Libraries & Culture* 23.1 (1988) 83–85.

73. I. Kikawada and A. Quinn, *Before Abraham Was.* *JAOS* 108.2 (1988) 310–11.

74. N. S. Fujita, *A Crack in the Jar.* *BA* 52 (1989) 54–55.

75. J. Harpur, *Great Events of Bible Times.* *BAR* 16.1 (1990) 12.

76. D. Wilber, *Persepolis.* *BA* 53 (1990) 236–37.

77. J. Walvoord, *Armageddon, Oil and the Middle East Crisis.* *CT* 35.5 (1991) 50–51.

78. R. A. Horsley, *Jesus and the Spiral of Violence.* *FH* 23 (1991) 111–13.

79. H. C. Kee, *Knowing the Truth: A Sociological Approach to New Testament Interpretation.* *Them* 17.1 (1991) 31.

80. E. Ferguson, ed., *Encyclopedia of Early Christianity.* *FH* 23 (1991) 80–87.

81. J. Bottéro, *Mesopotamia: Writing, Reasoning, and the Gods.* *NEASB* 37 (1992) 61–62.

82. M. Dandamaev, *A Political History of the Achaemenid Empire. Bibliotheca Orientalis* 49 (1992) 455–56.

83. L. Stadelman, *Love and Politics: A New Commentary on the Song of Songs. NEASB* 38 (1993) 61–62.

84. R. Charron, *Concordance des textes de Nag Hammadi: Le Codex VII. JECS* 2 (1994) 107–9.

85. S. H. Moffett, *A History of Christianity in Asia I: Beginnings to 1500. AHR* 99 (1994) 617.

86. L. H. Schiffman and M. D. Swartz, *Hebrew and Aramaic Incantation Texts from the Cairo Genizah.* In *Critical Review of Books in Religion,* 439–40. Atlanta: Scholars Press, 1994.

87. K. Armstrong, *A History of God. The Historian* 57 (1995) 192–93.

88. L. H. Feldman, *Jew and Gentile in the Ancient World. FH* 26 (1994) 72–74.

89. J. J. Buckley, *The Scroll of Exalted Kingship: Diwan Malkuta cAlaita. JAOS* 115 (1995) 526–27.

90. H.-J. Klimkeit, *Gnosis on the Silk Road. NEASB* 39–40 (1995) 132–33.

91. R. W. Ferrier, *The Arts of Persia. NEASB* 39–40 (1995) 133–35.

92. P. Cherix, *Concordance des Textes de Nag Hammadi, Le Codex VI. JECS* 5 (1997) 120–21.

93. G. L. Kelm and A. Mazar, *Timna: A Biblical City in the Sorek Valley. BAR* 23.6 (1997) 68, 70.

94. B. A. Pearson, edited, *Nag Hammadi Codex VII. JECS* 5 (1997) 587–88.

95. Bruce Kuklick, *Puritans in Babylon: The Ancient Near East and American Intellectual Life. Libraries & Culture* 32.4 (1997) 481–82.

96. P. L. Maier, *A Skeleton in God's Closet. NEASB* 41 (1996) 87–88.

97. R. E. Brown, *The Death of the Messiah. NEASB* 41 (1996) 88–90.

98. Jan Assmann, *Moses the Egyptian: The Memory of Egypt in Western Monotheism. FH* 27 (1997) 103–4.

99. J. J. Collins, *Daniel. JETS* 46 (1998) 124–25.

100. J. Bottero, *Mesopotamia: Writing, Reasoning and the Gods. NEASB* 43 (1998) 66–67.

101. J. Hoffmeier, *Israel in Egypt. Review of Biblical Literature* (May, 2001) web version.

102. E. Stern, *Archaeology of the Bible II: The Assyrian, Babylonian and Persian Periods. Bulletin for Biblical Research* 13 (2003) 297–98.

103. V. P. Long, D. W. Baker, and G. J. Wenham, eds., *Windows into Old Testament History. NEASB* 48 (2003) 65–66.

104. J. F. Bowman, *Ancient Israel and Ancient Greece. JETS* 47 (2004) 153–54.

105. P. Briant, *From Cyrus to Alexander: A History of the Persian Empire. NEASB* 49 (2004) 61–62.

106. J. J. Buckley, *The Mandaeans: Ancient Texts and Modern People. JAOS* 124 (2004) 136–37.

107. F. Rochberg, *The Heavenly Writing: Divination, Horoscopy, and Astronomy in Mesopotamian Culture. The Historian* 68.2 (2006) 398–99.

Edwin M. Yamauchi

Kenneth R. Calvert

❊EDWIN MASAO YAMAUCHI was born in the city of Hilo
on the island of Hawaii in February of 1937. In his youth Edwin's father,
Shokyo, died, leaving his mother, Haruko, to provide for his welfare and
education. Though his father had been a devout Buddhist, Edwin received only a nominal understanding of this Eastern philosophy. In his
early teens he attended an Episcopal boys' school where he obtained an
equally nominal understanding of Christianity. His earliest exposure to
an evangelical faith was through his classmate Richard Lum, who invited
Yamauchi to attend the Kalihi Union Church where a visiting basketball
player from Taylor University was presenting the gospel. In the autumn
of 1952 Theodore Yeh, an Episcopal minister from China, introduced
Edwin to Robert Hambrook, a retired British educator, who encouraged
Yamauchi toward a final Christian commitment.[1]

In his late teens Edwin worked summers on a missionary farm in
Wahiawa on the island of Oahu. Though Yamauchi had little aptitude
for farming, the administrator, Claude Curtis, influenced Edwin's early
faith and understanding of Scripture. Interests in fiction and math were
replaced by a love for Greek and linguistics, which formed the foundation of Yamauchi's scholarship.[2] At Shelton College he polished his abili-
ties while working on a B.A. in Hebrew and Hellenistics. There he held
his first teaching post as an instructor of Greek (1960-61). From 1961 to
1964 Yamauchi swiftly completed his graduate work in Mediterranean
studies at Brandeis University, while honing his linguistic and archeological skills through summer sessions at Brandeis University, the University
of Oklahoma, and Harvard.

In the 1960s biblical studies were dominated by higher criticism.
Few universities offered alternatives, making it difficult for scholars to

---

[1] Edwin M. Yamauchi, interview by author, 6–8 May 1994.

[2] Edwin M. Yamauchi, "Imprisoned in Paradise," *CT* 36.13 (Nov. 9, 1992): 11; by 1994
he had studied twenty-one languages.

1

enter into serious research without accepting Julius Wellhausen's documentary hypothesis and its broad influence. However, Cyrus Gordon of Brandeis University rejected this critical theory that neglected evidence tending to corroborate biblical and classical accounts.[3] A group of evangelicals were drawn to Gordon; Yamauchi emerged as one of the most prolific.

Elements of Yamauchi's earliest scholarly contributions were also influenced by Kimie Honda, whom he married in August 1962. In fact, her studies at Wheaton College on ancient slavery served as a foundation for his first paper at a scholarly conference and an article for the *Bulletin of the Evangelical Theological Society*.[4] This article displays his command of ancient languages and his focus on the historical and cultural settings of the biblical accounts.

The Early Monographs

Yamauchi's first monographs foreshadowed the themes of nearly his entire corpus of work. In 1966 and 1967 he produced two texts dealing with the application of higher-critical analysis to classical and biblical documents. In *Composition and Corroboration in Classical and Biblical Studies* he reviewed critical treatments of Homer and Herodotus as well as of the texts of Genesis and Daniel.[5] He questioned why classicists, in light of the evidence, had retreated from extreme critical methodology while biblical scholars stubbornly retained theories not corroborated

[3] Cyrus H. Gordon, *Ugaritic Literature* (Rome: Pontificium Institutum Biblicum, 1949); idem, "Higher Critics and Forbidden Fruit," *CT* 4.4 (Nov. 23, 1959): 3–6; idem, *The Common Background of Greek and Hebrew Civilizations* (New York: Norton, 1965); idem, *The Ancient Near East* (New York: Norton, 1965). Gordon proposed deciphering Linear A as a Northwest Semitic dialect; see "Notes on Minoan Linear A," *Antiquity* 31 (1957): 124–30; "Toward a Grammar of Minoan," *Orientalia* 32 (1963): 292–97; "The Decipherment of Minoan," *Natural History* 72 (Nov. 1963): 22–31.

[4] Edwin M. Yamauchi, "Slaves of God," *BETS* 9.1 (1966): 31–49 (esp. n. 41). Yamauchi regards Kimie, who earned a second degree from Columbia University, the most important influence on his faith. Their two children are Brian (b. 1966) and Gail (b. 1970).

[5] Edwin M. Yamauchi, *Composition and Corroboration in Classical and Biblical Studies* (Philadelphia: Presbyterian and Reformed, 1966).

by the data. His second monograph, *Greece and Babylon: Early Contacts Between the Aegean and the Near East,* focused primarily on the Book of Daniel.[6] Whereas S. R. Driver had asserted that the content and a few Greek words found in Daniel "demanded" a Hellenistic dating (c. 165 BC),[7] Yamauchi argued that Akkadian prototypes of the apocalyptic element in Daniel, etymological considerations, and, above all, the physical evidence of pre-Hellenistic contacts between the Aegean and the Near East all support an early date for this biblical text (sixth century BC). He postulated that the few Greek influences found in Daniel are better explained by centuries of cultural interaction than by the Hellenistic influx of Alexander and the Diadochoi (the lieutenants who succeeded him and split up his empire). These two works quickly placed Yamauchi among a number of evangelical scholars specifically questioning higher-critical theory.[8]

In 1967 Yamauchi published his dissertation, *Mandaic Incantation Texts.*[9] In 1970 he produced *Gnostic Ethics and Mandaean Origins.*[10] These two works marked his entrance into the field of Gnostic stud-

---

[6] Edwin M. Yamauchi, *Greece and Babylon: Early Contacts Between the Aegean and the Near East* (Grand Rapids: Baker, 1967); see also Bernard Goldman, review of *Greece and Babylon,* by Edwin M. Yamauchi, *Classical World* 61 (Jan. 1968): 181.

[7] S. R. Driver, *An Introduction to the Literature of the Old Testament* (New York: Meridian, 1956 reprint) 508; cf. Edwin M. Yamauchi, "The Greek Words in Daniel in the Light of Greek Influence in the Near East," in *New Perspectives on the Old Testament,* ed. J. Barton Payne (Waco: Word, 1970) 170–200.

[8] E.g., Kenneth A. Kitchen, *Ancient Orient and Old Testament* (Chicago: InterVarsity, 1966); see also Edwin M. Yamauchi, review of *Ancient Orient and Old Testament,* by Kenneth A. Kitchen, *Journal of the American Scientific Affiliation* 20 (1968): 94.

[9] Edwin M. Yamauchi, *Mandaic Incantation Texts,* American Oriental Series 49 (New Haven: American Oriental Society, 1967); see also Morton Smith, review of *Mandaic Incantation Texts,* by Edwin M. Yamauchi, *American Journal of Archaeology* 73 (Jan. 1969): 95–97; Edwin M. Yamauchi, "Aramaic Magic Bowls," *Journal of the American Oriental Society* 85 (1965): 511–23; idem, "A Mandaic Magic Bowl from the Yale Babylonian Collection," *Berytus* 17 (1967): 49–63.

[10] Edwin M. Yamauchi, *Gnostic Ethics and Mandaean Origins* (Cambridge: Harvard University Press, 1970) esp. 53–93; see also Kurt Rudolph, review of *Gnostic Ethics and Mandaean Origins,* by Edwin M. Yamauchi, *Theologische Literaturzeitung* 97 (Oct. 1972): 733–38.

ies. Here again Yamauchi brought physical evidence to bear on critical theory. The German scholars Richard Reitzenstein, Rudolf Bultmann, and Kurt Rudolph had used the modern Mandaean Gnostics of Iraq and Iran as evidence that crucial elements of ancient Christian doctrine were rooted in a pre-Christian Gnosticism.[11] Yamauchi's treatments of the data concluded that the Mandaean sect was a synthesis of a Mesopotamian cultic tradition and Gnostic teaching (it is possible that they were Jewish-Christian Gnostic Elkesaites). Central to this discussion was his dating of the evidence. The earliest he could date Mandaeism was the second century AD, much too late to be useful in source studies of the Gospel of John (contra Bultmann). Robert Grant of the University of Chicago wrote that Yamauchi's "restraint in an area where hypotheses have often overshadowed the evidence is highly welcome."[12]

By 1969, in addition to his monographs, Yamauchi had produced a number of scholarly and popular articles. His work was respected by colleagues within and outside of evangelicalism. However, this did not earn him due advancement. Denied tenure by Rutgers University, where he had been an assistant professor of history since 1964, he was hired by Miami University (Ohio) in 1969 and promoted to full professor in 1973.

In Oxford, Ohio, Yamauchi greatly influenced local evangelicals. Together with Bill Wilson he helped establish the Oxford Bible Fellowship, an active church with a large campus ministry. He also served as advisor for InterVarsity Christian Fellowship, and as coordinator for a group of faculty, graduate students, and staff members. He frequently gave public lectures on topics like "Easter—Myth, Hallucination, or

[11] Richard Reitzenstein, *Die hellenistischen Mysterienreligionen* (Leipzig: Teubner, 1910); Rudolf Bultmann, *Das Evangelium des Johannes* (Göttingen: Vandenhoeck & Ruprecht, 1964); Kurt Rudolph, *Die Mandäer,* 2 vols. (Göttingen: Vandenhoeck & Ruprecht, 1960–61).

[12] Robert Grant, review of *Gnostic Ethics* and *Mandaean Origins,* by Edwin M. Yamauchi, *Journal of Biblical Literature* 91 (1972): 281; see also George MacRae, review of *Gnostic Ethics and Mandaean Origins,* by Edwin M. Yamauchi, *Theological Studies* 32 (1971): 730: "It is important to have a position like this so clearly argued at a time when the hypothesis of a pre-Christian Western origin of Mandaeism risks becoming a dogma of the history of religions."

History?"[13] Such work earned him the admiration and sometimes the scorn of the university community. More important was his influence on Miami students who rose to positions of evangelical leadership, including Michael Maudlin, Managing Editor of *Christianity Today*, and Dorothy Chappell, Dean of the Faculty at Gordon College.[14]

In 1972 Yamauchi published *The Stones and the Scriptures: An Introduction to Biblical Archaeology*, outlining his convictions that archaeology produces confirmation as well as difficulties for the biblical texts.[15] He warns against fundamentalist abuses of archaeology, but at the same time emphasizes its strengths, which were sufficient to bring about William F. Albright's shift from a critical position to acceptance of biblical authenticity and William Ramsay's dramatic affirmation of Luke's accuracy on the basis of archeological data from Asia Minor.[16] In this work Yamauchi affirms that, though the evidence is often limited, an accurate analysis, including the three spheres of archaeological material, inscriptions, and tradition, will produce a better understanding of the religious and cultural environments of the Hebrews and early Christians.[17]

The central theme of The *Stones and the Scriptures* is a critique of higher-critical (literary or source) theory in contrast to lower (textual) criticism. Here Yamauchi affirms the values of limited critical techniques in ascertaining the text and background of the Bible, but refuses to accept approaches that include literary analysis unsupported by the evidence. He sternly warns against theories that argue from silence. He criticizes the Tubingen school and the theories of religious evolution affirmed by

[13] Edwin M. Yamauchi, "Easter—Myth, Hallucination, or History?" *CT* 18.12 (March 15, 1974): 4–7; 18.13 (March 29, 1974): 12–14, 16.

[14] Edwin M. Yamauchi, "God's Work at Miami U," *CT* 37.7 (June 21,1993):13.

[15] Edwin M. Yamauchi, *The Stones and the Scriptures: An Introduction to Biblical Archaeology* (Philadelphia: Lippincott, 1972); see also idem, "The Archaeological Confirmation of Suspect Elements in the Classical and the Biblical Traditions," in *The Law and the Prophets*, ed. John H. Skilton (Nutley, NJ: Presbyterian and Reformed, 1974) 54–70.

[16] Yamauchi, *Stones*, 24–25, 95–96.

[17] Ibid., 20–22, 25–26, 158–65.

the history-of-religions school.[18] For Yamauchi, the presupposition that the biblical text is always inaccurate causes essential errors. He suggests that no classicist, no Orientalist, and no Egyptologist would approach a text the way in which biblical scholars handle their data.[19]

The Major Work on Gnosticism

Yamauchi's most important work, *Pre-Christian Gnosticism: A Survey of the Proposed Evidences*, appeared in 1973.[20] The central question addressed in this monograph is whether Gnostic systems existed prior to and gave Christianity its "redeemer myth" (among other elements), as claimed by Reitzenstein and Bultmann, or whether proto-Gnostic components were drawn together by Christians and Jews into full-fledged Gnostic systems after the first century.[21] A related question is whether non-Christian Gnostic evidence necessarily points to a pre-Christian Gnostic presence. In opposition to scholarly orthodoxy, Yamauchi rejects the notion of a pre-Christian Gnosticism.[22]

The inability of scholars to define the word Gnostic is among Yamauchi's many points of contention.[23] More important is the dating of

[18] Yamauchi was influenced by Carsten Colpe, *Die religionsgeschichtliche Schule: Darstellung und Kritik ihres Bildes vom gnostischen Erlösermythus* (Göttingen: Vandenhoeck & Ruprecht, 1961); see also Edwin M. Yamauchi, "History-of-Religions School," in *New Dictionary of Theology*, ed. Sinclair B. Ferguson et al. (Downers Grove, IL: InterVarsity, 1988) 308–9.

[19] Yamauchi, *Stones*, 27–31, 92–97; idem, *Composition*, 32–37; see also Martha M. Wilson, review of *The Stones and the Scriptures*, by Edwin M. Yamauchi, *Library Journal* 97 (Sept. 1972): 27–42.

[20] Edwin M. Yamauchi, *Pre-Christian Gnosticism: A Survey of the Proposed Evidences* (Grand Rapids: Eerdmans, 1973; 2d ed., Grand Rapids: Baker, 1983); see also Edwin M. Yamauchi, "Some Alleged Evidences for Pre-Christian Gnosticism," in *New Dimensions in New Testament Study*, ed. Richard N. Longenecker and Merrill C. Tenney (Grand Rapids: Zondervan, 1974) 46–70.

[21] Yamauchi, *Pre-Christian Gnosticism*, 163–70.

[22] Ibid., 13–28.

[23] Ibid., 18. Of particular import was the Messina conference, "The Origins of Gnosticism," in 1966; see George MacRae, "Gnosis in Messina," *Catholic Biblical Quarterly* 28 (1966): 332. Even major proponents were frustrated; see James M. Robinson and Helmut

Gnosticism. All definitive data concerning Christian and non-Christian Gnostic systems come from the second to eighth centuries AD. For scholars to establish a pre-Christian Gnosticism, they have to extrapolate backwards from post-first-century-AD evidence. Among the data Yamauchi addresses are Patristic sources, hermetic literature, Syriac evidence, Coptic (Nag Hammadi) evidence, the Mandaic data, and Judaic sources, as well as his study of Manichaeism.[24] In each case Yamauchi reviews various theories and the failure to discover definite evidence of any pre-Christian Gnostic systems.[25]

First-century sources support Yamauchi's position. The New Testament (particularly the Johannine literature) and apocryphal texts certainly include Gnostic tendencies, but by no means point to a Gnostic system.[26] The Dead Sea Scrolls also come up for discussion, for they seem to teach a gnostic-like cosmological dualism (light vs. dark). Further, the baptismal elements found at Qumran have been seen as Gnostic influences on John the Baptist and early Christianity. Yamauchi points out, however, that Gnostic thought was manifestly anti-Jewish, including a non-Judaic dualism. In addition, Gnostic systems give evidence of only a limited knowledge of the Hebrew Scriptures (mainly Genesis). Consequently, whatever Gnostic elements the Dead Sea Scrolls and, indeed, any of the first-century evidence contain, are only a small part of the great variety of proto-Gnostic components found throughout the Mediterranean milieu from which Gnostic systems arose. So then, the Scrolls, while illuminating ancient Christianity, in no way reflect a pre-Christian Gnostic system at Qumran.[27] Yamauchi concludes by questioning the misuse of data and the generally poor methodology of his fellow scholars.[28]

Koeste, *Trajectories through Early Christianity* (Philadelphia: Fortress, 1971) 115–16.

[24] See also Edwin M. Yamauchi, "Jewish Gnosticism? The Prologue of John, Mandaean Parallels, and the Trimorphic Protennoia," in *Studies in Gnosticism and Hellenistic Religions*, ed. R. van den Broek and M. J. Vermaseren (Leiden: Brill, 1981) 467–97.

[25] Yamauchi, *Pre-Christian Gnosticism*, 56–142.

[26] Ibid., 29–55.

[27] Ibid., 152–56.

[28] Ibid., 151–62, 184–86.

Reviews of Pre-Christian Gnosticism were positive, affirming the critique of both general theory and methodology. Elaine Pagels stated that Yamauchi "has cleared the way for reevaluation of the basic issue, the relation of Gnosticism and NT Christianity. Whoever takes up this issue should find in his book an incisive account of the history of scholarship and a challenge to rethink critically one's own approach to the sources."[29] Of course, no paradigm shift occurred. So in 1983 Yamauchi published a second edition with a new chapter entitled "Pre-Christian Gnosticism Reconsidered a Decade Later."[30] Here he discusses the continued scholarly frustration regarding a definition for the word Gnostic, the failure to discover any pre-Christian Gnostic documents, and the fact that the Nag Hammadi texts present only a vague notion of Gnosticism.[31] Acknowledging that there is only limited support for his position, he exhorts his readers to consider the evidence and the work of other scholars who doubt pre-Christian Gnosticism.[32]

Among the supporters of Yamauchi's position was Alan Segal, whose *Two Powers in Heaven* examined reports by rabbis who were "among the closest, most expert, and most concerned contemporary observers of

[29] Elaine Pagels, review of *Pre-Christian Gnosticism*, by Edwin M. Yamauchi, *Theological Studies* 35 (1974): 776; other reviews include those of Hall Partrick, *Church History* 43 (1974): 97; John D. Turner, *Journal of Biblical Literature* 93 (1974): 482–84; R. McL. Wilson, *Expository Times* 84 (1972–73): 379; Gilles Quispel, *Louvain Studies* 5.2 (1974): 211–12; George MacRae, *Catholic Biblical Quarterly* 36 (1974): 296–97.

[30] Yamauchi, *Pre-Christian Gnosticism*, 2d ed., 187–249; see also Birger A. Pearson, review of *Pre-Christian Gnosticism*, by Edwin M. Yamauchi, *Religious Studies Review* 11.1 (Jan. 1985): 75.

[31] See also Edwin M. Yamauchi, "Pre-Christian Gnosticism in the Nag Hammadi Texts?" *Church History* 48 (1979): 129–41; idem, "The Word from Nag Hammadi," *CT* 22.7 (Jan. 13, 1978): 19–22; idem, review of *The Nag Hammadi Library in English*, by James M. Robinson, *CT* 23.1 (Oct. 6, 1978): 36–40, 42–43; idem, review of *The Gnostic Gospels*, by Elaine Pagels, *Eternity* 31 (Sept. 1980): 66–67, 69; idem, review of *Zur Sprache and Literatur der Mandäer* by Rudolf Macuch, Kurt Rudolph, and Eric Segelberg, *JAOS* 100 (1980): 79–82; idem, review of *The Gnostic Dialogue*, by Pheme Perkins, *Christian Scholar's Review* 11 (1982): 171; idem, "Pre-Christian Gnosticism, the New Testament and Nag Hammadi in Recent Debate," *Them* 10.1 (1984): 22–27; idem, "Gnosticism: Has Nag-Hammadi Changed Our View?" *Evangel* 8.2 (Summer 1990): 4–7.

[32] Yamauchi, *Pre-Christian Gnosticism*, 2d ed., 248–49.

Christianity and Gnosticism."[33] He concluded that they attributed dualistic sentiments ("two powers") to both Gnostics and early Christians. But "the evidence is that [rabbinic] opposition to Christian exegesis preceded opposition to extreme gnostic exegesis." Indeed, the controversy led to a Gnostic self-definition: "The radicalization of gnosticism [the concept of the two powers as antagonistic] was a product of the battle between the rabbis, the Christians and various other 'two powers' sectarians who inhabited the outskirts of Judaism."[34] Thus Gnosticism arose later than Christianity.

Among European scholars Yamauchi found support in Simone Pétrement, a friend and biographer of the Catholic mystic Simone Weil.[35] Yamauchi frequently cited Pétrement, who had long contested the critical approach to Gnostic studies. In turn her 1984 work *Le Dieu Séparé: Les Origines du Gnosticisme* (Eng. trans., 1990) cited Yamauchi as support for her contention that Gnosticism must have emerged from Christianity.[36]

Yamauchi's work was also acknowledged by an invitation to participate in the Second International Congress of Mithraic Studies, convened by the Empress of Iran during September of 1975. His paper, "*The Apocalypse of Adam*, Pre-Christian Gnosticism, and Mithraism" continued the critique of his contemporaries.[37] By this time his work in Mandaic

---

[33] Alan E Segal, *Two Powers in Heaven: Early Rabbinic Reports about Christianity and Gnosticism* (Leiden: Brill, 1977) 29.

[34] Ibid., 262, 265; see also Edwin M. Yamauchi, "The Descent of Ishtar, the Fall of Sophia, and the Jewish Roots of Gnosticism," *TynBul 29* (1978): 140–71; idem, "Christians and the Jewish Revolts Against Rome," *FH 23* (1991): 11–30.

[35] Simone Pétrement, "La Notion de gnosticisme," *Revue de métaphysique et de morale 65* (1960): 385–421; idem, "Le Colloque de Messine et le problème du gnosticisme," *Revue de métaphysique et de morale 72* (1967): 344–73; idem, "Sur le problème du gnosticisme," *Revue de métaphysique et de morale 85* (1980): 145–77; idem, *Simone Weil: A Life* (New York: Pantheon, 1976).

[36] Simone Pétrement, *A Separate God: The Christian Origins of Gnosticism* (San Francisco: Harper and Row, 1990).

[37] Edwin M. Yamauchi, "*The Apocalypse of Adam,* Pre-Christian Gnosticism, and Mithraism," in *Etudes mithriaques: Textes et mémoires,* ed. Jacques Duchesne-Guillemin (Liège: Bibliothéque Pahlavi, 1978) 4:537–63.

studies, general Gnostic theory, and archaeology had made Yamauchi an important voice within biblical and early Christian scholarship.

The 1980s: A Sense of Balance

During the 1980s Yamauchi began his work as a consultant for Scholars Press, the publisher for the Society of Biblical Literature and the American Academy of Religion. He also served on the editorial boards of several journals: *Bulletin for Biblical Research*, *Fides et Historia*, *Journal of the Evangelical Theological Society*, and *Journal of the American Scientific Affiliation*. Thus his influence was being felt within and outside of evangelical circles.

Most of Yamauchi's efforts during this period focused on biblical archaeology.[38] He produced *The Archaeology of New Testament Cities in Western Asia Minor*[39] and *Harper's World of the New Testament*.[40] In lectures at Western Conservative Baptist Seminary in 1980 he critiqued the work of various archeologists and reviewed the general field of Old Testament archaeology: "In the eight years since I published *The Stones and the Scriptures* the trends have not all been positive in confirming the Scriptures as I had anticipated."[41] In this admission there was a note of frustration. However, there were also some positive trends which, along

---

[38] E.g., Edwin M. Yamauchi, "Ramsay's Views on Archaeology in Asia Minor Reviewed," in *The New Testament Student and His Field*, ed. John H. Skilton (Phillipsburg, NJ: Presbyterian and Reformed, 1982) 27–40; idem, "Archaeology and the Gospels: Discoveries and Publications of the Past Decade (1977–1987)," in *The Gospels Today*, ed. John H. Skilton (Philadelphia: John H. Skilton, 1990) 1–12.

[39] Edwin M. Yamauchi, *The Archaeology of New Testament Cities in Western Asia Minor* (Grand Rapids: Baker, 1980); this was republished in 1987 under the title *New Testament Cities in Western Asia Minor*. See also idem, "Recent Archaeological Work in the New Testament Cities of Western Anatolia," *NEASB* 13 (1979): 37–116.

[40] Edwin M. Yamauchi, *Harper's World of the New Testament* (San Francisco: Harper and Row, 1981).

[41] Edwin M. Yamauchi, "Scriptures and Archaeology," Bueermann-Champion Lectures, Western Conservative Baptist Seminary, Portland, Oct. 1980, 1; see also idem, "Archaeology and the Scriptures," *Seminary Journal* 25 (1974): 163–241; Donald J. Wiseman and Edwin M. Yamauchi, *Archaeology and the Bible* (Grand Rapids: Zondervan, 1979).

with the burgeoning digs at Ebla and other new finds, gave Yamauchi continued confidence that archaeology would affirm the biblical accounts.[42] Despite the difficulties that the data sometimes presented to evangelical scholarship, insistence that theory be corroborated with evidence remained a central theme.[43]

An important balance to his negative evaluation of critical theory was Yamauchi's disavowal of idiosyncratic fundamentalist exegesis. He disapproved of the search for Noah's ark.[44] In response to apocalyptic exegesis as found in Hal Lindsey's *Late Great Planet Earth*,[45] he produced *Foes From the Northern Frontier*, a monograph clarifying various historical and geographical specifics of the Bible.[46] He discussed, for example, the location of Urartu (Ararat) and the anachronistic confusion of modern Russia with the ancient Scythians, or Chaldeans.[47] When Saddam Hussein came to blows with the United Nations in 1990-91, Yamauchi again countered apocalyptic fervor with a solid review of John Walvoord's *Armageddon, Oil, and the Middle East Crisis*.[48] Just as Yamauchi was willing to confront the poor methodology of some fellow scholars, he critiqued his fellow evangelicals as well.

A similar sense of balance was consistently reflected in Yamauchi's participation within evangelical scholarly spheres. He contributed to *The NIV Study Bible* and authored "Ezra-Nehemiah" in *The Expositor's Bible Commentary*.[49] Yamauchi also participated in the Institute for

---

[42] Edwin M. Yamauchi, "Unearthing Ebla's Ancient Secrets," *CT* 25.9 (May 8, 1981): 18–21.

[43] Edwin M. Yamauchi, "The Proofs, Problems and Promises of Biblical Archaeology," *Journal of the American Scientific Affiliation* 36.3 (1984): 129–38.

[44] Edwin M. Yamauchi, "Critical Comments on the Search for Noah's Ark," *NEASB* 10 (1977): 5–27; idem, "Is That an Ark on Ararat?" *Eternity* 28 (Feb. 1978): 27–32.

[45] Hal Lindsey, *The Late Great Planet Earth* (Grand Rapids: Zondervan, 1970).

[46] Edwin M. Yamauchi, *Foes From the Northern Frontier* (Grand Rapids: Baker, 1982).

[47] See also Edwin M. Yamauchi, "The Scythians: Invading Hordes from the Russian Steppes," *BA* 46.2 (1983): 90–99.

[48] Edwin M. Yamauchi, review of *Armageddon, Oil, and the Middle East Crisis*, by John F. Walvoord, *CT* 35.5 (April 19, 1991): 50–51.

[49] Edwin M. Yamauchi, "Ezra-Nehemiah," in *Expositor's Bible Commentary*, ed. Frank

Biblical Research, an organization established by E. Earle Ellis in 1970 to encourage evangelical research in the Hebrew and Greek Scriptures. In its evolution the institute became a moderating body between the liberal Society for Biblical Literature and the conservative Evangelical Theological Society.[50] Yamauchi served on the executive committee from 1974 to 1976; and as chairman from 1984 to 1989, he saw the organization double its membership from 150 to 300 fellows and associates. In the burgeoning inerrancy debate of the 1980s Yamauchi found that his position was more conservative than many faculty members from institutions like Fuller Seminary, but he was also comfortable with an eclectic and broadly defined doctrine of inerrancy. Though his work has always affirmed a strong confidence in Scripture, he has never published a position on this topic.

The 1990s: Continuity and New Interests

Yamauchi's work in the late 1980s and early 1990s reflected a continuity as well as movement in new directions. In 1990 he published *Persia and the Bible*,[51] the first volume of its kind since Robert North's *Guide to Biblical Iran*.[52] In this text Yamauchi brings together his work on Greek and Near Eastern contacts, a detailed analysis of Achaemenian history, a review of studies of Zoroastrianism and of the Magi,[53] as well as discussions of the confirmations, parallels, and difficulties that such studies have brought to the biblical text. Central to this monograph are continued confidence in classical texts such as Herodotus, and defense of an

E. Gaebelein (Grand Rapids: Zondervan, 1988) 4:565–771; see also idem, "The Reverse Order of Ezra/Nehemiah Reconsidered," *Them* 5.3 (1980): 7–13.

[50] It is important to note that Yamauchi has held office in the Evangelical Theological Society (chairman of the Eastern Section, 1965–66) and the related Near East Archaeological Society (board of directors, 1973– ; vice-president, 1978–79).

[51] Edwin M. Yamauchi, *Persia and the Bible* (Grand Rapids: Baker, 1990).

[52] Robert North, *Guide to Biblical Iran* (Rome: Pontifical Institute of Biblical Archaeology, 1956).

[53] See also Edwin M. Yamauchi, "The Episode of the Magi," in *Chronos, Kairos, Christos: Nativity and Chronological Studies Presented to Jack Finegan*, ed. Jerry Vardaman and Edwin M. Yamauchi (Winona Lake, IN: Eisenbrauns, 1989) 15–39.

early dating of Daniel.[54] While praising his scholarship, reviewers have often found fault with Yamauchi's conservative positions.[55]

In *Persia and the Bible* Yamauchi also delves deeply into the area of Mithraic studies. As in his work on Gnosticism, he confronts critical methodology, this time as represented by Franz Cumont's thesis that Mithraism had influenced early Christianity.[56] Though mainstream Mithraic studies have abandoned Cumont's analysis, Yamauchi provides a critique of the field, arguing that it is invalid to use data from the second and third centuries AD to postulate first-century influences on Christianity.[57] Possibly more than any of his previous studies *Persia and the Bible* illustrates Yamauchi's earlier emphasis (in *The Stones and the Scriptures*) that accurate analysis requires three spheres of evidence: tradition, inscriptions, and archaeology.

During this period Yamauchi also developed an interest in ancient Africa. In 1991 he participated in multicultural dialogues at Miami University relating to Asian- and African-American relations. Yamauchi criticized both the racism of past European scholarship, which ignored Afro-Asian elements in classical culture, and Afrocentric trends that exaggerated these influences. Of particular importance was his reaction to Martin Bernal's *Black Athena*, which in overstating the Near Eastern and African elements within Greco-Roman culture made use of the work of Cyrus Gordon.[58] Yamauchi's efforts in this field included organizing a conference at Miami University on "Africa and Africans in Antiquity," and preparing the presentations for publication.[59] Exploring the often

[54] Yamauchi, *Persia,* 379–94.

[55] Among the reviews of *Persia and the Bible* are Lester L. Grabbe, *Journal for the Study of Judaism* 22 (1992): 295–98; S. P. Brock, *Interpretation* 46 (Jan. 1992): 100–101; Joseph A. Fitzmyer, *Theological Studies* 52 (March 1991): 176; Paul-Alain Beaulieu, *Bibliotheca Orientalis* 50.3–4 (1993): 484–86; J. R. Russell, *Jewish Quarterly Review* 83 (1992): 256–61.

[56] Franz Cumont, *The Mysteries of Mithra* (Chicago: Open Court, 1910).

[57] Yamauchi, *Persia,* 502–4, 516–18.

[58] Martin Bernal, *Black Athena: The Afroasiatic Roots of Classical Civilization,* 2 vols. (New Brunswick, NJ: Rutgers University Press, 1987, 1992).

[59] *Africa and Africans in Antiquity,* ed. Edwin M. Yamauchi (East Lansing: Michigan

ignored or misinterpreted African elements in the biblical accounts, he also produced the monograph *Africa and the Bible*.[60]

In the mid-1990s, as an extension of his previous work in Mandaic and general Persian studies, Yamauchi began to research further the early developments of Christianity in the East.[61] His 1994 paper on "Adaptation and Assimilation in Asia," for example, discussed Hellenistic influences on Buddhist art in Gandhara, as well as the movement of Manichaean Gnostic and Nestorian Christian missionaries along the Silk Road.[62] In this paper he also distinguished between assimilation and syncretism in reference to cultural and religious interaction, an important point in his overall view of the development and spread of early Christianity.

So far, Yamauchi's interest in and ability to work with an extremely broad body of ancient evidence has been noted. To Miami University he has attracted graduate students interested in such wide-ranging fields as Mycenaean studies, ancient warfare, Judaica studies,[63] New Testament studies, and the study of Patristics.[64] His broad interests also served him well as a senior editor of *Christianity Today* from 1992 to 1994. His contributions in this capacity include an overview of the "power struggles, guerrilla publishing, and bizarre interpretations of the Dead Sea Scrolls."[65]

State University Press, forthcoming); the conference was held on 1–2 March 1991.

[60] Edwin M. Yamauchi, *Africa and the Bible* (Grand Rapids: Baker, 2004); idem, "The Archaeology of Biblical Africa: Cyrene in Libya," *Archaeology of the Biblical World* 2 (1992): 6–18; idem, "Afrocentric Biblical Interpretations," *JETS* 39:3 (1996) 397–409.

[61] See Edwin M. Yamauchi, review of *A History of Christianity in Asia*, vol. 1, by Samuel H. Moffett, *AHR* 99 (April 1994): 617.

[62] Edwin M. Yamauchi, "Adaptation and Assimilation in Asia" (paper presented to the Association of Ancient Historians, Dayton, 6–8 May 1994); see also Edwin M. Yamauchi, "Hellenistic Bactria and Buddhism," *Humanitas* 18.3 (Winter 1995): 5–10.

[63] See, e.g., Edwin M. Yamauchi, "Josephus and the Scriptures," *FH* 13.1 (1980): 42–63.

[64] See, e.g., Edwin M. Yamauchi, "The Crucifixion and Docetic Christology," *Concordia Theological Monthly* 46.1 (1982): 1–20.

[65] Thomas Jones, "Scroll Hype," interview with Edwin M. Yamauchi, *CT* 37.11 (Oct. 4, 1993): 28–31. Interest in the scrolls is also evident in Yamauchi, "Qumran and Colosse," *BSac* 121 (1964): 141–52; idem, "The Teacher of Righteousness from Qumran and Jesus

Continued willingness to address issues of biblical scholarship[66] has brought Yamauchi into conflict with the Jesus Seminar of the Westar Institute, which published a monograph entitled *The Five Gospels: The Search for the Authentic Words of Jesus.* This work, which represents an extreme of higher-critical methodology, makes an overall judgment as to which of the *logia* (sayings) in the four canonical Gospels and the Gnostic *Gospel of Thomas* are authentic words of the historical Jesus.[67] Yamauchi's response was published in *Jesus Under Fire*, a work representing a general evangelical rejoinder.[68] Here he deals with the Jewish, Roman, and early Christian evidence of Jesus. Crucial to his arguments is the fact that the "Fellows of the Seminar were equally skeptical about the *logia* of Thomas. They considered only three of its sayings that have no canonical parallels worthy of serious consideration."[69] Despite such evidence as Yamauchi outlines, the Jesus Seminar insists that the "sayings of Jesus in the Gospels were freely invented by the church."[70] In his conclusion Yamauchi applies a sharp critique to the seminar's methodology and presuppositions, likening them to the eccentric and idiosyncratic speculations of John Allegro, who claimed that early Christianity was rooted in a mushroom cult.[71]

of Nazareth," *CT* 10.16 (May 13, 1966): 12–14; idem, review of *The Dead Sea Scrolls and the New Testament,* by William S. LaSor, *CT* 17.25 (Sept. 28, 1973): 34–35; idem, review of *Qoumrân: L'Établissement Essenien des bords de la Mer Morte,* by E.-M. Laperrousaz, *AHR* 83 (1978): 136–37.

[66] Edwin M. Yamauchi, "The Current State of Old Testament Historiography," in *Faith, Tradition, and History: Old Testament Historiography in Its Near Eastern Context,* ed. A. R. Millard, J. K. Hoffmeier, and D. W Baker (Winona Lake, IN: Eisenbrauns, 1994) 1–35; idem, "Political Background of the Old Testament," in *Foundations for Biblical Interpretation,* ed. David S. Dockery, Kenneth A. Mathews, and Robert B. Sloan (Nashville: Broadman and Holman, 1994) 306–27.

[67] *The Five Gospels: The Search for the Authentic Words of Jesus,* ed. Robert W. Funk and Roy W. Hoover (New York: Macmillan, 1993) 1–34.

[68] Edwin M. Yamauchi, "Jesus Outside the New Testament: What Is the Evidence?" in *Jesus Under Fire: Modern Scholarship Reinvents the Historical Jesus,* ed. Michael J. Wilkins and J. P. Moreland (Grand Rapids: Zondervan, 1995) 207–29.

[69] Ibid., 218.

[70] Ibid., 219.

[71] Ibid., 222; see also Edwin M. Yamauchi, review of *The Sacred Mushroom and the Cross,* by John Allegro, *Eternity* 22 (Nov. 1971): 54–55.

In 1994 Yamauchi returned again to the field of Gnostic studies with an article for the anthology *Hellenization Revisited*.[72] As in his earlier treatments he maintained that "the more analytic approach sees only a rudimentary, inchoate Gnosticism at the end of the first century, and concludes that the developed system cannot be understood apart from its parasitic relationship to Christianity."[73] This article was immediately followed by a most interesting critique by Michel Desjardins: "Yamauchi's scholarship, while highly admirable, creates a false dilemma by oversimplifying the question. His distinction between full-blown Gnosticism and proto-Gnostic elements is too sharp; it does not allow a middle ground of a developing Gnosticism alongside early Christianity."[74] Desjardins then goes a step further by critiquing Yamauchi's conservative Protestant presuppositions: Yamauchi "does not view the material with a disinterested eye. Gnosticism for him was a dangerous perversion of the Christian understanding of God, the Bible, and Christ; humanity is better served by its absence."[75]

The close reader of Yamauchi's work will acknowledge that Desjardins is essentially correct on both points. First, Yamauchi, like Pétrement, has always maintained that Gnostic systems emerged specifically from first-century Christian and Jewish groups. For Yamauchi this "cut-and-dried" position is sustainable because it best matches the evidence. On the second point it should be noted that as early as 1966 Yamauchi had touched on the matter of faith.[76] And in *The Stones and the Scriptures* he was quite bold regarding his position: "The [Christian] will be encouraged to know that the biblical traditions are not a patchwork of legends but are reliable records of men and women who have responded to the revelation of God in history. . . . Archaeology may show to us the nature of Christ's tomb.

[72] Edwin M. Yamauchi, "Gnosticism and Early Christianity," in *Hellenization Revisited: Shaping a Christian Response within the Greco-Roman World*, ed. Wendy Helleman (Lanham, Md.: University Press of America, 1994) 29–61.

[73] Ibid., 30.

[74] Michel Desjardins, "Yamauchi and Pre-Christian Gnosticism," in *Hellenization Revisited*, ed. Helleman, 64–66.

[75] Ibid., 66.

[76] Yamauchi, *Composition*, 37–38.

But it can never be a substitute for that personal faith which carries the believer beyond the empty tomb to a living relationship with [Christ]."[77] That Yamauchi has consistently communicated his position stands in sharp contrast to the many scholars who have claimed objectivity while working from a subjective agenda. Even Leopold von Ranke, the German historian whose American followers claimed an ideal *Objectivität*, understood history as pointing toward a metaphysical teleology informing the nature of reality.[78] From 1966 Edwin Yamauchi has worn the hats of a historian, biblical scholar, classicist, Orientalist, archaeologist, innovator, spoiler, and apologist. And he has never been shy about the faith that has informed the entirety of this work.

On the Retirement of Edwin M. Yamauchi[79]

In 2004 the History Department of Miami University announced that Dr. Edwin Yamauchi would retire from full-time teaching duties at the end of the 2004-2005 academic year. While this announcement was certainly expected by those close to Dr. Yamauchi, the news was met with a feeling that an important era was coming to an end. Through thirty five years of service Edwin Yamauchi has become something of an institution among his peers at Miami University, as well as among the broader Christian community in Oxford, Ohio. His work with Campus Crusade and InterVarsity Christian Fellowship has encouraged and strengthened many students and colleagues in their Christian faith.[80] His efforts at

[77] Yamauchi, *Stones,* 165–66.

[78] Leopold von Ranke, "Idee der Universalhistorie," *Historische Zeitschrift* 178 (1954): 290–301; idem, "Einleitung zu einer Vorlesung über Universalhistorie," *Historische Zeitschrift* 178 (1954): 304–7; see also Georg G. Iggers, *The German Conception of History* (Middletown, Conn.: Wesleyan University Press, 1968) 63–89.

[79] This portion of the chapter is designed as a continuation of a biographical sketch list above which was first published in Walter Elwell and J.D. Weaver, eds., *Bible Interpreters of the 20th Century* (Grand Rapids: Baker, 1999) 398–410.

[80] Dr. Yamauchi has often been asked to lecture at Miami University (and across the country) on the resurrection of Jesus. In his treatment of the subject he provides historical evidence in favor of the resurrection as well as critiques of those who ignore the evidence. This speech was published in two parts by *CT* magazine. See E.M. Yamauchi, "Easter—

dialogue with those outside the Christian traditions have helped to create better relations within the University community. And Yamauchi's willingness to serve as a church leader at Oxford Bible Fellowship as well as through informal ministry to many outside the church has consistently impressed those who have come into contact with him. The strength of his humble service will be missed as he steps away from full-time teaching and ministry at Miami University.

It is equally true that Yamauchi's retirement marks the end of an era in the broader world of scholarship. Through his many books, articles, and students Yamauchi has provided consistent support for evangelical thought. He now stands as one of the most influential evangelical scholars of the twentieth century. Yet his influence has extended well beyond the parochial. Yamauchi's work has consistently served as a corrective to both extreme fundamentalist and liberal scholarship. In this work he has created something of a "school" of thought in which he has asserted that faith must be informed by an honest analysis of historical evidence. Dr. Yamauchi once wrote that, "This revelation (God revealed in Jesus) was mediated in a particular culture. . . . It is, therefore, an error to attempt a literal transfer of biblical passages to our own situations without understanding their contexts."[81] A balance being necessary in the light of historical evidence was applied by Yamauchi in his critiques of arguments

---

Myth, Hallucination, or History?" in *CT* 18 (March 15, 1974) 4–7; and 18 (March 29, 1974) 12–14, 16.

[81] E. Yamauchi, "An Ancient Historian's View of Christianity," in P. Anderson, ed., *Professors Who Believe: The Spiritual Journeys of Christian Faculty* (Downers Grove, IL: InterVarsity Press, 1998). Also, "Ramsay's Views on Archaeology in Asia Minor Reviewed," in J.H. Skilton and C.A. Ladley, eds., *The New Testament Student and His Field* (Phillipsburg, NJ: Presbyterian and Reformed Publishing, 1982) 27–40; Yamauchi's perspective on the use of tradition, inscriptions, and archaeological materials is best expressed in his early work, *The Stones and Scriptures: An Introduction to Biblical Archaeology* (Grand Rapids: Baker, 1972) 158; and of great importance, idem, "The Current State of Old Testament Historiography," in A. R. Millard, J. K. Hoffmeier and D. W. Baker, eds., *Faith, Tradition and History: Old Testament Historiography in Its Near Eastern Context* (Winona Lake, IN: Eisenbrauns, 1994).

on behalf of pre-Christian Gnosticism, the Bauer thesis, Afrocentric historiography, as well as unusual interpretations of the Bible.[82]

The balance that Yamauchi has brought to Biblical and ancient studies is widely recognized. His formal and informal leadership in such organizations as the Institute for Biblical Research, the Evangelical Theological Society, the Conference on Faith and History, as well as the Near East Archaeological Society has been instrumental in making these societies worthy of scholarly respect.[83] Eugene Genovese, a colleague from Yamauchi's days at Rutgers, invited Dr. Yamauchi in the mid-1990s to participate in The Historical Society, a scholarly organization designed to counteract the Marxian and politically correct obsessions that have dominated the study of history in recent years.[84] In the winter of 2004 Dr. Yamauchi contributed an article to *The Journal of The Historical Society* entitled, "The Reconstruction of Jewish Communities during the Persian Empire." In this article he again demonstrated his great talent for finding "a more balanced view" between those who have too much or too little confidence in the ability of archaeology to address "the historical veracity of biblical texts." An extension of his *Persia and the Bible*, this article sets out to test the "minimalist" view of biblical archaeology that assumes no evidence exists to verify the biblical text. Yamauchi offers his support of such scholars as William G. Dever who has "decried Postmodernism's influence" on biblical studies by using the evidence of Jewish communities in the Persian Empire as a "test" of these competing claims.[85] In

---

[82] Among his most important works criticizing unusual Biblical exegesis is his book, *Foes from the Northern Frontier: Invading Hordes from the Russian Steppes* (Grand Rapids: Baker, 1982). His most famous work criticizing liberal scholarship is his world-renown, *Pre-Christian Gnosticism* (Grand Rapids: Wm. B. Eerdmans Pub., 1973).

[83] Edwin M. Yamauchi, "Attitudes Toward the Aged in Antiquity," in *NEASB*, 45 (2000) 1–9.

[84] Eugene Genovese was among a number of academics who rejected communism and its many abuses after the fall of the Soviet Empire. His return to Roman Catholicism led Genovese to renew ties with Yamauchi who taught at Rutgers University in the late 1960s, a period in which Genovese was ardently communist and anti-Christian. This renewal of personal ties led, in part, to Yamauchi lending his support to The Historical Society.

[85] Edwin M. Yamauchi, "The Reconstruction of Jewish Communities during the Persian

this article, Yamauchi convincingly demonstrates that archaeological and extra-biblical evidence is plentiful not only for a corroboration of the biblical text (especially of Ezra and Nehemiah), but also for an understanding of the cultural and historical context of biblical events.[86] Yamauchi's obvious rejection of the minimalist approach in this article represents the continuation of a confidence he has maintained throughout his career that archaeology is capable of offering historical evidence in support of the biblical text.[87]

Yamauchi's efforts to address abuses of historical evidence have also played an important role in his critique of Martin Bernal's *Black Athena* series as well as of general Afrocentric thought.[88] As a student of Cyrus Gordon and fellow student of Michael Astour at Brandeis University, Edwin Yamauchi was trained in the Afro-Asiatic school of Aegean and Mediterranean interactions. Cyrus Gordon's approach to the subject is most evident in his book *The Common Background of Greek and Hebrew Civilization* (Norton, 1965). In this work he established a strong foundation for a more thorough understanding of Ancient Near Eastern influences upon the development of Greek culture. Such scholars as Gordon, Astour and, more recently, M. L. West introduced and strengthened the Afro-Asiatic model with good support from the schol-

Empire," in *The Journal of The Historical Society*, IV.1 (Winter 2004) 1–2, 4. See also E. Yamauchi and D. J. Wiseman, eds., *Archaeology and the Bible* (Grand Rapids: Zondervan, 1979).

[86] This article is also representative of Dr. Yamauchi's extensive study of Ezra and Nehemiah. See "Ezra and Nehemiah," in K.L. Barker and J. Kohlenberger, eds., Zondervan *NIV Bible Commentary: Old Testament* (Grand Rapids: Zondervan, 1984) 1.680–725.

[87] A further publication, edited with Al Hoerth and Gerald Mattingley, entitled, *Peoples of the Old Testament World* (Grand Rapids: Baker, 1994) again demonstrates Yamauchi's confidence in archaeology to support and inform the biblical text. This work stands in good company with the efforts of such colleagues as Alan Millard and Kenneth A. Kitchen of the University of Liverpool, and Donald J. Wiseman of the University of London. Indeed, this work is a successful addition to D. Wiseman, ed., *Peoples of Old Testament Times* (Oxford: Clarendon, 1973).

[88] Edwin M. Yamauchi, "Martin Bernal's 'Black Athena' Reviewed," in *Journal of Ancient Civilizations* (Volume 12, 1997) 1–10.

arly world.[89] Unfortunately, this scholarship has been misused by Martin Bernal and other proponents of Afrocentric models in their efforts to argue for Egyptian (hence, African) colonization and dominance in the Aegean during the third and second millennia BC. Yamauchi's most recent books *Africa and Africans in Antiquity* and *Africa and the Bible* are dedicated to the pursuit of a balanced, Afro-Asiatic model as compared to the more politically-driven Afrocentric perspective.[90]

Yamauchi's book *Africa and the Bible* takes the reader beyond a simple examination of connections between the biblical world and Africa. Such biblical figures as the Queen of Sheba, Simon of Cyrene, and the Ethiopian eunuch are analyzed along with other instances of Mediterranean, African and Near Eastern interaction. The fourth chapter of this book includes a helpful description of Kushite monarchs.[91] However, more central to the book is a discussion of the "curse of Ham" myth which had its roots in medieval and early modern European thought, and which has now been perpetuated in rather odd ways via Afrocentric arguments. As with his book *Persia and the Bible*, Dr. Yamauchi sets out to establish a reasonable perspective of ancient Africa and its influence on the context of scripture. Based upon available evidence, he has produced a typically Yamauchian balance in which the populations of Africa are understood to have been quite diverse—made up of Egyptians, Greeks, Macedonians, Libyans, Kushites and others. This mix of populations presents a variety of difficulties for the ancient historian. For instance, Simon of Cyrene was most likely of Greek descent, and evidence is unclear as to whether the Queen of Sheba was African or from the Arabian Peninsula. Nuances such as these fit neither a Eurocentric perspective nor an Afrocentric view

---

[89] Michael C. Astour, *Hellenosemitica*, (Leiden: E.J. Brill, 1965) and M.L. West, *The East Face of Hellicon: West Asiatic Elements in Greek Poetry and Myth*, (Oxford: Clarendon, 1997). Also of interest is Amélie Kuhrt, "'Greeks' and 'Greece' in Mesopotamian and Persian Perspectives," The Twenty-First J.L. Memorial Lecture, New College, Oxford (Oxford: Leopard's Head Press, 2002).

[90] Edwin M. Yamauchi, *Africa and the Bible* (Grand Rapids: Baker, 2004); idem, ed., *Africa and Africans in Antiquity* (East Lansing, MI: Michigan State University Press, 2001).

[91] This is difficult due to the heavy Egyptian influence and destruction in Kush.

of ancient African people groups. The Eurocentric scholar might be ignorant of the wealth of information available regarding complex sub-Saharan civilizations, while the Afrocentric scholar might be taken aback by the fact that not all important ancient African cultures were "black African" in their racial makeup. In this approach to ancient Africa Dr. Yamauchi has earned criticism from those who want to see their racial or ethnocentric theories affirmed. On the contrary, he has continued to gain respect from those who are interested in an honest evaluation of the evidence. In his foreword to Yamauchi's book, Kenneth Kitchen writes, "Dr. Yamauchi reviews understandingly and sympathetically the questions and claims raised by Afrocentrism, while seeking to weed out misconceptions that too easily arise when enthusiasm outruns knowledge."[92] In this work, Yamauchi brings to completion his observations on ancient Africa that first began to take shape in *Africa and Africans in Antiquity*, a collection of articles from such luminaries as Frank Snowden and Frank Yurco. A result of a conference on ancient Africa held by Yamauchi at Miami University in March of 1991, these papers represent the balance that Yamauchi seeks to promote on the subject.

Finally, two recent articles serve as excellent indications that Dr. Yamauchi will continue to promote the balance of archaeology, faith, tradition, and modern scholarship that has been so central to his life's work. In 1997 he participated in a festschrift for Michael Astour, whose *Helenosemittica* helped open the scholarly world to the Afro-Asiatic model. Yamauchi's article, "Herodotus—Historian or Liar?" again addresses the role of archaeology in giving support to ancient classical and biblical texts.[93] As he did in *Persia and the Bible*, Ed Yamauchi draws upon data collected from the wide variety of cultures under Persian rule and known to Herodotus. This is done to prove that while Herodotus was by no means perfect in his many accounts of ancient cultures, the archaeological evidence indicates that he had a firsthand knowledge of the cultures in question and gave reliable information to his readers. In short, Yamauchi

---

[92] Yamauchi, *Africa and the Bible*, 14.

[93] Edwin M. Yamauchi, "Herodotus—Historian or Liar?" in G. D. Young, M. V. Chavalas and R. E. Averbeck, eds., *Crossing Boundaries and Linking Horizons: Studies in Honor of Michael C. Astour on His 80th Birthday* (Bethesda, MD: CDL Press, 1987).

continues through this article to lend credence to the idea that Greeks in the Aegean not only had heard of African and Near Eastern cultures, but indeed had visited these cultures, were influenced by them, and could speak about them with reliable authority.

And in a further article, "Homer and Archaeology: Minimalists and Maximalists in Classical Context," Dr. Yamauchi returns to another favorite topic: that archaeological evidence can and does inform Homer's writings. As in his previous works, Ed Yamauchi provides a strong argument for an ability to understand Homer, his time, and context via archaeological data. On the reverse, it also indicates that Homer's works can be used to assist modern scholars in their understanding of Mycenaean culture. Relating this to the same debate raging in biblical studies he writes, ". . . the extreme skepticism of minimalists like Finley is not warranted, as it underestimates the range of possibly authentic elements which have been preserved in Homer. On the other hand, the extreme optimism of maximalists like Vermeule does not adequately account for the many (some would say majority of) materials in Homer that betray a Dark Age or even early Geometric origin," and "The implications of these positive archaeological confirmations of the Homeric text should not be missed by biblical scholars."[94]

In a recent email interview, Yamauchi wrote that his retirement will be spent with his mother, his children and his dear wife, Kimie.[95] Part-time teaching, travel and the completion of unfinished projects will also play their part in this next stage of his life. It would appear that Yamauchi's presence in the scholarly world will diminish during retirement. One suspects, however, that if Dan Brown, Elaine Pagels and the Jesus Seminar keep up their shenanigans the world will hear from our good friend, colleague and mentor.

---

[94] Edwin M. Yamauchi, "Homer and Archaeology: Minimalists and Maximalists in Classical Context," in J. K. Hoffmeier and A. Millard, The *Future of Biblical Archaeology: Reassessing Methodologies and Assumptions* (Grand Rapids: Eerdmans, 2004) 89.

[95] Monday, 4/4/05 at 11:16 a.m.

Is the Maker of Heaven and Earth the Father of Jesus?

Carl B. Smith II

❊THE MAIN THESIS of my book, *No Longer Jews*,[1] has three parts. First, that Gnosticism's most clearly identifiable innovation was its identification of the Creator, and consequently, the product of his creative activity, as evil and separated from, and hostile to, the highest God of light. Second, it argues that Jesus Christ was sent forth from the God of light to reveal knowledge that allowed those who possessed it (i.e., the Gnostics) to escape the power of the archons, the chief of whom was the God of the Old Testament. Finally, that the circumstantial events of history and literary evidences of the Jewish, Christian, Hellenistic and Gnostic worlds supported the conclusion that Gnosticism arose in the early decades of the second century, and very likely in the intellectual environment and hermeneutical space[2] of Alexandrian Egypt following the Jewish Revolt under Trajan (AD 115–117).

As this monograph was in the final stages of publication, I discovered a passage in the Apostolic Fathers that seemingly undermined a major contention of my thesis. The problematic passage, found in Ignatius of Antioch's *Letter to the Philadelphians*, admitted the church father's

---

[1] Carl B. Smith II, *No Longer Jews* (Peabody, MA: Hendrickson, 2004). My interest in Gnostic studies were inspired by Dr. Edwin Yamauchi's careful analysis of the issues in his *Pre-Christian Gnosticism* and numerous other related works. I am deeply indebted to "Dr. Y" for his scholarly guidance and personal support.

[2] I borrow this helpful term from Risto Uro, *Thomas: Seeking the Historical Context of the Gospel of Thomas* (New York: T. & T. Clark/Continuum, 2003), who further credits K. Syreeni. The term is useful in my mind to remove the inquiry from the vain effort to discover the *Sitz im Leben* of the Gnostic innovation, but rather to seek a place in history when the themes and ideas of Gnosticism were part and parcel of the conversations of the era. From this standpoint, the themes and ideas of Gnosticism are most readily apparent in the hermeneutical space of the first half of the second century and beyond.

knowledge of a group who alleged that Jesus Christ did not derive from the Creator God of the Jews, a clearly Gnostic idea. Hear his words:

> If any one confesses Christ Jesus the Lord, but denies the God of the law and of the prophets, saying that the Father of Christ is not the Maker of heaven and earth, he has not continued in the truth any more than his father the devil, and is a disciple of Simon Magus, not of the Holy Spirit. (*Phil.* 6.49b-50a)

At first glance it seems from this text that Ignatius, who likely died a martyr for Christ in a Roman arena sometime between AD 110 and 113, was admitting knowledge of a Gnostic adversary, and relating the origins of the heresy to Simon Magus, the infamous fountainhead of all heresy.

Fueled dually by an altruistic passion for truth and a fearful dread of academic disgrace, I was prompted by my discovery to pursue a careful reexamination of the Ignatian corpus. The research revealed that Ignatius' letters have been the subject of intense academic scrutiny over the past several centuries, particularly due to the fact that the letters have come down to us in three basic recensions: (1) a short form of three abridged letters (Polycarp, Ephesians, and Romans) extant only in Syriac;[3] (2) a middle recension which includes seven letters: those to the Ephesians, Magnesians, Trallians, Romans, Philadelphians, and Smyrnaeans, and one to Polycarp, bishop of Smyrna; and (3) a long form in which each of the middle recension's letters were expanded and six additional letters were attributed to the Antiochene bishop.[4]

---

[3] Schoedel states that this shorter abridgement was constructed for monastic purposes. See William R. Schoedel, *Ignatius of Antioch. A Commentary of the Letters of Ignatius of Antioch*, Hermeneia (Philadelphia: Fortress, 1985) 3.

[4] Lightfoot dated the Long Form to about the mid-fourth century and the Short Form not much earlier than 400 C.E. See J. B. Lightfoot, *The Apostolic Fathers,* Part II, *S. Ignatius and S. Polycarp* (London: MacMillan, 1889) I.273 and 326 respectively. Ford argues that "the interpolations and forgings of the Ignatian Long Form fit very well into the period of the last quarter of the third century as a polemic against Marcion Docetism and against the Monarchianism of the school of Theodotus and/or of Paul of Samosata, c. A.D. 260;" in Harold W. Ford, "A Comparison of the Recensions of the Ignatian Corpus," *The Iliff Review* 18 (1961): 31. [Note: This article is drawn from Ford's 1961 Th.D. dissertation at the Iliff School of Theology.]

Though there are several scholars who still do not embrace the majority view,[5] a general consensus, nonetheless, has emerged which holds that the middle recension of seven letters is the original corpus written by Ignatius prior to his martyrdom, and that the longer form is a later expansion of the middle, and that the shorter form is an abbreviation of three of Ignatius' original writings.[6] The research also revealed that the edition of the *Letter to the Philadelphians* that contained the problematic passage was not the middle recension, but the longer and later edition. Ignatius' letters had been used and expanded by later church leaders to address other heretical views as they arose, and thus the longer reading did not undermine the thesis of my book, but, in fact, very likely supported it. The problematic passage was a later expansion, and the original passage was primarily concerned with Christian adherence to Jewish laws and practices, an early doctrinal concern of proto-orthodox[7] Christianity. Ignatius himself did not counter a Gnostic adversary; rather, his successors did, later in the second century or even later,[8] and enhanced the context of Ignatius' attack upon Judaizers (and docetists in other Ignatian letters) to include Gnostic opponents as well.

It must be mentioned here that the definition of Gnosticism is crucial to this discussion and at the same time one of the thorniest issues

[5] Chiefly, Reinoud Weijenborg, *Les letters d'Ignace d'Antioche* (Leiden: Brill, 1969); J. Ruis-Camps, *The Four Authentic Letters of Ignatius, The Martyr* (Christianismos 2; Rome: Pontificium Institutum Orientalium Studiorum, 1979); and R. Joly, *Le dossier d'Ignace d'Antioche* (Université libre de Bruxelles, Faculté de philosophie et Lettres, 69; Brussels: Éditions de l'université de Bruxelles, 1979). See the discussion in Schoedel, *Ignatius*, 3–7; and idem, "Are the Letters of Ignatius of Antioch Authentic?" *Religious Studies Review* 6 (1980): 196–201.

[6] For a full discussion of the textual history of the Ignatian corpus, see Ford, 21–32; Schoedel, *Ignatius*; and more recently, Charles T. Brown, *The Gospel and Ignatius of Antioch*, ed. Hemchand Gossai. Studies in Biblical Literature 12 (New York: Peter Lang, 2000) 9, n.1.

[7] This term is used by Bentley Layton, *The Gnostic Scriptures*, ABRL (New York: Doubleday, 1987) xxii; and Larry W. Hurtado, *Lord Jesus Christ. Devotion to Jesus in Earliest Christianity* (Grand Rapids: Eerdmans, 2003), among others, to describe first- and second-century positions that would later be included in Christian orthodoxy.

[8] The exact dates of the longer recension are in debate, ranging from the late second to the fourth century.

of Gnostic studies. No consensus view has emerged on the definition of Gnosticism, in spite of several worthy proposals.[9] The debate has been so strong and seemingly irresolvable that Michael Williams encouraged the abandonment of the term "Gnosticism" and proposed a new category of "biblical demiurgy," which he describes as "an adaptation of tradition from Jewish or Christian Scripture that assigns primary initiative and responsibility for the creation of the cosmos to one or more creators lower than the highest divinity."[10] His proposal has been met with wide acclaim by scholars, and many researchers in the field have both abandoned the category of Gnosticism and along with it the search for Gnostic origins.[11]

This idea is rejected here, and I have proposed, instead, a definition of Gnosticism that identifies "biblical demiurgy" of a negative bent as the chief innovation of the Gnostic religion. That is, Gnosticism's primary innovation that is fundamental to its essence is an oppositional relationship between the highest God of light and the Creator of the world, typically identified as the God of the Old Testament. Further, it was not as proto-orthodoxy claimed that the God of the Old Testament sent Christ into the world to redeem sinners; rather, according to the Gnostics, the God of light sent Jesus into the world for the purpose of revealing secret knowledge to the elite so that they could discover their true identity and find their way back to the God of light. The conclusion of my study

[9] A colloquium of international scholars met at Messina in April 1966, and their papers and discussion were published in Ugo Bianchi, ed., *The Origins of Gnosticism: Colloquium of Messina, 13–16 April 1966* (SHR 12; Leiden: Brill, 1967). See also Birger Pearson's eleven-point definition in *Gnosticism, Judaism, and Egyptian Christianity* (SAC; Minneapolis: Fortress, 1990) 7–9. Definitions range from the narrow with extended lists of elements (Pearson) to very broad, encompassing only the possession of secret knowledge as necessary for salvation, a definition that is generally meaningless in religious studies. See my discussion in *No Longer Jews*, 7–18.

[10] See Michael A. Williams, *Rethinking "Gnosticism:" An Argument for Dismantling a Dubious Category* (Princeton: Princeton University Press, 1966) 218.

[11] For example, Karen King, *What Is Gnosticism?* (Cambridge, MA: Belknap, 2003). King's work is a sophisticated example of post-modern analysis. See also Marvin Meyer, *The Gnostic Discoveries: The Impact of the Nag Hammadi Library* (San Francisco: HarperSanFrancisco, 2005) esp. 38–43.

showed that this idea developed in Egypt following the Jewish Revolt under Trajan.

In light of this debate over definition, it is clear to see why many scholars see a Gnostic opponent in the New Testament and Apostolic Fathers as well as in early heterodox writings and teachers, while some, though few in number, reject this thesis based upon the contention that no evidence exists, either direct or polemical, that indicates a Gnostic adversary prior to the early decades of the second century.[12] Edwin Yamauchi has been a long-standing champion of this challenge to the consensus view, arguing that an anti-cosmic dualism of a Gnostic sort does not appear until the era following the Bar Kochba Revolt of AD 132–135.[13] Noting the presence of earlier proponents of Gnostic ideas in Egypt in the 120s, particularly Carpocrates, Basilides, and Valentinus, should encourage scholars to look to Egypt following the Jewish Revolt under Trajan (AD 115–117) as the hermeneutical space in which the God of the Old Testament and his creative work were rejected, his positive image inverted, and his high position as Jehovah demoted to the lowly demiurge.

This problematic passage spurred my further research into the connections between Christ and the Creator and creation in the first hundred years of the Christian era, that is, up to around AD 120. This study presents a general survey of Creator and creation concepts in late Second Temple Judaism, the New Testament, the earliest alleged "Gnostic" teachers, and the Apostolic Fathers, particularly as they apply to the development of Christology. Though the survey is of necessity brief, it demon-

---

[12] Though some elements that would later be included in Gnosticism were present in first-century literature and conceptions (e.g., Docetic Christology), they were not combined in a system with the unique Gnostic innovations prior to the second century. See "parts-for-the-whole" discussion in Edwin Yamauchi, *Pre-Christian Gnosticism* (2d ed.; Grand Rapids: Baker, 1983) 171–73.

[13] See Yamauchi, esp. 237–39. Yamauchi was influenced by Alan Segal's *Two Powers in Heaven: Early Rabbinic Reports about Christianity and Gnosticism* (Studies in Judaism in Late Antiquity 25; Leiden: Brill, 1977) in developing this thesis. See also Simone Pétrement's *A Separate God: The Christian Origins of Gnosticism* (trans. by Carol Harrison; San Francisco: HarperSanFrancisco, 1990).

strates that the preponderance of evidence still supports my earlier thesis of a second-century origination for the Gnostic innovation.

Walter Wagner contends, "[T]he challenge of understanding the Creator and the creation was the basic theological issue facing the church throughout the second century. . . ."[14] Though many might surmise that Wagner's statement is hyperbole, an analysis of the importance of the Creator and the creation in second-century polemics and debates, particularly with regard to the Gnostics and Marcion, proves otherwise. Wagner's comment should be nuanced by three further considerations: (1) the subject of the Old Testament itself and the relationship between Christianity and Judaism were likewise central in the debate, as Daniélou noted much earlier: "The problem of the Old Testament is central to the controversies of the second century;"[15] (2) the place of Christ with reference to the Creator God of the Old Testament is equally critical in the discussion, especially as he is the primary focus of devotion in each of the religious movements that we are considering; and (3) the foundations of the debate lie in the Hellenistic and Jewish speculations of the Second Temple period, including of course the earliest Christian literature of the first and early second centuries. It is there that we begin our survey.

Creator and Creation in Late Second Temple Judaism

The centrality of Jehovah as the sole Creator and Ruler of the universe is unambiguous in the Old Testament and Second Temple Jewish litera-

[14] Walter H. Wagner, *After the Apostles: Christianity in the Second Century* (Minneapolis: Fortress, 1994) 68.

[15] Jean Daniélou, *Gospel Message and Hellenistic Culture,* trans. and ed. J. A. Baker (Philadelphia: Westminster, 1973) 199. I owe this reference to Larry Hurtado, *Lord Jesus Christ,* 558. He comments: "For second-century Christianity, the most far-reaching issue was whether to cede the world and human history to a stupid and vain creator deity sharply distinguished from the true God, or to lay claim to them as the creation and rightful property of the true God." . . . "Those who urged a distinction between the Old Testament deity and the true God were not simply trying to be difficult; they were reacting to real issues" (among which he lists theodicy, tensions between Old Testament and Christian gospel, incompatibility between transcendent God and matter, etc.; see Hurtado, 559).

ture.[16] This fact needs no defense. However, it is also a well-established fact that some Jewish writers in the late Second Temple Period were speculating on heavenly figures and personifications who mediated God's activities with reference to the physical realm. P. Maurice Casey has identified these as messianic and intermediary figures,[17] and Alan Segal has classified them as "two powers in heaven"[18] conceptions. Whether due to their considerations of the transcendence of God, their interactions with the Hellenistic world with its theological speculations and aversion to anthropomorphisms, or some other factors, Jewish writers were willing to introduce mediating figures who carried out God's activities with reference to creation and humanity. These secondary figures include principal angels (Michael and Philo's Metatron), heavenly men (Moses, Melchizedek and Enoch), Son of Man motifs (such as those found in *1 Enoch* and Daniel), personifications (Spirit), and hypostases (such as Wisdom and Word/Logos).

Richard Bauckham provides a succinct evaluation of the evidences and scholarly theories regarding these mediators particularly in relation to New Testament Christology in his book, *God Crucified*.[19] He argues that there are two general approaches to the question of the development of Christology. First, some scholars identify Second Temple Judaism as

[16] Richard Bauckham has provided a catalog of references for these postulates in his *God Crucified: Monotheism and Christology in the New Testament* (Grand Rapids: Eerdmans, 1998). That YHWH is the sole Creator of all things, see Isa. 40:26, 28; 42:5; 44:24; 45:12, 18; 48:13; 51:16; Neh. 9:6; Hos. 13:4 ;Septuagint: 2 Macc. 1:24; Sir. 43:33; Bel 5; *Jub.* 12:3–5; *Sib. Or.* 3:20–35; 8:375–376; Frag. 1:5–6; Frag. 3 ; Frag. 5; *2 Enoch* 47:3–4; 66:4; *Apoc. Abr.* 7:10; *Pseudo-Sophocles*; *Jos. Asen.* 12:1–2; *T. Job* 2:4. (See *God Crucified*, 10, n.8). That YHWH is the sole Ruler of all things, see Dan. 4:34–35; Bel 5; Add. Est. 13:9–11; 16:18, 21; 3 Macc. 2:2–3; 6:2; Wis. 12:13; Sir. 18:1–3; *Sib. Or.* 3:10, 19; Frag. 1:7, 15, 17, 35; *1 Enoch* 9:5; 84:3; *2 Enoch* 33:7; *2 Bar.* 54:13; Josephus, *Ant.* 1:155–156. (See *God Crucified:*, 11, n.9).

[17] P. Maurice Casey, *From Jewish Prophet to Gentile God: The Origins and Development of New Testament Christology* (Louisville: Westminster John Knox, 1991).

[18] See Segal, *Two Powers in Heaven.*

[19] The following summary is from Bauckham, 2–3. In this work, Bauckham interacts repeatedly with Larry W. Hurtado's works, especially *One God, One Lord: Early Christian Devotion and Ancient Jewish Monotheism* (Philadelphia: Fortress, 1988) as well as other scholarly works.

strictly monotheistic such that no secondary power could have been granted divine status with Jehovah, and thus, early Christology in the New Testament does not affirm the deity of Jesus. In fact, they argue, the development of Christ's divinity was more the result of Hellenistic influences in the late first and early second centuries than of Jewish Christianity in the early first century.[20] Second, other scholars find in these intermediary figures exceptions to, and perhaps compromises of, the exclusive monotheism of Second Temple Judaism. Further, they contend that these intermediaries provide the conceptual framework for the development of Trinitarian doctrine, thus maintaining the foundations of Christology in Judaism, albeit a Judaism that was questionably monotheistic.[21] Bauckham poses a third option that embraces the vision of an exclusively monotheistic Judaism in the Second Temple Period, and sees the development of New Testament Christology not as dependent upon the various intermediary figures, but as a unique and unprecedented innovation of including Jesus in the divine identity of the one true God.[22]

While there was a large degree of vagueness in the relationship between these secondary powers and the true God, most of them were considered lesser beings who did not participate in the divine identity, who

[20] Bauckham cites A. E. Harvey, *Jesus and the Constraints of History* (London: Duckworth, 1982) ch. 7; P. M. Casey, *From Jewish Prophet to Gentile God*; idem, "The Deification of Jesus," *SBLSP* 1994, 697–714. See the discussion in Bauckham, 2, and 2 n.2.

[21] Among others, Bauckham cites, C. Rowland, *The Open Heaven* (London: SPCK, 1982) 94–113; A. Chester, "Jewish Messianic Expectations and Mediatorial Figures and Pauline Christology," in M. Hengel and U. Heckel, eds., *Paulus und Antike Judentum* (WUNT 58; Tübingen: Mohr [Siebeck], 1991) 17–89; M. Barker, *The Great Angel: A study of Israel's Second God* (London: SPCK, 1992); C. A. Gieschen, *Angelomorphic Christology* (AGJU 42; Leiden: Brill, 1998). He also cites further works from M. Hengel (*The Son of God* {tr. J. Bowden; London: SCM, 1976}), J. D. G. Dunn (*Christology in the Making* {London: SCM, 1980}), J. B. Green and M. Turner (eds., *Jesus of Nazareth: Lord and Christ* {Grand Rapids: Eerdmans, 1994}), and L. W. Hurtado (*One God, One Lord*). See Bauckham, 3 n.3. Of authors who question the strict monotheism of Second Temple Judaism, see Peter Hayman, "Monotheism—A Misused Word in Jewish Studies," *Journal of Jewish Studies* 22 (1990): 1–15, and Alan Segal, *Two Powers in Heaven*.

[22] Bauckham, 3–4. Bauckham calls the appeal to intermediary figures "misleading" (4), "distorted" (18), and "a fiction" (19). He concludes, "This alleged precedent for Christology should be forgotten" (19).

were servants of the will and desires of Jehovah, and who were not generally offered and refused to receive worship due to their secondary status
compared to Jehovah. Equally important, according to Bauckham, is the
small amount of evidence for these secondary figures in Second Temple
Jewish literature, such that Bauckham accuses scholars in their search for
the roots of New Testament Christology of making too much of too little
evidence from this period, especially when posited against the manifold
declarations of the uniqueness and singularity of Jehovah in literature
from this same period. Bauckham concludes, "However diverse Judaism
may have been in many other respects, this was common: only the God
of Israel is worthy of worship because he is sole Creator of all things and
sole Ruler of all things. Other beings who might otherwise be thought
divine are by these criteria God's creatures and subjects."[23] Yet, there are
several images in the Second Temple Period that most scholars, including
Casey and Bauckham, are willing to admit cross the boundaries into the
realm of divinity. These include the Son of Man in the *Parables of Enoch*
(*1 Enoch* 61:8; 62:2, 5; 69:27, 29; cf. 51:3),[24] Word/Logos (Philo calls
Logos "the second God" in *Qu in Gen* II,62) and Wisdom (*2 Enoch* 33:4;
1 Enoch 84:2–3; Wis. 9:4, 10).[25]

A feature of Second Temple Judaism that possibly demonstrates the
separateness of Jewish thought and categories from Hellenistic ones, or
at least engenders caution in the equating of the two, is the usage of language for the Creator in the Greek translation of the Old Testament, the
Septuagint. This is particularly noteworthy with reference to the Greek
term *demiourgos*, which the Greek philosophers, beginning with Plato,
used for a secondary power who was lower than the highest God and
who created the universe.[26] Apart from a few references of a neutral na-

---

[23] Bauckham, 11.

[24] Bauckham calls this "the sole example of an angelic figure who has been included in
the divine identity" (20).

[25] Bauckham concludes that these personifications and hypostatizations are "participants
in the divine identity" and "that these Jewish writers envisaged some form of real
distinction within the unique identity of the one God" (22).

[26] Beginning with Plato's *Timaeus* (28f), through Neo-Platonism. See the discussions by
W. Foerster in *TDNT*, III, 1023–1028, and I. H. Marshall in NIDNTT, I, 387–389.

ture in three apocryphal books,[27] the use of *demiourgos* is absent from the Septuagint. This is somewhat surprising given the creativity of Jewish circles in Egypt, where the Septuagint was produced, and their proclivity for and proximity to Middle Platonic thought. Philo and Josephus both used *demiourgos* in their writings, giving evidence of Hellenistic influence; yet, the negative and diminishing overtones that accompany the words as apparent in later Gnostic literature are absent from their works.[28] Both Philo and Josephus used the term with reference to the creative work of Jehovah himself.

What also must be kept in mind, particularly when considering a trajectory toward Gnosticism, is that the intermediary figures in each of these accounts is in harmony with the highest and only God, Jehovah. Though they share in his power, they do not share in his status as the sovereign God of the universe or in his unique identity as a divine being, of course, with the exception of the Son of Man, Wisdom, and Word, as noted above. When we come to Gnosticism in the second century, lesser beings are present within the divine pleroma as emanations from the highest God, and the creation is the product of a fall or rebellion. The God of the Old Testament does not occupy the position of the highest God; rather, he has been demoted to the lesser being who creates, usually with accomplices, the physical universe against the will of the highest God. Jesus is not a participant in this creative process, but rather comes as a revealer to free those who are held captive through their ignorance by the God of creation, the demiurge, and his fellow archons. What accounts for this demotion of the God of the Jews from the highest rank of divinity to the lower realm of the demiurge, and what accounts for the adoption of "demiurgical" language for him, are the crucial quests of this study.

---

[27] Wisdom 15:13, 2 Macc. 4:1 and 10:2, and 4 Macc. 7:8.

[28] For Philo, see *Op. Mund.* 10, *Mut. Nom.* 29–32 and *Som.* 1.76. For Josephus, see *Ant.* 1.155, 7.380 and 12.23.

Christ, Creator, and Creation in the New Testament[29]

The New Testament, as a collection of books originating from a Jewish environment, shares with the Old Testament and Second Temple Judaism a strong commitment to monotheism and a high regard for the Creator and the physical creation. This, again, is unambiguous.[30] However, there is a large degree of indefiniteness with regard to the relationship between Second Temple Jewish conceptions of messianic and intermediary figures and those that developed regarding Christ. While many scholars argue for a line of dependence between these figures and the images of Christ developed in the early Christian centuries,[31] there are several scholars who argue quite convincingly that the doctrine of Christ was in many ways a unique innovation of the first century that posited the person of Christ within the divine identity itself, thus preserving monotheism, while at the same time differentiating Christ from God the Father.[32] Richard Bauckham, for example, makes an important case for the understanding that these early developments in Second Temple Judaism were not the basis of New Testament Christology. These prior figures were not

[29] I read a paper at the November 2003 meeting of the Evangelical Theological Society in Toronto, Canada, entitled, "'No Longer Jews': Gnostic Origins and Their Implications for Early Christian Studies." Copies of this paper can be requested from Zondervan Publishers online at http://www.etsjets.org/meetings/2003/2003-papers-3.html.

[30] Any hints of anti-creation rhetoric revealed in the New Testament, whether directly or polemically, are uniformly in passages that are associated with themes of asceticism and law-keeping (e.g., Col. 2:20–23; 1 Tim. 1:3–5; 4:3). What should be noted here is that the theology of the New Testament raised ascetic themes beyond the realm of law-keeping to one's new identity in Christ (e.g., Col. 3:1–4; 1 Tim. 1:3–11; 4:1–5). Christians are able to be holy before God only as they allow Christ to live his life through them through the power and control of the Holy Spirit and as a manifestation of the "new creation." The Gnostics took this theme a step further, once the God of the law was dissociated from the true God of light. They related ascetic success to realizing one's identity in the higher God of light, and Christ (or another revealer figure) became the bearer of that message. The Gnostic was not dependent upon Christ for ascetic holiness; in fact, in their despite for the archons, they could very well rise above Christ. See below, under the teachings of Carpocrates as represented by Irenaeus (*Haer.* 1.25.1–6).

[31] For example, P. M. Casey, *From Jewish Prophet to Gentile God.*

[32] Bauckham, *God Crucified*, and Hurtado, *Lord Jesus Christ*, 2, where he speaks of a "mutation" in Jewish monotheism, and an "explosion" in devotion to Jesus.

included in the divine identity of God himself, with the exception of the Son of Man motif of *Enoch* and the hypostases of the Wisdom and Word of God. Larry Hurtado, in his recent works on Christology, concurs with Bauckham on these essential points.

It must be admitted, however, that the existence of these messianic and intermediary figures, and the development of language regarding them, at least created categories for the development and understanding of Christological themes that are found in the New Testament and early Christianity, especially in those movements that were later to be categorized as heterodox, or heretical. Further, whether one defines the development of Christology as innovative, "evolutionary," or as a "gradual unfolding" (Dunn) process, the point of the matter is that development was involved in Christological understandings from the time of Jesus' ministry through the early Christian centuries. What is most significant is that though development is observable, a high Christology nonetheless is in evidence from the earliest decades of the Christian movement.[33]

Below is a brief summarization of the New Testament evidence for Christ and his relationship to the Creator and creation. When the New Testament is analyzed as a unity of texts, Jesus Christ himself, the central figure of the New Testament, is posited very positively with reference to the Creator and creation. Jesus is clearly portrayed as a physical and historical person, linked dramatically with God's redemptive purposes and, subsequent to his resurrection, linked fundamentally with God's work of creating and sustaining the universe and worshipped together with him. Hurtado calls this "binitarian worship."[34] This image is consis-

---

[33] This point is a major contention of Hurtado in *Lord Jesus Christ*. See also Colin E. Gunton, *Christ and Creation: the Didsbury Lectures, 1990* (Grand Rapids: Eerdmans, 1992) esp. 10, where he quotes Moule, among others.

[34] A frequent term in Hurtado's *Lord Jesus Christ*. See also, idem, "The Binitarian Shape of Early Christian Worship," in *The Jewish Roots of Christological Monotheism: Papers from the St. Andrews Conference on the Historical Origins of the Worship of Jesus* (ed. C. C. Newman, J. R. Davila, and G. S. Lewis; JSJ Sup 63; Leiden: Brill, 1999) 187–213. Hurtado makes a significant point in relating that devotion to Jesus was very prevalent and important in the first several centuries of the Christian era, whether the ones who held that devotion were proto-orthodox, heterodox, or heretical. For some reason, Jesus Christ became a major focus of speculation with regard to Jewish ideas of history, redemption, creation,

tent from the earliest to the latest New Testament writings, though the emphases are not entirely even throughout the books, and certain themes show definite diachronic development. The evidence for this connection between Christ and the Creator and creation is demonstrated in several particular ways throughout the New Testament, indicating the breadth and depth of this reality.

First, there are innumerable texts that clearly indicate the physical nature of Christ, including his birth, life, limitations, suffering, death, resurrection, and exalted state. In this case, the Creator has become a full participant in his own creation (see Lk. 2:52 and 1 Tim. 2:5). Second, there are texts that demonstrate Christ's lordship over creation through his miracles and wondrous works. On certain occasions the works of Jesus elicit responses of wonder and amazement such as, "What kind of man is this? Even the winds and the waves obey him!" (Mt. 8:27). A third and related category includes passages indicating that Christ's redemptive purposes and future ministry extended to the entirety of creation, not just to humanity. Colin Gunton argues in *Christ and Creation* that nearly every dimension of the life and work of Jesus Christ, from incarnation to miracles and parables, speaks with a unified voice to the unity of creation (vis-à-vis the Hellenistic dualism of matter and spirit) and the reign of God in creating and redeeming it.[35] The ministry of Christ is thoroughly connected with creation in origination, sustentation, incarnation, redemption, and glorification (see Rom. 8:19–22).

Fourth, certain texts make direct statements regarding Christ's pre-existence and his role in creating and sustaining the universe. These texts include John 1:1–5, 1 Corinthians 8:6, Colossians 1:15–16, Hebrews 1:2–3, 10–12, and Revelation 3:14. These passages are found in some of the earliest books of the New Testament (1 Corinthians; possibly Colossians), and the earliest reference is arguably the most spectacular. In 1 Cor. 8:6, Paul utilizes the language of one of the strongest expressions of Jewish monotheism, the Shema, and transforms it into a statement to

---

etc., with many of these speculations taking a negative stance toward the "mother" faith of Judaism. This includes Christianity as well as Gnosticism.

[35] This work is the published version of the 1990 Didsbury Lectures at Nazarene Theological College.

argue for a plurality in the Godhead with direct reference to the work of creation. "[Y]et for us there is but one God, the Father, from whom all things came and for whom we live; and there is but one Lord, Jesus Christ, through whom all things came and through whom we live." This development is highly innovative and occurs within twenty to thirty years of the crucifixion and resurrection of Jesus Christ. The speed with which this developed in a Jewish context, penned by a highly-trained Jewish Pharisee, is nothing short of amazing. Of these texts Bauckham states,

> What is noteworthy is that in three of these cases (1 Corinthians, Hebrews, and John) the purpose, in my view, is precisely to express Jewish monotheism in Christological terms. It is not that these writers wish to say anything about the work of creation for its own sake or even that they wish to say anything about the relationship of Christ to creation for its own sake, but that they wish to include Jesus Christ in the unique divine identity. Including him precisely in the divine activity of creation is the most unequivocal way of excluding any threat to monotheism— as though Jesus were a subordinate demi-god—while redefining the unique identity of God in a way that includes Jesus.[36]

The extended summary of Gunton is also worthy of consideration:

> When passages such as those which have been discussed are added to the passages in which the preexistence and eschatological future of the Christ are introduced without direct reference to his relation to the creation, it seems clear that we have here more than a few proof texts culled arbitrarily to prove a dogmatic point. The facts that they come strategically at the beginning of treatises like those of John and Hebrews, that they appear to be used unselfconsciously as part of the fabric of early Christian belief, and that they are not inconsistent with—to understate the matter—the

---

[36] Bauckham, 36. In his arguments, Bauckham does an excellent job of exegesis in explaining how themes from Psalm 110:1 and Isaiah 40–55 emerge in the New Testament to demonstrate that the authors were intentional in connecting the uniqueness of the God of Israel with Jesus, both in his humiliation and exaltation. Further, his analysis of the prepositions used in 1 Cor. 8:6 compared to those of Rom. 11:36 indicate another point in which Jesus is included in the divine identity (40).

lordship over creation depicted in Synoptic narratives, are point-
ers to something of considerable significance. Whatever we may
wish to make of them—and of the Old Testament and other
background—in 'the modern age', and I want to make much
of them, there can be little doubt that, for whatever reason, they
bulked large in early Christian response to the resurrection of
Jesus from the dead. It may be our weakness, not that of the
New Testament, that so little has been made of these passages
constructively in recent christology.[37]

The consistent image of these New Testament texts is that Jesus, the one
through whom God acted to save the world, is also the medium through
whom He created and sustains that same world.

Fifth, there are innumerable passages that indicate a harmonious
relationship between God the Father (i.e., the God of the Old Testament)
and Jesus Christ, and that include the latter as an equal in the divine
identity and participating in divine activities. These texts are positively
stated with Jewish language, images, and conceptions (e.g., "only-begot-
ten Son" of John 1:18 is derived from Psalm 2:7). Though many of these
texts do possess an element of subordination of function (e.g., Jesus' obedience to the Father), the subordination is not stated with reference to
person. Jesus and the Father are distinct, and Jesus obeys the Father, but
they are one. Sixth, and last, there are numerous texts in which Jesus is
offered and receives worship, a clear indicator that Jesus stood apart from
the messianic and intermediary figures of the Old Testament and Second
Temple Period (see Lk. 5:8 and Jn. 20:28; compare with Acts 14:11–18
and Rev. 22:8–9).[38]

The Christology of the New Testament is phrased in Jewish terms
and crafted in Jewish constructs. It is not rooted in Hellenistic or syn-
cretistic images as proposed by the German *relgionsgeschichtliche Schule*.[39]

---

[37] Gunton, 24–25.

[38] This aspect of devotion to Jesus is a major point of Larry Hurtado's most recent work
on Christology, *Lord Jesus Christ*, where he argues that the debate should not center
primarily upon doctrinal or creedal concerns, but rather on the liturgical and worship
traditions revealed in the documents.

[39] "The History of Religions School," as defined by R. Reitzenstein, W. Bousset, and

Though many of the original presuppositions of this school of research have been overturned by subsequent scholars, there are still deep strains present in contemporary scholarship.[40] To the contrary, the divinity of Jesus is rooted deeply in Jewish soil, culled from images and patterns defined in the Hebrew Scripture and Second Temple Judaism. Beyond this, the authors of the New Testament and the earliest Christian communities and authors created several innovations that had no prior antecedents in the Jewish or Hellenistic worlds. Fundamental to the earliest Christian community was a tenacious commitment to monotheism, derived obviously from the "mother" faith of Judaism. Doubts about the exclusive monotheism of Second Temple Judaism are dispelled upon careful reflection on the texts. An absence of Hellenistic terms is equally evident, particularly the absence of the typical Greek terms *demiourgos* and *demiourgein*, with the single exception of its use in the New Testament appearing in Hebrews 11:10 where it is used with reference to the heavenly city. If Greek culture and philosophy were responsible causes for the development of New Testament Christology, as many claim, the absence of these terms is difficult to explain.

Mediation of Angels in the New Testament

Though it does not appear that the New Testament authors depended upon the angelic and intermediary figures for their Christology, they were not totally unaware of these developments in Judaism. In fact, it appears that the angelic mediation of the Law of Moses was a significant point in the development of Paul's theology of Christ's superiority to the Torah in Galatians 3:19. Hebrews 2:2–3 likewise addresses this theme when it argues for the superiority of the revelation that came through Christ over that mediated by angels to Moses. This theme was entirely absent from the chronicles of Exodus, but it did surface in the speculations of Second

R. Bultmann. For an overview of the issues and literature pertinent to this school, see Edwin Yamauchi, "History-of-Religions School," in *New Dictionary of Theology* (ed. S. B. Ferguson, D. F. Wright, and J. I. Packer; Downers Grove, IL: InterVarsity, 1988), 308–9. See also the extended discussion in Hurtado, *Lord Jesus Christ*, Introduction.

[40] The primary influence in the American academy is felt by professors Helmut Koester and James M. Robinson.

Temple Judaism in *Jubilees*.[41] This theme of the angels mediating the Law is later adopted by the Gnostics and expanded by them to include the prophets and the creation itself. Among the angels/archons who created the world is the God of the Old Testament, the giver of the Law and the inspiration of the prophets, the One who holds humans captive through their physical bodies and his commandments.

Christ and the Old Testament Prophets

The Gnostic contention that the angels inspired the writing of the prophets should not be overlooked. Mediation was initially used as a means to provide distance between the transcendent God and the physical domain. The New Testament authors used the prophets to argue for the vital connection between the incarnate Christ and the God of the Old Testament. Not only was Christ sent by Jehovah, but his coming was prophesied repeatedly in the Old Testament books, establishing it as the culminating event of the divine plan of redemption. The importance of the prophets was established in their usage by the canonical Gospels to validate Jesus as the Messiah, and continued to be of primary importance in the exegetical and apologetic work of the early Christian Fathers.[42] The Gnostics, on the other hand, used mediation not just to create distance, but a separation between the highest God and the physical domain, and to isolate the God of the Old Testament as an evil, arrogant, and ignorant archon.[43] The law is banal, the prophecies are false, the creation is a

---

[41] Casey outlines the development of Moses into a mediatorial figure in Second Temple literature in his *From Jewish Prophet to Gentile God* (83–84). *Jubilees* 1:27—2:1 attributes an expanded version of part of the Pentateuch to the angel of the Lord who communicated it to Moses on Sinai. *T.Mos.* 1.14 speaks of Moses as the "mediator of his covenant." *Jubilees* is dated to the second century BCE in J. H. Charlesworth, ed., *The Old Testament Pseudepigrapha* (2 Vols.; New York: Doubleday, 1985) 2.35, 42–44.

[42] For a discussion of the early Christian use of prophecy, see Oskar Skarsaune, *The Proof from Prophecy: A Study of Justin Martyr's Proof-Text Tradition Text-type, Provenance, Theological Profile* (NovTSup 56; Leiden: Brill, 1987) and more recently, the collection of essays in Craig A. Evans, ed., *From Prophecy to Testament: The Function of the Old Testament in the New* (Peabody, MA: Hendrickson, 2004).

[43] In *No Longer Jews* (127–28, n.40), I raised the possibility that the Gnostics may have attributed the prophets to the archons, one of whom was the God of the Old Testament,

mistake, and the body is a trap. All of these elements are manifestations of a break/rebellion in the pleroma, and the means by which the archons, led by the God of the Old Testament, keep souls enslaved to their principles. Christ is essentially a revealer (not a redeemer) figure whose primary role is to reveal knowledge to the elect so that they can escape the archons' enslavement. There is very likely a time factor in this issue. If the Synoptics are late, and the development of prophecy lists was an even later development, then the Gnostics' reaction to them must have been even later still.

Without engaging a thorough discussion of early Christology, several conclusions from the New Testament are foundational to this study. First, development was undeniably involved in Christological understandings from the beginning of Jesus' ministry, throughout the writings of the New Testament, and to the end of the first century and far beyond. Second, a high Christology is evident very early in this development, including statements of Jesus' divinity, "binitarian" and proto-trinitarian formulas, the inclusion of Jesus in divine activities, and the offering of worship to and the reception of worship by Jesus. Third, the relationship between Jesus and the God of the Old Testament is one of familial harmony and cooperation in divine activities. There is no sense of relational division between them, and Jesus is included in the divine identity with the Father, though distinct from him. Fourth and last, Christ is identified very early to be a participant in the activity of creation along with his Father, most typically in the role of divine agency. Nowhere is this more dramatic, clear, and early than in 1 Cor. 8:6 where Paul uses the Jewish Shema to elucidate plurality of persons in the Godhead with reference to the work of creation. This creative role is clear in other New Testament passages as well, but this theme is nearly absent from the Apostolic Fathers. Further, it is completely denied in Gnosticism.

as a deliberate attempt to undercut the defense of the Christian faith offered by the apologists and to posit the "Great Church" as under the dominion of the archons.

Christ, Creator, and Creation in the Early "Gnostic" Teachers

The individuals identified by the second century Heresiologists as the earliest Gnostics are difficult to classify with reference to their views regarding Christ and creation. This is largely due to the lack of primary material related to them and the fact that their images, projected to us through the lenses of the Heresiologists, are highly polemical, inconsistent, and expansive over time.[44] On the latter point, an examination of each of the so-called Gnostic figures prior to the 120s when Carpocrates, Saturninus, Basilides, and Valentinus first appear, demonstrates that later Heresiologists at times amplified the images presented by their predecessors. For instance, the image of Simon Magus becomes more and more Gnostic over time in the treatment of the subsequent heresy hunters. This factor begs the question of what we really can know about the earliest "Gnostics." The situation is such that Hurtado begins his discussion of Jesus devotion among radically diverse Christian movements with Valentinus, a relative late-comer to the Gnostic scene, with a full-blown Gnostic system.[45] This is particularly troubling in that some scholars see Valentinus providing a corrective to the radical anti-cosmism and anti-Judaism of prior Gnostic conceptions.[46]

In spite of the polemical nature of the portraits of the first Gnostics and the disparity of details among the varied accounts, it is only through an analysis of the works of the Christian Heresiologists that we can really analyze these earliest so-called Gnostics. Though the codices discovered at Nag Hammadi allow us to analyze Gnostic teachings first-hand, the works are very late and their textual traditions are uncertain. No clearly Gnostic text from Nag Hammadi is datable with any certainty before AD 120,[47] and the vast majority were likely composed any time from

[44] See my review in *No Longer Jews*, 120–42. This section serves as a basis for what follows here.

[45] Hurtado, *Lord Jesus Christ*, 523.

[46] Petrement, 270–78, for example. See also, Layton, 217–22.

[47] See my discussion of the dating and historical significance of the Nag Hammadi Library in *No Longer Jews*, esp. 115–16. *The Gospel of Thomas* may deserve special attention since many scholars date the work to the first century and posit its significance as equal to if not greater than the canonical gospels (see the discussion in Meyer, 61–74). Yet, many other

the late second through the fourth centuries AD, much beyond the time period under consideration in this paper. Thus, the representations of the Heresiologists and the works of the Apostolic Fathers are our most important witnesses for this period, as meager and prejudiced as they may be.

There are several teachers identified by the Heresiologists of the second and third centuries as the first "Gnostics." Of these very little is known for certain. In the following survey, the accounts will be examined for the following crucial issues: (1) a separation of the creator(s) from the highest God, attributing the creative work to lower emanations, angels, or the demiurge; (2) the identification of the God of the Old Testament/ God of the Jews with the creator(s)—thus, demoting him to a secondary status; (3) the presence of an oppositional relationship between the creator(s) and the highest God, indicated through a statement of rebellion or the salvific goal of overcoming the creator's (or creators') enslavement; and (4) the derivation of Christ from the highest God of light as opposed to from the God of the Old Testament, particularly revealed through a rejection of the prophets and identifying the source of their inspiration, or rather deception, as the angels/archons. Justin Martyr captures these criteria in his *Dialogue with Trypho*:

> My friend, there were, and still are, many men who, in the name of Jesus, come and teach other atheistic and blasphemous doctrines and actions; we call them by the name of the originator of each false doctrine. (For each has his own particular method of teaching how to blaspheme the Creator of the universe, and Christ, whose Advent was foretold by Him, and the God of Abraham, and of Isaac, and of Jacob. They are all outside of our communion . . .) Some of these heretics are called Marcionites, some Valentinians, some Basilidians, and some Saturnilians, and others by still other names. (*Dial.* 35)

scholars do not find this dating historically credible, such as Risto Uro who dates *G. Th.* to the "hermeneutical space" of the 120s in Syria (see his *Thomas*, Epilogue, 134–38, esp. 134–35). Further, *G. Th.* has few references to the Creator and creation, and the sayings that do relate to the creation are ambiguous at best (e.g., 12, 77 and 113) and do not further the purposes of this study.

Our survey begins with the arch-heretic, Simon Magus (fl. AD 40–65) from Samaria. Simon is one of the most difficult alleged Gnostics to identify and classify because of the variety of accounts that evidence progressive embellishment. Obviously, Acts 8 is the earliest testimony of Simon's existence and teachings, meager as it is. In the account of Irenaeus (*Haer.* 1.24.1–3), Simon, through Helen, his first Thought (*Ennoia*), created the angels and archangels who in turn created the world. Simon is both the "Father above all" whom the angels deny, and the "Christ" who comes into the world to provide salvation through knowledge, freeing men from enslavement by the angels. Thus, in Irenaeus we encounter Simon and the Simonians, his followers, as true Gnostics, "promoting an oppositional relationship between the creator-angels and the 'Father above all,' a Docetic Christ, a negatively valued creation, prophets who speak by inspiration of the archons, and, of course, libertine ethics."[48] Epiphanius's account includes "an elaborate system of emanations," and a "'defectively constructed' creation" (*Pan.* 1.2.21). From the accounts of the Heresiologists, it appears that in their quest to establish antiquity the Gnostics appealed to Simon as their founder. Yet, for different purposes, the proto-orthodox teachers likewise appealed to Simon as the founder of the Gnostics, primarily to establish their own historical priority, since Simon appears after Peter in the account of Acts and is denounced by him only to disappear into oblivion. Yet, the highly developed nature of the Gnostic scheme attributed to Simon appears forced and anachronistic, indeed more complex than those of his alleged students.

The next supposed Gnostic teacher was Menander from Samaria who taught in Antioch, Syria (late first, early second c. AD). Menander is the alleged disciple of Simon and teacher of Saturninus (Satornilus) and Basilides. According to Irenaeus (*Haer.* 1.23.5), the first Power sent Menander to be the Savior. The world was created by angels, brought forth by *Ennoia*. Menander's role was to conquer the angels who created the world through his magical arts. It is not clear that this is an oppositional dualism, and the Old Testament God is not identified among the angels. This picture is less developed than Simon's, leading Reimer

---

[48] *No Longer Jews*, 128.

Roukema to conclude that it is "even simpler and is perhaps even older" than Simon's myth.[49] This factor may have implications for the accuracy of Simon's portraiture as a Gnostic as considered in the account above.

Cerinthus was an alleged Gnostic teacher in Asia Minor in the late first or early second century AD, and there are two very diverse accounts regarding his teachings. The first is found in Irenaeus (*Haer.* 1.26.1; 3) followed by Hippolytus (*Haer.* 7.21; 10.21.1), who both portray him as one who separated the first God from the creator, a lower power who was likely an angelic being and ignorant of the higher God. There is also evidence of adoptionistic Christology with the Christ descending upon Jesus, the son of Joseph and Mary, who actually died and rose again. Christ was impassible, since he was pneumatic (spirit). The second account is found in Eusebius (*Hist. eccl.* 3.28), who claims two alternative sources, Gaius of Rome's *Disputation* (AD 160–230) and Dionysius of Alexandria's *Promises* (AD 190–264). The account portrays Cerinthus as a chiliast who espoused a future earthly kingdom of Christ, a position Eusebius finds "revolting." Though Charles C. Hill has attempted to reconcile the two accounts,[50] most scholars remain skeptical of discovering the "historical" Cerinthus because of the varied accounts.[51] For our purposes, we will consider Irenaeus' account since it is the most "Gnostic" in orientation, limited as it is. There is no identification of God of the Old Testament with the power or angel that created, nor is there a clear oppositional relationship between the creator(s) and the first God, though there is ignorance. This portrait is consistent in the first three individuals examined. They have "two power in heaven" conceptions, but the God of the Old Testament is not mentioned, and there is no oppositional relationship between the creator(s) and the first God/Power, though there is ignorance on the part of the angels/archons. The only exception to this is

---

[49] Reimer Roukema, *Gnosis and Faith in Early Christianity: An Introduction to Gnosticism* (trans. by John Bowden; Harrisburg, PA: Trinity Press International, 1999) 23.

[50] Charles C. Hill, "Cerinthus, Gnostic or Chiliast? A New Solution to an Old Problem," *JECS* 8 (2000): 135–72.

[51] See the comments of A. F. J. Klijn and G. J. Reinink, eds., *Patristic Evidences for Jewish-Christian Sects* (Supplements to Novum Testamentum 36; Leiden: Brill, 1973) 19.

the account of Simon's teaching, which we have good reason to hold with a large degree of skepticism as an anachronistic reconstruction.

When we arrive at Carpocrates, who lived In Alexandria, Egypt (AD 120s), we are much more solidly on Gnostic soil. Irenaeus (*Haer.* 1.25.1–6) includes in Carpocrates' teachings creation by angels who are inferior to the unbegotten God, Satan as present among the archons, the transmigration of souls, and libertine ethics. Jesus was born naturally, but his soul was strong and pure because it "remembered what it had seen in the regions of the unbegotten God." Because of this remembrance, he had power to escape the world-creators. Anti-Judaism is evident as Jesus is described as being "lawfully" nurtured in Jewish traditions, but despised them and obtained power to vanquish his passions. He likewise despised the creator-archons themselves, a model for others to follow. The presence of the God of the Old Testament among the archons is inferred, and he may be identified as the "Prince" who is first among the world-creators (1.25.4). Clement (*Strom.* 3.2.5, 3.2.10) describes Carpocrates with a libertine image as well. Hippolytus (*Haer.* 7.20) gives indication of a clear antagonism present between the highest God and the world-creators. Minor details are added in the accounts of Eusebius (*Hist. eccl.* 4:7) and Epiphanius (*Pan.* 27.3.3–4), but Carpocrates and his followers are clearly among the earliest Gnostics.

With Basilides, Saturninus, who lived in Antioch of Syria (AD 120s??), is described as a disciple of Simon through his master Menander.[52] In Irenaeus' account (*Haer.* 1.24.1–2), Saturninus taught that the Unknown Father created angels, powers, and principalities, and these angels, in turn, created the world. The angels imitated a shining image to create man, but he could not stand, and the supreme power, taking pity upon man, sent a spark of life that enabled him to stand erect. The angels/archons desired to destroy the Father, and the God of the Jews was identified as one of these archons. The Savior, a Docetic Christ, came from the unknown Father for the express purpose of destroying the

[52] There is a timing issue here in that Menander is supposed to have flourished around the turn of the century and Saturninus and Basilides are described as beginning their ministries in the 120s or 130s. A gap of time seems evident for direct contact, a factor that may also impact the alleged relationship between Simon and Menander.

God of the Jews. Asceticism is evident in abstinence from marriage and procreation, which are of Satan. Hippolytus (*Haer.* 7.16) adds that the prophets spoke by the angels, though some were inspired by Satan.

Finally, there is Basilides (AD 120s-150s) of Alexandria, Egypt, who taught that there were 365 emanations from the highest God before arriving at the final pair of angels who created the world. The angels divided the nations among them, the chief of who was the God of the Jews. This God incited the Jews to rebel against the nations, such that the other nations were antagonistic toward the Jews. Salvation history was initiated because of this plight, so the highest God sent the first-born Nous (= Christ) to free those who believed from the creators. Docetic and adoptionistic ideas are present. A polemic against Christianity is evident with the challenge that one cannot confess both the crucified Christ and the Docetic Christ. Salvation is for the soul only, not the body. The prophetic writings originated from the rulers, and the law came from the chief of the Jews. Basilides and his followers are described as "no longer Jews; on the other hand, they have come to be no longer Christians."[53] Hippolytus' account (*Haer.* 7.20.1–7.27.13) is much more philosophical. In it, a lower ruler is said to have spoken to Moses. The lower rulers think they alone are God, and there is a confusion of three Sonships. Jesus was illuminated. With the account of Clement of Alexandria, the image of Basilildes is more moderate and Platonic than Gnostic. The opposition between the creator(s) and the highest God is reduced. Whether this moderation is a true reflection of Basilides himself or that of his followers is difficult to ascertain.

What can we conclude regarding these early "Gnostic" teachers? First, there is demonstrable evidence of "two powers in heaven" conceptions, as angels are immediately responsible for creating the world in every system. The highest God is clearly not the creator in any of these systems,

---

[53] I take the title for my book from this text in Irenaeus (*Haer.* 1.24.6). Bentley Layton corrects Irenaeus via Epiphanius to state that the Gnostics are "no longer Jews; on the other hand, they have come to be no longer Christians" vs. Ignatius' Latin version, where the text reads: they say they are "no longer Jews; on the other hand, they are not yet Christians." Layton uses the term "erroneously" of the Latin text. (See *The Gnostic Scriptures*, 425, 425 n.f).

and quite frequently the angel-creators are ignorant of him. The relationship between these angels and the highest power/God is not always clear, but a progression seems evident, moving from general ignorance in the earliest teachers to outright rebellion in the later. References to the God of the Old Testament are absent in the earliest Gnostic teachers (with the exception of the anachronistic reconstructions regarding Simon Magus), but become more prominent in the systems of those who arise in the AD 120s (Carpocrates, Saturninus, and Basilides). Concepts of Christ are mixed, with Simon and Menander both identifying themselves as savior-figures who impart knowledge. Later teachers posit Christ as sent forth from the highest God to illumine those enslaved by the archons. Depending upon whose account is read, the Heresiologists identify Docetic, adoptionistic, and modalistic conceptions in the Christology of these early figures. In each, the Savior/Christ takes on a revealer role and not a redemptive one. He has no connection at all with the creator, and is very often removed from any real contacts with the creation (either by birth, body, death, or resurrection).

There appears to be a marked trend to disassociate the true Christian "Gnostic" faith from Judaism, the Old Testament, and its God through a demotion of the God of the Old Testament, a rejection of creation, a rejection of the Law of Moses, and the attribution of the prophets' inspiration to the angels/archons. In the latter regard, it is likely that the prejudice against the prophets is a reaction against Christianity, which was seeking quite actively at the time to exploit the archives of the Old Testament to find prophecies and types that demonstrated the connections between the God of the Old Testament and Christ, as well as Christ's significant place in his unfolding plan of redemption.[54]

Beyond these factors, the early Gnostics seemed willing to take up two elements in their conceptions that the New Testament authors seemed reticent to do. The first was to accept the mediation of creation by angels, a Second Temple Jewish theme that seems to bypass the New

---

[54] See S. G. Wilson, *Related Strangers: Jews and Christians 70–170 C.E.* (Minneapolis: Fortress, 1995) 209–10, where he attributes the development of Marcion's teachings to this type of environment where a polemical battle over the use of the Old Testament and related issues existed between Jews, Christians, and Marcion and his followers.

Testament conceptions. The second was to take up the philosophical term *demiourgos* and *demiourgein* in their creation rhetoric. Though almost entirely absent from the Septuagint and the New Testament, the terms appear readily in Gnostic texts and reports about these Gnostic teachers.[55]

Christ, Creator and Creation in the Apostolic Fathers[56]

With what was later defined as the New Testament canon finalized by earliest estimates by the last decade of the first century (i.e., with Apocalypse of John), there was a relatively short window of time for other proto-orthodox writings to be produced prior to AD 120. However meager the list, there are several works from this period that can be considered for what they say and do not say about Christ and his relationship with the Creator and creation. An interesting feature of the writings of the Apostolic Fathers is that the connection between Christ and creation is not a prominent theme. This is not to say that the creation is portrayed in negative terms, it is not; nor that the Creator/Maker has a negative image, he does not. Creation in general is viewed quite positively as the product of God the Father, but the occurrences of this theme do not seem to be offered in response to any challenges to the doctrine of creation, or as polemic against false concepts. Further, and of special interest to this study, Christ's agency in creation is nearly absent. A major point of concern in light of Docetic challenges is the reality of the flesh of Jesus in his virgin birth, physical life, redemptive death, and victorious resur-

---

[55] A casual reading of the *Nag Hammadi Library* and the reports of the Heresiologists evidences the popularity of demiurgical language among the Gnostics. For the latter, see Irenaeus, *Haer.* 1.5.2–3 and 1.7.2–5 for Valentinus and 1.26.1 for Cerinthus. See also Hippolytus, *Haer.* 7.23.1–7, 7.26.9 and 7.27.9 for Basilides.

[56] For an excellent general overview of the apostolic Fathers, see Clayton N. Jefford, et al., *Reading the Apostolic Fathers: An Introduction* (Peabody, MA: Hendrickson, 1996). In *No Longer Jews*, I surveyed each of these sources with reference to anti-Jewish attitudes and possible polemics against Gnosticism (168–80). Here, I examine them more for their Christological perspective, particularly with reference to the Creator and creation. Unless otherwise indicated, all translation are from Michael W. Holmes, ed., *The Apostolic Fathers* (2d ed.; translated by J. B. Lightfoot and J. R. Harmer; Grand Rapids: Baker, 1989).

rection. Thus, texts that do make the connection between Christ and the work of creation are especially significant and may provide a datable benchmark for Gnostic concerns. The following is a brief survey of five important works potentially datable to this period.

The Didache (a.k.a. *The Teaching of the Twelve Apostles*) was composed by an unknown author very likely in Antioch, Syria, anytime from the late first century to as late as AD 140, though the former is the more probable date of composition. Known essentially as a church manual and a call to personal morality through an enumeration of the "Two Ways," there is very little by way of theological reflection in this work. God the Father is identified as the Creator, as in 10.3, "You, Almighty Maker, created all things for your name's sake." But Jesus is not associated with this work of creation. Typical Gnostic themes are absent, and there is no separation of Christ from the Father or of the creator from the highest God. A proto-trinitarian baptismal formula is accentuated by the practice of triune baptism (7.1–4), indicating the close connection between the Father, Son, and Holy Spirit. Themes and quotations from Jewish scriptures and traditions indicate a strong sense of continuity between Judaism and Christianity, though the former has definitely been superseded by the latter. A physical resurrection and the future kingdom of Christ are clearly anticipated, themes consistent with the New Testament but far from Gnostic in orientation.

The *First Epistle of Clement to the Corinthians* was probably written by Clement, bishop of Rome about AD 95. This letter from the Roman Church to its Corinthian counterpart, is perhaps the earliest extant extracanonical Christian document. Written to counter a major schism in the Church at Corinth, this letter is a call to Christian unity. The creation, though not a major theme in *1 Clement*, is viewed very positively both in terms of its purpose and design (e.g., 20, 33, 60). The creation is viewed as a gift to enjoy, and creatures are to live with respect and honor for their Maker (7.3). The Father and Master of the universe is the Maker and Creator of all things and as such is sovereign and to be obeyed. Numerous titles (e.g., Maker, Creator, Lord of all flesh) relate to the same individual, God the Father, who was the Creator of all. No indication is given that Christ mediates the creative order, as is found in the New Testament. Yet,

Christ's resurrection is deemed the basis of the believer's hope (24–26), and his identity as divine is well-established (36; note the proto-trinitarian formulas in 46.6 and 58.2), as is his messianic fulfillment of prophecy and patterns. Clement has a high view of scripture, and his knowledge and use of the Old Testament is often seen as evidence of the use of *testimonia,* or anthologies of Old Testament texts related to Christ.[57]

A significant point to consider is that Clement utilizes the Greek term for Creator that was generally absent from the New Testament, *demiourgos.* This word appears in both its noun and verb forms a minimum of eight times (20.6, 10, 11; 26.1; 33.2; 35.5; 38.3; 59.2), marking a significant departure from the Biblical traditions of the Septuagint and the New Testament. This Stoic term, generally translated "Creator," "Maker," or "Architect," and used by the Stoics of a lower power than the highest God, was stripped of its typical pagan connotations in its employment by Clement. He used it of God the Father as both the one who speaks the world into existence (*ktízo*) and then crafts it after his architectural design. The demiurge is not a lesser being or one separated from the Father, but the Father himself.[58] The word is used in a very positive, non-polemical manner, and does not betray any evidence of Gnostic influence or a Gnostic opponent.[59]

[57] See Jefford, 111.

[58] See the discussion in James A. Kleist, *The Epistles of St. Clement of Rome and St. Ignatius of Antioch* (Ancient Christian Writers 1, ed. J. Quasten and J. C. Plumpe; New York: Paulist, 1946) 108–9, n.68; and Foerster, *TDNT* II:62 and III:1026.

[59] I do not know of a single reference where Christ himself is called the demiurge until the time of *The Epistle to Diognetus,* which Jefford dates to the late second century (162; he gives the range of 117–310). In *Diog.* 7.2, the author speaks of the Creator (παντοκτιστη) who is Lord and God), who did not send a subordinate (angel or archon), but was the Designer and Architect (τεξνιτην και δημιουργον) of the Universe in person (himself). In *Diog.* 7.4, he is called both God and Man. This identity seems to be a response to a Gnostic challenge. It is surprising that this important term was not more prominent in proto-orthodox circles. This would especially be the case if Hellenism was a major force in the development of New Testament Christology, since in Greek philosophy the demiurge was an intermediary and secondary figure. Its nearly complete absence from the Septuagint and New Testament, is evidence of at least the Jewish orientation of the Septuagint and the New Testament and perhaps the avoidance of terminology that might confuse or diminish the significance of the creator in Jewish and Christian circles, though

Hermas, who lived in Rome, probably wrote the *Shepherd of Hermas*, which can be dated to the late first to early second century AD. It is an apocalyptic work manifested in visions, commandments and parables, which are revealed to Hermas by a variety of mediators, including angels and human figures. It is very moralistic in purpose and focus, as Hermas calls the faithful to purity, humility, and obedience, and the wicked and schismatics to repentance. It has a positive regard for marriage, as Hermas is a married man with children, but virginity is highly exalted as well. The creation is viewed in very positive terms, as is God the Creator who by his wisdom and great power "created out of nothing the things that are" (Vision 1.1; 1.6). The Son of God is defined as "older than all his [God's] creation," and functions as "the Father's counselor in His creation" (Parable 9.12; 89:2). He is also responsible for sustaining the entire world (Parable 9.14; 91.5). "The pre-existent Holy Spirit, which created the whole creation," is made by God "to live in the flesh that He wished" (Parable 5.6; 59:5). Angels also have a prominent role with reference to creation, being the first created beings. Following their creation, the Lord delivered unto them "all His creation to increase and to build it, and to rule over all creation" (Vision 3.4; 12.1). The angels are also given by the Son of God supervisory responsibility over men (Parable 5.6; 59.2), and responsibility for building the tower (= the Church; Vision 3.4; 12.2). Man's prominence in creation is extolled by naming him "lord of all the creatures of God" (Mandate 12.4; 47.2–3).

Thus, it is in the *Shepherd of Hermas* that we encounter very likely the first extra-canonical reference to the Son participating in the work of creation, and the first proto-orthodox work that includes the mediation of creation by secondary powers (Christ as well as the Holy Spirit and angels), though God the Father is still clearly the master Creator. In no sense is the God of the Old Testament demoted to a secondary status, and the creation is still highly valued. The angels mediate God's sovereignty and carry out his work, but they do not replace him or stand in opposition to him. Gnostic themes are entirely absent from the account, and *Hermas* seems to know no Gnostic opponents. The *Shepherd of Hermas* stands as

this argument from silence is highly speculative.

a clear witness to a simplistic Jewish-Christian tradition focused upon a strict morality based upon the commandments of God and manifesting Jewish themes (e.g., angelology, unbelievers as "Gentiles," and "Two Ways" theology).

The author of the *Epistle of Barnabas* is unknown. It was written in Egypt in the late first century or early second century up to the time of the reign of Hadrian (AD 120–130s). It is a much debated work, not only with reference to its dating and provenance, but also due to its extreme anti-Jewish rhetoric and its possible mention of a rebuilt Jewish Temple.[60] If it were composed in the late first, early second century in Egypt (as I contend), it stands as an almost solitary witness to proto-orthodox Christianity in this region prior to the late second century.[61] The author exhibits a deep concern regarding Jewish-Christian relations, and exhorts the Christian community to faith, unity, and morality. The author has special spiritual insights into the text of the Old Testament, which he quotes and paraphrases freely, adopting an allegorical approach to the text vis-à-vis the literal and mistaken understanding of the Jews who are blinded by the Evil One (see 9.4). *Barnabas* has a high view of scripture, but the author claims to have special insight into the fact that the prophets spoke by parables and types such that the Jews did not understand their own scriptures or their place as the people of God. In fact, he states that the Jews were never the true people of God in that Moses destroyed the stones of the covenant upon his descent from Mount Sinai (4.6–8; 14). The covenant was ultimately offered through Jesus, and

---

[60] For the latter, see my discussion of the primary issues and arguments in *No Longer Jews*, 175–78. See also Wilson, *Related Strangers*, 131–36; William Horbury, "Jewish-Christian Relations in Barnabas and Justin Martyr," in *Jews and Christians in Contact and Controversy* (Edinburgh: T. & T. Clark, 1998) 127–61; P. Richardson and M. B. Shukster, "Temple and *Bet Ha-midrash* in the Epistle of Barnabas," in *Anti-Judaism in Early Christianity*, ed. P. Richardson, D. Granskou, and S. G. Wilson (Vol. 2; Waterloo, ON: Wilfrid Laurier University Press, 1986) 17–31.

[61] W. Bauer made much of the silence (interpreted by him as absence) of proto-orthodoxy in Egypt in his *Orthodoxy and Heresy in Earliest Christianity* (tr. and ed. R. A. Kraft, et al., 2d ed.; Philadelphia: Fortress, 1971). See the discussion in B. Pearson, "Christians and Jews in First Century Alexandria," in *Gnosticism and Christianity in Roman and Coptic Egypt* (SAC; New York: T. & T. Clark/Continuum, 2004) 90–95.

Barnabas is written to warn his hearers "not to fall short of that which we possess" (4.9; translation of first ed. of Lightfoot's *Apostolic Fathers*).

In light of this focus, it is not surprising that there are very few references to the Creator and creation in *Barnabas*. References to the "Maker" appear naturally and casually in the text (e.g., 2.10). An excursus in 5.10–6.7 explains the reality and necessity of the incarnation and suffering of Christ. In the midst of this section, the author appeals to the sovereignty and pre-existence of Christ at creation as a basis for understanding the value and plan of redemption. Barnabas exhorts those who follow the Way of Light, "You shall love him who made you; you shall fear him who created you" (19.2a); but those who follow the Way of the Black One are described as "not knowing him who made them" (20.2). They are also described as "corrupters of God's creation" (20.2). This can be seen as an obvious signal that Gnosticism was not a concern, because it posits one's relationship with the truth as having a positive relationship with the Maker of heaven and earth and following his ways of morality. Along the path of the Two Ways are stationed "light-giving angels of God" and "angels of Satan" respectively (18:1). *Barnabas* concludes, "And may God, who rules over the whole world, give you insight" (21.5).

Barnabas stands as a testament to a Christianity that is fully immersed in Jewish scripture, but greatly distanced from the Jewish people and their traditions. There is no sense of supercessionism as is found in some Pauline texts and Hebrews in the New Testament; rather, for *Barnabas*, the Jews never had the covenant of God. Yet, the Jewish God, scripture and covenant reach their culmination in the Christian community. There is no returning to Judaism; yet, neither is there any threat of Gnosticism. Barnabas and his community seem oblivious to any viewpoint that rejected the God of the Jews and his works of creating, law-giving and covenant-making. He is still the supreme God of the world and the Maker of heaven and earth, and Jesus, who was present with him at creation, shares in his sovereignty.

The letters of Ignatius of Antioch[62] were written by Ignatius, bishop of Antioch, Syria, who died between AD 110 and 113. Like *Barnabas*,

---

[62] All quotations are from Schoedel, *Ignatius of Antioch*.

the theme of the original creation is barely mentioned in Ignatius' letters. The author, preparing for his impending martyrdom, warns the churches against doctrinal opponents and schismatics, and encourages them to unity under the leadership of their bishops. The identity of his opponents is not entirely clear, but it is certain that he contended with Judaizing teachers who sought to encourage the observance of Jewish ways, and docetists who diminished the humanity of Jesus and the reality of his physical life, passion, and resurrection.[63] His attacks upon Docetism are limited to the physical reality of Christ's birth, life, death, resurrection, and appearances. He does not in any sense appeal to the goodness of creation, a fact that may indicate that Docetic concerns were not driven by philosophical speculations regarding the value of creation. Rather, the Docetism of Ignatius' time (and that of the Apostle John's for that matter) was centered upon Christological concerns, that is, the impossibility of the incarnation and the impassibility of God. Hurtado makes the point that the Docetism of Johannine literature and the Apostolic Fathers (though he rejects the category of Docetism as confused and misleading) was more than likely fueled by angels manifesting the presence of God in the Old Testament rather than the metaphysical and ontological concerns of Hellenism.[64]

Given these considerations, there are still a number of observations that can be deciphered from Ignatius' corpus of letters that are critical to understanding his theological content and context and their relation

[63] There has been a significant debate regarding the identity of Ignatius' opponents. Nearly all scholars admit the presence of Judaizers and docetists. More debatable is the presence of charismatic itinerant preachers (C. Trevett, "Prophecy and Anti-Episcopal Activity: A Third Error Combated by Ignatius?" *Journal of Ecclesiastical History* 34 {1983}: 1–18) and Gnostic teachers (H. Koester, *Introduction to the New Testament* {2 vols. 2d ed.; New York: de Gruyter, 2000} 2.289; and Ford, 25). Regarding the latter, most scholars are willing to admit that Ignatius did not encounter opponents with fully formed Gnostic systems; rather, they see in Docetic concerns an "incipient" Gnosticism similar to that found in the NT. See also, J. L. Sumney, "Those Who 'Ignorantly Deny Him': The Opponents of Ignatius of Antioch," *JECS* 1.4 (1993): 345–65, for a careful analysis of *Smy.*, *Phd.*, and *Mag.* where the author finds docetists and opponents who hold different views regarding Judaism, but not Gnosticism.

[64] Hurtado, *Lord Jesus Christ*, 636–37.

to Gnosticism.[65] On numerous occasions, Ignatius makes unequivocal claims regarding the divinity of Jesus Christ. This is most clearly found in titles that appear casually in and broadly across his letters. Examples of these are "Jesus Christ, our God" (*Eph.* salutation, *Rom.* salutation), "our God, Jesus Christ" (*Eph.* 18.2, where it reads "Jesus the Christ;" *Rom.* 3.3), and "Christ Jesus, the God who made you so wise" (*Sm.* 1.1). There are also passages that speak of his pre-existence with the Father. *Mag.* 6.1 speaks of "Jesus Christ, who before the ages was with the Father and appeared at the end." Likewise, *Mag.* 7.2 encourages the readers to hasten "to one Jesus Christ, who proceeded from the one Father and was with the one and returned (to him)." *Ephesians* provides several texts in which Jesus' divinity and humanity are equally emphasized. *Eph.* 1.1 provides an interesting reference to the "blood of God," and 19.3 speaks of "God being revealed as human to bring newness of eternal life." *Eph.* 7.2 provides a detailed Christological expression in which divine and human elements are juxtaposed: "both fleshly and spiritual, begotten and unbegotten, come in flesh, God, . . . both of Mary and of God, first passible and then impassible, Jesus Christ our Lord." In 20.2, Jesus came "according to the flesh . . . of the family of David, the son of a human and son of God."

The humanity of Jesus is a major concern of Ignatius, particularly in light of his Docetic opponents. Repeatedly, Ignatius provides testimony to the reality of Jesus' birth, sufferings, death, and resurrection as historical realities (e.g., *Mg.* 11, where these events took place under the rule of Pontius Pilate, things "truly and surely done"). *Tr.* 9.1–2 provides one of Ignatius' most detailed statements: "Jesus Christ, of the family of David, of Mary, who was truly born, both ate and drank, was truly persecuted under Pontius Pilate, was truly crucified and died, as heavenly, earthly,

---

[65] Schoedel rejects many of the identification of elements with Gnosticism as common themes in Hellenistic Judaism (see, for example, *Ignatius of Antioch*, 167). Though Mikael Isacson argues for a differentiated understanding of each letter, for the purposes of this paper, I will consider them as a unit. See M. Isacson, *To Each Their Own Letter: Structure, Themes, and Rhetorical Strategies in the Letters of Ignatius of Antioch* (Coniectanea Biblica New Testament Series 42; ed. by B. Holmberg and K. Syreeni. Stockholm: Almqvist & Wiksell, 2004).

and sub-earthly things looked on, who was also truly raised from the dead, his Father having raised him, in whose likeness his Father will also so raise us up who believe in him through Jesus Christ, apart from whom we do not have true life." The repetition of the adverbs "truly" and "surely" accentuates Ignatius' concern regarding those who say he suffered "in appearance" only (*Tr.* 10.1; see also *Sm.* 2.1). These ones are "apart from Jesus Christ" and are not "plantings of the Lord" (*Tr.* 9–10). *Sm.* 1.1–2 provides another Christological, anti-Docetic formula:

> . . . convinced as to our Lord (that he is) truly of the family of David according to the flesh, Son of God according to the will and power of God, truly born of a virgin, baptized by John that all righteousness might be fulfilled in him, (2) truly nailed for us in the flesh under Pontius Pilate and Herod the tetrarch—from the fruit of which are we, from his divinely blessed passion—that he might raise an ensign to the ages through his resurrection to his saints and believers whether among the Jews or among the Gentiles in the one body of his church.

Sm. 3.1 provides a rare statement regarding Jesus' post-resurrection appearances, in which he was "in the flesh even after the resurrection." In *Sm.* 3.2, Jesus is quoted as offering to the disciples, "Take, handle me, and see that I am not a bodiless demon." In *Sm.* 4.1–2, Ignatius calls his opponents "beasts in human form" (1) and Jesus Christ "the perfect human being" (2). These opponents Ignatius will not even give the dignity of naming (5.3), seeing that they are not persuaded of Christ's physical nature by the prophets, the law of Moses, the Gospel or even our own individual sufferings (5.1). They are further to be despised because they do not care for the physical concerns of widows and orphans (6.1–7.2; perhaps a caricature?).

Ignatius expresses a firm rejection of Judaism and its practices in his refutation of the Judaizers. *Mg.* 8.2 says that to "continue to live until now according to Judaism" is to reject grace and to follow erroneous opinions and old fables, which are useless. It continues, "Set aside, then the evil leaven, old and sour" and accept the new leaven which is Jesus Christ (10.2). "It is ridiculous to profess Jesus Christ and to Judaize;

for Christianity did not believe in Judaism, but Judaism in Christianity" (10.3). *Phd.* 6:1 adds, "But if anyone expounds Judaism to you, do not listen to him for it is better to hear Christianity from a man who is circumcised than Judaism from a man uncircumcised; both of them, if they do not speak of Jesus Christ, are to me tombstones and graves of the dead on which nothing but the names of men is written." In *Phd.* 8:2, Ignatius challenges those who say, "If I do not find (it) in the archives, I do not believe (it to be) in the gospel," to which Ignatius replies, "for me the archives are Jesus Christ."[66] For Ignatius, the Old Testament must be interpreted Christologically. For example, *Phd.* 9:1 states that Jesus Christ is the door of the Father through whom enter Abraham, Isaac, Jacob, and the prophets and the apostles, expressing the unity of all of redemptive history in Jesus Christ.

There are innumerable "binitarian" expressions in Ignatius' letter which demonstrate the close connection between the Father and the Son (e.g., *Eph.* 21.2). In *Mag.* 7.1, Ignatius emphasizes the unity between the Father and the Son: "The Lord did nothing without the Father—being united (with him)—neither by himself nor through the apostles." This unity is further stated in *Mag.* 8.2: "there is one God who revealed himself through Jesus Christ his Son, who is his Word which proceeded from silence,[67] who in every way pleased him who sent him." Further, there are also several proto-trinitarian formulas in Ignatius' works. *Eph.* 9.1 provides an analogy of the temple with the believers serving as "stones," an image used by Paul in his letter to the Ephesians (2:20–22), and Peter in his first epistle (2:4–8). Ignatius extends the metaphor by describing believers as those who are "made ready for the building of God the Father, carried up to the heights by the crane of Jesus Christ (which is the cross), using the Holy Spirit as a rope." *Mg.* 13.1 uses the Trinitarian formula "in the Son and the Father [and in the Spirit]," and again in 13.2, the

---

[66] Schoedel discusses the archives, and identifies them as the Old Testament scripture. See *Ignatius of Antioch*, 207; see also Idem, "Ignatius and the Archives," *Harvard Theological Review* 71 (1978): 97–106.

[67] Schoedel rejects the Gnostic interpretation of this expression, but suggests that the silence accounted for the inability of the Jews and Judaizers to understand Scripture; see *Ignatius of Antioch*, 122.

apostles are described as being subject "to Christ [and the Father and the Spirit]."[68]

Unlike those we have identified as possible early Gnostic teachers and those who were clearly Gnostic in the later decades, Ignatius provides numerous positive references to the prophets. In this, Ignatius is clearly in the trajectory of those who were developing Old Testament proof texts, or *testimonia,* for identifying Jesus as the Messiah and interpreting the Old Testament Christologically. In *Mag.* 8.2, Ignatius states, "the most divine prophets lived according to Jesus Christ." In this, Schoedel says that "Ignatius radically Christianizes the 'prophets' . . . and elsewhere also the law (*Sm.* 5.1)."[69] *Mg.* 9.2 states, "The prophets also were disciples in the spirit, {of} him to whom they looked forward as their teacher." *Phd.* 5.2 claims that the prophets made their proclamations with the Gospel in view, set their hope on him and waited for him, "in whom by believing they were also saved" (see also, *Phd.* 9.2). *Sm.* 7.2 appeals equally to the prophets and the gospel as sources for truth about Jesus.[70]

There are several interesting elements in Ignatius' epistles that are evident in (later?) Gnostic writings. For example, *Eph.* 19.1 speaks of the secrecy of Mary's virgin birth as well as the death of Jesus in order to elude the attention of the "ruler of this age."[71] In *Tr.* 5:2, Ignatius claims knowledge of heavenly things, "both the angelic locations and the archontic formations, things both visible and invisible." There are also numerous references to the "ruler of this age" beyond *Eph.* 19.1 mentioned above. *Eph.* 17.1 refers to his "teachings," which are "evil arts," "plots," and "scheming" associated with the Judaizers (*Phd.* 6.1–2). In *Tr.* 4.2, the

---

[68] It is interesting in each of the last two references that Christ precedes the Father.

[69] Schoedel, *Ignatius of Antioch*, 119.

[70] In this context, both the prophets and the gospel seem to be appealed to as items with specific content, perhaps written sources, though Schoedel disagrees with this last contention. See *Ignatius of Antioch*, 242.

[71] The theme of secrecy or silence regarding descent-ascent is found in several Nag Hammadi texts (e.g., *The Apocryphon of John* 20.19–27 and *The Three Steles of Seth* 127.6–20; compare Irenaeus, *Haer.* 1.24.6). Schoedel suggests that what eluded the "ruler" was not the knowledge of Jesus' birth and crucifixion (see *Mag.* 9.2), but their meaning. See *Ignatius of Antioch*, 87, esp. n.1. He also states that the importance of the knowledge of such mysteries was, in the time of Ignatius, "not yet markedly Gnostic."

disciples are taught that the "ruler of this age" is destroyed by gentleness. *Mg.* 1.3 encourages that if believers endure the whole of the abuses of the "ruler of this world" and escape, they shall attain God. It should be noted here that Ignatius' use of the term "ruler of this age" parallels Paul's usage in the New Testament (e.g., Eph. 2:2 and 2 Cor. 4:4) where the term is parallel to Satan, and juxtaposed to the true God and the gospel of Christ. In later Gnostic systems, the word becomes plural (rulers/archons), and includes the God of the Old Testament.

What of Ignatius of Antioch? One of the burdens of Ignatius was to defend the reality of Christ's physical being in his birth, life, suffering, death, and resurrection against those who would deny its reality. This he did with passion and clarity. Jesus' physicality was the means by which he provided redemption, and his passion gives meaning to Ignatius' own suffering and looming martyrdom. Jesus was the focus of the Old Testament prophets who both revealed him and believed in him for salvation. Jesus is divine as well as human; in fact, he is called God on numerous occasions, and was preexistent with God from eternity, proceeding forth from the Father's silence. Binitarian and proto-trinitarian formulas are prominent, giving evidence of the harmony and unity between Christ and the Father, as well as with the Spirit.

Ignatius was equally passionate against Judaizers as he was docetists, and his language and concepts, whether intentional or not, distanced the Christian faith from its Jewish roots. Christians should not follow Jewish practices, nor should they limit their understanding of God's ways to the Old Testament. Though the Old Testament is a valuable source of information about Jesus, the true "archives" are Jesus himself, and the gospel message of the apostles has equal authority for finding truth. He does show openness to Jewish Christian teachers who expound Christ to their hearers, but he would have nothing of Gentile believers who sought to enumerate on Judaism.

Though there are false teachers in the range of Ignatius' authority as bishop, he does not seem to be aware of Gnostic opponents. This is rather peculiar in that Menander is reported to have taught in Antioch, the city where he served as bishop, in the early second century, and Cerinthus was in Asia Minor, the destination of several of his letters, in the same period.

Ignatius makes no attempt to refute any secret knowledge, or to defend the connection between the God of the Old Testament and Jesus Christ. Christ was sent forth by the Father God of the Old Testament, and the purpose of his coming was to provide redemption through his passion, not to convey secret knowledge to his followers. In an innocent sort of way, Ignatius did address some themes that were soon to be themes of Gnostic teachers. His understanding of the descent of Christ and its secrecy with reference to the "god of this world" would later be employed by the Gnostics to refer to the world-creating archons whose deceptive powers Jesus came to destroy and free those who were ignorantly enslaved to them. Yet, his writing does not give evidence of knowledge of Gnostics or a polemic against them. His chief concerns were Docetic teachers who diminished the humanity of Christ and consequently his passion, Judaizers who emphasized Jewish practices and rituals to the ignoring and diminishing of Christ, and anyone else who might operate apart from the authority of the bishop(s).

The Apostolic Fathers considered above provide an important witness and context regarding the development of Gnosticism and Gnostic themes in the late first and early second centuries. These writings cover a relatively broad geographical scope, when both their originations and destinations are considered, including Antioch, Syria (*Didache*, Ignatius), Rome (*1 Clement, Shepherd of Hermas*, Ignatius), Corinth (*1 Clement*), Egypt (*Barnabas*), and various cities of Asia Minor (Ignatius). Though they are written for a variety of purposes, and are not in any sense theological treatises, most of them are concerned with unity in their churches which was grounded in theological considerations. Together they reveal a Christianity that was emerging from its Jewish roots, still struggling with issues related to Jewish practices, but firmly planting their understandings of God's purpose and Christ's identity in the Old Testament. The prophets are highly exalted as revealers of truths about Christ, and in these writings we see the first extra-canonical evidences of the development of *testimonia*. The Maker of heaven and earth is honored, and his creation is valued. Christ's identity as fully human is a passionate concern of several writers, and his identity as divine is also quite well attested, whether through direct statements of divinity or through "binitarian" or proto-trinitarian formulas or practices (e.g., triune immersion).

There is no clear evidence of themes or opponents that were clearly Gnostic in nature. Certainly elements and themes that were later included in Gnostic systems were present, such as Docetism, procession from silence, and an adversary identified as the "god of this world;" yet, none of these emphases is a definite feature of Gnosticism, or inconsistent with themes that were of concern to earliest Christianity as revealed in the New Testament texts. These texts betray no evidence of a separation between Jesus and the God of the Old Testament, otherwise called the Father, neither is there any evidence that the Creator is a lesser being than the highest God himself. The Old Testament prophets are still sources of truth originating from the highest God, revealing truth about his Son who came to redeem the world.

Did Ignatius of Antioch believe that the Maker of heaven and earth was the Father of Jesus? The answer is an unequivocal yes in every possible respect. And, it is not a far stretch to surmise that had there been a theological opponent who separated Christ from the Creator, lessened the value of the creation, and diminished Christ's and our identity with it, Ignatius would have been among the first to condemn him and warn of the disastrous implications of this teaching for personal redemption and spiritual meaning. The task of condemning this kind of teaching was carried out by the redactor of Ignatius' writings as Gnostic themes took shape and challenged apostolic doctrine in the subsequent decades of the second century.

Irenaeus, Pagels, and the Christianity of the Gnostics[1]

Daniel Hoffman

❋HUNDREDS OF THOUSANDS of people have discovered the important and pivotal early church era period with its many various sources through the numerous published works of Elaine Pagels.[2] My own study and research has benefited from Pagels' writing in several ways. My Master's thesis extended her general view that heterodox factions, Gnostics and others, influenced church writers like Ignatius, Justin, and Irenaeus in positive and negative ways.[3] Pagels, indirectly, also provided me with a unique and worthwhile dissertation topic: a thorough critique of her theory that Gnostic groups in the second and third century offered women higher status than was available in the general Christian community in that era.[4] Her 1979 bestseller *The Gnostic Gospels* (more than 650,000 copies sold) noted that various Gnostic philosophical and theological systems often included female deities or what she called "God the Mother" imagery. She argued that mythological systems that contained such feminine language and imagery led to higher status

[1] I would like to offer personal thanks to Dr. Yamauchi for his unfailing help and support through his teaching, guidance, encouragement, and advocacy on my behalf.

[2] Her most important popular works include: *Adam, Eve, and the Serpent* (New York: Random House, 1988); *The Gnostic Gospels* (New York: Random House, 1979); *The Origin of Satan* (New York : Random House, 1995); and *Beyond Belief: The Secret Gospel of Thomas* (New York: Random House, 2003) [Hereafter abbreviated *BB*].

[3] Daniel Hoffman, "The Eucharist and Docetism in Selected Second Century Orthodox Writings" (M.A. Thesis, Trinity Evangelical Divinity School, 1984).

[4] This dissertation was supervised by Dr. Edwin Yamauchi. Daniel L. Hoffman, "The Status of Women and Gnosticism in Irenaeus and Tertullian" (Ph.D. diss., Miami University, 1992). Later it was revised and published as a monograph, Daniel L. Hoffman, *The Status of Women and Gnosticism in Irenaeus and Tertullian* (Lewiston, NY: Mellen, 1995).

for women within Gnostic groups, in contrast to those women in groups where "God the Father" language and imagery were used.

Pagels' theory about the status of women found in *The Gnostic Gospels* was based upon philosophical and theological belief systems, and the images within them. Her work relied heavily upon her interpretation of these systems and beliefs which she saw as very important for people in religious groups in the second and third centuries—and in our own day. Her views, however, have now been modified and toned down in her most recent major book, another best seller, *Beyond Belief: The Secret Gospel of Thomas*. Here she is very critical of "philosophical and theological belief systems" and advocates moving beyond them.[5] She is primarily interested in going beyond orthodox Christian belief systems, not the belief systems of some Gnostics, whose views she still champions. Nevertheless, it was Pagels' writing that has prompted much of my own writing and research.

My focus here is Pagels' interpretation in *Beyond Belief* of the role of Irenaeus, the well known Christian writer and bishop of Lyon (Logdunum), in establishing Christian orthodoxy in the second century and following. Certainly Irenaeus rejected the doctrines and practices of Valentinians and other Gnostics that he knew, but more importantly, in contrast to Pagels' view, these Gnostics would most likely not have wanted to be identified with Irenaeus' church either.

Beyond Belief was published in 2003 and has been very well received by the mainstream media. It was highly praised, for example, by the *Los Angeles Times* as "a winning combination of sound scholarship, deep insight and crystal clear prose style." The prestigious *New York Times Book Review* said, "This packed, lucid little book belongs to that admirable kind of scholarship in which . . . the exhausting study of ancient fragments of text against the background of an intimate knowledge of religious history can be represented as a spiritual as well as an intellectual

---

[5] *BB*, 136. Much of my general review that follows appeared in a somewhat different form as "'Gnostic Christianity' Revisited: Seek Your Inner Light," *Christian Research Journal* 26.3 (2003) 54–56. That review is also available online: http://www.equip.org/free/DG045.htm.

exercise." *Publishers Weekly* said "In this majestic new book, Pagels . . . ranges panoramically over the history of early Christianity, demonstrating the religion's initial tremendous diversity and its narrowing to include only certain texts supporting certain beliefs."[6]

Many specialists in the early church have also been generous in their praise. Karen King, professor at Harvard Divinity School, called *Beyond Belief,* "a book many readers will treasure for its healing, its good sense, and its permission to think, imagine, and yet believe." Well-known religious writer Karen Armstrong said, "This luminous and accessible history of early Christian thought offers profound and crucial insights on the nature of God, revelation, and what we mean by religious faith." Krister Stendahl, Emeritus Professor of Divinity at Harvard, in a reference to the autobiographical information sprinkled throughout the book said, "It is as generous as it is rare that a first-rate scholar invites the reader to see and sense how her scholarship and her religious quest became intertwined. Elaine Pagels calls for a generosity of mind as she takes us into the world of those early Christian texts that were left behind but are now with us. Her very tone breathes intellectual and spiritual generosity too rare in academe."[7]

Not all reviews were completely positive, of course. For example, *The Atlanta Journal-Constitution* noted that the book was "an explosive and, some say, heretical look at the evolution of Christianity."[8] In academic circles, Pheme Perkins, Professor of New Testament at Boston College, indirectly raised a serious question about the accuracy of the general themes in the book. In a mostly positive review in *America: The National Catholic Weekly*, Perkins nevertheless noted that "since *Beyond Belief* is 'religion lite' for the PBS crowd, it would be unfair to debate Professor Pagels on scholarly details. Suffice to say that almost every gen-

[6] *BB*, back flap cover. These are the "standard" advertisement quotes for the book also available on numerous web sites, for example, http://www.amazon.com/gp/product/product-description/0375501568/002-7466405-3656063. This site also has links to many other reviews.

[7] Ibid. See also http://en.wikipedia.org/wiki/Elaine_Pagels for extensive biographical information about Pagels.

[8] Ibid.

eralization could be challenged or modified."[9] Unfair or not, the accuracy of "scholarly details" still determines the truth or error of any historical theory, and Pagels' generalizations, if they are incorrect in specifics as Perkins implied, should not go unchallenged just because they suit the interests of some readers.

In fact, challenging misleading generalizations that appear in *Beyond Belief* seem perfectly fair since Pagels clearly wrote to correct what she viewed as wrong generalizations about doctrines and practices in early Christianity. More specifically, the book attacked traditional Christian doctrines as too limiting for those seeking God, but supported selected Gnostic ideas in various ways. For example, in one important section, Pagels cited the *Gospel of Thomas* (Logion 70) which reads: "Jesus said: 'If you bring forth what is within you, what you bring forth will save you. If you do not bring forth what is within you, what you do not bring forth will destroy you.'" Then she gave this revealing commentary: "The strength of this saying is that it does not tell us what to believe but challenges us to discover what lies hidden within ourselves; and, with a shock of recognition, I realized that this perspective seemed to me self-evidently true."[10] Other personal commentary sprinkled throughout the book made it clear that Pagels' dislikes traditional Christian doctrines and creeds, but has sympathy toward inclusive religion. In various places, for example, she told of her participation in an evangelical church as a teenager, the later tragic illness and death of her son Mark, and her enjoyment of the community, friendship, and mystical nature of her current church, the Church of the Heavenly Rest (an Episcopal Church in Manhattan). Unfortunately, her early association with evangelical Christianity ended when, as she noted, "a close friend was killed in an automobile accident at the age of sixteen" and her "fellow evangelicals commiserated but declared that since he was Jewish and not 'born again,' he was eternally damned." Furthermore, she commented that since they

---

[9] Pheme Perkins, "Getting Past Orthodox Doctrine: A Book Review of Beyond Belief", *America: The National Catholic Weekly*, 189:1 (2003) 29 now available online at http://www.americamagazine.org/BookReview.cfm?articleTypeID=31&textID=3053&issueID=439.

[10] *BB*, 32.

allowed "no room for discussion" about "their interpretation" of his fate, she left that church group.[11] Elsewhere in the book she mentioned that she came to realize that there was "much that I love about religious tradition, and Christianity in particular—including how powerfully these may affect us, and perhaps even transform us." But there were still things that she could not love, namely "the tendency to identify Christianity with a single, authorized set of beliefs, however, these actually vary from church to church, coupled with the conviction that Christian belief alone offers access to God."[12] Unfortunately, her analysis of sources and presentation of that analysis in *Beyond Belief* clearly reflected these likes and dislikes.

Beyond Belief in many ways is a replay of themes from Pagels' *Gnostic Gospels*. Both were prompted by the amazing discovery of Coptic manuscripts in 1945 near Nag Hammadi in Egypt. These remarkable texts were first translated into English in 1977[13] and later revised by a team of scholars that included Pagels.[14] They provide an independent witness for many Gnostic beliefs previously known primarily from the refutations of them by church fathers such as Justin and Irenaeus. However, the Nag Hammadi texts have practically nothing to say directly about any individual teachers or actual groups that may have used them. They can only be linked with real teachers or groups based on what the church fathers said that they taught. For example, *The Gospel of Truth* and *The Gospel of Philip*, can correctly be called "Valentinian" because the views described in them closely match the descriptions of what Valentinus taught according to Irenaeus and other church fathers.[15] Since Pagels' theories are largely based on the interaction between historic Gnostic groups and those Christians who disagreed with them—like Justin and Irenaeus—she

---

[11] Ibid., 30–31.

[12] Ibid., 29.

[13] James M. Robinson, ed. *The Nag Hammadi Library in English* (New York: Harper & Row, 1977).

[14] Elaine Pagels contributed to Stephen Emmel, ed., Nag *Hammadi Codex III, 5, The Dialogue of the Savior* (Leiden: Brill, 1984) and Charles W. Hedrick, ed. *Nag Hammadi Codices XI, XII, XIII* (Leiden: Brill, 1990).

[15] See, for example, Pheme Perkins, "Nag Hammadi," in *Encyclopedia of Early Christianity*, ed. Everett Ferguson (New York: Garland Publishing, 1990) 636–37.

cited these church fathers in her work much more frequently than any Nag Hammadi texts including the *Gospel of Thomas* (despite the *Beyond Belief* subtitle).

Pagels assumed throughout *Beyond Belief*, based on the work of Walter Bauer and others, that there were no widely held or common standards for "correct" or "incorrect" Christian beliefs in the first centuries. She writes, for example, that Christianity existed for centuries "*before* Christians formulated what they believed into creeds."[16] However, this is true only if "creeds" were meant to denote large, formal, church councils, since these obviously did not begin until the fourth century. However, there were compact statements of key Christian beliefs that were widely accepted and used in the first century (e.g. 1 Corinthians 15:3–8). Pagels actually cited passages in Paul, John, Ignatius, and other sources that show the early existence of such beliefs, including the view that Jesus rose from the dead and was both human and divine. But she dismisses these by noting that they were not "universally accepted" and were interpreted to mean something quite different by those she calls Christians behind the *Gospel of Thomas* and other Nag Hammadi texts.[17] However, she omits details on what those differences sometimes included: a denial of the real humanity of Jesus by some who said He never had a physical body at all; a denial of his physical crucifixion and bodily resurrection by those who said it just seemed that these had occurred; and even a denial of his unique status as the only Son of God by those that said there were numerous deities in the heavenly realm, or Pleroma, and that Jesus or the Christ was just one of these. Pagels also omits, probably intentionally, any definition of her own use of "Christianity" or "Christian" based on doctrines, practices, or anything else—and she specifically rejects the fourth century and subsequent creeds as a valid description of what constituted Christianity in the earlier years. This makes it possible for her to use "Christian" throughout the book in completely indiscriminate ways.

---

[16] *BB*, 5. For a fairly comprehensive review of the Walter Bauer thesis, see Thomas A. Robinson, *The Bauer Thesis Examined: The Geography of Heresy in the Early Christian Church* (Lewiston, NY: Mellen, 1988).

[17] *BB*, 44–45.

On the other hand, there is one religious idea in *Beyond Belief* that she is willing to define partially, and advocate thoroughly. It is the theory that individuals should seek God by bringing forth the inner light or inventive consciousness, *epinoia*, that each person has within himself or herself according to her understanding of "The Secret Book of John" and some other Nag Hammadi texts. Pagels seems to believe that this *epinoia* can provide whatever essential spiritual awareness or link with the divine that a person might need. But this *epinoia* would not be limited to Christianity, no matter how it is defined, since Pagels argued it can be found in many other religious traditions.[18] Her universalistic emphasis actually contrasts somewhat with Gnostic teachings as described in the church fathers where the secret, higher, knowledge (*gnosis*) many viewed as necessary for salvation would have been reserved for the spiritual elite. Also, by advancing *epinoia* as a key element within otherwise diverse Gnostic groups, Pagels has actually made an important distinction between the essence of Gnosticism and the essence of Christianity according to Paul, John, Ignatius, Justin, Irenaeus and others.[19]

Of course, Pagels did not intend to make such a distinction, and would not have framed the issues in that way. She assumed that in the first and second centuries the many various groups that claimed some link with Christ were distinct only in a sociological sense: they had different leaders such as Peter, Philip, Thomas, Irenaeus, or others, and used different texts, or interpreted those they used differently. For example, she calls the groups that accepted and used the *Gospel of Thomas* "Thomas Christians,"[20] but as noted above, does not define what makes them "Christian." That is because her real concern is *how* such a definition

---

[18] Ibid., 74–76, 164–67.

[19] Forrest Schultz, "A Review of Pagels' *Beyond Belief*," *Chalcedon Report*, July 5, 2003, here he argues that Pagels inadvertently showed that "Gnosticism teaches that each one of us has divine light and a divinely given capacity to save ourselves so that we should look within and discover our light . . . to anyone with even this rudimentary understanding of Christianity and Gnosticism, it is crystal clear that they are antithetical to each other." Available now on "The Chalcedon Foundation" website, http://www.chalcedon.edu/articles/0307/030705schultz.php

[20] BB, 38–39, 58, 66, 72, 81, etc.

that seems to stress adherence to specific doctrines came to be empha-sized. Her proposed answer stressed sociological power struggles between the various heterodox factions that was won, unfortunately in her opin-ion, by the groups represented by John, Irenaeus, Tertullian, and finally Athanasius. The inherent truth or error of any particular view would be irrelevant or impossible to determine objectively in this era since Pagels does not recognize the existence of any valid standards, except perhaps whatever is "self-evidently true," to quote from the description of her own process for coming to truth.

Thus, she outlined the religious disputes of the second century as power struggles that involved the forceful suppression of "Thomas Christians" and others who stressed the vital *epinoia*. In particular, she argued that Irenaeus used the *Gospel of John* as an effective weapon in his struggle against various Gnostics. She contended that prior to Irenaeus, *John* was not widely accepted as authoritative by Christians who shared his outlook. Moreover, she theorized that Irenaeus used *John* to popularize the view that Jesus alone was God in order to refute Gnostic teachers who were troubling his church in Lyon. In the course of this conflict, Irenaeus helped to add *John* to the emerging canon, and promoted a rather literal interpretation of it to refute various Gnostic symbolic or spiritual inter-pretations of the book. Finally, Pagels believed that the work of Irenaeus bore fruit in the fourth century with the formulation and enforcement of the Nicene Creed on an otherwise much more diverse Christian scene.[21] Unfortunately, space does not allow for the refutation of all these general-izations in detail. But her theory that *John* would not have been accepted as canonical without the work of Irenaeus seems particularly weak or open to revision. However, briefly mentioning these generalizations does lay the groundwork for examining the comments of some Valentinians re-corded in *Against Heresies* 3.15.2. Pagels presented these as proof that the Valentinians were really misunderstood, and falsely maligned, Christians whose views were legitimate, or even preferable to those of Irenaeus and his church. Pagels ended *Beyond Belief* by quoting a command of Jesus

---

[21] *BB*, 114–81.

popular with Gnostics, saying to her readers, "seek and you shall find."[22] So heeding this command, the following discussion seeks out the details of Irenaeus' interactions with the Valentinian Gnostics to determine if "Christianity" is on both sides of the conflict as Pagels claims.

In this process, it would be helpful to be able to find objective historic standards, preferably ones that both sides accepted. Thankfully, Irenaeus provided plenty of information in this regard in his *Against Heresies,* and other works. In short, Irenaeus objectively defined true Christianity as those beliefs and practices which conformed to the historic "rule of faith," "the canon of truth," "apostolic doctrine," and Scripture (the OT or Hebrew Bible).[23] He presumed that his readers knew, or could find out whether doctrines or practices matched these, if they learned the content of the teachings in question. Irenaeus, furthermore, presumed that this apostolic faith was widespread, "scattered throughout the whole world,"[24] and that it included

> belief in one God, Father almighty, creator of heaven and earth, and the seas . . . and in one Christ Jesus, the Son of God, who became incarnate for our salvation, and in the holy spirit . . . . and the birth from a virgin, and the suffering and resurrection from the dead, and the heavenly ascension in the flesh . . . of our beloved Jesus Christ.[25]

Pagels knows these passages and arguments, of course, and even cited them. But she commented that "Irenaeus's vision of a united and unanimous 'catholic church' speaks more of *what he hoped to create* than what he actually saw in the churches he knew in Gaul, and those he had vis-

---

[22] *BB*, 185 (quoting Matt 7:7 and Luke 11:9).

[23] See Irenaeus, *Against Heresies*, 1.9.4; 2.27.1–2; 2.25.4; 3.1.1; 4.32.1 and *BB*, 151–52. All specific quotes from *Against Heresies* come from Alexander Roberts and James Donaldson, eds. *The Ante-Nicene Fathers, Vol. 1: The Apostolic Fathers—Justin Martyr—Irenaeus,* revised American edition, A. Cleveland Coxe (Grand Rapids: Eerdmans reprint 1981) [hereafter *ANF*] unless otherwise cited.

[24] *Against Heresies* 1.10.1 quoted in *BB*, 129.

[25] Ibid.

ited or heard about in his travels through Gaul, Asia Minor, and Italy."[26] Her psychoanalysis, as opposed to what Irenaeus actually said, seems to be based on the theory that the existence of Gnostics such as the ones Irenaeus encountered in Gaul, or knew about elsewhere, proved that there was no real doctrinal unity in the Christian community. The possible accuracy of her comment depends completely on her belief that these Gnostics, contrary to what Irenaeus claimed, were actually *within* the Christian congregations of Gaul and elsewhere whose doctrine he described. Otherwise, her comment would be about as logical as saying that the existence of Mormons shows that there is no doctrinal unity about the deity of Christ among evangelical Christians today! Irenaeus was in a better position to know what was widely believed in churches in his own day, and what groups were in it or what ones were not, than would any modern researcher.

Remarkably, in various places throughout the book Pagels admitted that Irenaeus had accurate and detailed knowledge of the doctrinal views and practices of at least some of the groups he described—those that used the *Gospel of Truth*, *Secret Book of John*, and the *Gospel of Philip*, for example.[27] She also explicitly recognized that Irenaeus sincerely believed that his Christian community held the same faith that had been taught by the apostles, and not a Gnostic version of it:

> I do not mean to suggest that he set out to deceive his audience. On the contrary, Irenaeus surely shared the conviction that made "orthodox Christianity" so compelling to him, as well as to many other Christians to this day: that the faithful as trustworthy stewards, hand down only what they, in turn, received from the apostles, without adding or subtracting anything.[28]

Since Irenaeus was in a position to know what true Christians believed, and Pagels admitted that he sincerely believed that it was essentially the same as what the apostles taught (not what the Gnostics taught), one can

---

[26] *BB*, 129.

[27] Ibid., 138.

[28] Ibid., 155.

only conclude that Pagels believed Irenaeus was deluded in his statements about widespread church unity.

However, on occasion elsewhere, Pagels seemed to accept that the Christian beliefs held by Irenaeus really were widespread. For example, she wrote that whoever authored books like the *Gospel of Truth* and the *Secret Book of John* "were implicitly criticizing, intentionally or not, the faith of *most* believers."[29] In describing the warnings expressed by Irenaeus against schism, she paraphrased his words, saying that by "devaluing what they held in common with other believers and initiating people into their own *smaller* groups, such teachers were creating potentially innumerable schisms."[30] Finally, in explaining the Valentinian Gnostic Heracleon's allegorical method of exegesis, Pagels noted that "Heracleon explains that *most* Christians tend to take literally the images they find in the Scripture."[31] If *most* believers did not have the kind of religious faith described by the *Secret Book of John*, and anyone who might leave Irenaeus' group would be moving to a *smaller* schismatic one, and *most* believers followed a rather literal method of interpreting Scripture in the second century, perhaps Irenaeus was neither as innovative as Pagels claimed, nor as mistaken about the relative size and doctrinal unity of the church as she theorized!

This brings us to *Against Heresies* 3.15.2, which is the main basis for Pagels' claim that Gnostics known to Irenaeus were actually Christians arguing for "redemption," or *apolutrosis* via second baptism from *within* the larger church community.[32] *Beyond Belief,* in both the original printing and the new version that included a translation of the *Gospel of Thomas* in an appendix, has a very troublesome rendering of what appears to be Pagels' own paraphrase of 3.15.2. After the passage saying that Irenaeus "hoped to create" unity, rather than seeing unity already present in the churches on key doctrines, Pagels wrote that Irenaeus encountered heretics in his various travels. She then wrote, "When he urged them to

[29] Ibid., 138, my italics.
[30] Ibid., 141, my italics.
[31] Ibid., 165, my italics.
[32] Ibid., 136.

return to the simple baptismal faith, *he says that they answered in words like this*:"[33] Then an indented and apparently direct quote of Irenaeus followed:

> We too have accepted the faith you describe, and we have con
> fessed the same things—faith in one God, in Jesus Christ, in the
> virgin birth and the resurrection—when we were baptized. But
> since that time, following Jesus' injunction to 'seek and you shall
> find,' we have been striving to go beyond the church's elementary
> precepts hoping to attain spiritual maturity.[34]

The argument then moved on to the *Gospel of Philip* where Pagels tried to show that Valentinians could have used words like virgin birth and resurrection to convey ideas far different from what was meant by this terminology in Irenaeus' church. There was no hint about where the above apparent quote may have come from until a few pages later when these different interpretations from *Philip* were linked back with Irenaeus. Here is an extensive quote from *Beyond Belief*, page 133:

> If Irenaeus read the *Gospel of Philip* he must have sharply rejected
> such teachings; for, as we have seen, when he demands that the
> believer "hold unmoving in his heart the rule of truth received
> in baptism," he specifically includes the "birth from a virgin, the
> passion, and the resurrection from the dead . . . in the flesh of
> our beloved Jesus Christ, our Lord" [with endnote citing *Against
> Heresies* 1.9.4 and 1.10.1] . . . Were members of Philip's circle

---

[33] Ibid., 129, my italics.

[34] Ibid. 129–30. *Beyond Belief* has no endnote number at the end of this ostensible quote from Irenaeus, nor does the any other endnote before or after tell where this apparent quote came from. I have run a search for every key word in this "quote" through a full text copy of *Against Heresies* of the *ANF* version and read every passage tagged, and have found no matchs. The closest for part of it is 3.15.2 and that is considered below. Irenaeus does say in a couple of other places that the Gnostics quoted "seek and you will find" but the surrounding text and meaning for that part of Irenaeus is completely different than what appears in this "quote." When reviewing this in 2003 I originally noticed this problem and emailed Dr. Pagels to ask for the source of this quote. She answered while on vacation and said that she did not have a copy of Irenaeus handy, and could not say for sure but guessed that this was "a paraphrase." She did not answer my follow up email comments and questions about it.

to answer that they confessed the same faith, Irenaeus would have replied, as he did to other Valentinian Christians, that although they "say the same things, they mean something different by them."[no endnote at the end of the quotation] Followers of Valentinus might readily have admitted that this was true; but they asked him, what is *wrong* with that? "When we confess the same things as you, why do you call us heretics?" [endnote given citing 3.15.2]. No doubt their interpretations *differed* from his, and from each other's; but why did Irenaeus think that these differences actually *endangered* the church? These questions are hard to answer . . ."[35]

Actually, these questions are easy to answer if Irenaeus is taken at his word. The Valentinians did not confess the same faith, and would not have claimed that they did if they were being candid. They might "say the same things" temporarily and superficially as a tactic to entice members from Irenaeus' church to listen to them. But the differences between what they actually taught in private and what Irenaeus and the rule of faith held to be true were extreme. It was that large disparity on central doctrines that brought the danger. Nor was it primarily a sociological danger, but one that involved the eternal destiny of real men and women.[36] Much of this is obvious when *Against Heresies* 3.15.1–2 is considered in more detail:

---

[35] *BB*, 133, Pagels own italics.

[36] Pagels, *BB*, 155 noted that Irenaeus was concerned about "eternal salvation" and cited *Against Heresies* 4.36.2–4 in note 38, page 221. The actual passage is 4.26.2–4 where Irenaeus warned against schismatics and said in part that those who "rise up in opposition to the truth, and exhort others against the Church of God, [shall] remain among those in hell (*apud inferos*)" and that "those who cleave asunder, and separate the unity of the Church, [shall] receive from God the same punishment as Jeroboam did." *ANF*, 1:497, with brackets, italics, and parenthesis in original. Pagels took this passage as further evidence that Valentinians, who she claimed were often priests, were being threatened. But the passage only compares schismatics to heretics, and does not describe the doctrine or practice of those who might separate from the church in any way that would certainly identify them as Valentinians. It is obvious that Irenaeus was concerned about maintaining unity in the church and that he recognized schism was possible and sometimes happened, but this passage does not prove that it was Valentinians who were viewed as this potential internal threat.

The doctrine of the apostles is open and stedfast, holding nothing in reserve; nor did they teach one set of doctrines in private and another in public. For this is the subterfuge of false persons, evil seducers, and hypocrites, as they act who are from Valentinus. These men discourse to the multitude about those who belong to the Church, whom they do themselves term "vulgar" or "ecclesiastic." By these words they entrap the more simple, and entice them, imitating our phraseology, that these [dupes] may listen to them the oftener; and then these are asked regarding us, how it is, that when they hold doctrines similar to ours, we, without cause, keep ourselves aloof from their company; and [how it is, that] when they say the same things [*et cum eadem dicant* according to Harvey[37]], and hold the same doctrines, we call them heretics? When they have thus, by means of questions, overthrown the faith of any, and rendered them uncontradicting hearers of their own, they describe to them *in private* the unspeakable mystery of their Pleroma [*his separatum inenarrabile plenitudinis suae enarrant mysterium*].[38]

Several points should be noted from this passage. Irenaeus never said that these Valentinians were once part of the "ecclesiastical" church and had separated from it. On the contrary, Irenaeus' church members were the ones who keep aloof from the company of the Valentinians mentioned here. Nor do the Valentinans ever claim to have been part of Irenaeus' group. Pagels apparently made that link in part by seeing in *dicant* a reference to the kind of confession of faith that new converts would make at their baptism. Irenaeus elsewhere does describe Valentinian baptism rituals, but these had only superficial similarities with those of his own "vulgar" church. For various reasons Pagels saw those Valentinian baptisms described elsewhere as *second baptisms* and presumed that most or all Valentinians had previously been baptized and made an essentially

---

[37] W. Wigan Harvey, *Sancti Irenaei, Episcopi Lugdunensis: Libros Quinque Adversus Haereses* (Cambridge: Typis Academicis, 1857) 2:80.

[38] *ANF*, 1:439 text and note 8 supplies the information that "vulgar" and "ecclesiastic" is *communes et ecclesiasticos* and that *communes* is the Latin translation based on the *katholikous* in the Greek original of Irenaeus. The Latin text is from Harvey, *Santi Irenaei*, 2:80.

orthodox baptismal *confession* in the church at some point before being forced out. That is probably why she translated *dicant* from 3.15.2 as "they confess" in most cases, rather than the more normal "they say." It was also apparently this theory which led her to create the very free paraphrase, or hypothetical dialogue, that appeared on pages 129–30 of *Beyond Belief,* looking as if it were a direct quote when it is not.

However, without that creative rendering of 3.15.2, there is nothing that indicates the Valentinians actually described by Irenaeus had ever been in the "common" church. Thus, there is little reason to believe, as Pagels does, that they "never intended to go their own separate way," but preferred to stay in that church and only left because they were forced out by Irenaeus or other church leaders.[39] In fact, Pagels repeatedly wrote that Irenaeus called "on his fellow believers to judge and expel heretics," sought to "expel them from the churches," told them "to abandon their heresy or be 'cut off,'" and demanded "that believers destroy" false writings and so forth.[40] However, in none of these cases did Pagels actually cite a passage where Irenaeus took such actions or made such demands! Based on the evidence in the sources that we have, he simply did not expel or excommunicate anyone from his church, or specify that any writings should be destroyed, nor did he ask others to do any of these things in their churches.[41] Furthermore, it is doubtful at this time wheth-

---

[39] *BB*, 158.

[40] *BB*, 141, 142, 147, 156, 157–58. Pagels does cite *Against Heresies* 1.20.1 in connection with her contention that Irenaeus urged that false writings be *destroyed* (*BB*, 147). However, that passage merely describes a number of apocryphal and spurious writings but does not contain any command by Irenaeus that such writings should be destroyed. The other claims that Irenaeus excommunicated, expelled, etc. do not include any cited passages from Irenaeus. No doubt some people did leave Irenaeus' church for various reasons—we know that some left to follow a Valentinian named Marcus, according to *Against Heresies*, 1.13.1–7, for example. But they left voluntarily. Irenaeus said that were duped by Marcus, but it is nevertheless clear that they were not excommunicated or expelled. In fact, some also returned voluntarily when they saw that Marcus was a fraud, and were welcomed back into Irenaeus' own church. There is no hint in this Marcus section that there were Valentinians *within* Irenaeus' church who wanted to stay but were forced out by him!

[41] See Matthew Gross, "Beyond Unbelief—A Critical Response to Elaine Pagels' *Beyond Belief: The Secret Gospel of Thomas*," *Reformed Perspectives Magazine* 6.16 (2004) at

er bishops would have been able to excommunicate anyone effectively, or compel the destruction of books. The position of the church within the Roman Empire was precarious, and Christian leaders certainly could not expect military or other *forces* to be available to compel obedience to their wishes. Indeed, it seems unlikely that Irenaeus would have taken the time and effort to make his massive refutation of heresy if he could simply have ordered heresy or heretics destroyed. In short, Irenaeus and other church leaders had available only moral and spiritual authority, not any kind of physical force.

Next, there is no basis in 3.15.2 or anywhere else for asserting that Irenaeus ever called any Gnostics "Christians," or considered them true believers. Pagels' *Vigilae Christianae* article upon which much of the Irenaeus material in *Beyond Belief* was based, unfortunately, was just as indiscriminate in the use of the term "Christian," and in the interpretation of 3.15.2, as the popular book whose "scholarly details" one would be unfair to debate. For example, Pagels wrote: "Irenaeus himself acknowledges that the Christians he accuses of divisiveness object to this charge, insisting that they, too, being baptized Christians, have received the same faith and 'confessed the same things' [3.15.2 cited] as other believers."[42] It should now be clear that Irenaeus calls them followers of Valentinus, not "Christians," does not directly say they had ever been baptized, presumes their argument about "saying the same things" was a mere ploy, and, above all, does not accuse them of divisiveness because he does not identify them as ever having been part of the church. Moreover, if Irenaeus' comment about the Valentinian pejorative references to his church as being "vulgar" and "ecclesiastic" are taken seriously, they themselves did not want to be identified with it either. Thus, they could not have been acting as a divisive element within it. In short, Irenaeus sees them, at least by the time of his writing *Against Heresies* in the late second century, as an *external* threat to the Christian church, not an internal one.

---

http://reformedperspectives.org/files/reformedperspectives/new_testament/NT.Gross. Matthew_BeyondBeliefbyElainePagels.html.

[42] Elaine Pagels, "Irenaeus, The 'Canon of Truth,' and *Gospel of John*: 'Making a Difference' Through Hermeneutics and Ritual," *Vigiliae Christianae* 56 (2002): 352.

Finally, Irenaeus himself uses "Christian" or "Christians" only three times in *Against Heresies*: in 1.24.6, 3.10.5 and 4.26.1. The first instance appears in a discussion of the doctrines of Basilides, a Gnostic from the early second century. Irenaeus says that followers of Basilides "declare that they are no longer Jews, and that they are not yet Christians."[43] Moreover, whatever their beliefs, he says that they stood "ready to recant" and would not be willing to "suffer on account of a mere name."[44] It is reasonable to conclude that they explicitly rejected being identified as Christians in order to avoid the danger that this name could bring in that era. Pagels seemed to have forgotten that danger in one very surprising section of *Beyond Belief* where she theorized about why those she called "Valentinian Christians" might stay in Irenaeus' church: "I would guess that the majority . . . rather than risk expulsion, chose the *safer* shelter of the church community"![45] There is little evidence that the Valentinians were *in* Irenaeus' church in the late second century, but even if there had been some in the church at that point, what threat did a hypothetical excommunication represent? It is laughable to think such persons would want to be identified as Christians by meeting and worshipping with people whose "elementary" views they no longer shared in order to gain *safety*! It was actually the Christians that Irenaeus described, and whose views he represented who were the most *unsafe* and the most likely to be persecuted or to suffer or die at the hands of the Roman authorities, or in pagan mob action. The Basilidians, at least, knew that people did not identify themselves as Christians if they sought *safety*!

A second passage where Irenaeus used the term "Christian," 4.26.1, is relatively incidental for our purposes, as Christians are contrasted with Jews, not Gnostics, and are said, unlike the Jews, to see the Law as "a treasure" that has been "brought to light by the cross of Christ."[46] However, the remaining instance where Irenaeus mentioned "Christians," 3.10.5, is on topic. It provides a fine place to conclude. In arguing against various

---

[43] Irenaeus, *Against Heresies* 4.26.1; *ANF*, 1:496–97.

[44] Ibid.

[45] *BB*, 158.

[46] Irenaeus, *Against Heresies* 1.24.6; *ANF*, 1:350.

Gnostic theories that distinguished between "God," and the "Father," and the being who created the heavens and earth, as did some Valentinians, Irenaeus said in this passage:

> God and the Father are truly one and the same; He who was announced by the prophets,
> and handed down by the true Gospel, whom we Christians worship and love with the
> whole heart, as the Maker of heaven and earth, and all things within.[47]

This usage implies, as would many other teachings in Irenaeus, that he would never have called Valentinians or other Gnostics "Christians." And, based on the Basilidian example among others, the Gnostics would not themselves have wanted to be called "Christians." Pagels' use of the term in *Beyond Belief* is not consistent with the historic beliefs or practices of either side in the second century based on the evidence in Irenaeus.

---

[47] Ibid, 3.10.5; *ANF*, 1:426.

Ante-Pacem *Christian Structures in the Levant*

Robert W. Smith

❊CHRISTIANS OF THE Levant have had a continuous history of using physical facilities in their advancement of the spiritual Kingdom of God. Christians of the Levant, before Constantine's singular rule over the whole Roman Empire in AD 324, used existing buildings that they could adapt, and even constructed new ones for their corporate purposes when possible. All of this happened in spite of their status as adherents to a religion that was not authorized by the Roman Senate. The Christians' employment of increasingly large and more public structures in the third century, as shown in Patristic sources and evidenced in archaeological discoveries in the Levant, challenges the prevailing image of a persecuted pre-Constantinian Church driven to find refuge underground in catacombs until liberated by Emperor Constantine. Previously, general and regional accounts of Ante-Nicene Church History have given little if any attention to the possible existence and use of publicly visible ecclesiastical structures,[1] but this is no longer excusable.

[1] Church historians, following the lead of Eusebius, have focused on the venerated martyrs and notorious heretics rather than the common experience of most Christians and the structures they employed. Classic resources like Henri Leclercq's *Dictionnaire d'Arché'ologie Chré'tienne et de Liturgie* (Paris: Letouzet et Ane', 1907–1953) make no significant comment on pre-Constantinian church facilities. The standard mid-twentieth-century texts such as Kenneth Scott Latourette's, *A History of Christianity* (New York: Harper & Brothers, 1953), make only passing mention of a church building at Dura-Europas from the third century (p. 79). William H.C. Frend's, *The Archaeology of Early Christianity: A History* (Minneapolis: Fortress Press, 1996), recounts the discoveries at Dura (p. 196f.), and points to the possibility of finding more evidence of the Christians from the third century (p. 386), but has no discussion of the developing utilization of buildings for Christian activities since none beside Dura were known. In W. C. H. Freund, *The Rise of Christianity* (Philadelphia: Fortress Press, 1984), there is no extended discussion of church architecture, but he shows an awareness of early third-century buildings mentioned by Origen (p. 429 nn. 43, 44). In Robert W. Smith's *Arabia Haeresium Ferax: A History of Christianity in the Transjordan to A.D. 395* Oxford, OH; Miami University Ph.D.

Some Christians in the Roman Empire lived in places where at times they could not meet publicly, and they were sometimes martyred for living their faith. The vast majority of Christians, however, would have been known as family, fellow workers, and friends whose religious eccentricity was tolerated in the religiously pluralistic society. Officially mandated persecution of Christians had to be enforced by busy local authorities who did not always understand the necessity for persecution as an effective means to restore the *pax deorum* or relish the task of enforcement.[2] Thus, when the Christian community in an area was extended *de facto* toleration, and it had sufficient resources from a large congregation or wealthy patrons, there was a proliferation of structures built for congregational functions as Christians awaited the *parousia* (return of Jesus Christ and the end of time).

Christians in the Hellenistic milieu of the first century saw themselves as a part of a singular collective spiritual entity they called the "*ecclesia*," which is translated in secular literature as the "assembly," but is translated in religious contexts as "congregation," or "Church."[3] As self-identified "resident aliens" (1 Peter 2:11) whose home was in heaven, the Christians had no desire to invest heavily in the physical world that they knew was going to burn (2 Peter 3:10–12). The assembly of believers, united spiritually by belief in the identity and work of Jesus Christ was,

dissertation 1994, (hereafter Robert Smith, *Arabia Haeresium Ferax*) written under the supervision of Dr. Edwin Yamauchi, there is no discussion of early Christian structures since none had yet been found, and the literary indications of these structures were yet to be brought to scholarly attention.

[2] The situation of Christians in the Roman Empire is analogous with the experience of unregistered Chinese Christians and congregations in the twenty-first century. Although officially suppressed, independent congregations like the Tu Du Sha Church in the Xiaoshan District of Hangzhou City, Zheijang Province, were able to grow from its beginnings in the 1930s through the Communist Revolution to 1500 members with a significant church building in June 26, 2003, when the building was reluctantly flattened by local authorities who had been badgered by members of the official Three-Self Church. For a video of the destruction of this structure see http://www.persecution.com/china. A written description of events can be read at http://www.persecution.com/china/media/Tu_Du_Sha.pdf as of March 1, 2006.

[3] Gerhard Kittel, *Theological Dictionary of the New Testament*, trans. and ed. Geoffrey W. Bromiley, (Grand Rapids: Eerdmans, 1976) (hereafter *TDNT*) III:501–36.

however, comprised of people with physical bodies that needed space. The early Christian practice of gathering regularly for corporate meetings was effectively a "family reunion" where affirmation of their mutual identity as brothers and sisters in Christ was enjoyed with conversation, food, song, and affirmation of shared belief and shared symbols (Acts 2:42). Their meetings had some elements of similarity with activities practiced in the Jewish community within synagogues from which many first-century believers came. Similarities are not surprising as the Jews, like the Christians, sought to retain a cultural distinctiveness in the greater community through corporate meetings. The apostolic era writings produced in the first century, and accepted by the orthodox Christian community as being divinely inspired, includes many allusions to corporate Christian gatherings of the assembly (Acts 2:42f) and a clear mandate for Christians to meet together (Hebrews 10:25). These earliest Christian source documents evidence a pragmatic view of the use of buildings in apostolic precedents reflected in the canonical writings, but there is no evidence of direct promotion of specific designs or prohibition of the use of buildings. Christian's use of architectural space to accommodate ritual, didactic, and fellowship activities is clearly evidenced in the earliest accounts of the Apostolic Church. However, no specific style of church architecture was expected in the Apostolic Church. The use of architectural space that included symbolic orientation, specific functional furnishings such as teaching chairs, communion tables, didactic frescos, and mosaics appears in later second- and third-century references to "Church-life," and is evidenced in physical remains from the third century. Thus it is seen that there was a trajectory towards a standardization of rituals and architecture within the Christian community.

The following study of textual references to Christian use of buildings and study of early church buildings in the Levant serves to correct the misconception that the Church was so dreadfully persecuted in the period before Constantine that it could not possibly have large and potentially recognizable public meeting places that were modified or even built for religious activities. This misconception is held first, by opponents of Christianity who wish to diminish the early societal impact of the Church; second, by Christians as an apologetic for the dearth of early church buildings; and third, by members of the primitiv-ist "House Church Movement" as proof that the church building is a post-Constantinian development that has hampered the subsequent nu-merical growth and spiritual focus of the Church.[4]

The apostolic era Christians did not confuse the varied meeting places of congregations with the Church itself. In the New Testament the congregations employed space, but the word *ecclesia* is always used in reference to either the local assembly of believers or the Church uni-versal. In canonical literature there is no confusion of the congregation with the place the congregation met. The practice of Christians employ-ing architectural space for religious purposes continued and expanded over the period prior to AD 324. The Church continued to anticipate Jesus' return and the complete realization of the Kingdom he had inau-gurated, but settled into becoming a more "resident" social institution. The movement of the Church away from the practice of "the priesthood of all believers" toward having a clergy class and a clerical performance of liturgical functions, promoted by a desire to protect orthopraxy and orthodoxy, contributed to the consecration of dedicated facilities.

The growth the Christian community and free practice of its faith, including its use of buildings, was impeded by the opposition of adher-ents to rival worldviews and the Roman state, which by the time of Nero identified Christianity as an illegal religion (*regio illicita*). Persecution that moved from sporadic local ridicule to systematic judicial prosecu-tion challenged the maintenance of public facilities for regular corpo-rate gatherings in places where the anti-Christian edicts were enforced. Systemic empire-wide persecution seems to have often run out of energy as it was decreed in Rome but not enforced elsewhere. Opposition to

---

[4] Howard Snyder writing about the first two centuries of the Church concludes, "In other words, the church grew fastest when it did not have the help or hindrance of church buildings." *Radical Renewal: The Problem of Wineskins Today.* (Eugene, OR: Wipf and Stock, 2005) 69. See also publications by Nate Krupp, *God's Simple Plan for the Church.* (Salem, OR: Preparing the Way Publishers, 2003); Robert J. Banks, *The Church Comes Home* (Peabody, MA: Hendrickson,1998); Frank Viola, *Rethinking the Wineskin: The Practice of the NT Church.* (Gainsville, FL: Present Testimony Ministry, 3d ed., 2001). Websites of proponents of the "House Church Movement" are common, and may be seen at www.homechurch.com, www.hccentral.com, or www.homechurch.org.

Christianity certainly forced some believers to gather in secret in obscure places like catacombs in Rome, but this was not the ubiquitous experience of Christians in provinces of the Levant.[5] The waves of opposition that crashed upon Christians in Rome were typically but a ripple in the Levantine provinces of Syria, Palestine, and Arabia. The impression that "church buildings" were largely a *post-pacem* creation that only came to be possible with the patronage of Constantine is a mistake perpetuated by the close association of "Basilicas" with church architecture. Recent archaeological discoveries and a close reading of patristic literature reveal that this was not the case. A more significant limiting factor than persecution on the construction of monumental church buildings in the third century was the terrible economic situation that existed in the time of the barracks emperors. In the Decapolis cities like Abila, Gadara, Gerasa, Hippus, Pella, Philadelphia, and Scythopolis many monumental structures were built in the second century, though few were built in the third century when the economy had deteriorated to the point where the cities could no longer afford the prestige of minting local bronze coins.[6] Christians were able to have worship places from their beginning in the first century through the singular rule of Constantine. Things that changed for the Church with the unified rule of Constantine over the entire Roman world in AD 324 were imperial patronage, an influx of people who did not have to fear persecution, and an improving economic situation.

Apostolic Era Use of Buildings by Christians

The Christian community was very flexible in finding ways to meet their need for space in the apostolic era. The Christians' need for space changed with their desired activities. Proclamation to non-believers could take

[5] J. Gordon Davies. *Origin and Development of Early Christian Architecture* (New York: Philosophical Library, 1953) 12.

[6] Augustus Spijkerman, *The Coins of the Decapolis and Provincia Arabia* (Jerusalem: Franciscan Printing Press, 1978). The catalogue of city-coins shows that most cities stopped production of coins after the reign of emperor Elagabalus. A few cities attempted a revival of coin production under emperor Gordianus. Bostra produced a few issues under Philip the Arab, Decius and Etruscilla in the mid-third century.

place person-to-person, in a variety of places, and in public venues with crowds. Devotional activities were more suited to private venues where the congregation, whether singing, praying, participating in communion, or listening to instruction, would not be disturbed by the activities and interruptions of the outside world. The prosperity of the first century probably restricted the availability of excess infrastructure.

Christians employed public venues when they engaged in proclamation of their message. Luke's account in Acts describes the Temple courtyard of Jerusalem as being a prominent venue for evangelistic meetings of the Christian community in the nascent days of the faith (Acts 2:46, 5:12), and as a venue for public events that publicized the faith such as a healing of the lame man (Acts 3:2), or apostolic public teaching under Solomon's Colonnade (Acts 3:11—4:3, 5:21, 25, 42). The synagogue similarly served as a semi-public venue to meet an audience that shared a common worldview. The Jewish response was divided over Jesus, and there is no indication that synagogues were ever totally converted into assembly places for Christians. Saul's search for Christians in Damascus was set up to begin in the synagogues,[7] and certainly it was in these same type of venues that he would later seek to find the receptive ears of proselytes. Among the pagans where there were no synagogues, quiet places of prayer like the riparian venue outside Philippi were sought out by Christians to make contacts (Acts 16:13). Public venues like the market place and the Areopagus were used in Athens (Acts 17:17–19) and other cities where discussions spilled out of the synagogues.

Christians typically employed the resources they had available, and thus commonly used their homes. Some homes were larger than others, and some would have had room configurations that were more conducive to larger corporate gatherings.[8] Large homes and small upper story apartments (Acts 20:8) could suffice as venues for private evangelistic and didactic encounters (Acts 5:42, 18:26). Regular corporate fellowship, and didactic and devotional time appears to have centered in homes (Acts

---

[7] Paul's technique of beginning his evangelistic work in the local synagogue is seen in Salamis (Acts 13:5), Pisidian Antioch (Acts 13:14–42), Iconium (Acts 14:1), Thessalonica (Acts 17:2), Berea (Acts 17:10), Athens (Acts 17:17), Ephesus (Acts 19:8).

[8] The home of Mary in Jerusalem had an entrance court (Acts 12:14).

2:46b). Prayer meetings also took place in homes and are seen in the house of Mary the mother of John when Peter was imprisoned by King Agrippa I (Acts 12:5). In order to root out Christians in Jerusalem, Saul of Tarsus had to resort to a house to house search in his effort to destroy the Christian community (Acts 8:3). While Christians were able at times to find venues like the lecture hall of Tyrannus in Ephesus (Acts 19:10) that they could use for their purposes, it is apparent that homes were the most common meeting place. "House Churches" were active in the homes of Jason in Thessalonica (Acts 17:7), Titus Justus in Corinth (Acts 18:7), Priscilla and Aquila in Ephesus (1 Corinthians 16:19), and for the same couple later in Rome (Romans 16:3–5), Nympha in either Laodicea or Hierapolis (Colossians 4:15), Philemon in Colosse (Philemon 1), and unnamed patrons who opened up their apartment for a late-night meeting in Troas (Acts 20:8–12).

L. Michael White identifies the "House Church" as the first stage in the development of Christian buildings.[9] In this stage Christians took advantage of the space affored in homes regardless of their configuration. While houses with an interior atrium would have provided extensive private space, and may have been the style of home owned by wealthy patrons like the luxury textiles merchant Lydia in Philippi[10] or the slave owner Philemon in Colossae,[11] the upper floor apartments in *insulae* and modest homes of crafts workers like Priscilla and Aquila were also employed as venues for congregations to meet. Such domestic structures are not easily identified in archaeological remains as they could only be differentiated from neighboring residences by the presence of Christian symbolism. The tables used for the Lord's Supper were employed for the occupant's daily meals. The seating included benches like those found in the adjacent homes of non-Christians. These nondescript "House Churches," with their limited space, promoted closeness in the Christian

[9] L. Michael White, *Social Origins of Christian Architecture. Volume I: Building God's House in the Roman World: Architectural Adaption Among Pagans, Jews and Christians; Volume II: Texts and Monuments for the Christian Domus Ecclesiae and Its Environment.* (Valley Forge, PA: Trinity Press International, 1997) I.105.

[10] Acts 16:15.

[11] Philemon 1:2.

community. In the Christian family, brothers and sisters enjoyed table fellowship and intruded upon each other's personal space. Their meeting in the close quarters of homes would arouse suspicions of sexual impropriety in later years.

The only alleged first-century "house church" that has been excavated and publicized is the "House of Peter" at Capernaum. Father Virgilo Corbo, who excavated beneath the fourth-century octagonal pilgrimage church in 1968, located what he interpreted to be the remains of Peter's home. This first-century domestic structure, consistent with a fisherman's home, has seen subsequent architectural modifications. Most important to identifying this structure as a house special to Christians are graffiti scratched into plaster layers on the walls in the second and third centuries. Corbo thus confirms the fourth-century account of Epiphanius that a pilgrimage church had been built in Capernaum.[12] Corbo's interpretation has been questioned by Meyers and Strange. They call for further study of the pottery fragments in the plaster to more tightly date the plaster layers and confirm the early use of the building as a house church.[13] White, following Testa, dismisses Corbo's dating of the graffiti and asserts, "There is no evidence of any sort that the buildings of Phase 1 were actually used by Christians prior to the beginning of the fourth century, either as a holy site (associated with Peter) or as a place of Christian assembly."[14] The site at Capernaum is nonetheless still widely accepted as being the site of a "house church." Debate about this site does not undermine the overwhelming literary evidence for House Churches.

Second-Century Use of Structures by the Church

In the second century Christians continued to meet together on the first day of the week for communion, thanksgiving, and confession. [15] The fellowship of the first century that was built upon the Apostles' doctrine

---

[12] Epiphanius *Panarion* 1.30.110.

[13] Eric M. Meyers and James F. Strange *Archaeology, the Rabbis and Early Christianity* (Nashville: Abingdon, 1981) 128–30.

[14] White II.159.

[15] *Didache* 14.1

and practice was increasingly restrained formalism. Traditions developed and were protected by changes in polity.[16] In the early second century, Christians typically continued to make do with their homes as places of assembly,[17] and to sometimes rent facilities.[18] Second-century apocryphal writings that purport to tell the stories of the Apostles depict Peter,[19] Paul,[20] and Thomas[21] in ways that probably reflect both memory of the past and contemporary practice.

L. Michael White's second stage in the development of the early church building is the *domus ecclesiae*, or "house of the Church," in which previously existing domestic structures were renovated. He dates this second stage as emerging at the end of the second century.[22] White logically attributes the change to having an enlarged central meeting room to the growth in size of local Christian communities and to changes in activities of the Christians. He highlights as an example the separation of the Eucharist from the Agape Meal. The adaptation of previously existing structures, and even homes for cult purposes, was not just a Christian practice. Jews and Pagans also did this.[23]

The apologist Minucius Felix created a fictive dialogue between a Christian named Octavius and his non-Christian friend, Caeclius, in which the lack of public Christian structures is a point of pagan criticism. "Why do they endeavor with such pains to conceal and cloak

[16] Ignatius of Antioch, *Epistle to the Smyrneans* 8, records that the presence of the monarchial bishop of Antioch in Syria was required to have baptisms and Eucharistic memorials.

[17] Justin Martyr testified c.165 to meeting in his upstairs apartment over a bathhouse in Passio sancti Justini et socii 3.1–4 and reprinted in White II.43.

[18] Passion of Paul 1 depicts Paul as renting a warehouse outside Rome as a place to teach.

[19] Peter addressed crowds in the house of Narcissus *Acts of Peter* 6–8, 19.

[20] Paul taught Thecla in the church that met in the house of Onesiphorus *Acts of Paul and Thecla* 7.

[21] *Acts of Thomas* 131 reports teaching, baptizing, and taking communion in the house of Siphor.

[22] White I. 111.

[23] Followers of Mithaism, Judaism, and Christianity all seem to have done this at Dura Europas.

whatever they worship? . . . Why have they no altars, no temples . . . ? Why do they never speak openly, never congregate freely unless for the reason that what they adore and conceal is either worthy of punishment, or something to be ashamed of?"[24] Octavius responds by admitting, " . . . we have not temples and altars,"[25] but continues to explain that Christian worship is not limited to temples and altars like paganism but is lived out in public daily by believers. While this discourse has been used by members of the "House Church Movement" to support their assertion that the Church did not have significant church buildings until after Constantine,[26] this dialogue demonstrates that the Christians did not equate the existence of monumental public structures with vitality. Smoke from animal flesh and incense burning on altars and cult statues standing in temples along the *cardo maximus*, while normal in paganism, were not a part of Christianity. Miucius Felix did not indicate that Christians repudiated the use of buildings; rather, he affirmed the earlier Pauline teaching that Christians themselves are the "Temple of God," and that the Christian community is not restricted to living out their faith in public buildings where there were idols and bloody sacrifices. Later, Origen and Lactantius would contrast Christianity and paganism, and similarly highlight that the Christians had no temples or idols. This statement should not be construed to mean that they had no large places to meet.

Clement of Alexandria, at the end of the second century, clearly distinguished between the place where Christians gathered and the Church,[27] but the assembly of believers was clearly associated with a place where one should be modestly attired.[28] The close connection between the assembly of believers and the place where they meet is increasingly

---

[24] *Octavius* 10, *The Ante-Nicene Fathers; translations of the writings of the Fathers down to A.D. 325*, ed. Alexander Roberts and James Donaldson, (Grand Rapids, Eerdmans, 1951) hereafter *ANF*, 4:178.

[25] *Octavius* 32, ANF 4:193.

[26] Andrew Strom, "Church Buildings are Not in the Bible" http://homepages.ihug. co.nz/~revival/lie-2.html.

[27] Clement of Alexandria, *Stromata* 7.5.

[28] Clement of Alexandria, *Paedagogus* 79.3.

evidenced in late second-century patristic writings. Tertullian, at the end of the century, speaks of the *"domus dei,"* "house of God," where one prays and communes.[29] Tertullian's characterization of the proceedings of such a place is expanded in his *Apology* where reading and exposition of Scripture, giving, singing and love feasts are added.[30] The *"ecclesia"* was increasingly understood to be a place that a person approaches and enters through doors.[31]

Third-Century Christian Use of Structures

The third century saw the transition from the Christian use of modified houses, or *"domus ecclesiae,"* to the construction of *aura ecclesiae,* "church halls."[32] These larger structures were socially more visible. The largest audience halls of the Roman world were courts adapted from the audience rooms of Hellenistic monarchs. It is likely that economics were a factor that restricted the wide-scale adoption of such monumental structures. Few monumental buildings were founded in the third-century Levant because of the civil wars and the economic inflation promoted by the barracks emperors, that would finally be addressed by Diocletian and Constantine.

In the early third century, in the period of the Antonnine Emperors, there are indications of some church houses and large church halls in the Levant. The sixth-century *Chronicle of Edessa* records that in AD 201, during the reign of Septimius Severus, "the holy building/temple of the Christians was washed away by a great flood that killed 2000 in the lower city."[33] The Pseudo-Clementine writings, which are preserved in early fifth-century manuscripts, are religious romances that tell stories of the ministry and teaching of the Apostle Peter through the fictive report

---

[29] Tertullian, *On Idolatry* 7.1 writes, "Does a Christian come from idols into the church, from the workshops of the adversary into the house of God?"

[30] Tertullian, *Apology* 39.1–20.

[31] Tertullian, *De fuga in persecutione* 3.2. De pudicita 3.4, 4.5

[32] White I.128.

[33] http://tertullian.org/fathers/chronicle_of_edessa.htm copies the translation of *The Journal of Sacred Literature,* Series 4, Vol. 5 (1864): 28–45.

of Clement, an early leader of the Christians in Rome. The *Clementine Recognitions* are generally dated to the period after Emperor Caracalla's extension of Roman citizenship in AD 212 and before AD 245 when Origen cites the work in his *Commentary on Genesis*. The Judeo-Christian elements in the work and its geographical content, suggest that this work could be a source that originated in the Levant.[34] If the *Clementine Recognitions* does come from the Levant in the early third century, and preserves a memory of the contemporary Christian experience projected back on the Apostolic past, it suggests the existence of mansions being utilized for Christian purposes. In Tripolis, the ministry of Peter is described as having been advanced by the response of Maro, a wealthy citizen, to the Apostle's appeal for a place to discuss Christianity. Maro donated his spacious hall that could accommodate five hundred people, as well as an adjacent garden.[35] After three months of teaching by Peter and his party, Maro was ordained as the Bishop of Tripolis.[36] The *Clementine Recognitions* describe a similar situation in Antioch. There the patronage of a prominent disciple named Theophilus included the dedication of a huge audience hall[37] within his villa complex as a meeting place where crowds could gather daily to hear Peter, who taught from a chair.[38] These apocryphal stories provided a claim for the congregations of Tripolis and Antioch for apostolic origins and blessing of their buildings and leadership. These apocryphal stories retroject post-apostolic polity of monarchial bishops, but may well preserve some clouded memory of names and places. At minimum they indicate that church buildings adopted from earlier structures were employed at the time when the *Clementine Recognitions* were finally redacted. The adoption of houses as structures

---

[34] Johannes Quasten, *Patrology. Volume I: The Beginnings of Patristic Literature* (Westminster, MD: Christian Classics, 1983) 59–63. An English translation of the *Clementia* by Thomas Smith can be found in Alexander Robert and James Donaldson Eds. *Ante-Nicene Fathers Vol. 8* American Ed. Rev. by A. Cleveland Coxe, (Peabody, MA; Hendrickson, 1994) 73–346.

[35] *Clementine Recognitions* 4:6, 7 and *Clementine Homilies* 10:8.

[36] *Clementine Recognitions* 4:15, *Homilies* 11:36.

[37] Rufinus preserves here in Latin "basilicam ecclesiae."

[38] *Clementine Recognitions* 10:71.

dedicated for use by the Church is attested in the Levant[39] and in the physical remains of a *domus ecclesia* found at Dura Europas. This structure excavated in 1933 is interpreted to be a typical private family house constructed in AD 233 that was renovated in 241 for use as a church until it was covered over in AD 256 to strengthen the city walls against attack.[40]

Emperor Alexander Severus (r. AD 222–235), who had Levantine family connections, apparently was a pluralist who kept a statue of Jesus. He had powerful women in his family who were sympathetic to Christianity, even hosting Origen in Antioch.[41] This emperor supported the claim of Christians to use a building in Rome when they were in a dispute with tavern owners.[42] In the Canons of the Church of Alexandria that have been erroneously ascribed to Hippolytus, it was anticipated that Christians would make daily visits to church-owned structures.[43] In the early mid-third century Origin's treatise, *On Prayer*, written in the Levant, evidences that the Christians' habit was to come together in church buildings to pray, and that it was thought that prayers in the churches were beneficial for the participants.[44]

Emperor Philip the Arab (r. AD 244–249), originally from south Syria, seems to have been even more sympathetic toward Christianity and tolerant of their buildings than the Antonnine Emperors. Eusebius reports that at the climax of a Paschal celebration, " . . . he (Philip) wished to share in the prayers of the Church along with the people, but the prelate of the time (Babylas, Bishop of Antioch) would not let him come in

---

[39] Gregory of Tours writing in the sixth century reports that in the middle of the third century Leocadius donated his home for the use of the congregation of Bourges (*History of the Franks* 1:29).

[40] C.H. Kraeling, *The Christian Building: Excavations at Dura-Europas, Final Report VIII.2.* (New Haven: Dura-Europas Publications, 1967).

[41] Eusebius 6.21ff

[42] Aelius Lampridius, *Life of Severus Alexander.* 29, 43,49.

[43] *ANF* 5:258.

[44] Origin, *On Prayer* 31.5. Hippolytus, writing in Rome in the same general time period, in *Commentary on Daniel* 1. 20.2 describes the actions of persecutors who invade "the house of God [*domum dei*] while all those there are praying and singing hymns to God."

until he made open confession."[45] This text identifies a church structure where there were separate places for penitent seekers and regular communicants.

Emperor Decius reacted against the *laissez-faire* policy of Philip the Arab towards Christianity and the deterioration of economic and military confidence by instigating empire wide persecution against the perceived Christian disruptors of prosperity and the *Pax Deorum*. His persecution is evidenced in *libelli* in Egypt, and in records of strife in Palestine where Origen was imprisoned. While Decius' persecution is characterized as being a systematic empire-wide persecution, it did not lead to the destruction of the church house in Dura Europa. His persecution probably did not touch many other ecclesiastical structures in the Levant as well.

In the third-century period of persecutions in North Africa, Cyprian in Carthage was preoccupied with the challenges facing the Christian community, and in his voluminous correspondence makes some passing allusions to the use of buildings. These allusions give archaeologists an idea of what might have been a simultaneous development in the Levant. In the buildings employed by the Church he mentions a raised platform from which teaching was dispensed by leaders,[46] and an altar and space that was in a "sacred and venerated gathering area."[47] His discussion also reveals that in the second half of the third century there were facilities for Christian initiation in at least some of the Christians' meeting places.[48]

From the time of Emperor Gallienus (AD 261–268), Eusebius preserves memory of the decree ending the persecution of Valerian. Specifically, Gallienius made a guarantee to bishops that, "All places of worship shall be restored to their owners."[49] This decree allows for a variety of "places of worship." Subsequently, in the time of Emperor Aurelian (AD 270–276) there was a theological dispute in Antioch. Paul

---

[45] Eusebius, *Church History* 6:34.

[46] Cyprian, *Letters*, 39.4.

[47] Cyprian, *Letters*, 59.18.

[48] Cyprian, *Letters*, 75.15. In particular Cyprian accepted clinical baptism of the sick by sprinkling as being equally valid to a convert's immersion in "the Lord's house."

[49] Eusebius *Church History* 7:13.

of Samosata's christological views led to his excommunication by the orthodox synod who replaced him with Domnus as bishop of Antioch in AD 265. In the messy aftermath Eusebius records, "Paul absolutely refused to hand over the church building," and that the matter had to be resolved in the civil courts and appealed to the Emperor (Aurelian) who eventually ordered the building be assigned to the orthodox faction.[50] By the end of the third century the *Didascalia Apostolorum* 12.44 evidences increasingly rigid expectations of church architecture and liturgy. This document that reflects Levantine practice shows a concern for an eastern orientation and symbolic seating arrangements.

In the late third century Christianity gained support as the populace and societal leaders stressed by political and economic tumult struggled with the perceived failure of the pagan gods, and found Christian ethics and teaching to be attractive. Eusebius indicates that congregational leaders were respected by Roman officials, and the Christians were permitted to assemble publicly. The Church in the Levant clearly thrived in the first two decades of the rule of Diocletian, and new buildings were built for many congregations. Eusebius found himself amazed at the expansion of freedom, and attributed it to divine providence:

> How could one describe those mass meetings, the enormous gatherings in every city, and the remarkable congregations in places of worship? No longer satisfied with old buildings, they raised from the foundations in all the cities, churches spacious in plan. . . . as long as the divine and heavenly hand sheltered and protected its own people.[51]

The architectural shape of these new spacious worship facilities is not clearly specified, but must have included a large space for corporate assemblies. Porphyry, a pagan who produced a diatribe against Christians in c. AD 270, testifies to the increasing prominence of church buildings as he belittles Christians: "But the Christians, imitating the construction of temples, erect great buildings in which they meet to pray, though there is nothing to prevent them from doing this in their own homes since,

---

[50] Eusebius *Church History* 7:30.

[51] Eusebius *Church History*, 8.1.

of course, their Lord hears them everywhere."[52] Other evidence for the existence of church buildings c. AD 295 is found in the street names of Oxyrhynchus, Egypt.[53] It is not clear what shape these great buildings took. Architectural historians have relegated the basilica to being a post-Constantinian development,[54] but this argument is based upon negative evidence, namely that no pre-fourth-century basilicas have been found.

Following the late third-century fluorescence of ecclesiastical structures, Eusebius saw the divine hand of protection removed because of pride and division in the Christian community, in a way analogous to God's treatment of Israel in Old Testament times. The result was the Diocletianic persecution. The first edict of Diocletian, in March of AD 304, testifies to the spread of formal church buildings as it decreed, "churches to be razed to the ground."[55] This edict was not just acted upon in Nicomedia,[56] but was enforced widely. In Palestine, Eusebius vividly recalled, "I saw with my own eyes the places of worship thrown down from top to bottom, to the very foundations."[57] A decade later Eusebius in Palestine would join in celebrating the resurrection of new ecclesiastical constructions "rising from their foundations high into the air, and far surpassing in magnificence those previously destroyed"[58]at such locations. Not all congregations in the early part of Diocletian's rule, however, employed large formal church buildings. The edicts promoting the tolerance and favor of Christianity by Constantine give evidence that all confiscated Christian meeting places and property were to be promptly returned to them.[59]

---

[52] White, II, 76. Porphyry, *Against the Christians*, frag. 76.

[53] White, II,164–66, *Oxyrhynchus Papyrus* 43.

[54] White, II, 8.

[55] Eusebius, *Church History*, 8.2.

[56] Lactantius, *On the Manner Persecutors Died*, 12, describes a gated Church building that was ransacked and then demolished by Praetorian Guards since it was feared that a fire would spread to the adjacent structures.

[57] Eusebius, *Church History*, 8.2.

[58] Eusebius, *Church History*, 10.2.

[59] Eusebius, *Church History*, 10.5.

The deliberate destruction of *ante-pacem* Christian structures, and the tendency of Christians to engage in reconstruction on the same sites, explain why physical evidence of *ante-pacem* churches is rare. Older archaeological investigations have produced early church buildings at Qirqbize, Syria and at Umm el-Jimal, Jordan, but an ante-pacem date of these structures is not clearly indicated.[60] Recent excavations in the Levant have, however, affirmed the existence of large, public structures that were constructed as church facilities late in the third century at the port city of Aila (Aqaba, Jordan), and the military center of Maximianopolis near Megiddo, Israel. Further claims have also been made for a church building at Rahab near Mafraq, Jordan.

The Aila excavations directed by S. Thomas Parker from 1994–2002 announced in 1998 their discovery of "the oldest structure known that was built specifically as a church." The expedition has continued its claims to have discovered "possibly the oldest purpose-built Christian church in history" at the conclusion of the expedition in 2002.[61] This complex covers an area of c. 25 x 15 meters, and has mud-brick walls that stand as much as 5 meters tall.[62] The physical evidence that this non-basilical structure was a church rests on the observation that the structure has a general east-west orientation; that it was illuminated by glass oil lamps; that a "collection box" and its contents of 100 coins dating from AD 337–361 were found on the floor buried by the collapse of the structure as a result of the earthquake of May 19, AD 363; that a 1m. by 0.65m sandstone liturgical table was found associated with the building; and that a cemetery containing a burial of a person with a cross was found adjacent to the structure. A badly preserved "Diocletianic" coin found in a probe of the building's foundations, together with diag-

[60] White II, 135–51.

[61] News release of October 31, 2002 by S. Thomas Parker and the Roman Aqaba Project, http//www.ncsu.edu/news/press_release/02_10/291.htm and presented within the workshop on the Roman Aqaba Project as "The Monumental Mud-Brick Structure at Aqaba: The Oldest Purpose-Built Church in the World?" at the Annual Meeting of ASOR in Atlanta, November 20, 2003.

[62] The best publicly available picture of the site is taken by S. Thomas Parker and may be viewed at http//www.archaeology.org/9811/newsbriefs/Aqaba/html.

nostic late Roman pottery sherds, provide the basis for the assertion that this structure was built as early as AD 290.[63] The assertion that this is a "purpose-built church" has not been argued extensively in print. Support for the excavator's assertion can be seen in the fact that the building was not subjected to large scale structural modification. Some doorways and niches were, however, walled up, and the size of the building is not beyond the size of a large home. While the excavators have described the building using basilical terminology such as a "nave", "chancel" and "side aisles," the function of the design remains to be clearly established. This building would fit into Michael White's typology as a *Domus Ecclesiae/ Church House* and not as a Church Hall or Basilica. This structure could have been the main meeting place of the significant Christian community, in Aila, that sent their bishop to represent them in the Council of Nicaea in AD 325.

The discovery of the pre-Constantinian Church structure at Aqaba was followed in 2001 with the announcement of Abdel-Qader al-Husan's excavation of an even earlier Christian structure at Rahab-al-Mafraq.[64] The written report of the excavation unfortunately fails to adequately substantiate the claims made in the media that a church building from the year AD 230 has been found.[65]

Rehab, the possible location of the Hellenistic city of Thantia,[66] sometimes associated with the Decapolis, was a prosperous stop near the frontier road, *Via Nova Traiana,* in late antiquity. The Church at Rehab, during the *post-pacem* Byzantine era, clearly grew to have a great influ-

---

[63] S. Thomas Parker, "The Roman Aqaba Project: The 1997 and 1998 Campaigns" *ADAJ* 44(2000): 383.

[64] See CNN report and video clip "Archaeologists Uncover Ancient Christian Church in Jordan" http://archives.cnn.com/2001/WORLD/meast/01/29/jordan.church.html

[65] Abdel-Qader al-Husan, "The New Archaeological Discoveries of the al-Fudayn and Raha-al-Mafraq Excavation Projects, 1991–2001." *ADAJ* 46 (2002): 71–94 (Arabic Section) (hereafter Abdel Qader).

[66] Abdel-Qader al-Husan p. 84 argues for this identification. Discussion of other possibilities like Umm al-Jimal and Thughrat al-jubb based on the Peutinger Map can be seen in G. W. Bowersock, *Roman Arabia* (Cambridge: Harvard University Press, 1983) 175–76.

ence as numerous ecclesiastical structures have been identified.[67] This city located on the fringe of the Roman-controlled world may have had a Christian tradition that reached back to the first century. Like other Hellenistic cities in the Transjordan where Jesus' name and teachings had been made known from the inception of the Church,[68] Thantia could have been the home of an early congregation. Like Pella, it could have been a refuge for Christians who fled the ravages of the Jewish War, which culminated in Jerusalem's destruction in AD 70.[69] There are no written records of early Christian traditions in Rehab and all discussion of first- and second-century Christian activity there is speculative. Abdul-Qader al-Husan has, however, excavated an ecclesiastical complex that he has interpreted to be a basilica from the year AD 230 built above a yet earlier literal "underground church." He suggests that the "Cave Church," which measures 11.2 meters by c. 7.5 meters and has a 3.2 meter diameter apse, could have been the meeting place of Christians in the first and second centuries.[70] The above ground building that he has identified as the "Church of Saint George," built in AD 230, is a 20 meter by 13 meter three-aisled basilica. The date of the building has been determined solely upon an inscription in the mosaic floor of the nave. The year 124 clearly appears to be indicated at the end of the fifth line, and is properly assumed to be calculated by the Bostran era of AD 106, when the province of Arabia was established. This gives the excavator the date of AD 230. This date is not consistent with many other pieces of evidence in the inscription, the architectural style, and the other church structures excavated at the same site.

---

[67] Gaetamo Palumbo ed. *JADIS: Jordanian Antiquities Database and Information System* (Amman: ACOR, 1994).

[68] Mark 5:1–20.

[69] The much discussed "Pella Flight Tradition" in Eusebius, *Church History* 3.5.3 has been maligned by persons who do not share the ancient Christian historian's interpretive perspective but never discredited by facts. The escape of some Christians from the ravages of war to the peaceful cities and countryside of the Transjordan, is most reasonable. See Robert Smith, *Arabia Haeresium Ferax?* 257–64.

[70] Abdel-Qader, 84.

The six-line inscription within the *tabula ansata* is difficult to translate since it employs many abbreviations, and the last two lines are compressed since the artisan was running out of space. The inscription indicates that the mosaic floor, and possibly the whole structure, was dedicated, "In the name of the holy trinity through the largesse of a group of 70 blessed individuals together with the head of the monastery, in memory of Saint George in November during the 18th indiction in the year 124, under the supervision of Sergius." [71]

The problems facing the excavator's interpretation are numerous. Problems for dating the inscription that arise from the words of the inscription include the anachronistic use of theological language, the anachronistic description of monasticism, the dedication of the church in memory of a person not martyred until AD 305, and the reference to the "eighteenth indiction" which refers to a system of dating using a fifteen year cycle that did not begin until AD 312, almost a century after the proposed date of the inscription. It is also problematic to date the building to AD 230 because the well preserved architectural elements of the structure indicate that it is of a "basilical" form. The use of this style of architecture has no other examples dating to the early third century but it is common about a century later. Also problematic is the marble chancel screen, a structure which segregates the laity from the Eucharistic table, in this building. The use of a chancel screen is unknown in the early third century but much more common in the early fourth century.

In Rehab there are several seventh-century church buildings that have inscriptions that are similar in orthography. These buildings are four hundred years older than the very similar "Church of St. George." The "Church of John the Baptist" is dated to the year AD 620 during the time when the Zoroastrian Sassanids had invaded the Levant. This inscription suggests a correction that needs to be made in the reading of the inscription from the Church of St. George that would bring the architectural and etymological evidence into line. While the inscription clearly reads *rho* (100) *kappa* (20) *delta* (4), the first part of the number

---

[71] The author produced this translation of the inscription based upon the rendering of the inscription in Abdel-Qader 87–88.

may have been poorly formed, and instead of being a *rho*, the letter is a misshaped *psi* (500). The vertical stroke, instead of bisecting the orb, was perhaps placed to the left side because of the restricted space. The year 524 would then indicate the year AD 630. This re-dating of the church building identifies it as a *post-pacem* structure built in the same time as other ecclesiastical structures in the city. The subterranean meeting room beneath the Church of St. George could be a venerated place used by Christians from an earlier time as suggested by the excavator. Caves are difficult to date. The existence of an apse with seating around the base suggests that the cave was finally shaped in the Byzantine era. If it was made to escape a threat, it could have been that posed by the Sassanids. Therefore, the reported evidence of a very early church building at Rehab must sadly be dismissed in future discussion of *ante-pacem* ecclesiastical construction in the Levant.

Most recently, in October of 2005, the Israeli Antiquities Authority announced that prison inmates directed by Yotam Tepper had excavated a late third-century Christian structure at Maximianopolis.[72] This announcement was met with opposition from scholars, who did not believe that church structures of this sophistication existed at that time. The ecclesiastical structure that has been exposed was built in the legionary town that rests on the earlier site of ancient Hadad Rimmon in the plain of Megiddo (Zechariah 12:11). It has a mosaic floor decorated with a medallion with fish, geometric shapes, and three inscriptions. The 9 meter by 5 meter mosaic covered a rectangular hall. This structure remains to be more fully excavated, but it appears to be an example of Michael White's "church hall type." While the date of the floor has yet to be confirmed by excavation below the floor, the pottery sherds found on the mosaic floor were of the late Roman period. The workmanship of the mosaics and the epigraphic evidence are consistent with a late third-century date. It is possible that the floor of this structure was preserved by the destruction of the building under the decrees of either Diocletian c. AD 305 or Licinius c. AD 320. The later prominence of the Christian community of Maximianopolis is seen when its Bishop Paul participated

---

[72] http://www.archaeology.org.il/newsticker.asp?id+24.

in the Council of Nicaea.[73] The northern inscription in the floor honors a centurion named Gaianos, also known as Porphyrio, who paid an artisan named Brouti to have the floor laid. This inscription suggests that Christianity was making inroads to the military while Christianity was not yet legal. Five patronesses of the church's construction were also memorialized in two inscriptions that are placed at opposite ends of a "mosaic carpet," possibly laid under a liturgical table. The inscription at the west side recalls, "The God-loving Akeptos donated this table in memory of the God, Jesus Christ." The evidence exposed by Tepper, unless overthrown by the discovery of clearly datable pottery or coins beneath the mosaic, affirms the existence of significant, ornate, public ecclesiastical structures in the Levant as indicated by Eusebius.

In the first three centuries of Christianity, the disciples of Christ met in a variety of structures, even as they do to this day. The Church as a spiritual entity was not able to be restricted to structures. People within the Church who lose their spiritual identity can become habituated to certain types of structures, and then find them to be essential. The Christian community as it grew more numerous, more hierarchical, more formal in its liturgy, more affluent, more established and accepted in society, became accustomed to using larger specialized structures. These structures were acquired through modification of previously standing structures, and building new buildings. In some places, where funding was lacking, open air gardens were employed for the growing assemblies of Christians that grew in the late third century prior to the effective legalization of Christianity and "peace of the Church" in AD 324.[74] The physical evidence of ecclesiastical structures of Aila in Arabia and Maximianopolis in Palestina Secunda expose the perception of a poor, persecuted Church driven from public view, to be erroneous.

The change in the legal status of Christianity and the imperial largess affected by Constantine accelerated the adoption of larger purpose-specific construction of church buildings. This fact is attested in the profusion of church construction projects that are mentioned in Post-

---

[73] Gelzer, *Patrum Nicaeorum Nomina,* lxi.
[74] Eusebius, *Church History,* 10.5.

Nicene literature and the many physical remains. Following the end of persecution, Eusebius describes "the re-establishment of the churches from the foundations" through divine providence.[75] "Cathedrals were again rising from their foundations high into the air, and far surpassing in magnificence those previously destroyed. . . ."[76] Eusebius in Caesarea Maritima reveled in the patronage of Constantine, and recorded details of the re-dedication ceremonies of the magnificent cathedral basilica of Tyre he witnessed in AD 313 on the site of the destruction and desecration of the earlier structure.[77] The opposition of the pagan co-emperor Licinius impeded church construction in the Levant from AD 314 until AD 324 when he was deposed. Constantinian era ecclesiastical construction in the Levant after the Council of Nicea built upon a long tradition of the Church using buildings. Three-aisled basilicas became the standard architectural form, but octagonal pilgrim churches and huge five-aisled buildings soon arose to meet the needs of the Christian community.

[75] Eusebius, *Church History*, 9.11.
[76] Eusebius, *Church History*, 10.2.
[77] Eusebius, *Church History*, 10.4.

Women, Slaves, and Society in Rome's Empire and the Early Church

John F. DeFelice

❋THE PRIMARY THESIS of *Roman Hospitality: The Professional Women of Pompeii*[1] was to dispel the common myth that any woman who worked in the hospitality or restaurant business was automatically a prostitute. Such assumptions were quite common, and the stereotyping was not at all difficult to document both in ancient and modern literature. However, in suggesting an alternative for these women's lives my thesis was far too idealistic. It charted a possible course for them from being despised slaves in a questionable industry to the possibility of becoming a Roman matron, complete with the potential for legal marriage (*conumbium*) as opposed to mere informal slave marriage (*contubernales*) or other informal relationships. One can still maintain that such a change in status was possible, but it is clear that it is not very probable. Even if women such as these attained legal marriages, it must be that it would not greatly improve their status. Freedwomen would continue to be hampered by their servile origins and the necessity of earning a living through trades that the Roman elite considered disreputable.

There are many reasons for this, but only a few are significant enough to discuss. Slaves, especially female slaves, occupied the lowest rung of the Roman social order, and the liabilities placed upon those of servile origin were legion. While there were legal possibilities of upward social mobility spelled out in surviving Roman law, the practical application of Roman law in the cases of these lower order women remains doubtful. There were a handful of obstacles that servile women faced while trying to achieve any major changes of status beyond the hope of manumission. However, for some women the alternate society of the early church provided a haven from the stigma of servitude.

[1] John F. DeFelice, *Roman Hospitality: The Professional Women of Pompeii*, Warren Center, PA: Shangri-La, 2001.

John F. DeFelice

The Non-Personality of the Slave: The Initial Barrier

The Romans, according to their own laws, viewed slaves as chattel or little more than two legged livestock, *res* rather than *persona*.[2] Legally a slave was a non-person and had no personality, and thus slaves were tortured if they were witnesses to or accused of a crime.[3] Slaves were considered fixtures, utensils, and part of the business they worked in, that is they were no different in the eyes of Roman law than a tool or a fixture. This, of course, is a legal fiction (though the pain of torture was not) created for the slave owners for the purposes of use and inheritance.[4] Pliny, in his *Epistle* 10.96, presents one such example, with the torture of two slave women who were attending a Christian meeting. There are numerous other examples from other sources.[5] Furthermore, Romans liked to believe the fiction that slaves were by nature morally inferior. They were "naturally" morally weak, and thus a master anticipated bad faith, theft, flight, fiscal mismanagement, and laziness as part of the day to day routine of being a slave owner. Occasionally a Roman writer would recognize that slaves were at times responding to the trials of servitude and perhaps a cruel master, but their view was neither consistent nor universal. The official ideology is best stated by Ulpian, that a slave is a *servus onerosus*,

[2] See Michael J. Brown, "Paul's Use of *Doulos Chistou Iesou* in Roman 1:1," *JBL* 120.4 (2001) 728. See also Orlando Patterson, *Slavery and Social Death: A comparative Study* (Cambridge: Harvard University Press, 1982) 5–7. Patterson developed the ideal of "natal alienation" to describe all that a slave is separated from when enslaved.

[3] Keith Bradley, *Slavery and Society at Rome* (Cambridge: Cambridge University Press, 1994) 165–73 discusses laws calling for the examination of slaves by torture, slave mortality during torture, the unreliability of information gained by torture, and several other examples.

[4] Patterson, *Slavery and Social Death*, 38. . L. A. Hart, *The Concept of Law* (London: Oxford University Press, 1961) 11. Here he describes the function of legal fiction. See *Corpus Juris Civilis, Digesta* 32.7.13 *Paulus, On Sabinus, Book 4* (henceforth the *Digesta* is abbreviated as "D" in notation followed by it chapter, paragraph and sentence numeration) where the slaves and equipment of a tavern are included as business property left to an heir.

[5] But this was not applied in a haphazard fashion. Note Ulpian's extended comments in D.48.18.1 (Book 8 on the *Duties of the Proconsuls*). See Alan Watson, *Roman Slave Law* (Baltimore: Johns Hopkins University Press, 1987) 86–89.

or a troublesome property.[6] By the time of the early empire, nearly every urban craft or profession was staffed and managed by slaves. Slaves were also used as prostitutes and to populate brothels. There was little if any choice for women in this matter. While there were clauses in sales contracts that could stipulate that a slave could not be sold as prostitute, such a prohibition, though upheld in Roman law, depended solely upon the good will of the seller.[7] But good will often proved insufficient. For example, Jennifer Glancy described a woman named Thermouthion who sued a donkey driver who injured her young female slave. This young girl was being trained as a musician, and most probably was headed to some kind of sex trade to support her mistress in her old age, despite the fact that her mistress said she loved her "as though she were my own little daughter"![8] While this may be a form of court pleading that is almost formulaic, in another law case, this one in fourth-century Hermopolis, a woman named Theodora sued for justice because her daughter, a prostitute and her only source of income, was murdered by a man named Diodemos. The prefect hearing the case ordered Diodemos executed and ten percent of his estate to go to Theodora. He further expressed sympathy for the poverty that brought a mother to the point of prostituting her daughter.[9] The poor lived by whatever means possible, and it was possible

[6] See Bradley, *Slavery and Society*, 122–25. The quote from Ulpian may be found in D.17.1.18.4.

[7] D. 1.12.1.8 dates from the time of Severus and offers some protection from slaves being subjected to prostitution or degrading acts. D. 18.7.6.pr indicates that if a slave is sold with a contract stipulating that she be forbidden to be prostitute, and such contract is violated, the woman will be manumitted by the state. This principle is repeated in D. 21.2.34. pr, D 27.14.7. pr, and D 40.8.6. this legal standard probably dates to the time of Vespasian. Roman law should be used with caution in exploring social history, as it may or not be connected to any social reality and has been subjected to editing. Note my comments in J. DeFelice, *Roman Hospitality: The Professional Women of Pompeii* (Warren, PA: Shangri-La, 2001) 39–43 and those of T. Wiedemann, *Slavery* (Oxford University Press, 1987) 19–20.

[8] Jennifer A. Glancy, "Burial Plots: Burying Slaves Deep in Historical Ground," *Biblical Interpretation* 10.1 (2002) 57–59. Text may be found in *P. Oxy.* L.3555.

[9] Glancy, "Burial Plots," 62–64. the text cited is *BGU* IV.1024 Col VI (BL 1. 88–89, 7.17, 9.25). See Jane Rowlandson, ed., *Women and Society in Greek and Roman Egypt: A Sourcebook* (Cambridge: Cambridge University Press, 1998) 201–2.

for widows and women of lowly means to own a slave or raise a foundling slave for the purposes of prostituting her, or for parents to prostitute their own children.[10]

Slaves were continually subjected to harsh punishments, whether these were beatings, brandings, chaining, or being condemned to the mines. Roman literature is full of references and allusions to slave beatings. The whip then, as in the American South, was a symbol of the master's complete authority[11] In the case of the death of their master by the hands of *any* slave in the extended household, all slaves were subject to the death penalty. According to Tacitus, in one notorious case, four hundred slaves (men, women, and children) were executed after the murder of their master by one of his slaves. This provoked protests and riots by the city's poor (which had more in common with the executed as opposed to the executioners). But that did not stop the Senate from voting to execute and most probably torture all four hundred slaves. At one point they even considered executing the master's freedmen and women as well![12]

Any slave was sexually available to their male masters. This was socially and legally distinct from prostitution (although the master was in a sense purchasing sex by purchasing the slave). Occasionally, children resulted from these unions, but the children would be born into the status of slavery, just like their mothers.[13] Male slaves, however, were not

[10] John K. Evans, *War, Women and Children in Ancient Rome* (London: Routledge, 1991) 140–41 provides several examples.

[11] See for example, Keith Hopkins, "Novel Evidence for Roman Slavery," in *Past and Present* 138 (1993) 3–27; and William Fitzgerald, *Slavery and the Roman Literary Imagination* (Cambridge: Cambridge University Press, 2000) 32–41 for numerous examples. See also Moses Finley, *Ancient Slavery and Modern Ideology* (New York: Viking, 1980) 93.

[12] Tacitus, *Annals* 14.40–45. Note the comments of M. F. Finley, *Ancient Slavery and Modern Ideology*, 102–3; and those of Keith Hopkins, *Conquerors and Slaves* (London: Cambridge University Press, 1978)120–23. All the slaves of the household were required to be tortured and killed if the master of the house was assaulted in the *SC Silanianum* of 10 CE. See Watson, *Roman slave Law*, 134–38.

[13] Thomas A. J. McGinn, *Prostitution, Sexuality, and the Law in Ancient Rome* (New York: Oxford University Press, 1998) 196–97; K. R. Bradley, *Slaves and Masters in the*

available to their female masters (matrons). There were dire social consequences for a matron (*domina*) to have sexual relations with any of her male slaves.[14] But in general, sex between master and slave was never prosecutable as adultery, and common enough for the elder Seneca to coin this aphorism: "Unchastity (*impudentia*) is a crime in the freeborn, a necessity for a slave, and a duty (*officium*) for the freedman."[15]

Slaves sometimes did have long term relationships that resembled marriage. However, they could not legally because all slaves lacked the legal capacity to marry (*conubium*). Slave relationships were not legally recognized. In other words, this "marriage," unlike *ius matrimonium*, had no legal power.[16] This type of informal marriage in known as *contuberium*, or tent companion marriage. It was similar to the informal relationships soldiers had with women when the law forbade them to have legal marriage.[17] Though this "marriage" between slaves did not have the force of legal marriage (in other words, one could not be charged with adultery in the case of infidelity, and any children born would not be Roman citizens), such a relationship could have the stability and emotion of a legal marriage. *Contubernium* is often commemorated on tombstones with the typical memorial language used by mourning spouses.[18] But these relationships could be broken up by the sale of one or both slaves at any time by the master, although Roman law noted the emotive issue raised by such acts.[19]

Roman Empire (Oxford: Oxford University Press, 1984) 117–19.

[14] Though beyond the scope of this work, the definitive word on this subject is by Judith Evans-Grubbs, "Marriage More Shameful than Adultery. Slave-Mistress Relationships, Mixed Marriages, and Late Roman Law," *Phoenix* 47 (19993) 125–54.

[15] Seneca, *Controversiesi* VI praef. 10 (Finley). See Finley, *Ancient Slavery*, 96, 170 n.15.

[16] *Tituli Ulpiani* 5.5 *Cum servis nullem est conubium.* "With slaves there is no *conubium*." Paul, *Sententiae* 2.19.6a. *Inter servos et liberos matrimonium no potest.* "Between slave and free, marriage is not possible." See Susan Treggiari, *Roman Marriage* (Oxford, Clarendon Press, 1991) 43–45, 53.

[17] Peter Garnsey, "Septimus Severus and the Marriage of Soldiers," *California Studies in Classical Antiquity* 3 (1970) 45–53.

[18] See Susan Treggiari, "*Contubernales* in *CIL* VI," *Phoenix* 35 (1981) 42–69.

[19] Bradley, *Slaves and Masters*, 47–50. See D.21.1.35. The breaking up of slave families may have resulted in the odd dedications of tombstones to wives by two living husbands.

Manumission

A slave's hope was in manumission. This could occur when a slave saved enough of his allowance (the *peculium*) to literally purchase him or herself, was manumitted in the will of his or her master, or freedom could be granted at anytime by the master him or herself.[20] But there was still no guarantee of manumission even with sympathetic or kind masters. While Cicero seemed to imply that a war prisoner would be enslaved for around seven years, Roman law made it difficult to manumit a slave before the age of thirty, and Cicero did not manumit his favorite slave, Tiro, until he was fifty years old![21] The *peculium* saved by a slave was technically his master's, and the price of manumission was not fixed by law. However, once a slave used it to purchase his or her freedom, it was a binding contract, providing the freed slave could show proof of payment.[22] In reality slaves were often bound for longer periods and were freed less often than Roman literature may indicate.[23] Women often would not be manumitted until they were thirty years old. With the high risk on female mortality during child birth, many simply would not live that long. Many would die in slavery or would only be freed if their deaths were immanent.[24]

The assumption that most slaves were manumitted cannot be validated. It is entirely possible that the promise of freedom that seldom came and the threat of the whip that visited often, were the "carrot and

See S. Treggiari and S. Dorken, "Women with Two Living Husbands in *CILVI*," *Liverpool Classical Monthly* 6.10 (1981) 269–72.

[20] An excellent summary of the *peculium* is found in Watson, *Roman Slave Law*, 90–101.

[21] Cic. *Epistulae ad Familiares* 16.6; See Bradley, *Slavery and Society in Rome*, 1–7. See S. Treggiari, *Roman Freedmen During the Late Republic*, (Oxford, Oxford University Press, 1969) 259–63.

[22] *Digest* 40 , 1: 'Manumissions'; 5 Marcianus, from *Institutes*, Book 2. See also Thomas Wiedemann, *Greek and Roman Slavery* (London: Croom & Canberra, 1981) 53. Although the price for manumission fluctuated, it was probably not tied to the current market price of a slave. See Hopkins, *Conquerors and Slaves*, 158–63, esp. 160 n. 46.

[23] T. Wiedemann, "The Regularity of Manumission at Rome," *CQ* 35 (1985) 62–75.

[24] Martial 1.101; Petr. *Sat.* 65.10. See Bradley, *Slavery and Society*, 164, Hopkins, *Conquerors and Slaves,* (Cambridge: Cambridge University Press, 1978) 115–30.

stick" ideologies the Roman elite used to assure slave conformity with a minimal amount of effort.

In most cases, manumission led to some kind of Roman citizenship, but slaves who underwent punishment as slaves continued with social prohibitions after manumission. If a slave had ever been in chains, or was branded, or had been sent to the mines, that slave was considered a subject (*dediticii*), not a citizen.[25] This had many consequences. First, a freedman of this limited social status was essentially useless to his or her former master as a client. They could not vote in municipal elections, and they most probably had a reputation of unreliability and rebellion. Secondly, they could never legally marry (have *conubium* or the legal capacity for marriage). They could, however, continue any the informal slave marriage (*contubernales*) indefinitely. Finally, they would to have the same status as a member of a conquered state for life. Thus they would still be subject to torture if they witnessed or were accused of a crime.[26]

Slaves manumitted who had a less turbulent past became Roman citizens of one kind or the other. Depending upon the type of ownership, a freed slave became a Roman citizen or a citizen with limited Latin rights. The status a freed slave gained is described in great detail by the second-century Roman jurist, Gaius.[27]

There appear to be three conditions for being manumitted and receiving Roman citizenship. First, the slave must be over thirty years of age. Secondly, his master must own him by Quiritary right.[28] Finally, he or she must be set free by the rod (*vindicta*), by census, or by Will.[29] Slaves manumitted without one of these qualifications would become Junian

---

[25] Wiedemann, *Greek and Roman Slavery*, 14–15 with reference to the *Lex Aelia Sentia*.

[26] Gaius, *Institutes*, Book 1, 13–15; 25–27. Additional causes of this penalty include fighting beasts and gladiators in the arena, or being remanded to custody for a crime.

[27] Gaius, *Institutes*, book 1, 8–55.

[28] In a sense, the master was clearly the legal owner of the slave under *ius civile* and the authority of the praetor. See Hans Julius Wolf, *Roman Law: An Historical Introduction* (Norman: University of Oklahoma Press, 1951) 77–78.

[29] "By census" referred to a master declaring his slave free before the censor at the time of the census, thus liberating and enrolling him or her as a citizen simultaneously. See K. R. Bradley, *Slavery and Society at Rome*, 155.

Latins and receive a limited citizenship. While this was less preferable, it was not necessarily a permanent condition. Junian Latins had the same status as those living in Rome's "ancient colonies," those states within Italy of the early Republic that had limited rights under the Roman legal system, and harsher punishments if in the Roman army. The courts imposed civil limitations on those who received manumission: these freed people could not make a will, be appointed as a guardian under someone else's will, or inherit a legacy. However, benefices could be held in trust for them (*fideicommissum*).[30] Roman Law describes a number of actions Junian Latins could take to become Roman citizens. The simplest process required that a freedman under the age of thirty marry a woman of equal or greater status in the presence of seven witnesses, have her bear his child, and then for the child to live a full year. The magistrate would then recognize all (father, mother, and child) as Roman citizens.[31]

The Burden of the Freed

Once manumitted, a slave was technically free, and if that slave served well, would be either a full or Latin citizen. However, their obligations to the former master would continue. The former master could claim a specific amount of free labor (*opera*) as well as continued loyalty and respect from his freed men or women (*obsequim*). The freed person would become a client of the former master, who would be considered the patron. Roman law demanded that freed persons continue to show respect for their former masters and specifically defines what an ungrateful freed person is: "An ungrateful freedman is one who does not give due respect (*obsequim*) to his patron, or refuses to look after the management of his master's property or to act as his child's guardian."[32]

---

[30] Gaius, *Institutes*, Book 1, 22–24.

[31] Gaius, *Institutes*, Book 1, 28–35 presents us with this and other methods to obtain full citizenship. These include six years of service in the *vigils* (police force), building a ship for grain transport and operating it for six years, building a mill and grinding corn for three years, building an expensive house in Rome, or if under thirty years old, repeating the ceremony of manumission on their thirtieth birthday.

[32] *Digest* 37, 14.19 from Pailius, *Opinions*, Book 1 (Weidemann).

Punishments for such behavior could end up being quite severe. After an initial warning, the "ungrateful" freed person could be subject to an unspecified "severe punishment." If one proved to be insolent and abusive, the punishment could result in exile. If any freed persons physically attacked their ex-masters, the penalty would be hard labor in the mines (a slow death sentence). Furthermore, the Roman State would punish freed people if they spread rumors about their former masters, initiated a law suit against them, or incited others to do so.[33] Roman masters considered both the slave and the freed person to be under the dominion of the *pater familias*, or in the absence of a husband, under the authority of the *domina*, the female head of a household.

Roman law prohibited former masters from forcing women to continue in "disgraceful" professions. The *Digest* in particular asserts that the former master could not force a freed woman to continue as a prostitute as part of her service obligation (*opera*) after manumission.[34] However, slaves were usually trained to perform specific profitable tasks. A woman waiting on patrons in a wine shop most probably continued to do so as a freedwoman, and a prostitute most probably continued as a prostitute. This is clearly the case of the famous informant, Hispala Faeccenia, during the Bacchanalian conspiracy.[35] It is probable that any woman in a slave profession continued in such a profession after manumission.[36] This would maximize a master's profit from her *opera* and the opportunity for training in a new profession may simply not have been a viable option. Often, considerable money was spent to school a slave, and most masters expected some kind of income from this even after manumission.[37] But to focus on the issue of continued prostitution should not

[33] *Digest* 37, 14: 'The Rights of Patrons;' I: Ulpian, from *The Responsibilities of Proconsuls*, book 9.

[34] See D.38.1.38.pr. See Orlando Patterson, *Slavery and Social Death* (Cambridge, Harvard University Press, 1982) 242–43.

[35] See Livy 39.8–19. It is possible that she was granted the right to legal marriage to a freeman as a reward for her information.

[36] Ulpian himself indicated that Rome's elite often ran brothels on their own property. See D.3.2.4.2, Ulpian, *Edict Book 6* citing Pomponius, an early second-century jurist.

[37] See A. D. Booth, "The Schooling of Slaves in 1st Century Rome," TAPhA 109 (1979)

obfuscate the real issue that limited social mobility. The real issue was the fact that these were women working in public, and that alone limited any potential of upward movement in Roman society. Seneca's comment, mentioned above, on the position of the freed and slave is close to reality: "Unchastity (*impudicitiai*) is a crime in the free born, a necessity for a slave, and a duty (*officium*) for the freed man."[38]

Discrimination Against those of Servile Origins

Roman law, custom, and literature proscribed women of servile origins and ringed their lives with prohibitions. A slave could not legally marry (although there may have been exceptions for the imperial slaves), and were universally available to be used sexually by their masters. Once freed, the mark of servile origin continued. While Romans from the lower orders frequently married manumitted freed women, from the time of Augustus those of the upper orders could not, and any children born from such unions could never be designated as legitimate heirs, especially if the father was of the senatorial class.[39] This law was extended by Constantine to include marriage prohibitions of female slaves, freedwomen, working women who had morally suspect occupations, and their daughters from marrying higher classed men such as senators, duumvirs, priests, and holders of several lesser offices. Morally suspect occupations included prostitution and being a woman of the stage. But it also included any woman who had charge of goods to be sold in public or who was a "degraded woman of the lower classes," in other words, it included any of those who had a servile occupation, best defined as work or trade outside of the home. This condemned the poor and working free, the freed, and the slave woman equally. Should any of the holders of these upper positions marry a lower order woman, they risked losing their citizenship and risked acquiring the stigma of *infamia*. Greenidge's classic 1894

11–19.

[38] Seneca, *Controversiesi* IV praef. 10. Note the comments of Moses Finley, *Ancient Slavery*, 96, 170 n. 15.

[39] D.23.3.44 pr., Paul *I ad Legem Iuliam et Papiam*. This is discussed in S. Treggiari, *Roman Marriage* (Oxford: Clarendon Press, 1991) 61–62.

definition says that: "*Infamia* . . . is a special disqualification, based on moral grounds, from public or quasi public functions."[40] Furthermore, the man's property would be confiscated and given to his heirs or family, and the woman herself would be examined by torture. Two cases are known that involved controversies over women who merely sold goods to the public.[41] Women of this sort were considered *humilis obiectaque persona*, too low for prestigious marriages. At the same time, these women could marry men of the lower orders. This type of marriage may even be considered a legal marriage in some cases, with *conubium*. Modestinus, a pupil of Ulpian, went as far as to write that living with a freed woman was *nuptiae*, a word often used as a synonym for *ius matrimonium*, which is legal marriage, providing that she was not a prostitute.[42] The *Lex Papia* of Augustus made it clear that all free men of the lower orders could marry freed women (. . . *libertinam uxorem habere licere*).[43] But for it to be legal marriage, a woman would not be able continue in the profession that she had as a slave, especially if it involved direct contact with the public. Being of servile origins, working in public, and working in several despised trades, and above all being landless in an agricultural economy limited the potential of freed people in general, and women in particular.

This raises the issue of the Roman elite's attitudes towards labor and particularly women's work outside the home. To the Roman elite it was well known that most forms of labor indicated servitude. Since slaves performed so many functions of Roman society, work itself was degraded as being servile. There are numerous references in Roman literature to the elite's assumptions of moral inferiority of those who worked in any type

---

[40] A. H. J. Greenidge, *Infamia: Its Place in Roman Public and Private Law* (London: Clarendon Press, 1894) 8 also provides a list of various kinds of disqualifications. See also Adolph Berger, *Dictionary of Roman Law* (Philadelphia: the American Philosophical Society, 1953) 500.

[41] See See *Corpus Juris Civilis, Codex Justinianus* 5.27.1 (henceforth the *Codex* is abbreviated as "C" in notation followed by it chapter, paragraph and sentence numeration) and *Nmarc* 4.1.1.

[42] Modestinus, *Rules*, Book *1*. D.23.2.24.

[43] Celsus, *Digest, Book 30*. D.23.2.23.

of trade. It seems that women who worked, particularly freed women, incurred considerable liability if they continued working at all. The same elite bias that consistently dehumanized slaves continually devalued both freed men and women and the free born plebeian that worked as well. Cicero considered the trades of cook, butcher, fisherman, and those of the entertainment industry as dishonorable (*sordidi*). Those engaged in retail sale were also dishonorable, as they were forced by circumstances to lie about their merchandise. This was not the work of the humble patrician gentleman farmer. Cicero did not maintain that these trades were unnecessary, but that they were servile.[44] Furthermore, any business that served slaves were off limits for the elite to visit. Juvenal mercilessly lampooned Lateranus in his eighth satire for just this kind of an offense. Lateranus, a Consul, drove a mule cart and hung out at a tavern owned or managed by foreigners who were assumed to be slaves just as were the patrons.[45] He is damned by Juvenal for his servile actions and associations, so he drove by night to avoid confrontations with his peers, and committing himself to drive in the daytime only when his term as Consul expired! The sin of Lateranus is clearly spelled out by Juvenal. He risked upsetting the carefully constructed social hierarchy of the elite, maintained by the fiction of blue blood morality as opposed to typical and unavoidable immoral impulses of the lower orders. Juvenal castigated the egalitarian society of the tavern as well: "No social distinction here: bed and board are in common, privilege is abolished, all men are free and equal."[46]

What could be more threatening to the elite? Actually, Lateranus is one of several prominent blue bloods Juvenal lampoons in this satire which disgraced their heritage for one reason or the other.[47] It appears

---

[44] Cicero, *Off.* I.150–51. Note the comments of Seneca, *De Vita* Beata 7.3. See Sandra Joshel, *Work, Identity, and Legal Status at Rome* (Norman: University of Oklahoma Press, 1992) 66–69.; C. Edwards, *The Politics of Immorality in Ancient Rome* (Cambridge: Cambridge University Press, 1993) 173–75.

[45] For the "corrupting" influence of foreigners, see C. Edwards, *Politics of Immorality*, 80, 100–103, 147–48, 176–78, 186–87.

[46] Juvenal, *Satire* 8. 177–78 (Humphries).

[47] See R. M. Ogilvie, *Roman Literature and Society* (New York: Penguin, 1980) 242–43 for their possible historical identities.

that the prohibitions ran in two directions. The elite were to do nothing to risk the loss of their stations, and the lower orders rarely, if ever, were allowed to matriculate to the elite. The elite looked upon the poor and the rich with servile origins with equal disdain.[48] Pedigree depended upon family and connections, not wealth, and those who were freed but successful still had no lineage, as Martial was delighted to point out as he castigated an ambitious freedman: "You are welcome to the Right of Children even seven, Zoilus, so long as nobody gives you a mother or a father!"[49]

Both slaves and freed people shared the distinction of having no lineage, that is, having no father, and no mother. Though this too was a legal fiction, it was one with devastating social consequences. It is stated in Petronius' *Satyricon* that for all the wealth Trimalchio amassed, and despite his vast estates and the size of his trading empire, he was, in the eyes of the Roman elite, just a freedman. Socially, it seems that Laternus, on his way down, and Trimalcio, on his way up, met at the border between blueblood and commoner that the Roman elite guarded with the ferocity of their northern border legions, that "None shall pass". That is not to say that there were never unique situations where this "border" was breached by the rare and exceptional circumstances of imperial decree, or by the slaves in the imperial household that had significantly higher status and more privileges than many freeborn Romans.[50] But this was a border crossed with the strictest supervision under the Roman legal system.

While doing research for my book, *Roman Hospitality*, it became clear that there were many marriage prohibitions lodged against women in the hospitality trades by Roman law. Women who worked in restaurants, wine shops, hotels, and businesses that combined these operations, are cited by profession again and again. There was an assumption, with which I disagree, that such women were universally prostitutes. This is more of an ideologically driven exaggeration than a reality. It could be

[48] As maintained by Ramsay MacMullen, *Roman Social Relations,* (New Haven: Yale University Press, 1974) 104–20.

[49] Martial, *Ep.* 11.12 (Bailey, Loebs).

[50] The standard exposition of imperial slaves is still P. R. C. Weaver, *Familia Caesaris* (Cambridge, Cambridge University Press, 1972).

that because food and sex were often linked in the classical world this was simply another expression of a cultural assumption, or it could be that these women were slaves or freed women who served men who traveled, and that masters wishing to increase the profits of their business would use them on occasion to provide entertainment as well as the hard labor of food preparation and room maintenance. Of course they fall into the classification of all women who accepted money from customers in the service and retail trades. That act put them in the class of women who "made a living from their bodies," thus classing them as low as prostitutes.[51] But in the end, while all these are factors, inns and wine shops, and restaurants were also the haunts of slaves. The reputable did not go to these places. So if the stigma of servility was to be imposed upon any woman, it would be put on those who served slaves on a regular basis. Women who worked in inns and taverns directly with customers could never gain *conumbium* (after manumission). This excluded them from legal marriage. They would be immune from charges of adultery, since Roman moral assumptions pronounced them as being incapable of fidelity. Only the actual owner of the business, employing women to work beneath her, was exempt from the stigma of servitude:

> It should be ascertained whether the woman who committed adultery was the owner of the inn or only a servant; and if by employing herself in servile duties (which frequently happens) she gave occasion for intemperance, since if she were the mistress of an inn, she would not be exempt from the liability under the law. Where, however, she served liquor. . . . she would not be liable to accusation. . . . on account of her inferior rank, and any freemen who have been accused (of adultery) shall be discharged, since chastity is expected only of those women who are in a lawful relationship as matron, while the rest are immune from the severity of the law, since their lowly way of life does not call for them to observe these requirements of law.[52]

---

[51] See DeFelice, *Roman Hospitality*, 88.

[52] C.9.9.28 (Fant) See M Lefkowitz and M. Fant, *Women's Life in Greece and Rome* (Baltimore: Johns Hopkins University Press, 1992) 117–18.; C. 9.9.23.pr; and I discuss *Contubernium* in DeFelice, *Roman Hospitality*, 60–69. I have since revised several of my

The distinction between the owner of an inn (who may be a Roman matron) and a mere worker (who could not) is made evident by the low expectation of morality Roman law had towards the latter. She was legally beneath marriage and adultery, and shared that status with many women of servile origins. Actresses, prostitutes, and other women were also condemned. Though men were considered servile by working, they were not subject to as much moral disregard as women in the same professions:

> It is not possible to ignore as base people those who deal in and sell objects of daily use, even though they are people who may be flogged by the aediles. Indeed men of this kind are not debarred from seeking the decurionate or some other office of their own *patria*; for they do not suffer from *infamia*. Nor are those who have been actually flogged by the *aediles* excluded from any office, even if the *aediles* were within their rights in performing that act.[53]

Thus, emancipated women experienced within Roman society a double measure of liability: their servile origins, and their livelihoods. Locked out of marriages beyond their class, often prohibited from legal marriage and from ever being a part of a citizen family by the nature of their labor, and even stigmatized and lampooned should they prove successful, social mobility for the vast majority was an impossibility. Inferior rank automatically rated an assumption of inferior morality, and those who held the power in Rome, a small minority of elite balanced at the peak of its steep social pyramid, kept it so. As Catharine Edwards remarked, "the discourses of morality in Rome were profoundly implicated in the structure of power . . . attacks on immorality were used by the Roman elite to exercise control over their own members and to justify its privileged position."[54]

---

conclusions and am working on a second edition as this article reaches publication.

[53] Callistratus, *Judicial Examination, Book 6.* D.50.2.12 (Watson).

[54] Edwards, *The Politics of Immorality*, 4.

John F. DeFelice

Slave and Freed in the Early Church: the Egalitarian World

Though socially conservative, the early church made an impact on the world of the despised lower orders by creating a counter-culture of egalitarianism that to some extent ignored the social conventions of Roman society. The church constructed a new paradigm that subverted the traditional rankings and values long maintained by Roman elite. It has long been recognized by scholars that the church from its inception presented such a radical shift, that had Roman jurists and leaders properly understood it there would have most probably been a more systematic movement to wipe out or severely regulate the practice of the Christian faith. The King James Version states it best in Acts 15:7: "They who have turned the world upside down have come here also!"[55]

The primitive church in particular turned the world upside down by bringing an alternate value system into Roman society. This system of values, in which Christians affirmed the value of work, and disregarded class, competed with the ideology long established by the Greco-Roman elite. In particular, the lack of personality and social status of the slave was subverted by the social values of the new faith. However, the church never developed a sense of mission to end the institution of slavery until the modern era.

First, work and the trades long despised by elite Romans was given meaning. Perhaps an echo of the more egalitarian society of the Hebrews came through in the preaching of Paul, who himself, despite his education and the value of his rabbinic training, was a tent maker.[56] Jesus himself came from a family of carpenters. In the eyes of the Roman elite, Jesus and Paul were servile and debased. The Christian veneration of those who were socially despised was quite a shock to the Roman elite. This religion had empathy with the poor, and considered both their work and their poverty virtuous. Few Romans would speak that way and the few who did speak of the virtues of poverty were quite rich themselves! The virtue of work alone made primitive Christianity a counterculture. Of course

[55] Acts 17:6.
[56] Acts 18:3, 1 Thess. 2:9, 2 Thess. 3:7–9, Acts 20:23–25.

examples abound in the New Testament of the new dichotomy between rich and poor, both in the parables of Jesus and the teachings of Paul.

More importantly, the status of slaves was changed once they entered the faith and the "egalitarian" community of the primitive church.[57] They were now brothers or sisters in Christ, and though they returned to slave status once they left the church doors, the meeting affirmed their value before God and man. While there was no wholesale call for abolition, slaves were welcomed in the fellowship, along with freed men and women and those born free. But the discourse of Paul on slavery is uneven. Paul in several places gives advice to slaves to conform to a very traditional standard of slave behavior, and some of the letters of Paul were used to justify slavery throughout history.[58] But there is a subversive element in Paul's teaching that must be reckoned with. While Paul chose not to confront the system of slavery and status in the Roman world, he did choose to ignore it. However, there is one particular case in which Paul got involved in a slave issue, and this is addressed in the *Epistle to Philemon*.

Philemon is a short personal letter that provides the reader with very little background information.[59] It concerns Onesimus, a typical slave with a typical slave name meaning "Useful," and his fate after running away from his Christian master, Philemon. The letter is addressed to multiple recipients: Philemon, Apphia, Archippus, and the church that meets in Philemon's home. It is obvious that what in the Roman world

---

[57] Well maybe not completely egalitarian. Note the comment of Petersen in *Philemon: Paul's Rhetorical Style Serves to Mediate the Paradox that the Egalitarian Social Structure of Paul's Churches is Complemented by a Hierarchical Axis.* Norman Petersen, *Rediscovering Paul,* (Philadelphia: Fortress Press, 1985) 133.

[58] 1 Corinthians 7:21–22; Ephesians 6:5–9 and Colossians 3:22—4:1 provides advice to slaves and masters; 1 Timothy 6:1–2; Titus 2:9; 1 Peter 2:18–25 advocate submission to masters, faithful service, and patience to slaves and master alike, and neither attack nor question the institution of slavery. Many of these passage have been used at times to justify slavery. Note the recent comments by Ronald C. Potter, "Was Slavery God's Will?" *Christianity Today* May 22, 2000, Vol. 44, No. 6, Page 80. This subject is discussed at length in Bradley, *Slavery and Society,* 145–53.

[59] Norman R. Petersen, "Philemon," in James L. Mays, Ed., *Harper's Bible Commentary* (San Francisco: Harper and Row, 1988) 1245–48.

was a matter for the *pater familias* is now a matter for the small Christian community that met at Philemon's home.

Onesimus was apparently a runaway slave. This type of offender was often severely punished in a variety of ways: receiving a severe beating, being branded, being forced to wear a slave collar, being bound in chains, being sold to work in the mines, or other such punishments. This punishment was always controlled by the master, with few limitations.[60] However, Paul sets in motion a new standard. He asks that Philemon, in the presence of witnesses, welcome Onesimus back as though he were Paul himself, as a brother, and as a man (as opposed to *res*, a thing), not a slave.[61] The debt he incurred (whether Onesimus failed to complete an important errand, stole something from Philemon, or Philemon spent time and money trying to track him down) is to be charged to Paul himself, and furthermore, Paul would like to have Onesimus come back to him and tend to his needs. Issues in this letter are more in harmony with the confession proclaimed in *Galatians* 3:28 than the other references to slavery in the New Testament: "There is neither Jew nor Greek, slave nor free, male nor female, for you are all one in Jesus Christ."

Some questions do arise from this request. What of the issues of Roman law? Was Onesimus over thirty? Was he to be formally manumitted? What of the rights the master had to *opera* and *obsequim*? Was Onesimus a client of Philemon now? Would Paul's request affect his status as a freedman? Was he now a citizen? Did Philemon's action limit him to being a Junian Latin? And how did Philemon respond to the demands of Paul? All of these options were so deviant, so un-Roman! Furthermore, while it seems in harmony with Galatians 3:28, what of the other passages which justify the *status quo* of the master-slave relationship? In other places Paul's advice to slaves employs rhetoric similar to what the Roman elite might have used with well behaved slaves. But in this short epistle, Paul lays down a choice to Philemon: he may be a slave master or he may

---

[60] Hopkins, *Conquerors and Slaves*, 144–47. But there are limitations, at least in later Roman law. See *Code of Theodosius 9,12,1:* On punishing slaves in T. Wiedemann, *Greek and Roman Slavery*, 174.

[61] Philemon, 16.

be a son of God! Not both.[62] In any case, it was an inconsistent message and its radical nature did not endure long. Slavery continued in both pagan and Christian Rome and slaves were pacified, the pious concentrating on submission and cheerful obedience rather than manumission and an end to the institution.[63]

Perhaps the greatest challenge would be to convince the slave holders in the church in late antiquity and the congregations that they attended that slavery, which is "cross culturally defined as an anti-kinship structure," was in fact "within a network of intimate family relationships."[64] Maybe this was unintentional, or perhaps this ideology reflected the ideal of the faithful household servant as seen in the Hebrew Bible in *Exodus* 21:2–6: the servant who chose to stay as part of his master's household had as a symbol of his permanent joining to his master, his ear pierced with an awl through to the doorpost of his master's house. But that was a different culture and age.

Sabine Bieberstein has found a partial solution to the contradiction of the glaring use of the New Testament to justify slavery and the demands for freedom and equality in *Philemon*. Paul, in numerous passages, had to deal with new churches that developed in Roman society with its "specific structures and values."[65] The case of Onesimus caused some "fissures" to appear in this system of values in regards to slavery. The conflict between the church values of egalitarianism, expressed in the terms "brother and sister," were in conflict with the "dominant reality of slavery." To Bieberstien, this short letter represents "a litmus test of liberating praxis based upon the gospel, requiring the Christian communities to find a path along the borders between two worlds..."[66] These two worlds have two sets of values: slavery, on the one hand, and an egalitarian faith on the other. By writing this letter *with* a community of

[62] Petersen, *Philemon*, 1247.

[63] Se Bradley, *Slavery and Society*, 151.

[64] Glancy, "Family Plots," 64.

[65] Sabine Bieberstein, "Disrupting the Normal Reality of Slavery: a Feminist Reading of the Letter to Philemon, " *JSNT* 79 (2000) 108.

[66] Bieberstein, "Disrupting the Normal Reality," 110–11.

believers (Timothy and five other senders in *Philemon*, 23–24) and sending it to another community in Philemon's house (including a woman, Apphia), this letter became a public document discussing a private issue. This makes *The Epistle to Philemon* one of the most un-Roman epistles of the New Testament: household slave issues were to be decided by the *pater familias* and no one else! Thus, in this one instance, and in this house church, a counter culture is born, one quite deviant from the standard of the elite Roman views of the role of the master and the status of the slave.

While Onesimus has no voice in the letter, it is one of the rare letters of Paul that breaks a major barrier and gives voice to a difficult social issue with a radical solution. But there is no enduring universal principle that came from this action, and many Christians find that very disturbing. And while Onesimus was probably saved by Paul and the community's intervention, what of the rest? What of the Christian slave prostituted by her master, and other such dilemmas? To some extent it seems the church after Paul tried to work within the system, eventually ordering slaves to marry, making sex with a slave count as adultery, making the church the site of manumission ceremonies, and gradually adding more and more protections for slaves in Roman law.[67] But the church was not the center of abolitionist agitation, nor did the church agitate for a dismantling of the rigid rules of Rome's class society. Eventually, slavery would be considered a payment for sin, and the church never really directly sought to end slavery as an institution.[68] In fact, the slave laws and laws concerning freedmen were codified under Justinian in a Christian Eastern Empire. Perhaps it was the early church's myopic other-worldly focus in the apocalyptic driven Christian lifestyle of the first century that caused them to miss the consequences of not addressing that brutal institution that existed in plain sight of them all.

---

[67] Bradley, *Slaves and Society,* 145–53, 156–59 with references. For Christian slave marriages see D.38.8.1, D.10.10.5; For marriage of slaves as a sacrament, see Basil, *Ep.* CXCIX.42, *Apostolic Const.* III.iv; VIII, xxxii, for sex with slaves counted as adultery, see John Chrysostom *In Ep. Ad Ephes, Hom* xxii.2. For manumission in the church see C. 1.13.1, *C. Theo* 4.22.

[68] See Augustine, *C.D.* 19:15.

Benevolent Physicians in Late Antiquity
The Multifaceted Appeal of the Anargyroi[1]

Jerry Pattengale

Introduction

❊THE TOPICS OF medicine and magic are deeply interwoven in Late Antiquity studies; healing serves as their prominent common thread. By the fourth century AD Roman society witnessed a transition from a magical to a science-based healing. In this context we find excellent examples of the interaction of faith and reason, and of religion and science manifesting both complements and tensions.

Although this transition to science-based healing was by no means complete in the fourth century, it was nonetheless the sign of a new dispensation. Among the scientific ranks were numerous physicians known for their ethics and benevolence, many of whom became canonized Christian saints of healing or the Christian *anargyroi*, literally meaning "without silver." That is, they practiced their craft for free to assist those in need during the first four centuries of Christianity.

The cult of the *anargyroi* developed during the fourth century. It continues today in the churches of Haghioi Anargyroi in Greece, and modern shrines to select *anargyroi* are found throughout the world, including a few cities in the United States.[2] During their lives *anargyroi* served as Hippocratic physicians. Posthumously they were venerated for their supernatural feats.

---

[1] This manuscript was presented at the 2005 Annual Meeting of the Near East Archaeological Society, Valley Forge, PA. It was also presented at the John Wesley Honors College Faculty Lecture Series, 2006, Indiana Wesleyan University (Marion, Indiana).

[2] M. G. Papageorgiou, "Incubation as a Form of Psychotherapy in the Care of Patients in Ancient and Modern Greece," *Psychotherapy and Psychosomatics* 26 (1975): 35–38. Familiarity with the *Anargroi* among 2006 audiences and societies is attested by over 15,000 website listings.

The rise and popularity of the *anargyric* shrines resulted not only from their subjects' endorsement of Christianity as propagated by hagiographers,[3] but for numerous other reasons. The evidence presented here clearly demonstrates the key role of a persistent Hippocratic ethic in the cult's rise despite the reoccurring theme among hagiographers that science and the Early Church were in opposition. This hagiographic *topos* is counterintuitive because the saints canonized were known as Hippocratic healers, and it also ignores other historical evidence. Pagans and Christians alike applauded benevolent rational healers who were more concerned for their profession than with profit. The *anargyroi's* rise in popularity may be ironic, that is, that canonized doctors were being celebrated for their supernatural powers, but it does not substantiate a Christian rejection of Hippocratic healing.

The Hippocratic ethic permeated Roman society, with physicians from various backgrounds serving all levels of society. Charges of avarice lodged by pagans and Christians highlighted an assumed ethical standard among physicians. Christian physicians found little difficulty embracing this professional ethic while advocating their personal religion. While the Church established *anargyric* shrines, it highlighted not only the careers of its physicians, but of its endorsement of the Hippocratic ethic as well. For the Church, however, the key issue was the placement of credit for healing, not the endorsement or indictment of Hippocratism.

A Closer Look at the Anargyroi and Their Profession

Christian writers nearly always employed the term *anargyroi* in reference to benevolent physicians who were martyred for their Christian beliefs and posthumously canonized by the Christian Church. As noted above, the term *anargyros* (singular) was derived from the Greek phrase, "without silver," and was employed in reference to physicians who performed medical service gratis. New Testament writers used *anrgyros* for denoting

---

[3] Peregrine Horden, "Saints and Doctors in the Early Byzantine Empire: The Case of Theodore of Sykeon," *Studies in Church History* 19 (1982): 10.

silver,[4] and *anrgyrion* as one of the words for money.[5] The fifth section of the *Book of Painters* from Mt. Athos[6] contains a select list of *anargyroi*, which includes Kyros and Ionannes (Cyrus and John), Panteleimon and Hermaolaos, Sampson and Diomedes, Photios and Antiketos, and Thallelaios and Tryphon.[7] Alternate lists survive, and some *anargyroi*, though well documented in ancient sources, including church records, escape most lists, for example St. Colluthus of Egypt.[8] Similar to the Menouthis scenario (described below), late antiquity witnessed a pervasive interest in healing. Numerous healing cults established centers that often served as the fulcrum of activity for their local communities.

Nearly every region hosted an Asclepion, Serapeum, or one of a myriad of other pagan shrines. By the late third century society was ripe for the founding of anargyric healing centers and for the corresponding worship of healing saints. Peter Brown provides a good summary of both of these topics in his *Cult of the Saints: Its Rise and Function in Latin Christianity.*[9] In his chapter entitled "Society and the Holy in Late Antiquity," Brown addresses the important issue of locality among healing cults and the role of saints in many important aspects of their com-

---

[4] Akin to *argos* ("shining"); Matthew 10:9, Acts 17:29; James 5:3, Revelations 18:12.

[5] Although it is used to denote money (Matthew 25:18, 27, 28:15, Mark 14:11, Luke 9:3, 19:15, 23, 22:5, Acts 8:20), *argyrion* is also used more literally to denote a piece of silver (e.g., Acts 3:6), and a silver coin (e.g., Matthew 26:15).

[6] Athos was home to several early monastic sects, including the Iveron monastery associated with Athanasios I (1230–35).

[7] Heinz Skrobucha, *The Patron of the Doctors* (West Germany: Aurel Bongers Recklinghausen, 1965) 9. The extended list in the appendix of the *Book of Painters* also ascribes the title of "gratis giver" to Sergios, Bakchos, Christophoros, Eugenios, Auxentios, Eustratios, MArdarios, Orestes, Menas Viktor, Vikentios, Akindynos, Pegasios, Aphthonios, Elpidephoros, Anempodistos, Ananias, Azaras and Misael, Kerykos, Ioulitta, Marina, Kyriake, Barbara, Paraskeve (Thaumatourgos), Thekla (Promotomartys), Aikaterina, Eirene, Theodora (Myroblytis), Maria Magdalena, and Ana.

[8] See Jerry A. Pattengale, "Benevolent Physicians in Late Antiquity: The Cult of the *Anargyoi*" (Ph.D. dissertation, Oxford, OH: Miami University, 1993).

[9] Peter Brown, *Cult of the Saints: Its Rise and Function in Latin Christianity* (Chicago: University of Chicago Press, 1981).

munities.[10] He also notes the regional differences in these roles, such as Syrian saints being more involved in community affairs than Egyptian saints. Although he does not address the *anargyroi*, his study certainly gives direction in measuring the importance of the historical and legendary healing figures.

Much has been written on healing and healing cults, and the treatment of the cult of Asclepius by Emma J. and Ludwig Edelstein is of particular importance.[11] The Edelsteins designate Asclepius as the main healing opponent of Jesus "The Great Physician." Their respective cults were in conflict for centuries.[12] The implications of parallels between the success factors of the cult of Asclepius and the *anargyroi* are many.

Greco-Roman and Patristic sources provide rather thorough contemporary accounts of the issues related to benevolent physicians. Both prominent and obscure writers have left us an adequate basis for an interpretation of these physicians' roles in their society and profession. Such authors include Apollonius of Tyana, Aretaeus, Aristides, Basil, Cassiodorus, Celsus, Cicero, Eusebius, Galen, Hippolytus of Rome, Isidore of Pelusium, Jerome, John Chrysostrum, Josephus, Largus, Libanius, Macarius the Egyptian, Palladius, Procopius of Caeserea, Scribonius Gelasius, Seneca, Socrates, Sophrinus, Soranus of Cos, Tatian, Theodoret of Cyrrhus, Theodore of Sykeon, and Valentinian I. An important and interesting aspect of this ancient dialogue is the evaluation of the medical profession and the religious healing centers (some which employed medicine, or at least systematic treatment). Weighing the physicians' self-evaluation against that lodged by their contemporaries provides a critique of fourth- and fifth-century medicine. A clear distinction can be made between the physician and pagan healing priest, and the benevolent physician and his later *anargyric* status.

---

[10] Peter Brown, *Cult of the Saints: Its Rise and Function in Latin Christianity* (University of California Press, 1982).

[11] Emma J. and Ludwig Edelstein, *Asclepius: A Collection and Interpretation of the Testimonies* (2 vols.; Johns Hopkins Press, 1945).

[12] Ibid., 132–38. See also Alice Walton, *Asklepios: The Cult of the Greek God of Medicine* (Chicago: Ares, reprint ed., 1979).

The Christian physician emerged in a world in which science and ethics had already been fused. The economic chasm between the masses of Romans and the elite was ever increasing, and the need for health services for the poor was never more pronounced. Christian apologists, along with some pagan factions, were continually evaluating the moral and ideological basis of Roman society, and usually finding it wanting. Roman institutions, even buttressed by imperial decrees, were failing to provide basic public services, including health programs. State-funded doctors were only a token expression of concern from euergistic politicians who were part of an unofficial political arrangement between patron and client. The benefactor (*euergetes*) funded projects not in a spirit of benevolence, but for the sake of public recognition. The title of *euergetes* "did not simply state a fact but conferred a status, indicating that the person on whom it was conferred was in credit, as it were, in respect of the balance of friendly acts."[13]

Medicine, with its Hippocratic ethic, at least gave the average citizen hope for treatment. While some physicians threw ethics to the wind and pursued money, most Hippocratic physicians, like devoted Christians, operated under a mandate to assist the poor. With the physician-patient ratio, any reputable physician could devote him or herself to wealthy clients. For most physicians, Christian and pagan, generosity to the poor involved taking time to serve them and then accepting whatever remuneration followed. It is little wonder that when practitioners of an art in such demand dedicated themselves to helping the poor, and that when the *anargyroi* did so freely, that they gained Rome's attention. It is one thing not to ignore the poor, yet quite another to devote a life to serving them. If Edward Gibbon is correct, the latter devotion was a major factor in the eventual triumph of Christianity over paganism. On a somewhat different note, the former attitude was manifest in the average Roman physician (and Asclepiada priests), which made the commitment of the *anargyroi* a logical extension of their profession and religion, a commitment which could thus be appreciated by both pagans and Christians.

---

[13] A. R. Hands, *Charities and Social Aid in Greece and Rome* (Ithaca: Cornell University Press, 1968) 36.

Veneration of the *anargyroi* reflected praise from equally diverse factions of society.

The Financial Practices of Healers in Late Antiquity

Were the *anargyroi* similar to many other physicians? Were their actions unique to themselves or merely reflections of the medical ideal? Ludwig Edelstein contends:

> For in regard to every craft it is necessary to distinguish between its common characteristics and those which belong to the individual [or small group] practicing it. Failure to make this distinction is bad logic, irreconcilable with the tenets of Plato and Hippocrates alike.[14]

The *anargyroi* were not preceded by a rich medical heritage in Rome. Tradition holds that in 219 BC, Arcagathus, the first doctor (*medicus*), arrived in an appreciative city.[15] However, he was soon rejected because of his ill-fated surgeries. As Pliny notes, he was branded as *carnifex*, or "executioner," and driven from the city.[16] The next physician in Rome was also a Greek, Asclepiades, (ca. 100 BC), as were many of their successors through the end of Roman Antiquity.

Epigraphical and literary sources attest to the Greek dominance of the profession. During the first three centuries AD, over ninety percent of the doctors in Rome were Greek (or Greek pretenders). For the same period, around seventy percent of the doctors of the rest of Italy, Spain, and Provence were Greek.[17] Thus, when Julius Caesar banned foreigners from Rome, he exempted physicians.

[14] Ludwig Edelstein, "The Professional Ethics of the Greek Physician," in *Ethics in Medicine: Historical Perspectives and Contemporary Concerns,* ed. Stanley Joel Reiser, et. al. (Cambridge: MIT Press, 1977) 44.

[15] Arcagathus ("a good beginning") was known for his surgery, and initially referred to as Rome's *vulnerius;* John Watson, *The Medical Profession in Ancient Times* (New York: Baker and Godwin, 1956) 13.

[16] Pliny, *Natural History,* XXIX, 6.

[17] H. Gummerus, "Der Arztestand im Romischen Reiche," *Soc. Sci. Fennica, Comment, Hist. et Litt.* 3.6, Helsinki, 1932. See also Vivian Nutton, "Murders and Miracles:

The influx of Greek physicians undoubtedly propagated the Hippocratic ideal. Hippocratic doctrines accompanied the migration to Rome, and subsequently the Roman medical world known to the *anargyroi* was dominated by Hippocratism. Although several sects of Hippocratism surfaced alongside non-humoralistic schools, in the late second century Galen developed Roman medicine into a unified science.[18] Adaptations of the Hippocratic humoralism and the Hippocratic medical ethic found a new defender and propagator in Galen, and likewise became part of the medical curriculum of Stephanus of Athens in the sixth century. Thereby a form of Hippocratism persisted in medical training throughout the Middle Ages. Stephanus claimed to be a practitioner, and also branded all non-Hippocratic physicians as lacking professional knowledge (literally, "*idiotai*").[19]

Classifying physicians by their means of subsistence may be of the most assistance in clarifying the profile of Roman medical personnel in which the *anargyroi* surfaced. Four general types of Roman physicians were in the mainstream of society: the public physicians, those attached to the emperor's retinue, those serving wealthy families, and the independent practitioners. The priest-physician served a different role from the rational physician (*medicus*); nonetheless, he or she was commonplace in most Roman cities, though they practiced mainly on the outskirts of the city. A vast network of military, sports and gladiator medical personnel also existed. But these physicians, however important, were usually inaccessible for service to lay persons, and are therefore excluded from this study.

The first three categories may be classified as "dependent physicians," setting them apart from the independents, the vast majority of practitio-

Lay Attitudes Towards Medicine in Classical Antiquity," in *Patients and Practioners: Lay Perceptions of Medicine in Pre-Industrial Society,* edited by Roy Porter (Cambridge: Cambridge University Press, 1985) 44.

[18] Vivian Nutton, "Portraits of Science: Logic, Learning, and Experimental Medicine," *Science* 1 (February 2002) Vol. 295, no. 5556, 800–801. See also Nutton, God, Galen and the Depaganization of Ancient Medicine" in Peter Biller and Joseph Ziegler, editors, *Religion and Medicine in the Middle Ages* (Rochester, NY: York Medieval Press) 2001.

[19] Stephanus of Athens, *Commentary on Hippocrates' Aphorisms* 1.27, *Corpus Medicorum Graecorum* XI 1, 2.

ners. Legitimate doctors may be defined as those who were perceived as being trained in rational medicine, and who conducted themselves in accordance with the Hippocratic ethic. A definition more stringent than what the Romans themselves employed is both unnecessary and undesirable. Unless the inscriber qualified the "physician" as a quack, we can only assume that the *medicus* in question was "legitimate" according to the foregoing definition.

The need for independent physicians was apparent enough; the public physicians simply could not pretend to care for all of their city's inhabitants. The patient to *archiatros* ratio can be estimated at higher than thirty thousand to one! For example, according to the decree issued by Valentinian I (AD 366), Rome assigned an *archiatros* to each of its fourteen districts. At that time 500,000 people lived in the city, which amounts to a 35,000 patient load. The same load may be true of Constantinople, though the evidence only substantiates that civic physicians existed.[20]

It is clear that a Hippocratic-Galenic medical ethic pervaded late antiquity, transcending socioeconomic barriers, even within the profession of medicine. During the selection of the *archiatroi*, ethics were as crucial as skill. Both imperial and personal physicians were esteemed only if their successful treatments were complemented by trustworthiness and *philanthropia*. Independent physicians took great measures to establish a good reputation, often serving gratis.

It is important to note that when people turned to Asclepius priest-physicians they had usually looked earlier to a physician, whether a public, household, or independent practitioner. While the method of Asclepion healing changed with the progression of technology, the remuneration practices did not. Patients gave according to their ability, and those healers associated with Asclepia expressed concern first for the patients, not the purse.

Imperial decrees rarely matched reality, but at the very least attention to the medical needs of the poor was addressed at the highest level.

---

[20] Vivian Nutton, "Archiatri and the Medical Profession in Antiquity," *Papers of the British School at Rome* 45 (1977): 210–12.

Although no objectives were put into place to make such medical care a reality, the intention was still known to the body politic. The provisions for *archiatroi* to treat the poor alongside, but not to the exclusion of the rich, reflected the spirit of Hippocratism, a preoccupation also among Christians and their physicians.

The *anargyroi* surfaced in a society sorely needing medical help, aware of the benefits of medicine, but short of physicians. These saints saw both affluent and impoverished patients embrace rational medicine. The former paid their practitioners' bills, the latter afforded them the opportunity to acquire the reputation for character which attracted such patrons. *Anargyroi,* their medical colleagues, and even their pagan-priest counterparts were part of professions which embraced the notion of assisting the poor.

The Early Church's Reaction to Physicians

The same hagiographical texts venerating the *anargyoi* present a rather negative view of secular physicians. "The despair of doctors, in cases where the saint eventually triumphs, becomes a *topos* of hagiographical invective."[21] The hagiographers' intent to venerate the holy man in opposition to pagan philosophies explains such *topoi.*

Their view of secular medicine contains the same negative perception of medicine attributed to the early Church by Vivian Nutton, a view that is inconsistent with the sources. His work is remarkable contribution to the study of the history of medicine,[22] but his conclusions on this particular matter problematic. He begins his argument:

> The early apologists of Christianity laid stress on the effectiveness of Christian cures, and their message of hope to the sick was a major factor in the eventual triumph of Christianity over other cults.[23]

[21] Horden, "Saints and Doctors," 10.

[22] For this appreciation, one need look no further than his *Ancient Medicine* (London and New York: Routledge Press 2004). See also the important review by John Scarborough in the *Bryn Mawr Classical Review,* 2005.07.74.

[23] Vivian Nutton, "Murders and Miracles: Lay Attitudes Towards Medicine in Classical

With less support he conjectures that:

> ... from its inception Christianity offered itself as a direct competitor to secular healing. In Christ, God incarnate, it had the saviour on earth, the great physician, whose help was available to all believers, and at no monetary cost.[24]

This logic is faulty. The existence of (and/or strong faith in) supernatural healing is not mutually exclusive with confidence in secular (or rational) medicine.[25] Were priests at the Asclepieia in direct competition with Hippocratic physicians? No.[26] Following this rationale, the Tiber Asclepion would have been in competition with the Roman physicians, which, as we have already observed, simply was not the case. Incurable patrons commonly sought Asclepius on Tiber Island as a last resort.

Nutton cites as a proof text Mark 5:6: "The woman with the issue of blood had spent all her savings on doctors and drugs, yet she was not cured by them, but by merely touching the hem of Christ's robe."[27] Nutton fails to cite the variation of the Marcan passage, which is found in the synoptic account of Luke 8:43. The latter records that the woman "could not be healed by anyone," i.e., "all sectors of the health care system."[28] In this case, no competition with physicians took place, nor with the entire array of healers. The woman simply had an incurable illness, that is, outside of miraculous intervention.

Antiquity," in *Patients and Practitioners: Lay Perception of Medicine in Pre-Industrial Society,* edited by Roy Porter (Cambridge: Cambridge University Press, 1985) 23–53. (Hereafter referred to as Nutton, "Lay Attitudes," [in Porter].)

[24] Ibid.

[25] This view is unpacked in various modern writings, see: Willem Van De Merwe, "Modern Science and Faith" in J. Bradley Garner and Jerry Pattengale, editors, Becoming World Changers Resource Guide (Marion, Ind.: Indiana Wesleyan University, 2006) 128.

[26] J. Neusner, et al, *Religion, Science, and Magic* (New York: Oxford University Press, 1989) 125.

[27] Nutton, "Lay Attitudes," (in Porter) 48.

[28] John J. Piltch, "Sickness and Healing in Luke-Acts," in Jerome H. Neyrey, ed. *The Social World of Luke-Acts: Models for Interpretation* (Peabody, MA: Hendrickson Publishers, 1991) 193.

Most of Christ's cures were for otherwise incurable ills, which is another obstacle in accepting Nutton's thesis of competition. The pivotal role of "miracle cures" in Christian proselytizing is a familiar assessment, long established by Edward Gibbon, "perhaps the only English writer [at least through 1845] who has any claim to be considered an ecclesiastical historian."[29] Healing miracles were one of the key contributing factors in the rapid expansion of Christianity,[30] but the stampede to the new religion was not an exodus from Hippocratic healing. Gibbon, himself an "unbeliever" and rationalist, finds it puzzling nonetheless that such a display of supernatural healings did not evoke more of a response from the philosophers. Gibbon claims they remained indifferent, a far cry from Nutton's "competitor" status.[31]

Nutton also cites the lives of *anargyroi* Cosmas, Damian, and Artemius in support of third-century lay persons choosing Christianity over secular physicians.[32] This is a false opposition. With these *anargyroi* they were choosing both, not either-or. The later legends predictably highlight miraculous cures of desperate cases, but along with the earliest sources, they also note the ("secular") profession of *anargyroi*. The bishop of Cyrrhus, protector of one of the chief healing shrines for Cosmas and Damian, recruited numerous physicians to his city while openly embracing the power associated with *martyria*. In this city, the prolific bishop,

---

[29] John Henry Newman, *An Essay on the Development of Christian Doctrine* (New York: Doubleday, 1960) 35.

[30] Cf. Jarslov Pelikan, *The Excellent Empire* (San Francisco: Harper and Row, 1987) 15–40 *passim;* Pelikan qualifies Gibbon's statements on the disinterest of adherents of science in supernatural events.

[31] Nutton and Gibbon cannot both be correct. Ironically, Gibbon, the more "popular" writer, sides more closely with the facts in this instance, while it is Nutton, whose reputation is firmly established in the rigors of primary research, who is mistaken. See also Edward Gibbon, *The History of the Decline and Fall of the Roman Empire,* edited by J. B. Bury, 7 vols. (London: Metheun, 1896–1900) chapter 15 (Bury: 2:69–70).

[32] Nutton, "Lay Attitudes," (in Porter) 50, text to not 91. Cf. Stephen D'Irsay, "Christian Medicine and Science in the Third Century," *Journal of Religion,* 526–27, 534–35, 543–44.

Theodoret, certainly offered cooperation between scientific and faith healing, not an opposition.[33]

Nutton concedes that "a compromise" between religion and medicine was reached by the fourth century onwards "by most Christian writers."[34] However, evidence is found among the Patristic Fathers that does not suggest a need for such a compromise. They showed a marked difference of attitude from that of hagiographers towards physicians. It was the Church Fathers who were "foremost" in the effort "to keep alight the torch of Greek science," and "who became the guardians of the medical tradition."[35]

Church Fathers integrated science in their presentation and defense of biblical truths, with at least one major representation in every century of late antiquity: Tertullian (ca. 160–230) and in a qualified sense, Clement of Alexandria (ca. 200) in the second century;[36] Origen (185–254) in the third century[37]—an era which was less favorable to scientific integration,[38] but nonetheless also witnessed the practical application ("pastoral medicine") of Cyprian (d. 258) during an African epidemic;[39] Lactantius[40] and Methodius of Olympia (ca. 311) in the fourth century,[41]

---

[33] Theodoret, *Epistles*, 13, 112–15. Cf. *Indem, Dialogues*, 3.

[34] Nutton, "Lay Attitudes," (in Porter) 49.

[35] Charles Singer and E. Ashworth Underwood, *A Short History of Medicine*. Second Edition (New York: Oxford University Press, 1962) 67. Cf. Frings, *Medizin und Arzt bei den Griechischen Kirchenvatern bis Chrysostomos* (Dissertation, University of Bohn; Durk: Rheinische Friedrich Wilhelms, 1959) 8–24; Frings' dissertation thesis is that the Patristic Fathers embraced Hippocratic medicine.

[36] "In a qualified sense," this integration can be found in some hygienic treatises of a contemporary unknown to Tertullian, Clement of Alexandria, along with select statements from the latter's colleagues at the Alexandrian Christian College (the Didasalion).

[37] Origen declares that there is "no doubt" about the use of rational medicine, and what better example of "knowledge from God" could exist than that pertaining to health? (Origen, *In Numeros Homilae* 18.3; Migne *PG*, I12: col. 715B).

[38] Stephen d'Irsay, "Patristic Medicine," *Annual of Medical History* 9 (1927): 368.

[39] Pontius the Deacon, *The Life and Passion of Cyprian, Bishop and Martyr* 9 (in *The Ante-Nicene Fathers*, vol. 5) 270.

[40] Cf. his endorsement of the physician Diocles in *De opificio Dei*.

[41] Cf. *The Resurrection (De resurrectione)*.

followed by Jerome (ca. 347–420),[42] Ambrose,[43] and Augustine.[44] In the works of Isidore of Sevile we find a collection of many early Christian manuscripts in his science-faith integration.[45]

The Case of Menouthis: The Conflicts between St. Cyrus and Gesius, and the Conversion of Paralius

Before proceeding with a discussion of the Hippocratic persistence among Christian physicians and the interplay between faith and science, one should consider first the healing centers near Alexandria. In the case of St. Cyrus and Gesius, both were rational (Hippocratic) physicians from the same area, but by Gesius's time Cyrus had *anargyric* status. And in the case of Paralius (ca. 485–487), his conversion affords a look at the interplay between the pagan and Christian incubatory sites.

Near Canopus, only twelve miles east of the fallen Alexandrian temples, was an academy of sorts for both Christian and pagans.[46] This small town of Menouthis was very much involved with the events both in Canopus and Alexandria, and would later host the *anargyric* shrine of Saints Cyrus and John.[47] Bishop Cyril of Alexandria informed the Menouthis residents that they would no longer be invoking the name of "the lady," the *Kura,* i.e., Isis. Rather, they would invoke the more deserving and powerful personage of the martyr St. Cyrus (*Kuros*).[48] In AD 414 he translated the last sanctuary of Isis into their reliquary.[49]

---

[42] Jerome, *Adversus Lovinianum* [the monk Jovinian] 6.6–12.

[43] St. Ambrose, *Hexaem* 6.9 (Migne, *Patr.* Lat. XIV, cols. 264–71).

[44] St. Augustine, *Sermons* 243.6–7; 249.4; *The Animal* 2.4.

[45] St. Isidore of Sevile [Bishop of Sevile; not the son and disciple of the Gnostic Basilides], *Etymologiae* 4, 10.2.

[46] Herbert G. May, editor, et. al., *Oxford Bible Atlas,* 3d edition (Oxford: Oxford University Press, 1984) 89–91.

[47] T. Nissen, "De SS. Cyri et Iohannis Vitae Formis," *Analecta Boliandiana* 57 (1939): 68–70.

[48] St. Cyril, "Anargyroi," *PG,* 77.1104. For various examples of miracles credited to Sts. Cyrus and John, see Bollandists, *Les Recueils Antiques de Miracles des Saints* (Brussels, 1925) 8–73.

[49] O. Meinardus, "A Coptic Anargyos: St. Colluthus," *Studia Orientalia Christiana* 14

St. Cyrus' local heritage undoubtedly factored significantly in the sudden popularity of this healing cult. He was a physician of renown in Alexandria before his conversion, and was martyred near Alexandria in AD 303 after offering his medical services to Christian women facing martyrdom in Canopus. Along with St. John, another physician who joined him on his medical mission, he was initially buried at St. Mark's Church in Alexandria. These *anargyroi* had already developed a significant following before their translation to Menouthis. The legendary accounts of St. Cyrus boast that St. Cyrus "healed not only the bodies of the sick but also precious souls from whatever diseases had befallen them."

The Alexandrian doctor, Gesius, challenged the miraculous status of cures credited to Sts. Cyrus and John, only to suffer an embarrassing prognosis himself. Gesius charged that these cures were all natural and were actually found in the Hippocratic corpus (thus, discrediting divine intervention). But then an unknown incurable disease reportedly struck him, forcing his request of the Saints' healing power. His penance was public. Wearing a bell around his neck, and with a packsaddle on his back and a horse's bit in this mouth, he circled the church exclaiming, "I am a fool!"[50]

The interplay between faith and reason can be seen in the historic and legendary accounts of St. Cyrus. During his lifetime his reputation as a Hippocratic practitioner preceded his reputation as a Christian, and his missionary zeal. After translation, his popularity was on the rise, with his historical Hippocratic reputation now inextricably linked with his supernatural healing powers. Whether supernatural healing took place at his shrine is an issue beyond the scope of this discussion, but the societal belief in such occurrences, like earlier with Asclepius and Isis centers, reflects the endorsement of "magical" healing. It is clear that Cyrus the

(1970–1971): 357. Sophronius claimed to have been cured by Sts. Cyrus and John, and claimed that the temple of Isis sank into the sand, see "Kyros and John," *Oxford Dictionary of Byzantium*, vol. 2, 1164. St. Cyril of Alexandria [became patriarch in 412], "*Anargyroi*," Migne, *Patrologia Graeca*, 77.1100–1105. Quasten, *Patrology*, vol. 3, 116–42.

[50] H. G. Magoulaias, "The Lives of the Saints as Sources of Data for the History of Byzantine Medicine in the Sixth and Seventh Centuries," *Byzantinische Zeitschrift* 57 (1964): 130–31.

physician was both a respected scientist and a devout Christian. The exclamation point for his personal alignment is found in his willingness to be both openly, and his willingness to pay the ultimate sacrifice.

At the same location we learn of a relative peace between students of both the pagan and Christian healing shrines, that is, before the explosive story of Paralius. The details of a battle between the last remnant of the pagan healing cult at Menouthis and the patrons of the *anargyroi* come to us through the conversion experience of Paralius, recorded by Zacharias Scholasticus in his *Life of Severus, circa* 512–518. The *Life of Isidoris* by Damascus also corroborates portions of this account.[51] Menouthis was located in the resort area of Canopus, where thousands of Alexandrians and other Egyptians traveled annually for both religion and relaxation. Numerous pagan temples dotted the landscape of this city known for its Canopic funeral vases.[52]

Over a century earlier, one of Alexandria's last great pagan teachers, Antoninus, had taken refuge in Canopus and immediately attracted throngs of pagans. In turn, this was a significant factor in the ensuing wrath of St. Cyril. Nonetheless, even after the translation of the *anargyoi*, the cult of Isis managed to survive in Menouthis until the time of Paralius. While the relics of *anargyroi* were being translated, the surviving patrons of Isis seem to have transformed the crypt of an old temple into their secretive headquarters. Although the details are lacking, the general proximity can at least be ascertained: the Isis cult and that of the *anargyroi* were both in Menouthis, and interacted with each other.

As the decades passed, and as the Isis worship regained quasi-acceptance, disciples from both camps studied at least grammar together. Paralius and Severus had mingled freely with members from wealthy Asia Minor families, both pagans and Christians. In Menouthis, Paralius studied paganism while interacting with Christians. Perhaps he learned under descendants of Antonius; it is certain that he sat under the gram-

---

[51] P. A. Chuvin, *A Chronicle of the Last Pagans,* translated by B. Archer (Cambridge: Harvard University Press, 1990) 111; see 170, n. 14.

[52] These are beautifully crafted jars (for containing viscera), usually with animal heads such as the one found in King Tut's tomb.

marian Horapollo (who admired "demons and magic").[53] It is less certain how often both Christians and pagans had enrolled with Horapollo, but both groups were well aware of the others' daily affairs.

It is important to remember that Menouthis had become the host of the *anargyric* healing center—the "Church of the Evangelists," the Church of Sts. Cyrus and John. While a core of pagans had maintained a last stronghold in this resort area, the same Menouthis phenomenon of the past centuries had persisted, and had done so literally since the founding of Alexandria. That is, Menouthis had kept its magnetic appeal for the religious, but now the pilgrims were nearly all Christians rather than pagans. This phenomenon continued until the shrine was moved to Constantinople in the seventh century, after the Arab conquest of Egypt.[54] Ironically, a century after the "cleansing" of the pagan temples, and after St. Cyril's translation of the *anargyroi's* relics to Menouthis, one of Egypt's biggest collections of idols and strongest chapters of the Isis (Serapis) healing cult remained next door to one of Egypt's most re-nowned Christian healing centers.[55]

Zacharias recalls his youth in an attempt to acquit his teacher, Severus', testimony of pagan leanings. As a result, we have the details of the Menouthis incident as it involved Paralius, Severus' colleague. Paralius frequented the fugitive Isis sanctuary, a building covered with hieroglyphics, and whose patronage also included pagan professors and students. Like the patrons over in the Church of the Evangelists, Paralius exhibited confidence in incubatory revelation; he slept in the sanctuary of Isis in order to benefit from dreams. Both the *anargyric* center and the makeshift Serapeum had incubatory sanctuaries similar to those of

[53] G. Fowden, "The Pagan Holy Man in Late Antique Society," *Journal of Hellenistic Studies* (1982): 33–59.

[54] P. Peeters, *Analectia Bollandiana*, 25 (1906): 233–40.

[55] For the vestiges of pagan shrines in Roman North Africa, see David Riggs, "Pagans and Christians in Central North Africa: Reconsidering the Growth of Christianity from Cyprian to Augustine," dissertation for Oxford University (2005); also see Riggs forthcoming work with Oxford University Press on the same (in press, working title is "Divine Patronage in Late Roman and Vandal Africa: Reconsidering a Local Narrative of Christianisation). See also Sozomen, *Ecclesiastical History,* 2.5.6; and Eusebius, *The Life of Constantine,* IV.39.

other *anargyric* centers like that of St. Colluthus in Antinoe. In one instance at the *anarygric* shrine, a patron from Damascus was only "fully" cured after dreaming that the patron saint of his hometown assisted in the miracle.[56]

After revealing a fraudulent "fertility" miracle bestowed upon an impotent couple from his own hometown, and following contradictory advice from the priestess of Isis while supposedly dreaming, Paralius turned against the cult.[57] The Christian students in Menouthis rescued him from the ensuing scuffle and near-fatal blows from pagan classmates; an anti-pagan conflagration ensued. This clash resulted in the razing of the Isis center, which uncovered a secret treasury of idols, including several that had been salvaged from the Iseum in Memphis. The Christians routed the pagans and then carted twelve camel loads of idols to the Alexandrian public square for a ritual burning. The events at the *anargyric* center were well known in the patriarchal see. Monks from Canopus and *philoponoi* from Menouthis dismembered the idols, shouting "their gods have no surgeons!"[58] This is a fitting epithet exclaimed by the victor in a war between healing cults.

The story of Paralius played out many times at various locations. While religious differences between pagan and Christian healing centers existed, and ultimately ended the pagan institutions, the cultural acceptance and familiarity lingered. Following Owsei Temkin's lead, the rise of *anargyroi* is best understood by identifying the common concerns of patients and their praises of physicians which persisted from the era of the benevolent physician to that of his *anargyric* cult.[59] Elements found in pagan healing centers which can be identified and categorized not only

---

[56] *Miracula Sanctorium Cyri et Hohannis, PG* 87, 3664B ff.

[57] The Isis priestess gave the couple her own newborn child, but the "new" mother failed to produce milk, disproving the "miraculous" origin of the baby.

[58] "Surgeons"—Coptic, *karoumtitin,* "bone-setters." Zacharias, *Life of Severus,* 20–22. *Philoponoi* refers to energetic laymen.

[59] Owsei Temkin, *Hippocrates in a World of Pagans and Christians* (Baltimore: Johns Hopkins University Press, 1991) 126–45; he also edited the classic work on the history of medicine, Ludwig Edelstein's *Ancient History,* also by Johns Hopkins Press (1967, reprint 1987).

persisted well into the Christian era, but were manifest in the *anargyric* cult itself.

Benevolence and scientific healing were applauded and inextricably linked, and informed cultural expectations. In Paralius' conversion we find a societal disdain for fraudulence among healers, regardless of scientific endorsements by those particular healers. G. E. R. Lloyd reminds us that "it must be recognized that *but* for the ancients' assumptions of its value-ladeness—and of its value as contributing to the good life—there would hardly have been any science then at all."[60] Concomitantly the veneration of saints, the preoccupation with healing, the resurgence of magic, "incurable diseases," and strong remnants of pagan healing cults were dynamics also facilitating the rise of the *anargyric* shrines in late antiquity.

Conclusion: The Multifaceted Appeal

The *anargyroi* attracted large followings for numerous reasons. The hagiographers erroneously credit their supernatural powers as their reason for popularity, while also miscasting the Church in opposition to Hippocratism. There was also no rampant competition between science and Christianity as Nutton contends.

This study has shown several historical dynamics that shed light on understanding the *anargyroi's* appeal. 1) We only know of the *anargyroi* because they were Hippocratic physicians, making it counterintuitive to contend the Early Church's disdain for science. As reputable physicians the *anargyroi* commanded respect for their skills during their lifetimes. 2) While the Hippocratic physician was committed to being fair in representing his trade, and to keep the patient's needs as the key concern, he was not expected to do this gratis, and few did. The very term "*anarygros*" reveals the ancient's recognition that they were indeed a subset of the profession. 3) The paucity of physicians created a high demand that could have exacted considerable fees. As compassionate physicians their patrons respected their ethic. 4) As famous local physicians they earned

[60] G. E. R. Lloyd, *Science and Morality in Greco-Roman Antiquity: An Inaugural Lecture* (Cambridge: Cambridge University Press, 1985) 3.

respect as celebrities. 5) A substantial case has been made that a wide assortment of clients venerated these physician-saints in large part because they respected physicians in general. The wide assortment of patrons, and the Church as benefactor, institutionalized healing centers that, among other things, openly endorsed the medical profession. 6) Though not addressed in detail due to its trite place in medical history, it is clear that the candid and open criticism of dishonest physicians implied a standard for the profession. And, 7) it is clear that Christian and pagan physicians interacted even after the legalization of Christianity, a dynamic detailed above during the discussion of Menouthis.

The evidence shows a persistence of scientific healing in Christendom. The same hagiographic accounts condemning secular medicine ironically reveal the Church's endorsement of it. Stories of gratis giving were believable in large part because of the well established ethic of Hippocratic medicine. Patrons attended the shrines after consulting physicians who practiced with the Church's blessing, and who exhibited a professional ethic resembling the saints' standards. Although the *anargyros* was depicted in the role of *alter Christus,* evidence supports the notion that his virtues were just as likely rooted in a pre-Christian Hippocratic ethic. Spyros G. Marketos and Constantin Papaeconomou assert that in Ancient Greece the relationship between the Hippocratic physician and his or her patients "was dictated by human, rather than religious, concepts . . . practiced in accordance with scientific laws and felt bound by ethical and humane precepts of his [or her] profession."[61] The implication is that the same is true for modern physicians, that is, an incompatibility exists between religious and "human" concepts, or at least that they are mutually exclusive—a conclusion seriously challenged by this study. For the Christian physicians, both religious and human concepts could dictate their course, as both concepts were in agreement.

It is not important whether any of the specific acts of the *anargyroi* can be proven, but only that evidence informs us that from the fourth century on various communities embraced and championed the

---

[61] Spyros G. Marketos and Constantin Papaeconomou, "Medicine, Magic, and Religion in Ancient Greece," *Humane Medicine* 8 (January 1992): 43.

vitae of the *anargyroi*. These resumes were believable, acceptable, and commendable. The positive aspects of physicians and pagan priests were common before the advent of *anargyric* shrines. For example, the universal acceptance policy at *anargyric* shrines had precedence not only in Hippocratism, but also in former pagan centers such as the Asclepia.

Rational medicine, with its unofficial ethic, persisted through the religio-political transitions of the fourth and fifth centuries. During these centuries, societies under the umbrella of the Roman-Byzantine rule endorsed the general ethic of Hippocratism. Opinions, condemnations, praises, and passing references about scientific healing support this supposition. This common ethical standard spoke well of the profession, but branded many physicians as "bad," a condemnation which nearly always implied avarice. For the good independent physicians, which included the *anargyroi*, this ethic was one of the only two criteria for establishing and sustaining practice in a community, the other being medical training. The behavior of both dependent and independent physicians became a matter of public scrutiny. The records of city councils even attest to the high priority of a physician's reputation. Roman society had its ideals, and judged harshly those physicians and healers who transgressed them. The Christians made the parameters of ethics even more stringent, and elevated the physicians who not only best represented the Roman ideal, but who also provided the best contrast to errant Roman medicine.

The dynamic of martyrdom, veneration of saints, and *praesentia* significantly increased the fame of these doctors. Their veneration, attested in both private and institutional form, while promoting Christianity, also reveals an orchestrated endorsement of what was good in Hippocratic medicine. In communities whose highest prize and leading civic center was a shrine, what better compliment could have been given to Hippocratism than to venerate its ideal physicians? These physician-saints were not praised for converting from a disreputable profession to Christianity, but for perfecting their profession for the cause of Christianity. People from all social backgrounds and races could identify good physicians. Thus these legendary physician-saints came to be identified as trustworthy advocates with the divine, especially when the best physicians could not proffer a cure.

While the poor were the likely beneficiaries of Hippocratic standards, the physicians' benevolence did not escape the notice of the more fortunate. The educated citizen was familiar with medicine, and held that the title "physician" itself was an honor. Medicine in the abstract, with its accompanying lofty ethic, was secondary to the practical application of a medicine couched in benevolence. The latter produced some of the most popular figures in many late antique communities. Christians in these communities calculated that their best chance to supplant popular pagan healers rested with popular healing saints. In general, and in the cases of some saints in particular, the pervasive preoccupation with healing in late Roman society made the *anargyroi* prime candidates for such substitutions.

The Stars in their Courses Fought Against Sisera[1]

Astrology and Jewish Society in the Later Roman Empire

Lester Ness

Introduction

❈Dr. Yamauchi is well known for his work on a corpus of Mandaean incantation bowls[2] and his interest in Gnosticism of all sorts.[3] This chapter is on a related topic: astrology and Jews in the Roman Empire. My purpose is to discuss a puzzling group of archaeological finds, that is, the zodiac mosaics found in several Jewish synagogues in Israel, dating to the later Roman Empire period, the fourth through sixth centuries AD. A look at the history of astrology in the Biblical world and the Roman Empire will demonstrate that the pictures of the signs were a way of praising the Almighty and his power in the universe, an alternative to showing the invisible God Himself.

Astrology as it is known in the twenty-first century is clearly a mixture of ideas and practices from many different sources. Perhaps we might compare it to a Chinese hot-pot dish, where everyone adds a bit of meat or vegetable or mushroom to a hot broth to cook, and the mixture becomes something that none of the ingredients were individually.[4]

[1] Judges 5:20.

[2] Edwin M. Yamauchi, *Mandaic Incantation Texts*, American Oriental Series 49 (New Haven, CT: Yale University Press, 1967).

[3] Edwin M. Yamauchi, *Pre-Christian Gnosticism; A Survey of the Proposed Evidences*, 2d ed. (Grand Rapids: Baker, 1983); Edwin M. Yamauchi, "Gnosticism," *New Dictionary of Theology*, ed. Sinclair B. Ferguson, & David B. Wright (Downers Grove, IL: Intervarsity, 1988) 272–74; Edwin M. Yamauchi, *Gnostic Ethics and Mandaean Origins* (Piscataway, NJ: Gorgias, 2004) are only his best known publications.

[4] There are too many general histories of astrology to list all of them here. Franz Cumont, *Astrology and Religion among the Greeks and Romans* (New York: Putnam, 1912; repr., NY:

The most fundamental idea is nearly universal: that events in Nature, here and now, are messages from some thing or things greater than us, telling us to beware that omens exist, in other words. These include events in the sky, such as eclipses, comets, and bright planets drawing close or away from each other, against the background of the fixed stars. Mesopotamian academics made lists of sky omens, as they did of many other things.

Looking for omens in the sky was neither astronomy or astrology in our current sense of the word. Astronomy was part of regulating the lunar calendar. To be able to look at the moon's phase and judge that it was time to collect the rent was handy for Mesopotamian businessmen. But the phases of the moon do not fit the seasons of the year well. Payments due at wheat harvest had to take the path of the sun into account as well. Reconciling solar and lunar information required accurate observations and mathematical analysis. A by-product of this became the observation and analysis of all the other planets as well. A further by-product was the ability to predict planet omens in advance. By the seventh century BC the Neo-Assyrians could predict solar and lunar eclipses,[5] and by the Persian Achaemenian dynasty (sixth to fourth centuries BC) the horoscope had been invented. A horoscope is a calculated map of the sky, showing where the planets were, relative to any given place and time. This map allowed one to observe omens which had not yet occurred. Soon other mathematical practices were invented, especially elections. Elections involve

Dover, 1960), also at http://www.sacred-texts.com/astro/argr/index.htm, and Auguste Bouché-Leclercq, *L'Astrologie Grecque* (Paris: Press Universitaire de France, 1898) are the classic accounts. Perhaps the best recent account is Tamsyn Barton, *Ancient Astrology* (London: Routledge, 1994). I refer the curious reader to my on-line bibliography of astrology and history, http://www.smoe.org/arcana/astrol1.html, for many more titles.

[5] David Brown, *Mesopotamian Planetary Astronomy-Astrology* (Groenigen: Styx Press, 1999) Ulla Koch-Westenhol, *Mesopotamian Astrology: An Introduction to Babylonian and Assyrian Celestial Divination* (Copenhagen: Carsten Niebuhr Institute of Near Eastern Studies: Museum Tusculanum Press, University of Copenhagen, 1995) are the most up-to-date accounts of the history of astronomy and astrology in Mesopotamia. Otto Neugebauer, *The Exact Sciences in Antiquity* (2d ed., Providence, RI: Brown University Press, 1957) is the classic introduction.

using calculations to choose the moment most favored by the planets for some activity such as a marriage, for example, or an appointment.

The oldest known horoscope is on a clay tablet, and dates to 410 BC, the time of Socrates and Plato, Buddha and Confucius. A fair number of horoscopes on clay tablets survive, mostly from the Hellenistic era, often made for individuals with Greek names. However, Mesopotamian astral science clearly interested some Greeks. We do not know the details (save for some stories about the Babylonian priest, Berossus), but a great deal of Mesopotamian astronomical observational data was transferred to Greek astronomers. So was the horoscope. The Greek scientists then proceeded to interpret it all in the light of their own physics, philosophies, and religion. This is why the astrology that we know in the twenty-first century explains the powers of the planets in terms of the four elements of Greek physics, not the arbitrary desires of Mesopotamian gods. Likewise, we use the Greek (actually Roman) names for the planets and the signs of the zodiac.

The zodiac was and still is the celestial foot-ruler, with the signs being the inches. It was probably invented in Neo-Assyrian Mesopotamia, although proof is lacking. The zodiac wheel is a belt or ring in the sky, with the twelve signs being named for constellations. But the zodiac is primarily a tool for calculation. The constellations vary in size, while the signs are always thirty degrees long, or one day's journey of the sun. (The face of the full moon is half a degree across.) The sun's annual path, the ecliptic, runs through the center of the zodiac, which extends six degrees above and below it. The official beginning point started with the sign of Aries, defined as the point where the ecliptic crossed the celestial equator. The sun crossed this point on the vernal equinox, Babylonian (and Jewish) New Year, 1 Nisan, or the twenty-first of March on our calendar. The 12 signs are: Aries, the Ram; Taurus, the Bull; Gemini, the Twins; Cancer, the Crab; Leo, the Lion; Virgo, the girl; Libra, the scales; Scorpio, the Scorpion; Sagittarius, the Archer; Capricorn, a creature half goat, half fish; Aquarius, the Water Carrier; and Pisces, the two Fish.

The names and the iconography of the signs ultimately come from Mesopotamia. Goat-fish, for example, are common in Mesopotamian art. However, there were some variations over the centuries. Greeks, for example, usually called Libra the Claws of the Scorpion.[6]

Likewise, there have been many other identifications over the centuries and millennia. For example, the twelve signs have been identified with the twelve Olympians of Greek mythology; the twelve sons of Jacob; the twelve apostles; and recently, the twelve animals of the Chinese calendar. Almost any group of twelve has been identified with the signs by someone.

There are also many subdivisions, such as the decans (thirds of a sign, from the Egyptian calendar)[7], the dodecatemoria (twelfths of a signs),[8] and the terms (segments of the signs, of various lengths)[9], and alternatives, such as the lunar mansions, and the twenty-eight segments of the zodiac, corresponding to the daily journey of the moon.[10] The iconography of the signs is very striking, and has often been used in art from Neo-Babylonian times onwards.

Astrology has come into and gone out of respectability several times in its 2500 years. It was certainly respectable in the Roman Empire. Most of the practices and approaches of astrology that are familiar today were developed in Ptolemaic Egypt, and became known to Romans as their expansion brought educated Greeks to Rome. Major philosophers and scientists were divided over its validity. Carneades, leader of the Platonic Academy in the third century BC, formulated many arguments against its validity, while Stoic philosophers usually defended astrology. The early Christian Fathers were usually against the practice of astrology, usually on the grounds that determinism degraded moral responsibility, and some-

[6] Auguste Bouché-Leclercq, *L'Astrologie Grecque* (Paris: Presses Universitaires de France, 1899) 141–42.

[7] Bouché-Leclercq, 1899, "The Decans," 215–36, passim. Neugebauer, *Exact Sciences in Antiquity*, 1956, 81–82.

[8] Bouché-Leclercq, 1899, 216, 3, and many other places, passim; Abraham Sachs and Otto Neugebauer, "The 'Dodekatemoria' in Babylonian Astronomy," *Archiv für Orientforschung* 16 (1952): 65–66.

[9] Bouché-Leclercq, 1899, "*Confins* ou *Termes*," 206–15.

[10] Ibid., 463, note 2.

times on the grounds that it was a form of idolatry.[11] Astrology was a part of everyday life in the Roman Empire and almost everyone was familiar with astrological ideas and practices, perhaps in the way that modern Americans are familiar with popular television shows.

One use of astrology which was common in the Roman Empire was to symbolize political or religious power. Augustus put his sign, Capricorn, on some of his coins, perhaps hinting that is was his destiny to rule.[12] Nero's Golden House, his palace in Rome, had a round banqueting hall with a rotating ceiling, decorated to look like the night sky. Through the openings guest were showered with jewelry, perfume, and even horse dung.[13] This conveyed the message that Nero was the center of the universe, and that he could dispense both good and bad things, just as the planets did. Everyone knew the symbolism.

One can find the same message in several other religious settings, such as the ones found at the temple of Bel in Palmyra in modern Syria, or at the temple of Jupiter in Heliopolis (Baalbek) in modern Lebanon. Mosaic floors (the bourgeois art of antiquity) often had zodiacs with some favorite deity in the center, Dionysus, perhaps, praised as Cosmocrator or Master of the universe.[14]

---

[11] Bouché-Leclercq, 1899, "L'Astrologie et la Disussion Dogmatique," 593–609 and "L'Astrologie et l'Orthodoxie Chrétienne," 609–27, give detailed accounts. Dom Emmanuel Amand's *Fatalisme et Liberte dans l'Antiquite Grecque; Recherches sur la Survivance de l'Argumentation Anti-Fataliste de Carneade chez les Philosophes grecs et les Theologiens Chretiens des Quatre Premiers Siècles* (Louvain: Dissertation, 1945) is the classic work on philosophical arguments for and against astrology.

[12] Suetonius, *Aug.*, 94; Bouché-Leclercq, 1899, 373 note 2 and 549.

[13] Suetonius, *Lives of the Twelve Caesars,* "Nero," XXXI; Henri Stierlin, *L'Astrologie et le Pouvoir de Platon á Newton* (Paris: Payot, 1986) 42–43.

[14] Lester John Ness, "Astrology and Judaism in Late Antiquity" (Ph.D. diss., Miami University, 1990) 110–90 is an over-view (hereafter Ness, 1990). This work was later published as Lester J. Ness, *Written in the Stars: Ancient Zodiac Mosaics* (Warren Center, PA: Shangri-La, 1999). For Mithraic astrological art, Franz Cumont, *The Mysteries of Mithra* (New York, Dover, 1956), is the classic starting point, available online at Perhaps the best introduction to Palmyra's astrological art is Malcolm A. R. Colledge, *The Art of Palmyra* (Boulder, CO: Westview Press, 1976), while for Baalbek, see Yousseff Hajjar, *La triade d'Heliopolis-Baalbek; Iconographie, Theologie, Culte, et Sanctuaires* (Montreal: Université de Montreal, 1985).

The Synagogue Zodiacs

One example, rather surprising to the modern observer, is the use of the zodiac in synagogues. At least six examples are known, all dating to Late Antiquity, from the fourth through sixth centuries AD. Other examples may still await discovery. The first example of a zodiac mosaic was discovered in a synagogue at Naaran, near Jericho, in 1918, during a battle in World War I. In 1920, it was excavated by the Dominican Brothers Vincent and Carriere of the Ecole Biblique, in Jerusalem. Following the archaeological techniques of the day, they concentrated on drawing an architectural plan of the ruins rather than on the stratigraphy. As a result the building was dated solely on its artistic style to the fourth or fifth centuries AD. The meeting room, or the synagogue proper, was part of a larger complex. To reach it one had to walk through about ten meters of courtyard, which included an atrium with a pool, and a narthex. The meeting room was approximately fifteen meters wide and perhaps twenty-two meters long (only nineteen meters survive.) Ten square pillars held up the roof and divided the space into a large center aisle and two side aisles (the basilica plan).

The mosaic floor had four panels. The first panel, which had an appearance of a carpet, with images of plants and animals, was enclosed by polygons. The zodiac is in the panel, near the entrance. Like most of the other zodiac representations it is square (4.05 m. by 4.05 m) in shape, with an image of a woman representing one of the four seasons in each corner. Inside the square are two concentric circles. The inmost (1.6 m in diameter) holds a figure of Sol Invictus in a schematic chariot. The outer circle (diameter 3.5 m) holds the zodiac images in pie slice shaped borders. The third panel shows Daniel in the lions den as well as several Hebrew inscriptions. The fourth panel holds Jewish symbols such as menorahs, and the bookcase, or ark, which held the Biblical scrolls. Unlike the zodiacs of today, these signs are not coordinated with the seasons. The artistic style of the zodiac is oriental Hellenistic, the sort of thing common in Palmyrene art and many places in Mesopotamia, and which eventually became Byzantine art.[15] Unfortunately, all of the Naaran figures were vandalized in ancient times.

The next example of a synagogue mosaic was discovered at Beth Alpha, west of Beth Shan, on the lower slopes of Mt. Gilboa. This is the best known and best preserved zodiac, and it is often shown to tourists. It was discovered by kibbutzniks digging an irrigation canal in 1928, and was formally excavated by E. Sukenik, for Hebrew University. The complex includes a courtyard, narthex, and a meeting room, all very much like the complex at Naaran. The meeting room was in the basilica style (10.74 m. by 12.4 m), with pillars separating the nave and the side aisles. The apse was located so it pointed towards Jerusalem. It was built in later fifth century AD, based on the pottery found in the wall plaster, a coin hoard discovered in the apse, and the mosaic inscriptions. It was renovated several times. At entrance D there are mosaics by the mosaicists, Marinos and Hanina, artists known from other mosaics in Beth Shan area.

Located on the floor there are three mosaic panels, all well preserved. The first shows the sacrifice of Isaac, the second contains the zodiac symbols, and the third has the ark, menorahs, and other Jewish symbols. The zodiac panel is 3.55 m. by 3.75 m. and resembles the Naaran zodiac in most ways. The style is oriental. There are depictions of the seasons (labeled with the names of the Hebrew months) in the corners, and two concentric circles. The inner circle held Sol Invictus, the outer one, zodiac signs, labeled in Hebrew.[16]

The third example is the Husifa zodiac discovered in 1930 on Mt. Carmel, in a village twelve kilometers from Haifa. The site was excavated by Makhouly and Avi-Yonah in 1933. Perhaps about one half of the original synagogue building survives. One complete wall, 10.1 m. in length and two incomplete walls 6.2 m. and 5.5 m. in length are all that remain of what was probably a square building. One line of column bases also survives. The mosaics have mostly been destroyed, but recognizable

---

[15] Ness, 1990, "Naaran," 224–30. Cf. L.-H. Vincent and A. Carrière, "Le sanctuaire juif d'`Ain Douq," *Revue Biblique* 30 (1921): 442–43 for the report of the excavators.

[16] Ness, 1990, "Beth Alpha," 231–37. E. Sukenik, *The Ancient Synagogue of Beth Alpha* (Oxford: Oxford University Press, 1932) is a book-length account by the excavator.

menorahs indicate it was a synagogue. Only one edge of a zodiac mosaic remains, located in the center of the three panels. The zodiac panel is 2.76 m. by 2.76 m., and the outer circle, if reconstructed, most likely would measure 1.38 m in diameter. The zodiac panel contains fragments of the signs from Sagittarius to Aries. No inscriptions survive. The artistic style is oriental again, reminiscent of Naaran and Beth Alpha, and dates the mosaic to the same Byzantine era. No other datable materials were found.[17]

The fourth clear example of a synagogue mosaic was found at Hammath-Tiberias, another site often visited by tourists. Hammath-Tiberias served as a resort town for Tiberias, and is located on the shores of the Sea of Galilee. Its zodiac is not as well-preserved as the one at Beth Alpha; however, it is better preserved than the zodiacs at Naaran and Husifa. Moreover, the artistic style is of a higher quality classical style rather than the provincial oriental style of the examples mentioned above. The Sol Invictus representation, discovered in 1947, is particularly impressive. The major excavation at the site was conducted by Moshe Dothan from 1971–1973.

This synagogue went through several phases of use; the zodiac mosaic was discovered in the second phase of use. Dothan dated phase II to the late third or early fourth centuries AD, based partly on the mosaic inscription and partly on its artistic style. The meeting room of the synagogue was roughly rectangular in shape, with none of the corners at right angles or its walls having the same length. The zodiac panel, however, is similar to the others mentioned above. There is a roughly squared panel, 3.3 m. by 3.26 m., with a feminine figure representing one of the four seasons in each of the corners. The two concentric circles are 3.2 m. and 1.4 m. in diameter. The inner circle holds Sol Invictus, the outer one, the signs of the zodiac.[18]

---

[17] Ness, 1990, "Husifa," 237–40. Michael Avi-Yonah, and N. Makhouly, "A Sixth-Century Synagogue at `Isfiyâ," *Quarterly of the Department of Antiquities of Palestine* 3 (1933): 118–31.

[18] Ness, 1990, "Hammath-Tiberias," 240–50. Moshe Dothan, *Hammath-Tiberias: Early Synagogues and and the Hellenistic and Roman Remain, Final Excavation Report*, Vol. I (Jerusalem: Israel Exploration Society, University of Haifa, Department of Antiquities,

The most recently discovered synagogue zodiac mosaic was un-earthed in Galilee at Sepphoris in 1993. The mosaic floor (14.02 meters by 4.88 meters) has three panels. One is of Abraham and Isaac, one is of the Tabernacle and the Temple in Jerusalem, and the third is an intact zodiac wheel. It closely resembles the other zodiac mosaics mentioned above. A square panel has figures of the seasons in the corners, and two concentric circles within it. The center circle has Sol Invictus, the outer circle has figures of the signs surrounded by pie slice shaped figures. One unusual feature is that Sol Invitus is not in the form of a human figure, but rather is represented by a disc located towards the top of a pole. The meaning of this representation is not clear. It might be an attempt to rep-resent a lighthouse, like the Pharos of Alexandria. On the other hand, it might represent a mountain with the sun above, and refer to the Cosmas Indicopleustes. But what is clear, is that the representation stands in a chariot drawn by four horses, as in the other zodiacs. The four seasons are labeled in both Greek and Hebrew, but the signs are labeled only in Hebrew. The artistic style is the familiar oriental style of Beth Alpha, Naaran, and Husifa. [19]

Possible Synagogue Zodiacs

The five synagogues mentioned above, Naarum, Beth Alpha, Husifa, Hammath-Tiberius, and Sepphoris, contain clear examples of zodiacs. Besides these definite examples of synagogue zodiacs there are a number of other partly preserved mosaics in synagogues that might have repre-sentations of zodiacs. Three of the most promising examples were found during the excavations at Susiya, Yafia, and En Gedi.

The first site is Susiya, which is located in southern Israel, near Hebron. It was first examined in the nineteenth century by Conder and Kitchener, but the major excavations at the site were carried out by Gutman, Yeivin, and Netzer, of the Israeli Department of Antiquities,

---

1983).

[19] Zeev Weiss and Ehud Netzer, *The Sepphoris Synagogue: Deciphering an Ancient Message Through its Archaeological and Socio-Historical Contexts* (Jerusalem: Israel Exploration Society: Institute of Archaeology, Hebrew University of Jerusalem, 2005).

from 1971 to 1972. The synagogue had a complex history, and was in use from the fifth to the eighth or ninth centuries AD. The main mosaic belongs to the second phase of construction. At the edge of the surviving mosaic, the very edge of a wheel and a dividing line are clearly visible, but no zodiac images appear. What remains resembles the wheel found at Hammath-Tiberias. It is possible that the destroyed floor contained images of the months, or representations of the labors of the seasons like the mosaic floor at Hammath-Tiberius, rather than the typical zodiac signs, but since the rest of floor is destroyed, it cannot be ascertained. A positive date is also hard to decide on, but since it resembles the genuine zodiacs in overall style it is probably safe to date it to the same period, Late Antiquity, the fourth through sixth centuries AD.[20]

The second site, Yafia, is located in the Galilee region, very close to Nazareth. It first came to scholars' attention in 1921, when Vincent published some sculptured lintel fragments from the site. More thorough excavations at Yafia were conducted by Sukenik and Avigad in 1951. The mosaics found here include an unusual representation of a zodiac wheel. This mosaic has the usual two concentric circles (1.9 m and 3.8 m in diameter). But instead of the usual pie-slice shapes between them, there are smaller circles. Only one of the small circles survives intact, and it encloses a picture of a bull. The image of the bull is not labeled Taurus and there are no surviving circles with other images such as Aries or Gemini, so it is not certain that this is meant to be a zodiac. This image could be just a decorative animal, which is not rare in mosaic art; or perhaps the bull is to be identified as a representation of one of the Israelite tribes. Three Hebrew letters, *rym*, perhaps the last letters of Ephraim, were found in the fragments of a neighboring mosaic circle. If these letters are part of the word Ephraim then this would give support to the idea that the bull is meant to represent one of the twelve tribes of Israel. It is also impor-

---

[20] Ness, 1990, "Susiya," 250–53. Gutman, E., Netzer, S., Yeivin, Z. "Excavations in the Synagogue at Horvat Susiya," *In Ancient Synagogues Revealed*, ed. Lee I. Levine (Jerusalem: Israel Exploration Society; Detroit: Wayne State University Press, 1982) 123–28. Gutman, S., Netzer, E., Yeivin, Z. "Susiya, Khirbet," *The Encyclopedia of Archaeological Excavations in the Holy Land*, 4 Volumes, ed., Michael Avi-Yonah (Englewood Cliffs, NJ: Prentice-Hall, 1975) IV, 1124–28. These last two are by the excavators.

tant to remember that when the twelve tribes of Israel were symbolized by animal figures, these animal figures were sometimes identified with zodiac signs as well.[21]

The final site for consideration in this category is En Gedi, which is located at an oasis near the Dead Sea. The synagogue at this site has a mosaic inscription listing the signs of the zodiac, without any pictorial representation of a zodiac. The inscription is actually a lengthy list which includes the signs of the zodiac. The En Gedi synagogue was discovered in 1966 by local farmers, and excavated during the years 1970–1972 by Barag, Porat, and Netzer for the Israel Antiquities Authority and the Hebrew University.

The synagogue building was rectangular, measuring 12 m. by 15 m. The structure was first built in the third century AD, and it was destroyed by fire approximately AD 530. The mosaic inscription of interest to this study dates to the last phase of occupation. The western aisle of the synagogue contains a group of five inscriptions, two in Hebrew and three in Aramaic. These include a list of antediluvian patriarchs, Adam to Japheth; the twelve signs of the zodiac; the twelve months of the Jewish calendar; blessings upon several different groups of individuals; and an unclear injunction to keep certain secrets from non-Jews.

This inscription is unique. Pictures of the zodiac are common throughout the Roman Empire, and relatively common in Jewish art, but this is the only list of the zodiac signs. This list causes speculation as to any possible significance of putting a list of twelve zodiac signs between a list of thirteen patriarchs and a list of the twelve months. The inscription mentions secrets that are to be hidden from the Gentiles. Scholars can only speculate about what these secrets were, and if they are hidden still from us today. Also yet to be determined is the relationship of these five inscriptions to each other.[22]

---

[21] Ness, 1990, "Yafia," 253–58. E. L. Sukenik, "The Ancient Synagogue at Yafa Near Nazareth, Preliminary Report" *Bulletin of the Louis M. Rabinowitz Fund for the Exploration of Ancient Synagogues* 2 (1951): 6–24.

[22] Ness,1990, "En Gedi," 258–64. Lee I. Levine, "The Inscription in the `En Gedi Synagogue," *In Ancient Synagogues Revealed*, ed. Lee I. Levine (Detroit: Wayne State University Press; Jerusalem: Israel Exploration Society, 1982) 140–45. D. Barag, Y. Porat,

All of the examples of zodiacs mentioned above have been found in Palestine. There are no known examples of synagogue zodiacs from the Jewish Diaspora. However, in one of the Jewish catacombs of Rome, along the Via Nomentina, there is a grave with a painted representation of the sun and the moon, along with two menorahs, an ark for the biblical scrolls, and other Jewish symbols.[23]

Other Examples of Jewish Zodiac Imagery

There are other less likely examples of Jewish uses of zodiac imagery. One such example is the marble carving from Baram which some have conjectured was decorated with images of the zodiac. Other examples include mosaics of the four seasons without a zodiac, which Goodenough thought were shorthand zodiacs. But one interesting recent discovery is a wooden zodiac. While it is certainly a zodiac, it is not certain if it comes from a Jewish context or even that it comes from an ancient setting.

This is a fragment of a wooden disc. Enough survives to determine clearly that there is a representation of a zodiac wheel on one side of the disc which is similar to those found at Beth Alpha and elsewhere. Sol Invictus is clearly visible on the disc, and he has an image of Aries over his head, and images of Scorpio and Virgo under his feet. This is such a typical zodiac scene that the rest of the zodiac wheel can be easily reconstructed from other examples. On the other side of the disc there is a curious eight-sided figure and what appears to be a small incense altar.

There are three problems in connection with the wooden zodiac. First is its uncertain provenance, second is its date of its manufacture, and lastly its uncertainty of being of Jewish origin. The disc was published by

and E. Netzer, "En Gedi," *Encyclopedia of Archaeological Excavations in the Holy Land*, ed., Michael Avi-Yonah (Englewood Cliffs, NJ: Prentice-Hall, 1975) II, 378–80; D. Barag, Y. Porat, and E. Netzer, "The Synagogue at En-Gedi," *Ancient Synagogues Revealed*, ed. Lee I. Levine (Jerusalem: Israel Exploration Society; Detroit: Wayne State University Press, 1982) 116–22.

[23] Ness, 1990, 263. Harry Joseph Leon, *The Jews of Ancient Rome* (Philadelphia: Jewish Publication Society, 1960/5721) 207, 209, and fig. 43; E. R. Goodenough, *Jewish Symbols in the Greco-Roman Period*, 13 Volumes (NY: Pantheon; Princeton, NJ: Princeton University Press, 1953-68) VII.2, 175.

A. Ovadiah and S. Mucznik, who reported that the disc was owned by an anonymous private collector. They did not give details of its provenance, but said it had supposedly been found near Caesarea Maritima along the Mediterranean coast.

It would be quite unusual for a small piece of wood to be so well preserved after 1500 or 2000 years. This raises suspicions that the zodiac is a fake since it is in an excellent state of preservation, yet, fakes are usually created to obtain money and notoriety, but this artifact has not brought much fame or cash. The art work on the disc looks ancient, although that is no guarantee of its antiquity. However, ancient coins have often washed up on the beach of Caesarea Maritima. If the wooden zodiac were a sailor's amulet, as Ovadiah and Mucznik think, it might have been preserved underwater in an ancient wreck. Ancient wooden ships have sometimes avoided extensive decay. So it is not impossible that a bit of ancient wood might have washed up on Caesarea's beach by the same storms that wash up coins. While a carbon 14 test might reveal the age of the disk with certainty, it would also cause some damage to the artifact. However, up to this time the anonymous owner has not offered a sample of the disk for dating.[24]

Conclusion

The Psalmists asks, "Why do the wicked flourish like a green tree?"[25] Roman astrology writers like Manilius or Firmicus Maternus said it was because of astrology or *Fata regunt orbem*: Fate rules the world.[26] Fortune was a very popular goddess, and was sometime shown with a zodiac, symbolizing her ability to control events and people. The zodiac from Khirbet Tannur, now in the Cincinnati Art Museum, is one example.[27]

[24] Ovadiah, Asher and Mucznik, S., "A Fragmentary Roman Zodiac and Horoscope from Caesarea Maritima," *Studium Biblicum Franciscanum* [Jerusalem], *Liber Annuus* 46 (1996): 375–80, ills. [Also available online].

[25] Psalm 32.

[26] M. Manilii Astronomica IV, 14, at http://www.gmu.edu/departments/fld/CLASSICS/manilius4.html.

[27] See Nelson Glueck, *Deities and Dolphins* (New York: 1965) passim, and also Ness, 1990, 153–211 and fig. 44.

The famous astronomer, Claudius Ptolemy, could say that one the chief uses of astrology was to help us be reconciled to the inevitable.[28]

However, not everyone has always agreed. There was a philosophical opposition, beginning with Carneades (third century BC), and perhaps best seen in Sextus Empiricus and the early Christian writer, Hippolytus of Rome.[29] This opposition was not as impressive to most Romans as to modern people. The early Christian writers generally opposed astrology as deterministic, following Carneades and others, and hence immoral. Jewish writers, both Hellenistic and Rabbinic, accepted that the planets had powers, but they rejected the common determinism held by the pagan writers. *YHWH* controlled the planets along with everything else.

In the Bible, in the Book of Genesis, we are told that *YHWH* created the sun and moon to be for signs and seasons, but elsewhere Israelites were also instructed not worship the sun, the moon and all the host of heaven.[30] Isaiah mocks the Mesopotamian diviners who did not realize that *YHWH* was in control.[31] Jeremiah argues with Judean worshippers of the Queen of Heaven.[32] Daniel out-does the astrologers and dream interpreters at Nebuchadnezzar's court because YHWH tells him what is what.[33]

Later writers in the biblical pseudepigrapha, from Hellenistic and Roman times, have the same attitude towards developed Hellenistic astrology. Both Josephus and Philo say that the menorah's seven branches symbolized the seven planets, and that there were twelve loaves of shew

---

[28] Claudius Ptolemy, *Tetrabiblos*, ch. III. is a convenient English translation.

[29] Empiricus, Sextus, *Adversus Astrologos* in *Adversus Mathamaticos* 5, Loeb Classical Library, ed. and trans., R. G. Bury (Cambridge, MA: Harvard University Press, 1949) and Hippolytus, *The Refutation of All Heresies* in Roberts, Alexander and Donaldson, James eds., *The Ante-Nicene Fathers* (Grand Rapids: Eerdmans,1978). There is major anti-astrology polemic in Book IV, Chapters I-XXVII, which is word for word the same as the criticisms of Sextus Empiricus.

[30] Gen. 1:14–19; Deut. 17:2–7.

[31] Isaiah 47:12–15.

[32] Jer. 44:15–20.

[33] Daniel 2:27; 4:7 [4:4 in the Hebrew]; 5:7; 5:11.

bread everyday in the Temple because of the twelve signs.[34] Several magical texts are particularly good examples of this same concept. Both the "Hygromancy of Solomon" (also known as "Letter to Rehoboam" and dating to the same times and region as the New Testament)[35] and the *Sepher Ha-Razim* (the Book of Secrets, fifth-century Rabbinic in origin)[36] invoke the angels and demons of the planets, ordering them in the name of *YHWH* to obey the magician. The planets (like all other things) are operated by divine emissaries or angels, as we are told in many works from I Enoch onwards. Because the Israelites are specially chosen by *YHWH*, they may control the planets (with His help) and not vice versa. (The Babylonian Talmud records a debate over whether or not the planets affected the Israelites, but without reaching a conclusion.)

This is the mental background of the zodiac mosaics. It is clear that zodiac lists and symbols do appear in a number of Jewish settings, including synagogues. This raises the question of how to explain the Jewish use of zodiac symbols in synagogues, given the prohibitions against divination and images in the Hebrew Scriptures. Certainly Christians opposed the use of zodiac symbols based upon their understanding of Biblical references of the Hebrew Scriptures. One might expect the Jewish Rabbis and the Christian early Church Fathers to have similar attitudes toward astrology. Both movements had their origin in the religion of Second Temple period. But attitudes during the Second Temple period were

[34] Flavius Josephus, *Jewish War*, V, 217–18; Philo Judaeus, *Questions and Answers on Exodus*, 75, 112–14.

[35] All Greek texts of the "Hygromantia Salomonis," or "Letter of Rehoboam," have been brought together in the appendices of Pablo Torijano, *Solomon the Esoteric King: From King to Magus, Development of a Tradition*, supplements to the *Journal for the Study of Judaism* 73 (Brill, 2002). An English translation and analysis of one text, in VIII.2, of *Catalogus Codicum Astrologorum Graecorum*, ed. D. Olivieri, et al., 12 volumes in 20 parts (Brussels: Academie Royale, 1898-1953) was published by Dr. Scott Carroll in *The Journal for the Study of the Pseudepigrapha* 4 (1989): 91–103.

[36] *Sepher Ha-Razim. The Book of Mysteries*, tr. by Michael A. Morgan, (Chico, CA: Scholars Press, 1983); *Sepher Ha-Razim: A Newly Recovered Book of Magic from the Talmudic Period, Collected from Genizah Fragments and Other Sources*, [Title and text in Hebrew] edited with introduction and annotation by Mordecai Margalioth (Jerusalem: Yediot Aharonot, 1966). The Hebrew text was translated by Rabbi Morgan.

mixed too, and the Rabbis and the Church Fathers followed different paths. The Church Fathers are almost uniformly oppose to astrology, partly because of the determinism common in Roman period astrology, and partly because using astrological symbols in a religious setting seemed idolatrous to them. The Rabbis, however, were less interested in philosophy, and many were prepared to tolerate the use of astrology, albeit in its undeterministic forms. The Babylonian Talmud[37] records a debate over whether or not there was a star for Israel; in other words, they debated whether or not the planets ruled the Jews the way the astrologers said they ruled everyone else. They were never able to come to an agreement. Other stories in rabbinic literature make it clear that the sages thought that if astrology worked, it did so because it was a part of the Will of God. Likewise, in its non-determinative forms, astrology was tolerated, if not always welcome.

The meaning of the zodiacs in their Jewish synagogue contexts has been much debated. Some earlier scholars dismissed them as meaningless, but this is due more to the complete rejection of astrology in the early twentieth century than their scholarship. Some scholars, like Meir and Bar Ilan, for example, think they were used in Jewish liturgies in connection with poems called *piyyutim*.[38] *Piyyutim* do often mention the zodiac signs. Other scholars such as Michael Avi Yonah thought that they were connected somehow with the Jewish calendar. It is true that the modern version of Jewish astrology does equate the twelve months with the twelve signs, but this cannot be shown definitively to be an ancient concept, likely as that might be. The scholar Goodenough thought they were evidence of a hypothetical Jewish mystery religion in the Greco-Roman Near East. However, he convinced no one but himself that this mystery religion actually existed.[39]

My explanation of the Jewish use of zodiac signs is that they represented the Almighty God, the God of Israel, as cosmocrator, or ruler of the universe. The signs and planets were certainly thought to be an-

[37] Tractate *Shabbat* 156a and 156b.
[38] Personal communication.
[39] Ness, 1990, 265–77.

164

gels, working under the instructions of the Almighty. There is abundant evidence of this in Jewish texts, including magical texts. Likewise, in non-Jewish society, the zodiac was often used to praise a god or a ruler as cosmocrator. It seems likely that Greco-Roman Jews took the zodiac, a familiar work of popular art, and adapted it to their own needs.

The Clever and the Cunning

Finding Eurasian Nomads in Premodern History[1]

Darlene L. Brooks Hedstrom

Introduction

❊THEIR TRIBE AND kinsfolk had harshly abandoned them. A rival khan had murdered their father, Yesugei, and the rest of the tribe abandoned their leader's family. Now with only their recently widowed mother, Högelun, to protect them, the young brothers had to band together to seek food to keep their family alive.[2] As on most days, the brothers left the *ger* to find food. One day Temüjin was out fishing in the Onon River with his brother and half-brothers. Not satisfied with his own catch for the day, Bekhter, a half-brother, stole Temüjin's fish. In

---

[1] The ideas found in this paper were first explored as part of my graduate research on the Nomadic *logoi* for a seminar paper on Herodotus with Dr. Yamauchi in 1997. I later presented a segment of this paper at a panel at the Ohio Academy of History in 1998 and benefited from the comments of Jack Balcer who served as a commentator for the panel. The role of nomads in world history is a topic I have pursued since this time through my teaching of premodern world history and in upper-level seminars. Thanks to my early exposure to the literary constructs of nomad history, I was able to participate in a 2002 NEH institute on Eurasian history. I used the research I conducted on Eurasian nomads during the institute to design three upper-division seminars for Wittenberg University. In particular I focused on the role of nomads in premodern history and how to interpret literary and archaeological evidence. The students in *Herodotus, The Archaeology of Nomadic Empires* and *The Great Mongol Khans* should receive recognition for their willingness to grapple with difficult material and for taking pleasure in exploring new ways of understanding the past with enthusiasm and good humor. It is to those students that I dedicate this paper in honor of my mentor, Dr. Yamauchi, who encouraged me to pursue the often forgotten people of the Steppe. Through his encouragement, I have found numerous ways to pursue my archaeological research while exploring key historical questions that reflect the value of using material culture to better understand the premodern world.

[2] *Secret History of the Mongols*, 74.

response to this violation, Temüjin and his blood brother, Kasar', killed Bekhter with an arrow.[3]

The *Secret History of the Mongols*, the Mongolian account that recounts this story and the life of Temüjin, later known as Chinggis Khan, is a rare document that reflects a nomadic voice amidst the sea of pejorative accounts of nomadic culture and history by sedentary empires.[4] The story of the murder of Bekhter is often used to illustrate Temüjin's early brutality that would be a central characteristic for his later rise as the Great Khan over all the other nomadic tribes. However, this story more significantly reflects the cultural values of nomadic communities and what characteristics of behavior are needed for communities to survive and maintain their autonomy. The importance of loyalty to the strongest member, and fairness in procuring provisions for the community, are the central themes in this story. Temüjin's method of punishment for the violation of the codes of loyalty and mutual support is secondary to the lesson of what is valued in nomadic culture, even when only a mother and her sons define that community. The justness of Temüjin's actions are found in Bekhter's recognition that he has violated the rules, and does not run away or seek to defend himself from the punishment. His only request is that his brother, Belgutei, not be punished.[5]

[3] *Secret History of the Mongols*, 77–78.

[4] The *Secret History of the Mongols* is available to us as a later Ming translation of a Uighur original. A German translation is Erich Haenisch, *Die geheime Geschichte der Mongolen* (Leipzig, 1948). William Hung, "The Transmission of the Book known as The Secret History of the Mongols," *Harvard Journal of Asiatic Studies* (1951): 433–92. Textual analysis is by Igor de Rachewiltz, "The Secret History of the Mongols," *Papers on Far Eastern History* 1 (1971): 115–63; idem, 5 (1972): 149–75; idem, 10 (1974): 55–82; idem, 13 (1976): 41–75; idem, 16 (1977); and idem, 18 (1978): 43–80. A poetic rendering in English of the *Secret History* is Paul Kahn *A Secret History of the Mongols* (Boston: Cheng & Tsui, 1998).

[5] Paul Ratchnevsky observes that the historicity of this murder should not be doubted since it is omitted from the court histories in an attempt to preserve the reputation of Chinggis Khan for his conquered communities. However, too many Mongols were witnesses to Chinggis' past to permit an omission from an exclusively Mongolian account. Ratchnevsky also sees the incident with Bekhter as a direct rejection of Temüjin's authority as elder male in the tribe. Paul Ratchnevsky, *Genghis Khan: His Life and Legacy*, trans. and ed. Thomas Haining (Oxford: Blackwell, 1991) 23.

The sedentary empires that would face Chinggis Khan and his successors could never fully understand that Mongol success in battle and conquest sprouted from these two roots of unquestionable loyalty for one's leader, and equity in the division of all provisions for sustaining the health of the community. This ignorance on behalf of the thirteenth-century empires, such as the Qin and the Khwarizm Shah, is what gave the advantage to nomadic warriors. Without understanding their cultural structure and values, it was then impossible for states to find ways to use diplomacy to halt the Mongol conquest, leading the two empires into battles that played to the strengths of the nomads.

The great sedentary empires of Asia were not alone in their failure to comprehend their enemy. They had simply shared in the collective ignorance of all prior empires that had faced nomadic warriors such as the Scythians, the Xiongnu, the Avars, and the Uighurs. Sedentary empires could not bridge the cultural differences between themselves and the nomadic communities enough to understand what nomads valued and how they might defeat them rather than be conquered or exploited by the barbarians. From the time of Herodotus (fifth century BC) to the time of John de Plano Carpini (thirteenth century AD), the nomadic warrior was the cunning barbarian and he was forever a terrifying mystery to those who lived in a city.

The perplexity that overshadowed the nomads of old is still present in our general understanding of how to incorporate nomads into the wider story of global history. Rereading premodern nomadic history, such as the story from the life of Chinggiss Khan, is now part of the expanding field of global history in which non-traditional empires are being assimilated into the metanarrative of the evolution of the human community. The challenge for the world historian is to cull the appropriate sources from a wide array of specialists across the fields of Eurasian history, and to consider how to incorporate nomads into a story of the past that will have cohesion. [6] In an attempt to do just this, Thomas D. Hall examines

[6] For a survey of the nomad throughout history in Afro-Eurasia see the following. The ancient Near East: V. H. Matthews, *Pastoral Nomadism in the Mari Kingdom* (Missoula: Scholars, 1978); David C. Hopkins, "Pastoralists in Late Bronze Age Palestine: Which Way Did They Go?" *Biblical Archaeologist* 56.4 (1993): 200–211; M. B. Rowton,

the role of nomads in light of the hierarchy of the core/periphery world system.[7] He concludes that the shifting nature of status within nomadic hierarchies makes it almost impossible to ascertain a world system that one could assess as one can with sedentary empires. He writes: "Since, by definition, the wealth of nomads is portable, wholly nomadic core/periphery hierarchies probably would have been very fragile, and marked by a very shallow gradient of hierarchy."[8] As with historians before Hall, the nomads of premodern history are still elusive.

The primary sources that are available for examining any particular period in premodern history are generally limited. This problem is even

"Dimorphic Structure and the Problem of the 'Apiru-'Ibrim," *Journal of Near Eastern Studies* 35 (1976): 13–20; Mattanyah Zohar, "Pastoralism and the Spread of the Semitic Languages," in *Pastoralism in the Levant: Archaeological Materials in Anthropological Perspectives*, ed. by Ofer Bay-Yosef and Anatoly Khazanov (Madison, WI: Prehistory Press, 1992) 165–80. For late antiquity: Patricia Crone, "The Tribe and the State," in *States in History*, ed. by John A. Hall (Oxford: Basil Blackwell, 1986) 48–77; Fred M. Donner, "The Role of Nomads in the Near East in Late Antiquity (400–800 CE)," in *Tradition and Innovation in Late Antiquity*, ed. by F. M. Clover and R. S. Humphreys (Madison, WI: University of Wisconsin Press, 1989) 73–85; Steven A. Rosen, "The Case for Seasonal Movement of Pastoral Nomads in the Late Byzantine/Early Arabic Period in the South Central Negev," in *Pastoralism in the Levant: Archaeological Materials in Anthropological Perspectives*, ed. by Ofer Bay-Yosef and Anatoly Khazanov (Madison, WI: Prehistory Press, 1992) 153–64; idem and Gideon Auni, "The Edge of the Empire: The Archaeology of Pastoral Nomads in the Southern Negev Highlands in Late Antiquity," *Biblical Archaeology* 56.4 (1993): 189–99. For contemporary history: Jorge Silva Castillo, ed., *Nomads and Sedentary Peoples: 30th International Congress of Human Sciences in Asia and North Africa* (México: Colegio de México, 1981); Alan Keohane, *Bedouin: Nomads of the Desert*, translated by Julia Crookenden (London: Kyle Cathie, 1994); A. M. Khazanov, *Nomads and the Outside World* (Cambridge: Cambridge University Press, 1984); Cynthia Nelson, *The Desert and the Sown: Nomads in Wider Society* (Berkeley: Institute of International Studies, University of California, Berkeley, 1973); Emrys L. Peters, *The Bedouin of Cyrenaica: Studies in Personal and Corporate Power*, ed. by Jack Goody and Emanuel Marx (Cambridge: Cambridge University Press, 1990); Adolf Reifenberg, *The Struggle between the Desert and the Sown* (Jerusalem: Department of the Jewish Agency, 1956).

[7] Thomas D. Hall, "The Role of the Nomads in Core/Periphery Relations," in *Core/Periphery Relations in Precapitalist Worlds*, ed. Christopher Chase-Dunn and Thomas D. Hall (Boulder, CO: Westview, 1991) 212–39.

[8] Hall, *Role of the Nomads*, 228.

more acute for the field of nomadic societies; the sources for reconstructing a particularly nomadic worldview are scarce. The bulk of the nomadic evidence comes from the blurred literary accounts of historians from empires threatened by their unruly opponents. The charged nature of these accounts has added to the difficulty of interpreting the evidence of nomads found in the archaeological record; when sites are identified as nomadic they are almost exclusively from remarkable, but problematic, burials. Frequently the tombs were robbed or excavated hastily at a time when methods and theory were of little consequence to archaeologists.[9] Only in the last decades, with the adoption of new archaeological techniques and methods, do we see a more theoretical approach to the excavation and interpretation of nomadic material culture and settlements.

The historian faces, then, many levels of challenges and questions in the pursuit of Eurasian nomadic history. First, the reading of the nomadic portraits in the literary sources poses its own problems. How does the historian read and interpret portraits of an enemy and distill out what is useful? Without documentary sources from the nomadic world, how can one temper the biases found in the accounts of Sima Qian, the historian of the Han, or Ibn Fadlan, the traveler to the Rus'? Are these accounts so unreliable that nothing is to be gained except for what the portraits tell us about the authors who created these histories? In a post-structuralist milieu, such readings are sufficient, and yet, in nomadic studies, greater effort is now directed at rereading these sources in conjunction with the contemporary archaeological research to create a composite history that is far richer and more nuanced than any study of nomadic history in previous decades.

For global historians, studying nomadic history is valuable, and much is possible when considering a selection of these empires with an eye for rereading premodern world history in light of textual and archaeological evidence. For a textual rereading of the literary it is important to consider the archetypal nomad as found in the western Eurasian source of the *History of the Persian Wars* by Herodotus. Based upon the conclu-

---

[9] P. P. Tolochko and S. V. Polin, "Burial Mounds of the Scythian Aristocracy in the Northern Black Seas Area," in *Scythian Gold: Treasures from Ancient Ukraine*, ed. Ellen D. Reeder (New York: Henry Abrams, 1999) 83–91.

sions from this text and how scholars might mine such polemical sources for reflections of nomadic life, it will be necessary to examine a selection of current archaeological research on Eurasian nomadic communities from the Bronze, Iron and Uighur periods. The examples will all provide evidence of the expanding field of nomadic history and the fruitfulness of populating the early maps of premodern history with these communities that had a significant impact upon the empires more traditionally recognized as the forces who shaped the human community.[10]

The Nomadic Typos: Herodotus and the Nomadic Logoi

Herodotus's *History of the Persian Wars* (hereafter *Hist.*) contains several digressions that could be classified as ethnographic and geographic passages; they interrupt the main narration of the history of the Persians and their eventual war with the Greeks in the fifth century BC. Herodotus, however, suggests that these digressions are somehow significant to the central narrative. The secondary histories, in which ethnographic components are imbedded, contain valuable descriptions of societal customs from premodern Afro-Eurasia—including people from Europe, Central Asia, India, Egypt, Arabia and Libya.[11] Frequently these sayings, or *logoi*, deal with nomads; the inclusion of the fascinating and bizarre customs appear to be purely for entertainment purposes.[12] After analyzing the nomadic *logoi* in the *Hist.* it will become evident that Herodotus used the

---

[10] This study is not intended to be all inclusive, but rather, selective in order to demonstrate the ways in which the history of nomadic society has been understood and the ways in which nomads can and should be placed as central characters in premodern history.

[11] Many of the customs or usages recorded by Herodotus have been questioned because of their often bizarre nature (ex. Scythians using hemp, ants carrying gold on their backs, etc.). For a critical assessment of Herodotus' reliability see Detlev Fehling, *Herodotus and His 'Sources'* (Leeds: Francis Cairns, 1989); in defense of Herodotus and a response to Fehling's critique see W. Kendrick Pritchett, *The Liar School of Herodotus* (Amsterdam: J. C. Gieben, 1993).

[12] J. A. K. Thomson argues for three types of *logoi* found in Greek narrative form: history, fiction and unconscious fiction. Idem, *The Art of the Logos* (London: George Allen and Unwin, 1935). For an analysis of the Lybian *logoi* as it relates to the narrative structure of the *Hist.*, see Henry R. Immerwahr, *Form and Thought in Herodotus* (Cleveland: Press of Western Reserve University, 1966) 111–13.

logoi to communicate his assessment of the Persian rise to power and their interaction with nomadic tribes who lived on the frontiers of the ancient Mediterranean world.[13] The nomadic *logoi* are used as a rhetorical device by Herodotus to express the power relations between the Persians and those nomadic people whom they sought to assimilate into their empire. His primary concern was to offer a foreshadowing of Persian defeat at the hands of nomads. Only at a secondary level are the *logoi* used to provide a culture summary.

One of the more debated issues of Herodotean studies is whether Herodotus is a reliable historian, an artistic liar, or an undiscriminating recorder of hearsay.[14] Therefore, it is necessary to consider the value of Herodotus for investigating nomadic history, and how his work might be used to incorporate nomads into a global history. Within the *Hist.*, Herodotus describes several nomadic tribes, including the Scythians,[15] some Persian tribes (1.125; 7.85), the Massagetae (1.216),[16] Ethiopians (2.29)[17] Indians (3.98–99), and Libyans (4.168–199). The Scythians and Libyans are, by far, the two major groups of non-Greeks he identifies as nomadic in the *Hist.* The tribes are all one cultural entity, for each contains the qualities of the archetypal nomadic figure who is defined by five standard characteristics.[18]

---

[13] François Hartog, *The Mirror of Herodotus: The Representation of the Other in the Writing of History*, trans. Janet Lloyd (Berkeley: University of California Press, 1988). Hartog will argue that Herodotus' description of the Scythians is actually a commentary on Greeks themselves.

[14] See J. A. S. Evans, "Father of History or Father of Lies: The Reputation of Herodotus," *Classical Journal* 64 (1986): 11–17.

[15] Herodotus identifies the Scythians as nomadic in eleven passages (1.15; 1.73; 4.2; 4.11; 4.19; 4.55; 4.56; 4.109; 6.40; 6.84; 7.10A). Book Four of the *Hist.* extensively covers the Scythian communities.

[16] The Massagetae are not explicitly identified as nomadic; however, their characteristics match those given by Herodotus for all the other nomadic tribes and they will be regarded in this study as nomadic.

[17] Geographically speaking, *Ethiopian* is used by Herodotus as a regional term "for the entire area south of the Asswan (sic)" Alan B. Lloyd, *Herodotus II*, (Leiden: Brill, 1988) 120. See also Strabo, *Geog.* 17.1.53.

[18] Two of these characteristics are found first with Homer (*Iliad* 13.5–6) and are later

To the Greeks, to be a nomad was to be a wanderer. *Nomas* literally means to roam around for pasture; the term applies in Greek to both animals and humans. This appellation suggests that one characteristic of the archetypal nomad is that they are not associated with the city, the *polis*. However, more important than being a wanderer is the opinion that nomads do not till the soil (4. 191); they are not farmers who have made a commitment to a particular area of land. A third characteristic that nomads generally share is that they "eat meat and drink milk" (4.186).[19] This demonstrates that they are not agriculturalists or tillers, *aroteres*. A fourth characteristic is that nomads prefer impermanent dwellings; because they move from oasis to oasis, or travel through different regions with their flocks, they do not create or desire an established residence.[20] They are not defined by their allegiance to the *polis*, but rather define themselves by their family allegiances and their defense of their consumable goods. A final characteristic of these nomads in the *Hist.* is that they are located on the edges of inhabited areas; Herodotus explains that the nomads frequent geographic areas that are sandy deserts, or large open areas, and that tillers are located near wooded and more mountainous country (4.191).

Although the Indian, Massagetae, Persian, and Ethiopian nomads are only briefly mentioned, their customs and lifestyle reflect the essential Greek perception of how the one who wanders is fundamentally different from the one who is settled—in this case, the farmer.[21] One Indian

expanded by Herodotus.

[19] All English quotations of the *Hist.* are taken from A. D. Godley's translation unless otherwise stated. Idem, *Herodotus. I-IV* (Cambridge: Harvard University Press, 1921–22) 389. Hereafter referenced as *Hist.*

[20] Classical authors identify the Libyans as charioteers (7.184). Pausanius explains the formidable nature of the Libyans as the product of their use of horses (8.43.3). See Camps, *Berbers*, 63–66. Herodotus identifies only the Arabians, Indians, and Persians as camel riders (1.80, 1.133, 3.9, 3.102, 3.105, 7.83, 7.86–87, 7.125.) Bactrian camels, for example, are visually represented on the Black Obelisk of Shalmanezer III. On camels in Arabia see, Ilse Köhler-Rollefson, "Camels and Camel Pastoralism in Arabia," *Biblical Archaeology* 56.4 (1993): 180–88.

[21] The Dai, the Mardi, the Dropici, and the Sagartii are collectively identified as nomads (1.125) in contrast to the other tribes of tillers (*aroteres*).

tribe, the Padaei, eats raw flesh (3.99). This custom separates them from sedentary people whose diet consists of harvested grain, vegetables, and fruits. The fact that the meat is eaten raw suggests that the nomads have no hearth on which to cook their food. The hearth reflects the physical sign of permanent residence within a house or *oikos*. Because nomads wander, their residence is always changing, and their cooking procedures, or lack thereof, will reflect their unstable, and non-*Hellene* lifestyle. The dichotomy of the raw versus the cooked is a key cultural difference between those who are settled and those who move with their flocks.

The Massagetae, located beyond the Araxes River, are a nomadic group that Cyrus wanted to conquer after he had subdued Babylon; they are the first empire, sedentary or nomadic, to be the target of an extensive Persian assault (1.201–215).[22] The Massagetae are sometimes confused with the Scythians, however, Herodotus explains that this is an inaccurate association. What is particularly interesting about the Massagetae is that they are not explicitly identified as nomadic. While Herodotus does not use *nomas* to identify these people, his description of their occupation and customs resonates with the major characteristics of the archetypal nomad. They drink milk, reside in wagons, and never sow the land. They are also warriors of a great nation (1.201). One reason why Herodotus may not have included *nomas* in the description of the Massagetae is that he assumes from the context of his description that the term may be redundant. Based upon the language used by Herodotus to describe nomads, the Massagetae should also be regarded as nomadic and not as an anomalous tribe.

Cyrus was unsuccessful in his battle with the Massagetae and their queen, Tomyris (1.201–216). The Persian conqueror had provided an invitation to Tomyris to become his wife in exchange for the Massagetae land; upon her refusal Cyrus advanced to the Araxes River to attack.

---

[22] Cyrus' campaign against the Massagetae was motivated by pure imperialism, and in the end Cyrus would die at the hands of the Massagetaen army. J. A. S. Evans writes, "Cyrus, who founded Persian imperialism, was in the end driven by it to his death, and the treatment that the queen of Massagetae accorded his corpse is a wry comment on his life. But there is no great sense of tragedy." Idem, *Herodotus, Explorer of the Past* (Princeton: Princeton University Press, 1991) 71. Strabo 11.6.2, 11.8.2, 11.8.6–8, 15.1.6.

Croesus the Lydian had warned that a victory over the Massagetae was not worth the risk of losing everything. He says: "[I]f you lose the battle you lose your empire also, for it is plain that if the Massagetae win they will not retreat back but will march against your provinces" (1.207).[23] Herodotus describes the battle between Cyrus and Tomyris as one of the fiercest fought between barbarians in history (1.214). Cyrus was killed, the Persian army suffered a debacle at the hands of the Massagetaen army, and the region remained unconquered by the Persians.

Unlike the Massagetae, the Sagartians are identified explicitly as nomads. They speak Persian and "dress in a manner half Persian, half Pactyan" (7.85).[24] Herodotus recognizes these nomads as bicultural, suggesting that the Sagartians may represent a different kind of nomadism. The Sagartians are one example of nomads who lived in the semi-peripheral zones of Persia and were more integrated with customs of settled communities than those who were located on the remote frontiers, like the Massagetae (1.215). The semi-peripheral nomads reoccur elsewhere where Herodotus describes nomads who have two cultural influences. They may speak Scythian, but dress Greek, or they are Libyan nomads, but follow Egyptian customs.[25]

---

[23] Godley, *Herodotus II*, 261.

[24] Pactye is a town in Thrace.

[25] In anthropological terms there has been a dual nature to some sedentary areas during the second millennium BC in which both nomadic and settled people bring their own customs to a city. This "diomorphic society," as Michael B. Rowton coined it, is a society that characterizes a part of the progress of a settled area into an urban city. This classification was popular during the 1970s and 1980s, and was adopted by Syro-Palestinian archaeologists to describe nomadic pastoralism and its effects on the settled areas. However, in the 1990s the importance of nomadism has been used to explain the rise of the city-states in Palestine in opposition to theory of the conquest of Israel after the Exodus. These archaeologists have used Rotwon's theory of relationships, but have adopted a more world-historical terminology to express their ideas. See Israel Finkelstein and Nadav Na'amn eds., *From Nomadism to Monarchy: Archaeological and Historical Aspects of Early Israel* (Jerusalem: Israel Exploration Society, 1994); William G. Dever, "Ceramics, Ethnicity, and the Question of Israel's Origins," *Biblical Archaeologist* 58.4 (1995): 200–213; Michael B. Rowton, "Autonomy and Nomadism in Western Asia," *Orientalia* 42 (1973): 247–58; idem, "Urban Autonomy in a Nomadic Environment," *Journal of Near Eastern Studies* 32 (1973): 201–15; idem, "Enclosed Nomadism," *Journal*

These communities serve to outline the geography of the Herodotean world and allow us to see the inhabitants of the world from Persia to Greece. In many ways, Herodotus provides a very global perspective to his world by incorporating several tribes and peoples who are non-Greek. With his brief descriptions of nomadic tribes in Eurasia, Herodotus populates the spheres in which the Persians would travel on their path to conquest. However, he devotes more time to his discussion of the Libyans and, more significantly, to the Scythians. In both cases, the nomadic tribes played a crucial role in the development of world history as Herodotus defined it for his fifth-century audience.

The Libyan *logoi* in 4.168–199 are an example of Herodotus's application of rhetorical language to describe a region that is only marginally under the control of the Persians.[26] The Libyan *logoi* abruptly interrupt Herodotus's account of the queen mother of Cyrene,[27] Pheretime,

of Economic and Social History of the Orient 17 (1974): 1–30; Juris Zarins, "Pastoral Nomadism and Settlement in Lower Mesopotamia," *Bulletin of the American Schools of Oriental Research* 280 (1990): 31–66.

This anthropological model has not been adopted into Classical studies; rather, historians are employing world-system constructs such as core/periphery to express symbiotic relationships. For example, J. Harmatta asserts that Herodotus conceptualized the *oikoumene* as a complex relationship between the hegemonic cores and the frontiers: "According to his (Herodotus') conception of cultural history the most developed high cultures occupy the central territories of the *oikomene*, the sedentary cultures of tillers take the zone around them while the next zone outwards is inhabited by populations of stock-breeders: in the northern hemisphere we find the equestrian nomads, and in the outermost zone, the periphery of the *oikoumene*, occur the food-gathering tribes" (Idem, "Herodotus, Historian," 117).

[26] Herodotus's treatment of Libya, with the exception of the *Libukoi logoi*, aligns well with the general perceptions that were familiar to most Greeks. First, that Libya was located next to Egypt. Second, that Libya was one of the continents of the known world. Third, that Libya was the home to the famous oracle of Ammon, the Greek colony of Cyrene, and a land in which several mythical heroes had had adventures (Heracles, Jason, Perseus).

[27] Archaeological excavations of Cyrene have supported the foundation accounts in Herodotus and place the Greeks at Cyrene in the late seventh century BC (ca. 631). For a survey of the archaeology of Cyrenaica see J. Boardman, "Evidence for the Dating of Greek Settlements in Cyrenaica," *Annual of the British School in Athens* 61 (1966): 149–56; idem, "Bronze Age Greece and Libya," *Annual of the British School in Athens*

as she requests, and is granted an army from the Persian satrap of Egypt, Aryandes, to attack the rebels in Barce who had killed her son, Arcesilaus (4.165–67).[28] Herodotus provides descriptions of the Libyans's dwelling areas, dress, diet, sexual practices, hairstyles, medical treatments, religious beliefs and practices, animals, and occupations. However, found within these passages are references which have caused some historians to doubt the veracity of Herodotus's information.[29]

63 (1968): 41–44; D. Buttle, "The Architecture and Planning of the City of Cyrene," in *Cyrenaican Expedition of the University of Manchester 1952*, ed. by A. Rowe (Manchester: Manchester University, 1956) 27–47; Karen Chance and Marcia Bloom, "Seven Recently Discovered Sculptures from Cyrene, Eastern Libya," *Expedition* 18 (1976): 14–32; Brayek A. Ejteily, "Cyrenaica 1972–1980: Work done by the Department of Antiquities at Shahat (Cyrene)," *American Journal of Archaeology* 87.2 (1983): 207–8; R. Goodchild, J. Pedley, and D. White, "Recent Discoveries of Archaic Sculpture at Cyrene. A Preliminary Report," LA 3–4 (1966–67): 179–88; Susan Kane, "The Sanctuary of Demeter and Persephone in Cyrene, Libya," *Archaeology* 32.2 (1979): 57–59; D. White, "An Archaeological Survey of the Cyrenaican and Marmarican Regions of Northeast Africa," in *Africa and Africans in Antiquity*, ed. E. Yamauchi (E. Lansing, MI: Michigan State University Press, 2001); idem, "Cyrene's Sanctuary of Demeter and Persephone: A Summary of a Decade of Excavation," *American Journal of Archaeology* 85.1 (1981): 13–30; idem, *The Extramural Sanctuary of Demeter and Persephone at Cyrene, Libya* (Philadelphia: University Museum, 1984); Edwin Yamauchi, "The Archaeology of Biblical Africa: Cyrene in Libya," *Archaeology in the Biblical World* 2.1 (1992): 6–18. For a structural analysis of the foundation myths of Cyrene see Claude Calame, "Narrating the Foundation of a City: The Symbolic Birth of Cyrene," in *Approaches to Greek Myth*, ed. by Lowell Edmunds (London: John Hopkins University Press, 1990) 277–341; idem, *Mythe et Histoire dans l'Antiquité Grecque* (Lausanne: Payot, 1996); idem, ed., "Mythe, Récit E'pique et Histoire: Le Récit Hérodotéen de la Foundation de Cyréne," chapter in *Métamorphoses du Mythe Grece Antique* (Genève: Labor et Fides, 1988) 105–26.

[28] Immerwahr, *Form and Thought*, 112–13. For additional information on Pheretime, see Deborah Gera, *Warrior Women: The Anonymous Tractatus de Mulieribus* (Leiden; New York: Brill, 1997). This short Greek tractate recounts the life accomplishments of 14 warrior women from the fifth and fourth centuries. The text is dated by Gera to the end of the second or early first century BC.

[29] For example: the Trans-Saharan route from Thebes to the Pillars of Heracles (4.181), oxen with horns that would get caught in the soil (4.183), and women of Cyrauis who collect gold dust from rivers with feathers (4.195). For a defense of the reliability of the caravan route see Rhys Carpenter, "A Trans-Saharan Caravan Route in Herodotus," *American Journal of Archaeology* 60 (1956): 231–42.

The Libyan *logoi* contain a catalogue of inhabitants on the semi-periphery and periphery zones of the Sahara desert region of North Africa (2.34). Several of these tribes, *ethnoi*, reside in the desert, or in the "uninhabited area," and all of these tribes are identified as being nomadic.[30] Herodotus uses the term nomad in twelve passages for the Libyans. He is very specific as to which groups are nomadic; he identifies explicitly where they are located and what characteristics constitute the nomadic lifestyle. The Libyans who live on the seacoast form the first group of nomads (4.181), with the exception of the region of Cyrene (4.199). Twelve tribes comprise the eastern, coastal region (4.168–181).[31] The second group of nomads is located more inland along the Trans-Sahara caravan route (4.181–186), which connected several oases; the most important of these oases was the Siwa Oasis where the Egyptian oracle of Ammon

---

[30] See E. F. Gautier, *Sahara: The Great Desert* (New York: Columbia University Press, 1935).

[31] They are the Adrymachidae (4.168), Pliny the Elder 5.39; Ptolemy 4.5.12; Gsell, *Hérodote*, 120–21. The Giligamae (4.169), Strabo 17.3.23. W. W. How & J. Wells believe the Marmaridae are descendants of the Giligamae. Idem, *A Commentary on Herodotus in Two Volumes* (Oxford: Oxford University Press, 1912), 356; Gsell, *Hérodote*, 121–23. The Asbystae (4.170) Herodotus 4.170; Pliny 5.34; Ptolemy 4.4.6. Gsell, *Hérodote*, 123. The Auschisae (4.171) Diodorus 3.49; Ptolemy 4.5.12. Gsell, *Hérodote*, 124. The Nasamones (4.172), Strabo 17.3.23; Diodorus 3.49; Pliny 5.33, 7.14. Gsell, *Hérodote*, 124–26. The Psylli (4.173), Pliny the Elder 7.14; Strabo 2.5.33, 13.1.14, 17.1.44, 17.3.23; Ptolemy 4.4.6. Gsell, *Hérodote*, 126–28. The Garamantes (4.174) Pliny 6.45; Strabo 2.5.33, 17.3.19, 17.3.23; Ptolemy 4.4.6. Gsell, *Hérodote*, 128. The Macae (4.175), Pliny the Elder 5.34; Ptolemy 4.3.6. Gsell, *Hérodote*, 129. The Gindanes (4.176), Strabo 3.4.3, 17.3.17. Gsell, *Hérodote*, 130–31. The Lotophagoi (4.177), Strabo 17.3.8. How and Wells associates these "Lotus-eaters" with the Giridanes who are "mentioned by no other ancient geographer except Stephen of Byzantium, following Herodotus." (Idem, *Commentary*, 359). Gsell, *Hérodote*, 130–31. The Machlyes (4.178), Pliny 6.15. Gsell, *Hérodote*, 132. The Auseans (4.180), Gsell, *Hérodote*, 132–33.

was located.[32] Four nomadic tribes are located in the interior of Libya along this route.[33]

Unlike the Scythians, the Libyans and Indians were nomads who occupied two frontiers whose land was not central for the Persians in their establishment of a hegemonic state. Herodotus lists Libya and India as two regions that are part of Darius's satrapies (Libya is in the sixth province and India is in the twentieth province [3.89–94]); though considerable tribute was sent, Herodotus maintains that these regions, like those of Massagetae and Scythia, were not completely under Persian control.[34] In discussing the Indian nomads, Herodotus makes it clear that the Indians in the south "were no subjects of King Darius" (3.101).[35] The Libyan nomads are also presented as being resistant to Persian authority; Herodotus suggests that the military expedition led by Amasis and Badres to revenge the slaying of Arcesilaus was a pretext. The real reason for the invasion into North Africa was to establish a firmer control on the Libyan tribes "[f]or the Libyan tribes are many and divers kinds, and though a few of them were the king's subjects the greater part cared nothing for Darius" (4.167).[36] Herodotus claims that none of the Persian kings, from Darius to Artaxerxes, were successful in assimilating the Libyan tribes into their empire: "[T]he Libyans whom we can name, and of their kings the most part cared nothing for the king of the Medes

---

[32] See Carpenter, *Beyond the Pillars*, 113–33; idem, "Trans-Saharan Caravan," 233–35. The Siwa Oasis appears to have held both religious and commercial importance in antiquity. This combination of the spiritual and commercial is similar to the history of the city of Mecca during the pre-Islamic and early Islamic periods. Mecca can be a useful example for comparative history with the Siwa Oasis in their combined importance for religious ritual and the exchange of goods along caravan routes.

[33] The tribes along the route include the Ammonians, the Garamantes, the Atarantes and the Atlantes. The Garamantes occur in both lists which suggests that they were an important tribe in Libya since they had control of one of the oasis stations. Charles Daniels, *The Garamantes of Southern Libya* ([Stoughton, WI]: Oleander Press, [1970]); T. Monod, "Le mythe de l'émeraude des Garamantes," *Antiquites Africaines* 8 (1974): 51–66.

[34] Yamauchi, *Persia and the Bible* (Grand Rapids: Baker, 1990) 154, 162.

[35] Godley, *Herodotus II*, 129.

[36] Ibid., 373.

at the time of which I write, nor do they care for him now" (4.196).[37] Not only were the Persians under Amasis and Badres unsuccessful in asserting their authority over the Libyans, the nomads attacked the Persians as they made their march back to Egypt, killing the stragglers for their clothes and possessions (4.203). The brutality of the Libyan nomads in killing the Persians reflects the belief that nomads engage in attacks that exploit the weaknesses of their opponents.

In contrast to these vignettes of nomadic culture, we have the lengthy description of the Scythian culture and how their history relates to the Persian empire. The Scythian *logoi* are excellent passages for comparison with the other nomadic *logoi* because the Scythians played a prominent role in the Persian struggle for hegemonic control of the Middle East.[38] Edwin Yamauchi described the Scythians in *Foes from the Northern Frontier* as "among the most skilled horsemen ever known."[39] And certainly despite their non-Greek customs, Herodotus equally lauds them as the most cunning warriors:

> I praise not the Scythians in all respects, but in this greatest matter they have so devised that none who attacks them can escape, and none can catch them if they desire not to be found. For when men have no stablished (sic) cities or fortresses, but all are house-bearers and mounted archers, living not by tilling the soil but

[37] Ibid., 399. The Egyptians, led by Inarus, a Libyan, and Amyrtaeus of Sais, rebelled against Artaxerxes from ca. 461–451 (Thuc. 1.104; Diod. 15.29; Xen. 3.1.7). The Greeks who provided naval support aided the Egyptians. See Hdt. 3.12, 3.15.

[38] J. Harmatta classifies the role of the Scythians in the *Hist.* as twofold: first, as "masters of "Upper Asia' for 28 years (1.130; 4.1–3) and second, as "adversaries of the Persians and victors over Darius" (4.1–142). See further idem, "Herodotus. Historian of the Cimmerians and the Scythians," in *Hérodote et les Peuples non Grecs*, ed. by Walter Burkert, et al, (Vandoeuvres: Fondation Hardt, 1990) 121–22. For further bibliography on the Scythians see Hartog, *Mirror of Herodotus;* Edwin Yamauchi, *Foes from the Northern Frontier* (Grand Rapids: Baker, 1982); idem, "The Scythians: Invading Hordes from the Russian Steppes," *Biblical Archaeologist* 46 (1983): 90–99.

[39] Edwin Yamauchi, *Foes from the Northern Frontier* (Eugene, Oregon: Wipf and Stock, 2003) 67.

by cattle-rearing and carrying their dwellings on wagons, how should these not be invincible and unapproachable? (4.46)[40]

Herodotus continues to maintain the rhetorical language used to identify the nomads even in the context of praising their ability to escape Persian assimilation; later Graeco-Roman rhetoricians would not retain this neutral, if not positive, estimate of nomadic life. Herodotus is not concerned to focus on their non-*Hellene* nature; instead he elevates Scythian nomadism, for their culture makes them a difficult opponent for the Persians.

We learn from Herodotus that the Scythians are the nomads who pushed the Cimmerians from their homeland.[41] The Scythians were then hired by Cyaxares to instruct the young Median boys in the art of archery, a skill that was used for hunting game.[42] These same nomads would later overrun the country and seize power from Cyaxares for twenty-eight years (1.73, 4.12). After capturing Babylon, Darius marched against the Scythians in order to punish them for their rule over Media that had been unchallenged by the Medes (4.1).[43]

Herodotus describes the Scythians as people who do not till the soil (4.2).[44] Their diet, as with the Indian nomads, reflects their activity of wandering; they drink mare's milk (4.2), which can be used to

[40] Godley, *Herodotus II*, 247.

[41] According to Herodotus the nomadic Scythians live in Asia (4.11), the Hypacuris River flows through part of their territory (4.55) and the Gerrhus river divides the nomadic Scythians from the Royal Scythians (4.56). It is still not clear based upon archaeological evidence whether the Cimmerians were nomadic. See A. M. Leskov, "Die skythischen Kurgane," *Antike Welt* 5 (1974): 54–55 and Yamauchi, *Northern Frontier*, 51.

[42] For a review of Scythian archery in Greek art see M. F. Vos, *Scythian Archers in Archaic Attic Vase Painting* (Groningen: Wolters, 1963).

[43] Jack Balcer, "The Date of Herodotus IV.1: Darius' Scythian Expedition," *Harvard Studies in Classical Philology* 76 (1972): 99–132. Thomas Nowak, "Darius' Invasion into Scythia: Geographical and Logistic Perspectives," M.A. Thesis, Miami University, 1988.

[44] Later when Xerxes and Artabanus, Xerxes' uncle, reflect upon the launching of the Persian attack against the Greeks, Xerxes tells Artabanus that the troops will not be in need of food since they will have an ample supply of grain because "our enemies, remember, are not nomad tribes (*like the Scythians*)—they are agricultural peoples (*the Greeks*)" (7.50). Italics are my addition.

make cheese and other products. However, not all Scythians are nomads. Herodotus identifies some as tillers who sow corn (4.17), and others as farmers (4.18), *georgoi*. The nomadic Scythians are distinguished from these other tribes because they neither sow nor plough (4.19).

The Scythians frequently live in lands where there are no trees (4.19). The nomads are herders who lead their flocks through pasture and desert areas. As with his other references to nomads, Herodotus again provides another dichotomy for the pattern of the nomad in comparison to the tiller and city-dweller. As seen in previous *logoi*, nomads are particularly different from other people because they elect to not reside in or identify with a city (7.10A). However, the fact that nomads are void of a common regional identification or allegiance does not mean that they are easily conquered, as Darius's unsuccessful attempts against Scythia demonstrate.[45]

Nomads in the Histories: Ethnography or Literary Construct

As seen in the *logoi* above, the Herodotean nomad is a figure who is characterized by a list of binary opposites.[46] Nomads are wanderers who usually travel through pastures or desert areas; they transport their dwellings on top of wagons, and are not tied to a specific location–they are willfully non-urban. These pastoralists raise cattle and move with their herds; they are free to roam, unlike farmers who are tied to the land that they harvest. Nomads are skilled warriors who use a variety of weapons, including the lasso and the bow. Even their diet distinguishes them from others; they

---

[45] When Artabanus tries to dissuade Xerxes from bridging the Hellespont and engaging the Greeks in battle, he argues that there was only disaster when his father bridged the Ister and crossed over into Scythia. He warns Xerxes that the battle with the Greeks may bring even higher casualties than when his father fought with the Scythians. Artabanus continues to allude to the military and technological superiority of the Greeks in contrast to the nomads and suggests that Xerxes should reconsider his advance into Greece.

[46] The use of opposites to explain the structure of the world was a common feature of early Greek thought; even the human body was viewed as a substance that needed balance in order to be healthy. See G. E. R. Lloyd, *Polarity and Analogy: Two Types of Argumentation in Early Greek Thought* (Cambridge: Cambridge University Press, 1966).

drink milk from either mares or cows, eat hunted game or herded cattle, and gather berries along their path.

The nomadic Libyans, Scythians, Massagetae, Indians, and tribes of Europe and Persia all share these basic characteristics. Herodotus is, therefore, consistent in his description of those who are nomadic both in his extensive treatment of two nomadic areas, Libya and Scythia, and in his abbreviated references to less central tribes in Persia, India, and Europe.

After considering the typical Greek perception of the nomad in the fifth century as Herodotus first represents it, the question arises whether his portraits are a realistic characterization of nomadism, i.e., true ethnography. Or is Herodotus using the nomadic figure to express relationships of power between the Persians and their enemies as they struggle to establish and to maintain a hegemonic state?[47] The evidence leads this author to contend that the structure of the rhetorical language reflects a conscious decision by Herodotus to primarily use the nomad *logoi* as an expression of the actual lack of power that the Persians had. Only on a secondary level does the *logoi* provide a geographic or ethnographic guide to Eurasian nomadism.

In examining the Libyans in relationship to their neighbors, both sedentary and pastoral, Herodotus reveals his conscious choice to represent the Libyans as nomads who have only tenuously agreed to comply with Persian authority (3.91). Both the elusive Scythians and the Libyans are portrayed as being groups that needed to be conquered by Persia.

---

[47] Herodotus was not the first historian or geographer to refer to nomads living in these areas, although only fragments remain. Hecataeus of Miletus (b. ca. 549), who wrote a geographical work, and is the only source referred to by name in the *Hist.*, and Hellanicus of Mytilene (d. ca. 411), who wrote a history of the major kingdoms of the known world, are two of the contemporary sources. For Hecataeus see FGrHist 1 F 334–35 and for Hellanicus see FGrHist 4 F 67. Some commentators believe Herodotus borrowed extensively from Scylax of Caria (ca. 550), a geographer and mathematician. Herodotus only refers to Scylax as an explorer (4.44). See Lionel Pearson, *Early Ionian Historians* (Oxford: Clarendon, 1939) 90–96. Pearson explains that Herodotus was dependent upon Hecataeus for geographical data about Libya. While Hecataeus certainly referred to the Libyan tribes as nomadic, he did not employ the rhetorical language of a typos as is seen in Herodotus.

They are not critical for the empire's success, in Herodotus's agrarian-based opinion, since their regions contained no valued resources, such as grain (7.50).

Herodotus's presentation of nomads was fashioned from various sources: "personal observation, the evidence of other observers, inference, and the application, *a priori*, of an 'ideal' model of space."[48] Similar in his use of *nomas*, Herodotus maintains the spatial dimensions of the known world from the Greek perspective; however, he does not adopt the belief that the environment ultimately predetermines one's manner of life, as is represented in *On Airs, Waters and Places* from the Hippocratic Corpus.[49] An entrenched symmetry of space that keeps all the geographical elements in balance is demonstrated by the physical description of Scythia and Libya as squares. Scythia is a "four-sided country, whereof two sides are sea-bound, the frontiers running inland and those that are the sea make it a perfect square" (4.109, cf. 4.99).[50] The region of Libya is not a quadrilateral area like Scythia, but it is occupied by four groups of people whose presence provides symmetry; "two are aboriginal and two are not; the Libyans in the north and the Ethiopians in the south of Libya are aboriginal, the Phoenicians and Greeks are later settlers" (4.197).[51] As if bothered by a lack of balance even in areas where nomads are located, Herodotus creates an artificial equilibrium by weaving tillers and farmers into the remote steppe lands to balance the nomadic inhabitants.

Are Nomads Barbarians?

Those who are not Greek are identified generally by the term *barbaroi*. This term is imbued with a range of meanings in our modern period,

[48] John Gould, *Herodotus* (New York: St. Martin's Press, 1989) 92.

[49] W. H. S. Jones, *Hippocrates*, 4 vols. Loeb Classical Library (Cambridge: Harvard University Press, 1923) 65–138. Unfortunately the manuscript is missing the section relating the customs of the Libyans and Egyptians (12 & 13).

[50] Godley, *Herodotus II*, 303. Herodotus even remarks that Scythia's physical dimensions are similar to those of Attica (4.99).

[51] Ibid., 399 and 401. Fehling asserts that Herodotus' decision to represent Libya as a square allowed him the freedom to use the Trans-Saharan Caravan as the southern edge of the square. Idem, *Herodotus*, 228.

and even already with the Athenian tragedians, the term was altered to become a standard pejorative appellation.[52] Edith Hall explains that the preoccupation with the inclusion of barbarians by the tragedians was "an exercise in self-definition."[53] Like the polarization between the nomad and the tiller represented by Herodotus, the Athenian tragedians accentuated the binary of the barbarian and Hellene. Hall writes:

> [T]he polarization . . . was invented in specific historical circumstances during the early years of the fifth century B.C., partly as a result of the combined Greek military efforts against the Persians. The notions of Panhellenism and its corollary, all non-Greeks as a collective genus, were more particularly elements of the Athenian ideology . . . and subsequently the Athenian empire. The image of an enemy extraneous to Hellas helped to foster a sense of community between the allied states.[54]

Originally, *barbaros* was used adjectivally to refer to incomprehensible speech, a language which was not Greek (e.g. 1.57, 1.58, 2.57).[55] In what ways did Herodotus then view the nomads since they certainly spoke languages other than Greek?

Herodotus uses *barbaros* (s.)/*barbaroi* (pl.) in two distinct ways. First, in Books 1–4 of the *Hist.*, Herodotus applies a generic meaning to barbarian as someone who is a foreigner, or non-Greek.[56] Herodotus explains that even the Egyptians use *barbaros* to describe those who are non-Egyptian speakers; here again, Herodotus is consistent in his identifications of ethnicity as pre-determined by language usage (2.158).[57]

---

[52] See Edith Hall, *Inventing the Barbarian: Greek Self-Definition Through Tragedy* (Oxford: Clarendon, 1989); H. H. Bacon, *Barbarians in Greek Tragedy* (New Haven: Yale University Press, 1961); B. Cunliffe, *Greeks, Romans and Barbarians: Spheres of Interaction* (New York: Methuen, 1988); T. Long, *Barbarians in Greek Comedy* (Carbondale: Southern Illinois University Press, 1986); D. J. Mosely, "Greeks, Barbarians, Language and Contact," *Ancient Society* 2 (1971): 1–6.

[53] Hall, *Inventing the Barbarian*, 1.

[54] Ibid., 1–2.

[55] See Joel Wilcox, "Barbarian *Psyche* in Heraclitus," *The Monist* 74.4 (1991): 624–37.

[56] See 1.4, 1.6, 1.10, 1.14, 1.58, 1.60, 1.173, 1.214.

[57] Herodotus also identifies Greek places or people by whether the name is of Greek

Frequently, *barbaros* is used in contrast to *hellene* to convey the collective idea of the entire known world.[58]

Second, the opening passage to the *Hist.* announces the subject matter to be "deeds done by Greeks and foreigners" (1.1), and "why they warred against each other."[59] Within this military context, Herodotus implies *barbaroi* to mean the Persians, and not just non-Greeks in general. This exclusive identification of *barbaroi* with the Persians is explicit with the beginning of Book 5 and continues until the end of his discussion of the Persian Wars in Book 9. Books 1–4, however, contain only the history of the growth of the Persian empire under Cyrus, Cambyses, and Darius; within this Persian context *barbaroi* refers not to the Persians themselves, but to other non-Greeks with whom they come into contact or about whom Greeks have talked (e.g. "Persians claim Asia for their own, and the foreign nations that dwell in it" [1.4]).[60]

Herodotus's conscious modification of the word *barbaros* to aid his narrative demonstrates his diligence to craft a work of literature that is more complex than it may appear at first. If *barbaros* is part of a dichotomy between Greek and non-Greek, why does Herodotus not classify the nomad as a barbarian more explicitly? Are his readers to assume that the term *barbaroi* should apply to nomads since they are collectively non Greek speakers? Is Herodotus describing the nomads as the "ultimate barbaric human type,"[61] as people who "become progressively less sophisticated the closer they live to the western *eschatiai* of the inhabited world,"[62] and increasingly more savage?[63] Becoming less sophisticated, as

origin, such as the Eridanus River, which Herodotus says is a mythical river invented by a Greek poet and not a foreign river as he was told by others (3.115).

[58] "Darius conquered Samos, the greatest of all city states, Greek or barbarian (foreign)" (3.139). "I have now related this other tale, which is told alike by Greeks and foreigners" (4.12). Godley, *Herodotus II*, 173 and 213.

[59] Ibid., 3.

[60] Ibid., 7.

[61] Brent D. Shaw, "'Eaters of Flesh, Drinkers of Milk': The Ancient Mediterranean Ideology of the Pastoral Nomad," *Ancient Society* 13/14 (1982–83): 6.

[62] Lloyd, "On Egyptians and Libyans," 236.

[63] Klaus Karttonen, "Expedition to the End of the World," *Studia* Orientalia 64 (1988):

Lloyd puts it, conversely leads to one becoming more savage or barbaric. This interpretation may resonate well with the Athenian tragedians, but to attribute these same associations to Herodotus is to confound his portrait of the nomad with a negative characterization that is not found in the text. Instead of classifying nomads as savage or as varying degrees of uncivilized, Herodotus is the appreciative observer who applauds the nomads who have become an obstacle to the Persians.[64]

For Herodotus the nomads, therefore, are not the savage barbarians referred to in the *Hist.*; rather, the nomads are the *cunning* barbarians who elude the hegemonic power of the Persians. The nomad is smarter than the ordinary barbarian. Herodotus juxtaposes these warrior tribes with the Persians, the barbarians *par excellence,* and concludes that the nomadic warriors are the superior of the two. By casting such a judgment, Herodotus uses the resilient nomads to prepare his audience for the climactic defeat of the Persians by the Greeks. In an author's aside, he explains that Greeks have been distinguished from barbarians because they are clever and free from silly foolishness (1.60, 4.46).[65] But, the nomads are just as clever and free from silliness as the Greeks. For example, Herodotus praises the Scythians for their cleverness and assiduity for "none can catch them if they desire not to be found."[66] If the Scythian, Massagetae, Indian, and Libyan nomads are too difficult to be overcome, are they not somehow more cunning and astute than the Persians, the archetypal barbarian?

Due to our own predisposed notions of savagery and barbarianism, Herodotus's descriptions of the nomadism have often been read as a discursive report that has no harmony, with the implication that

177; Michéle Rosellini and S, Said, "Usages de Femmes et autres Nomoi chez les 'Sauvages' d'Hérodote: Essai de Lecture Structurale," *Annali della Scuola Normale Superiore di Pisa: Classe di Lettere e Filosofia* 8 (1978): 959–61.

[64] Similar assessments of "others" have been made by Tacitus of the noble Germans, in *Germania*, and by al-Jahiz of the Turks, in his letters entitled "Exploits of the Turks and the Army of the Caliphate in General."

[65] Not surprisingly, the Athenians are identified as the most clever of the Hellenes (1.60).

[66] Godley, *Herodotus II*, 247.

Herodotus does not deserve the title "Father of History." However, if the nomadic *logoi* are read within the context of a commentary on the power struggle between the Persians and other nations of Afro-Eurasia, Herodotus upholds the nomadic people, as typified by the groups such as the Massagetae, the Scythians, and Libyans, as those who prepared the Persians for their most crucial encounter with the Greeks. The latter, as agriculturalists, will eventually defend their land, their grain, and their cities because they are settled people.

For Herodotus, the Persian Wars involved numerous tribes, and was a truly global war as he defined the world. Herodotus is able to demonstrate that the premodern world was indeed populated by numerous nomadic and sedentary communities that interacted with each other on a regular basis. While he does not detail the mundane contact, his work evinces the importance of conquering or resisting incorporation of one group into the other. By indicating the cultural values of these communities, their practices, and their military techniques, Herodotus provides a foundation for reconsidering the role that nomads play in premodern history. Rather than simply providing a list of non-civilized characteristics for his audience, Herodotus inadvertently provides a complex view of nomadic and sedentary interactions, and demonstrates that even in a time when there were numerous nomadic tribes, defining nomadism was not easy.

The Uncivilized Nomads in Strabo's Geography

Not all historians or geographers shared Herodotus's tolerant view of nomads. Writing nearly four hundred years after Herodotus, Strabo's description of nomads in *Geography* illustrates the belief that those who were not associated with urban life and politics were inferior beings. [67] There is no trace of Herodotus's earlier praises for the cunning of nomadic warriors who escaped Persian authority; for Strabo the nomads and their lifestyle prohibit individuals from experiencing the blessings of the gods.

[67] All quotations are from H. J. Jones, *The Geography of Strabo*. 8 vols. Loeb Classical Library (Cambridge: Harvard University Press, 1917–35).

From a position of self-appointed accuracy in reporting, Strabo responds to the writing of earlier historians and geographers; he frequently argues against opinions which he deems unfounded. Books 1 and 2 are an extensive introduction to the *Geography*; this prologue allows Strabo sufficient time to defend his contention that Homer is a reliable geographer. Within this comprehensive argument is a smaller debate that relates specifically to nomads and whether Homer was aware of the Scythian nomads. Strabo argues that Homer knew of the Scythians (Il 13.5–6) because he gave them three specific tribal names: the Hippemolgoi, the mare milkers; the Galactophagi, the curd or milk eaters; and the Abii, the resourceless people (1.1.6, 7.3.2–3, 7.3.6–7, 7.3.9, 12.3.26).[68] Elsewhere, Strabo offers further explanation that the name Abii implies that people are "without hearths" and "live on wagons" (7.3.4). Strabo's defense of Homer demonstrates that the archetypal nomad in Greek thought was identified by his diet of milk, his lack of resources, his unsettled lifestyle, and his use of the wagon as a place of shelter. All of these characteristics were also used to describe the nomad in Herodotus's *Histories*.

A large component of Strabo's defense of Homer's accuracy includes detailed accounts of nomadic people found in Scythia, India, Arabia, and Africa.[69] These people are generally referred to as "the Nomads" (6.4.2), "the Tent dwellers" (6.4.2) or "the Wagon-Dwellers" (7.3.2, 11.2.1). Although they may serve his purposes to challenge the theories of his opponents, the nomads hold little value for Strabo. They "are of no use for anything and only require watching" (6.4.2).[70] The nomads are fickle warriors in Strabo's opinion, because they "are always attacking their neighbors and then in turn settling their differences" (11.8.3).[71] In spite of Strabo's frank assessment of the nomads as ferocious people (7.3.6)

[68] In 7.3.7., Strabo preserves a citation of Eratosthenes who recorded Hesiod, identifying the Ethiopians, Ligurians and Scythians as Hippemolgi.

[69] The term Numidae (i.e. Numidians) is a modification of *nomades* and was used to identify the inhabitants of North Africa in the region of modern Algeria (Sallust, *War with Jugurtha*, 18.1–9). See also Gabriel Camps, Berbères: Aux Marges de l'Histoire, (Paris: Éditions des Hespérides, 1980) 90–92.

[70] Jones, *Geography III*, 145.

[71] Jones, *Geography V*, 261.

who are constantly attacking others and preventing them from farming
(11.4.5), the rhetorical language for the archetypal nomad, as articulated
by Herodotus, is still maintained even though the purpose of the nomadic figure in the narrative has changed.

The critical components of the nomad typos are actually more explicit in Strabo's *Geography* than in the *Histories* since Strabo is trying to
unequivocally prove that Homer was the first to describe Scythians and
other nomadic people. For example, the Suevi, a German tribe located
between the Elbe and Vistula Rivers, can migrate with ease because they
have a meager existence and do not till the soil (7.1.3). Strabo associates the rejection of agricultural settled life with a conscious decision
to ignore the land (11.4.3). In Homer, heroes could be easily classified
as glorified nomads who travel without the encumbrance of herds; but
what saves them from the nomadic appellation is that they exploit the
people and lands they come into contact with.[72] The nomads live in environments where they could establish resources or exploit them, but
they choose not to. Strabo calls the Arabian Sabaeans "lazy" because they
do not feel compelled to harvest the abundant fruits found in their surrounding area (16.4.18). Unlike Herodotus, Strabo provides us with the
negatively charged view of nomadic life, and reflects the methods of assessing nomadic communities that will appear in several literary accounts
of nomadic enemies in premodern history.

The nomadic diet and dwellings remain the same in Strabo as in
Herodotus. They spend their lives "traveling on wagons" (7.3.2, 7.3.7,
7.3.17,11.2.1) that are equipped with felt tents.[73] They continue to drink
mare's milk and eat cheese (7.3.3, 7.3.7, 7.3.9, 7.3.17, 7.4.6, 11.2.2, and
16.4.17).[74] In the *Hist.*, Herodotus explains that the nomads eat flesh,

---

[72] János Harmatta, "Prolegomena to the Libykoi Logoi of Herodotus' Histories," *Acta
Classica Universitatis Scientiarum Debreceniensis* 27 (1991): 3–7.

[73] Jones, *Geography III*, 223. There are some variations, however, in this pattern of living;
the Suevi live in small huts (7.1.3), some Tanais area tribes live in tents (11.2.1), and the
Troglodytes, Ethiopian nomads, live in caves (16.4.17)

[74] Strabo describes the Troglodytes who mix blood with their milk, and another tribe
which prefers to drink sour milk (7.4.6). This same preference for fermented milk was
attributed to the Mongol tribes of the Central Steppe.

or raw meat. This suggests that they are hunters (1.73), and their skill as warriors on horseback and as archers would also suggest this interpretation; however, Strabo explains that the nomads are primarily pastoralists who are deeply tied to their flocks, and from these animals the nomads derive their sustenance (7.1.3, 7.3.7, 7.3.17, 7.4.6, 11.2.2, 16.4.17).

Strabo, inadvertently, elucidates for us the relationship of the nomad to the semi-periphery and the core (the Parthian empire in this case). With the territorial expansion of the Roman Empire, urban merchants and soldiers had more contact with these nomadic people. Strabo argues that the Parthians were the main rival to the Romans because they have accumulated so many lands. These lands and "the whole of the neighboring country was full of brigands, nomads and deserted regions" (11.7.2).[75]

The reason for Parthian success is "their mode of life, and also their customs, which contain much that is barbarian and Scythian in character, though more is conducive to hegemony and success in war" (11.9.2).[76] In reading Strabo's complaints of the Parthians, one might think that they are distasteful to him simply because the Parthians have assimilated some nomadic customs and behaviors. Some of these modes of life included guarding trade routes through less populated areas. For example, the Suevi were known to lead their goods for trade on their wagons (7.1.3). Wagon-dwellers and nomads peddled their wares in order to acquire goods they needed from the urban areas (7.3.7). In the Tanaïs region, there is a common emporium at which nomads and non-nomads exchanged goods. Nomads would trade slaves and leather hides; the Greeks would offer clothing, wine, and "other things that belong to civilized life" (11.2.3).[77] While these interactions between the frontier people with people in urban areas may suggest that the Parthians could have had a strong economic center, Strabo believes that they are fundamentally weak because they have too many nomadic tribes within their empire.

[75] Jones, *Geography V*, 253.

[76] Ibid., 275.

[77] Some of the nomadic goods come from diverse areas like India and Babylon and were exchanged for transport to Armenia and Media.

Unlike Herodotus's rhetoric in which the nomad is the cunning warrior who uses his freedom to out-maneuver the Persians, the nomad evolved into a warrior who fundamentally lacked commitment and would undermine any concerted effort at acculturation and assimilation. In the decades following Herodotus's death, the archetypal nomad evolved into a portrait which disguised Herodotus's rhetoric with more colorful, but culturally-biased imagery of nomadic life. The Scythians in *On Airs, Waters, and Places* are poorer nomads, migrating in order to survive:

> They (their wagons) are covered over with felt and are construct-
> ed, like houses, sometimes in two compartments, and sometimes
> in three, which are proof against rain, snow and wind. The wag-
> ons are drawn by two or by three yoke of hornless oxen. They
> have no horns because of the cold. Now in these wagons live the
> women, while the men ride alone on horseback, followed by the
> sheep they have, their cattle and their horses. They remain in the
> same place just as long as there is sufficient fodder for their ani-
> mals; when it gives out they migrate. They themselves eat boiled
> meats and drink mare's milk. They have a sweet meat called hip-
> pace, which is a cheese from the milk of mares (18).[78]

Despite the degeneration of a positive view of the archetypal nomad within Greek thought, later historians, geographers, and observers, in describing nomadic tribes, would adopt the same characteristics used by Herodotus.

By looking briefly at Strabo, it becomes clear that Herodotus's rhetoric had a significant impact upon how nomadic people would be discussed by later authors.[79] Regardless of whether one had reliable infor-mation about a particular tribe or not, if you described the tribe as wan-derers, milk drinkers, tent or wagon dwellers, or as those who do not sow the field, your readers would know that the tribe was a difficult group to handle—for Herodotus, this was an admirable characteristic, one which would highlight the weakness of the Persians; for Strabo, it would be a

[78] Jones, *Hippocrates I*, 119 & 121.

[79] Authors who demonstrate an appreciation, if not outright adoption, of Herodotus's nomadic accounts are Diodorus, Pliny the Elder, and Ptolemy.

factor that weakened the Parthian empire. Regardless of their differences, both authors commented extensively upon behaviors and activities such as food consumption, modes of travel, and lack of agricultural actions such as tilling and harvesting. None of their activities would leave a mark on the premodern world. Their behaviors would disappear silently with the actors.

Nomads in the Archaeological Record

As with most premodern fields of inquiry, theoretical models often spawn different questions as historians continue to examine textual sources, such as Herodotus and Strabo, as well as physical remains. Ongoing archaeological research is producing fascinating results which are revising traditional notions of the past, even our notions about the very origins of civilization.[80] Nomadic archaeology, in particular, has reaped the benefits of the *new archaeology* that considers processes and meaning behind the production of settlement plans and the distribution patterns that place materials across a room or site.[81] More recently social archaeologists have appropriated interdisciplinary methods to consider how archaeological evidence can reflect ethnicity, gender, and religion.[82] The concern is no

[80] Archaeological work in northern Syria and Iraq has provided evidence that the rise of civilization might not be found exclusively in southern Iraq, as has been believed for decades. The excavations at the sites of Tell Brak and Hamoukar in Syria point to the emergence of urbanism far earlier than that of the classical cities of Uruk and Eridu in southern Iraq. Andrew Lawler, "North Versus South, Mesopotamian Style," *Science* 312 (June 2006): 1458–63.

[81] For an introduction to processual and post-processual archaeological theory see Ian Hodder and Scott Hutson, *Reading the Past: Current Approaches to Interpretation in Archaeology*, 3d ed. (Cambridge: Cambridge University Press, 2003) and K. R. Dark *Theoretical Archaeology* (London: Duckworth, 1995). Some samples of this work include K. W. Kintigh and A. J. Ammerman, "Heuristic Approaches to Spatial Analysis in Archaeology," *American Antiquity* 47 (1982): 31–63; M. Parker Pearson, "The Powerful Dead: Archaeological Relationships between the Living and the Dead," *Cambridge Archaeological Journal* 3 (1993): 203–29; and J. F. Simek, "Integrating Pattern and Context in Spatial Archaeology, *Journal of Archaeological Science* 11 (1984): 405–20.

[82] Margarita Díaz-Andreu, Sam Lucy, Stasa Babic and David N. Edwards, *The Archaeology of Identity: Approaches to Gender, Age, Status, Ethnicity and Religion* (New York: Routledge, 2005).

longer with the elites, but with the ideas and behaviors that produced the sites found in the archaeological context.

As an example of such progressive research, Roger Cribb, in *Nomads in Archaeology*, provides methodological guidelines for documenting and assessing nomadic settlements.[83] His first challenge is to face the central assumption that we can know nothing of nomadic civilization as voiced by Gordon Childe in 1936: "Pastoralists are not likely to leave many vestiges by which the archaeologist could recognize their presence."[84] Cribb's response to this common assumption is that we need to redesign our view of distribution processes at settlements and consider that consumption of goods will vary from site to site. For example, we must recognize that there are varying degrees to which material items exist at a site. For Cribb this means considering items as being *fixtures*, borrowing from Lewis Binford's concept of "site furniture," and those that are *portable* items which might be moved from site to site, such as rugs. The second category includes items that have longevity and are therefore *durables*, in contrast to those items that are *perishable* and less likely to surface in the archaeological record. The third category includes artifacts that are *valuables*; this means that the items are difficult to acquire and therefore move with the communities. These *valuables* differ from those that are *expendables*, or are more frequently discarded at sites before moving to a new location.[85] With these categories of material remains, Cribb concludes: "[I]tems which are portable, perishable and valuable (like carpets) will have virtually zero archaeological visibility. Fixtures which are both durable and expendable and of low intrinsic value (such as stone hearths) will be site-specific and have a much higher visibility quotient. Intuitively one would expect nomad sites to contain a very high proportion of fixtures as opposed to portables and expendables as opposed to valuables."[86] The imbalanced record of what constitutes nomadism is seen in the liter-

---

[83] Roger Cribb, *Nomads in Archaeology* (Cambridge: Cambridge University Press, 1991).

[84] Gordon Childe, *Man Makes Himself* (London: Watts, 1936) 81.

[85] Cribb, *Nomads in Archaeology*, 68.

[86] Ibid., 69.

ary evidence in which behaviors were known in a general sense and very little knowledge existed of tangible nomadic material culture.

Testing the hypothesis of material culture with an ethnographic study demonstrates that the artifactual remains can be divided into these categories and therefore help us in interpreting and categorizing the relative value of the items that may or may not be found at nomadic settlements. Cribb's research has convincingly demonstrated that the archaeologist needs to develop an appreciation for the variables that will influence the finds that can be recovered in the nomadic context. Testing hypotheses at modern campsites of nomads has proved invaluable in creating models for assessing and interpreting stratigraphic deposits exposed through archaeology. Although not explicitly stated by Cribb, the underlying assumption is that nomadism, in its various forms, has a cultural continuity that exists throughout time.[87] This means that archaeologists can put forward a few preliminary hypotheses to test out while excavating ancient nomadic sites, and examine how modern campsites bear out theories of past behaviors of deposition and abandonment of material remains.[88]

An example of one category of finds will help explain Cribb's reasoning. Pottery is one of the most important artifacts that the archaeologist can recover to understand premodern societies. How it is distributed in a context can tell a story of human activity and help with dating and interpreting the world of those who used and produced the vessels. Just as with settled sites, pottery can provide a wealth of evidence for understanding nomadic culture and what was valued. With the recovery of ceramic evidence, Cribb provides four observations about the skewed distribution and typology of ceramic finds in comparison to settled areas. By drawing attention to this limitation, Cribb seeks to alert us to a sensitivity for considering patterns of nomadic usage and consumption.

---

[87] An example of assessing contemporary practices in light of archaeological remains is P. J. Ucko, "Ethnography and Archaeological Interpretation of Funerary Remains, *World Archaeology* 1 (1969): 262–77.

[88] R. L. Tapper, "The Organization of Nomadic Communities in Pastoral Societies of the Middle East," in *Pastoral Production and Society* (Cambridge: Cambridge University Press, 1979) 43–65.

First, the intensity of scattered pottery will be less. Second, the range and types of pots used will be smaller. Third, the distribution of scattered sherds will be "bimodal," meaning that one will recover "many sherds from large vessels (fixtures) and a smaller concentration at the lower end of the size spectrum."[89] Fourth, the pottery will only represent a particular end of the spectrum since the size distribution will be unfairly represented. These four observations are crucial for considering the processes of how the pottery has accumulated at a site and what it can reveal about the habits of the nomads at that site. Cribb's models are a useful starting point for considering how material remains in a nomadic setting will differ from the more traditional sites of premodern urban communities.

To begin assessing nomad evidence we need to take Cribb's work a step further by considering the assumptions that are made about culture and how we can interpret nomadic material remains. It is important to recognize that the physical depth of stratified layers of occupation at nomadic sites can be limited to just a hearth or a midden.[90] With this knowledge it is perhaps understandable that the excavation of burial sites with much deeper stratified contexts have captured the attention and imagination of archaeologists from the amateurish ones of the seventeenth century to the methodical investigators of the present. In particular, Russian archaeologists have excavated the most significant nomadic settlements and burials in Eurasia.[91] With their adoption of current theoretical approaches to excavation and interpretation, the world of premodern nomadism is starting to find definition apart from comparisons with their settled counterparts.[92]

---

[89] Cribb, *Nomads in Archaeology*, 76. In evaluating his hypotheses, Cribb notes: "Many campsites observed by myself and other archaeologists appear to contain very few sherds, widely scattered and of small size. . . .

[90] Ibid., 80.

[91] N. M. Vinogradova and E. E. Kuz'mina, "Contacts Between the Steppe and Agricultural Tribes of Central Asia in the Bronze Age," *Anthropology and Archaeology of Eurasia* 34.4 (1996): 29–54.

[92] For a general overview of theoretical shifts in Russian archaeology see P. M. Dolukhanov, "Archaeology in Russia and Its Impact on Archaeological Theory," in *Theory in Archaeology: A World Perspective*, ed. P. J. Ucko, (London: Routledge, 1995) 327–42.

One example of the current research is represented by the work of Ludmila Koryakova, who argues that: "Attempts to identify nomadic cultures by using a certain material complex have been rarely successful. The same can be said about the evolution of nomadism. Ethnography indicates that pure nomadism is extremely rare. . . . Besides, nomadic societies, represented by their material objects are traditionally considered to be asymmetrical."[93] The asymmetry is the difficulty that Cribb highlights with his examination of pottery remains at nomadic sites. Despite this limitation, past archaeologists have used common indicators to point to the identification of a site as being nomadic. Koryakova states that nomadism is often equated with the presence of "a kurgan burial ground; the relative absence of permanent settlements and house or the presence of camp sites; the absence or a very limited scale of farming; wheeled transport; and the bones of animals who were capable of traveling long distances and grazing all year round, and artifacts which would have been used for exploitation of these animals."[94] Koryakova's research into ceramic production and use in nomadic sites prompted her to reexamine assumptions made by earlier excavators about how nomadic burials and settlements were identified. She highlights the difficulties with using older models for identifying nomadic sites:

> [N]omadic material culture is characterized by some specifics that are recognizable as ethnographic models. . . . All of these types of nomadism were known historically, yet if we look at them from the point of view of their material culture, we will not notice any great differences between them. This illustrates the principal archaeological problem—the necessity to recognize the variety of nomadic types found in the archaeological assemblages.[95]

---

[93] Ludmila Koryakova, "Some Notes About the Material Culture of Eurasian Nomads," in *Kurgans, Ritual Sites, and Settlements: Eurasian Bronze and Iron Age*, ed. Jeannine Davis-Kimball, Eileen M. Murphy, Ludmila Koryakova and Leonid T. Yablonsky (Oxford: BAR International Series, 2000) 14 (hereafter Koryakova, *Eurasian Nomads*).

[94] Koryakova, *Eurasian Nomads*, 14.

[95] Ibid., 15.

Perhaps the most frequently cited feature of a nomadic settlement is the kurgan, or burial mound. Several of the kurgan sites have been excavated, and have produced artifacts that form the basis for much of what we know about nomadic life and culture. One of the more famous of these nomadic burials are the tombs at the site of Pazyryk, located in the Altai Mountains.[96] Initially the tombs were excavated in the 1920s and later in the 1950s for the Hermitage Museum. The tombs had all been robbed at one time, and thus the burial chambers had been exposed to the elements. This fact created a unique environment for water and rain to accumulate in the tombs and then to later freeze, thereby preserving artifactual evidence, such as textiles and skins, that would otherwise have perished if left in an unsealed state.[97]

As more excavations provided more reliable contexts for dating artifactual evidence, Esther Jacobson considered the ways in which scholars identify an iconography of nomadic art. In particular she has narrowed her research exclusively to the Scythians who were so richly incorporated into the world of Herodotus.[98] Based upon the funerary remains from the frozen tombs, most scholars viewed nomads as preferring an iconography that commemorated animals. They concluded that nomads created "animalism" as an art form in contrast to figural art of the settled communities. It is not until the Scythians relocate to western Asia that their art incorporates more Greek forms. After tracing the movement of the Scythians from Siberia to their later homeland around the Black Sea in the eighth century, Jacobson was unconvinced that the Scythians were only adopting Greek methods of artistic convention. She looked more extensively at the Scythian homeland where she examined petroglyphs of figural representations from the site of Pazyryk. Here, Jacobson saw

[96] M.I. Artamonov, "Frozen Tombs of the Scythians," *Scientific American* 212 (1965): 101–9.

[97] S.I. Rudenko, *Frozen Tombs of Siberia: The Pazyryk Burials of Iron-Age Horsemen* (Berkeley: University of California Press, 1970) and V. Schiltz, *Les Scythes et les Nomads des Steppes* (Paris: Gallimard, 1994).

[98] Esther Jacobson, "Early Nomadic Sources for Scythian Art," in *Scythian Gold,* 59–69 and idem, *The Art of the Scythians: The Interpretation of Cultures at the Edge of the Hellenic World* (Leiden: Brill, 1995).

that nomads were incorporating some story or event in rock carvings that would eventually resurface once the tribes had migrated further east. Rather than looking to the Greeks as a source for figural representations, Jacobson concludes that the Scythians merely borrowed the manners of producing human forms to represent their own tales: "In the case of Scythian art, an object may indeed look Greek, or at least Hellenized, but its underlying narrative reference may be quite different, from a vastly different place and time, and from a very different set of cultural values."[99]

Jacobson's conclusion accords well with Koraykova's conviction that the earlier interpretations made of nomadic material culture need to be carefully scrutinized. The assumption that sedentary communities are always influencing nomads reflects a modern bias that cultural influence can only flow from the urban communities to those who are in need of urbanization—the uncivilized nomads.[100] This prejudice toward the superiority, or exceptionalism, of the settled communities has hampered our ability to find nomadism in the premodern world. However, if we are aware of this natural predilection to trust the sedentary sources, how can we consider new ways of interrogating the physical sources to consider nomadic culture?

Nomadic Funerary Practices

The extensive nomadic burials of sacrificed horses and accompanying equipment has fostered a rich story of kurgan funerary rituals. The foundation for these reconstructions is often found in the stories of Herodotus who recounts that the Scythians, for example, dig square-shaped graves and bury the deceased with a roof of twigs (*Hist.* 4:72). He provides a vivid account of sacrificed attendants who were stuffed and placed atop sacrificed and stuffed horses in a circular formation on a kurgan (4.73). While this story has value, the actual kurgans now exposed for study

---

[99] Jacobson, *Scythian Art*, 69.

[100] J. Harmatta, "Nomadic and Sedentary Life in the Great Steppe-Belt of Eurasia," in *The Archaeology of the Steppes: Methods and Strategies*, ed. B. Genito (Napoli: Istituto Universitario Orientale, 1994) 565–71.

provide even more information about the variety within funerary practices.[101] For example, dendrochronology has demonstrated that much of the timber used in kurgan construction was cut during the winter months and likely moved to the burial site across the frozen waterways. This fact suggests some interesting possibilities about the activities of nomads during the winter season and the planning involved in constructing funerary sites.[102] Extensive recovery of grave goods become all the more important given the difficulty in finding and then interpreting the domestic nomadic settlements.[103] Even though Herodotus describes some domestic behaviors of nomadic tribes, the most memorable sections of his account are the gruesome details of scalping and of sacrificial rituals.

The location of the kurgans and the reuse of these structures for subsequent burials indicate that we can begin to articulate the behavior and beliefs of early nomadic societies. Bryan Hanks looks specifically at the Iron Age kurgan burials that date to the time of the eighth to fifth centuries BC, or to the Sauro-Sarmatian period.[104] In particular, Hanks considers the theoretical issues involved with distilling meaning from the burials, and how we might reconstruct premodern rituals in the nomadic milieu. Fundamental to Hanks's work is the recognition that scholars have inferred rituals merely on the basis of grave goods and the quality of those goods. For Hanks such research does not "accurately represent or acknowledge the complexity which burial ritual and subsequent variability are composed."[105] In order to start exposing the rituals of the past, one must consider theoretical models that will foster the right questions for investigating the evidence.

[101] B. Lincoln, *Death, War, and Sacrifice: Studies in Ideology and Practice* (Chicago: University of Chicago Press, 1991).

[102] Koryakova reports on the research of N. V. Polosmak who published these results in 1994. See Koryakova, *Eurasian Nomads*, 15.

[103] For a representative report on the finds of a nomadic burial see L. T. Yablonsky, "Burial Place of a Massagetan Warrior," *Antiquity* 64 (1990): 288–96 and N. A. Bokovenko, "Tomb of Saka Princes Discovered in the Sayans, Siberia," *New Archaeological Discoveries in Asiatic Russia and Central Asia* 16 (1994): 48–53.

[104] Bryan Hanks, "Iron Age Burials of the Eurasian Steppe: A Discussion Exploring Burial Ritual Complexity," in *Kurgans, Ritual Sites and Settlements*, 19–30.

[105] Hanks, *Burial Ritual*, 19.

For archaeologists, tombs have always served as a problematic source of information by providing a wealth of information about a particular moment in time, while simultaneously giving way to almost an immediate story of the moments of the deceased with the living community. Assumptions immediately surface. If the grave is large and filled with items, does it reflect an elite member of society? How do the burials reflect class and societal divisions? Are the inhabitants ordinary folk, or do they exhibit signs of being royal? What would the funerary assemblages of either group look like? Are the items within the tomb indigenous to the region? Do the grave goods include luxury goods, and how were the acquired? Were the luxury items gifts or, in the case of nomads, were these items the results of successful raids on sedentary lands? How do the burials of sacrificed animals factor into reflections of who was buried with them, and their value in society?[106]

Such questions seem routine, and yet they are imbued with a theoretical, hierarchical bias toward interpreting the evidence as to the value of the physical structures and goods contained therein. Hanks explains: "Arguably, theoretical approaches such as these presuppose a nearly direct correlation between the grave materials present and the respective deceased's rank and status within the previous life. In other words, these attempts explicitly seek to frame vertical societal relationships believed to be present within past societies."[107] Additionally, Hanks notes that Jeannine Davis-Kimball's work on the burials of warrior women at Pokrovka, Russia, has produced a similar theoretical structure, only her framework considers how the burials reflect status within the community.[108] Davis-Kimball deliberately jettisoned the evidence of finds of high frequency such as pottery, faunal evidence and iron knives. With these variables removed, she then assessed what items were found within the graves of men and women. Her conclusions present these roles within society: warriors, priestesses, hearth women, males buried with children, and males bur-

---

[106] G. R. Tsetskhladze, "Who Built the Scythian and Thracian Royal and Elite Tombs?" *Oxford Journal of Archaeology* 17.1 (1998): 55–92.

[107] Hanks, *Burial Ritual*, 20.

[108] Jeannine Davis-Kimball and Leonid T. Yablonsky, *Kurgans on the Left Bank of the Ilek: Excavations at Pokrovka 1990–1992* (Berkeley: Zinat, 1995).

ied with few grave goods. Again, Hanks sees Davis-Kimball's theoretical assessment as reflecting a preference to discern societal hierarchy from funerary assemblages, although she seeks to avoid a direct hierarchical analysis.

Hanks's response to these older models of interpretation is to draw upon the theoretical framework and questions framed by the post-processual archaeologists such as Ian Hodder. This means that Hanks seeks to consider the role of the kurgans in a broader context than just the sites as the only point of analysis. He begins his analysis by asking how the living nomadic community interacted with the burials, and what meaning the ritualized spaces had to those who lived around them. In considering the role that living members might have in the deposition of goods into a grave, Hanks draws upon the work of K. R. Dark who suggests that goods might be placed in a grave to appease the needs of the living members or to reflect the status of the living individual.[109]

With the sacrifice of over 160 horses at the site of Arzhan in the Sayan Mountains of Tuva, it is understandable that there is temptation to interpret the deceased men as royal elites with an elaborate kurgan. The number of sacrificed animals certainly was thought to indicate that person's value in society. However, current research indicates that it is likely that the animals may not only reflect the status of the deceased men who occupy the tombs but those who built them as well.[110] In fact, it is possible that the tomb and its associative items relate more to those who built the tombs than those who are buried there. The layout of kurgans with adjoining stone circles indicates that the funerary sites included areas for

---

[109] Dark, *Theoretical Archaeology*, 92.

[110] Excavation at Arzhan was initially undertaken by M. P. Gryaznov in the 1970s. His work produced the spectacular finds of Scythian nomads from the ninth and eighth centuries BC. Since the 1990s the Deutsches Archäologisches Institut has resumed excavations and has produced equally informative finds. See K. Čugunov, H. Parzinger and A. Nagler, "Der Fürst von Arzhan: Ausgrabungen im Skythischen Fürstengrabhügel Arzhan 2 in der Südsibirischen Republik Tuva," *Antike Welt* 32.6 (2001): 607–14; idem, "Der Skythische Fürstengrabhügel von Arzhan 2 in Tuva. Vorbericht der Russisch-Deutschen Ausgrabungen 2000–2002," *Eurasia Antiqua* 9 (2003): 113–62; idem, "Arzhan 2: La Tombe d'un Prince Scythe en Sibérie du Sud. Rapport Préliminaire des Fouilles Russo-Allemandes de 2000–2002," *Arts Asiatiques* 59 (2004): 5–29.

both the living and the dead. Therefore, the roles of nomads who might host the funerary rituals in honor of the deceased, as well as and what actions they performed in order to fulfill the obligations of the community should be considered.[111] To assume that all items that are placed in the grave are tied exclusively to the deceased may lead to incorrect assumptions about a society. Hanks concludes with these words of caution:

> Rather than seeing the burial evidence as simply a direct reflection of the deceased's status . . . there are a host of possible alternatives which can be seen to play a part in the process of the construction of the burial structure, the preparation of the body, and the inclusion/non-inclusion of artifacts with the corpse . . . it is necessary to consider that the material remains of the burial may indeed represent not only rank . . . but also a multitude of possible characterizations of the roles which this individual may have assumed. Additionally, one should be aware of the possible powerful resource not only on the corpse, but the site of the burial itself, . . . may have provided the *living* members of the community.[112]

The role of the living in funerary rituals and how their activities might impact the accumulation of artifacts in a given location is being illustrated in current excavations across Eurasia. The results of excavations of Scytho-Sarmatian sites exhibit the importance of this work for uncovering the nomads of Eurasia. At the Ustyurt Plateau in Kazakhstan, a series of forty Sarmatian burials were identified and surveyed for the first time in 1989.[113] The burials are located near oval or semi-rectangular earth mounds that are thought to have functioned as spaces for funerary feasts.[114] Between the mounds and the tombs, over one hundred anthro-

---

[111] N. A. Bokovenko, "Le Kourgane 'Royal' d'Arjan et son Tempe," *Les Dosseiers d'Archéologie* 194 (1994): 30–37.

[112] Hanks, *Burial Ritual*, 25.

[113] V. Yu. Zuyev and R. B. Ismagilov, "Ritual Complexes with Statues of Horsemen in the Northwestern Ustyurt," *New Archaeological Discoveries in Asiatic Russia and Central Asia* 16 (1994): 54–57.

[114] Jean-Paul Roux, *La Mort Chez les Peoples Altaïques Anciens et Médiévaux* (Paris: Librairie d'Amérique et d'Orient, 1963).

pomorphic stone sculptures were found facing the earth mounds.[115] The more complete sculptures represent males, at least .80–3 m in height, with a hand on the side of the hip, and the other reaching across to a sword. Based upon comparable material found in the Ural Mountains, the burials are dated to the fifth to third centuries.

The position of these sculptures indicates particular choices by the nomadic communities that erected them between the burial graves and the areas for the funerary feasts. In her reassessment of the monuments, Valery Olkhovskiy seeks to consider the purpose of such an elaborate display of anthropomorphic sculpture. The anomaly of figural, three-dimensional art seems independent of other Scythian art, and is certainly distinctive from all other kurgan burial settlements. Olkhovskiy is able to reconstruct the exact location of these pieces on the basis of the foundation bases that are still *in situ*. From this evidence she concludes "that the statues had been positioned in groups composed of two to four monuments, and that each group had been located approximately 1–2 m from the next. The number of sculptures located in each sanctuary ranged from one or two up to as many as 35."[116]

With a closer examination of the individual sculptures, it is clear that these figures are our closest photo of male Eurasian nomads from the Scythian-Sarmatian period of the Iron Age. They wore a wide belt, carried a doubled-edged sword, and had a quiver attached to the belt. The location and placement of these sculpted, nomadic warriors then might reflect views of the afterlife and nomadic spirituality. The statues are placed on the south side, and face the north or west. Olkhovskiy explains that these directions are important spatial alignments that reflect "Indo-Iranian and Indo-European mythological systems."[117] By facing to the north or east, the warriors are facing the world of the dead, and

---

[115] Valery S. Olkhovskiy, "Ancient Sanctuaries of the Aral and Caspian Regions: A Reconstruction of Their History," in *Kurgans, Ritual Sites and Settlements*, in *Kurgans, Ritual Sites, and Settlements: Eurasian Bronze and Iron Age*, ed. Jeannine Davis-Kimball, Eileen M. Murphy, Ludmila Koryakova and Leonid T. Yablonsky (Oxford: BAR International Series, 2000) 33–38.

[116] Olkhovskiy, "Ancient Sanctuaries," 34.

[117] Ibid., 35.

possibly represent heroic figures of nomadic history. In attributing these sculptures to a particular nomadic tribe, Olkhovskiy is cautious; however, she does posit an intriguing possibility that these burials might belong to the Ustyurt nomads who faced Alexander the Great, and were thereby influenced by Hellenism to construct a military sanctuary.[118]

Another example of funerary research in Eurasian nomadic history is the ninth-century-AD kurgan in the Egyin Gol valley of Mongolia.[119] The France-UNESCO Permanent Archaeological Mission in Mongolia drew upon both the older method of using ethnography to interpret current rituals and the newer method called the sociology of archaeology which studies the sociological factors that would produce a site as it is preserved in the archaeological record. The team consulted ethnographic accounts of nomadic funeral feasts from the nineteenth century AD and the analysis of stratified burials to reconstruct a plausible story of pre-modern funeral rituals of a Uighur community.

The Mongolian burial site includes at least fifty kurgans; a survey of the site and the burials suggests the area was used for nomadic burials from the Bronze Age to the period of the Mongols. EG IV-2 was elected for excavation and proved to be the burial for a woman, whose date of inhumation was projected to the eighth or ninth century. The excavators note that the burial assemblage is "atypical," with only a few grave items included. The position of a bone comb was suggestive of use in the woman's hair. Only one item, a spindle whorl, bore a recognized pattern of nested squares. This pattern is identified as Uighur in origin, and thus the occupant has been identified as being ethnically Uighur.[120]

[118] The uniqueness of the Ustyurt burials might be explained then as the by-product of cross-cultural exchanges between the Hellenizing Macedonians and the nomadic tribes. While Olkhovskiy seeks to distance herself from the assumption that nomads are recipients of Greek ideals, her replacement of a Hellenizing influence still underscores the preferential view that sedentary empires infuse new ideas into nomadic culture.

[119] E. Crubézy, H. Martin, et. al., "Funeral Practices and Animal Sacrifices in Mongolia at the Uigur Period: Archaeological and Ethno-historical Study of a Kurgan in the Egyin Gol Valley (Baikal Region)," *Antiquity* 70 (1996): 891–99. The longevity of the kurgan in nomadic funerary complex is attested to by the discovering of these late Uighur burials.

[120] The assumption here that one spindle whorl reflects ethnicity or community identity is problematic given the cautions of interpretative frameworks listed above. The presence

With the exception of the minimal artifactual finds the real area of interest and research in premodern nomadism comes with the documentation of the bones of humans and animals in the kurgan. The excavators explain that great attention was given to these deposits "with the aim of reconstituting in detail the actions and practices that were performed during the burial."[121] One way in which bioarchaeology and dental examination contributed to reconstructing these rituals was to ascertain that the horse, whose bones were visible below the topsoil on the kurgan, was killed in the winter season.[122] The bones of the three year-old horse were divided between two contexts: first, the head, rib bones, and right scapula were found in the upper part of the grave; and second, the hindquarters, rib cartilages, and incomplete forelegs were found at the bottom of the grave.

The recovering of the bones of this single animal raised questions about what processes or rituals might explain the eventual location of these bones. No signs of cutting were left on the bones, although the excavators noted that "cutting could have been done with sharp instruments which have not left a mark on the bones, or they may have been boiled, as is still done in Central Asia."[123] Additional caprine (goat) remains were found near the body and the equine bones, indicating that part of the burial ritual included the deposition of these animals into the fill. Using the results of the stratigraphic excavation the excavators concluded that the grave was filled in stages, with the hindquarters of the horse being deposited beside the deceased, and then the ribs were placed near the sealed surface of the grave. The presence of the skull on the very surface implies that the summit of the kurgan was marked by the horse's skull, most likely mounted on a post. Is it possible that Herodotus's account of the Scythian burial rituals around the Bronze and Iron Age kurgans is an accurate description of Eurasian nomadic life?[124] Despite

of a Uighur spindle whorl could be explained by a variety of factors.

[121] Crubézy, "Funeral Practices," 893.

[122] Ibid., 894.

[123] Ibid., 897.

[124] The discovery that Herodotus is a reliable source for Scythian material culture is not a new observation. Discoveries from the tombs of Pazyryk, discussed above; Melitopol';

Herodotus's reasons for incorporating the nomads into his history, does the correlation between the literary and archaeological evidence mean we should rely upon the accounts of sedentary communities for portraits of nomadism?

Conclusion

Clearly it is important to bring together these two very different methods of reading and interpreting sources for writing a history of premodern Eurasian nomads. Neither approach is particularly unique or new to historians. And yet together, the analysis of Herodotus's rhetoric and the applications of theoretical models for interpreting material culture, provide ways to construct the lives of nomads who are frequently omitted from the stories told in world history classrooms. Traditionally, the nomads surface when needed to explain the difficulties that sedentary empires would face and need to grabble with;[125] and eventually the nomads are the heroes of the story with the conquests of Chinggis Khan who surpasses all the victories of his predecessors.

For the global historian, the challenge is to reconfigure and contextualize this portrait of nomadic history. Rather than consider history as merely an evolving map of imperial states, the world historian calls us to consider all the people who lived along side the "greats" of antiquity. By peopling the early maps, the global historian draws attention to the fact that the territory between the Greeks and the Persians or the Han and Roman empires was not a no-man's land. Rather it was home to numer-

and Gaimanovo Mogila. In many excavation reports, Herodotus is used as confirmation for nomadic identifications. The best example would be the apparatuses for smoking hemp found in the Pazyryk tombs. For a brief overview see Yamauchi, *Foes from the Northern Frontier*, 109–24.

[125] The Xiongnu, for example, were a continual source of frustration for the Han. Eventually Emperor Han Wudi would seek to enlist help from rival nomadic tribes to try to limit the strength of the Xiongnu along the northern border of the Han. See the following works by Nicola Di Cosmo "The Origin and Rise of the Xiongnu Empire," in *The Turks*, eds. Hasan Celal Güzel et al. (Ankara: Yeni Türkiye Yayinlari, 2002) 217–27; *Ancient China and Its Enemies: The Rise of Nomadic Power in East Asian History* (Cambridge: Cambridge University Press, 2002).

ous nomadic tribes who were actively engaged with those empires, and had a history that was unique from the sedentary communities.

Herodotus, for all his faults and limitations, is the accidental world historian. He seeks to tell a tale of the Persian defeat at the hands of a group of Greek city-states. As he weaves his tale of digressions, histories and asides, he includes accounts of Eurasian nomadism. Some nomadic tribes would be too difficult to incorporate into the hegemonic Persian Empire, and others would accentuate the weaknesses of Persian confidence. The world, for Herodotus, was not simply defined by the barbarian imperial states. If anything, the reader of the *Hist.* realizes just how populated the fifth-century world was, and might wish that Herodotus had omitted a few of the empires he takes time to describe for his audience. The determination to include all the tribes illustrates the importance of nomads in premodern history in addition to their interactions with sedentary people. By rereading Herodotus and other authors we can sketch the ways in which sedentary communities saw themselves in light of the very populated world that included a large array of nomads.

While sedentary reports or histories can provide valuable insight into nomadic behavior and movements, these accounts are limited in providing depth to the history of Eurasian nomadism. Little is found in Herodotus, Sima Qian, or Ibn Fadlan of the material culture of nomads. Therefore, nomadic archaeology becomes all the more crucial for writing a history of the nomads as individuals. Rather than conceiving of the tribes as faceless entities that moved across maps and territories, archaeological work should seek to create daily activities, beliefs, and actions of individuals within the nomadic landscape.

The appropriation of recent theoretical models for interpreting material remains has been most effective in making nomadic life more tangible and less dependent upon the writings of outsiders who preferred the urban life and its cultural practices. It is perhaps fitting that the nomads who were so elusive to their contemporaries are still a mystery for the modern historian. However, the recent applications of historical inquiry in textual and archaeological studies can bring the spotlight onto the clever nomad.

The Aten Cult at Memphis[1]

Steven M. Stannish

❋MANY EGYPTOLOGISTS SEE pharaoh Akhenaten's (ca. 1352–1336 BC) religion, Atenism, as an austere form of solar monotheism, and judge his art to be grotesque and monotonous.[2] They believe that his ideas appealed only to a fawning inner circle, and that they vanished shortly after his death. In contrast, it is argued here that Akhenaten spread his religion in Memphis, 250 kilometers north of his residence at Amarna. It will be demonstrated that the king established offerings for his god in this city before his third year and that he built temples there by his ninth. Furthermore, it is shown that a modified Aten cult remained in Memphis long after his demise. It is not claimed here that Akhenaten was a beloved monarch or a brilliant statesman. Rather, it is contended here that many elites entertained his ideas—some perhaps for political gain, but others for more profound reasons.

Several scholars have asserted that Akhenaten secluded himself at Amarna and ignored the wider world.[3] They point to the king's promise,

---

[1] One of the qualities that I admire in Professor Yamauchi is his diligence in integrating recent discoveries into his teaching and scholarship. Under his direction at Miami University, I used old and new evidence to study the reign of the heretic pharaoh Akhenaten (ca. 1352–1336 BC).

[2] Examples of this thinking include J. H. Breasted, *A History of Egypt from the Earliest Times to the Persian Conquest* (New York: Scribner, 1909) 369; A. H. Gardiner, *Egypt of the Pharaohs: An Introduction* (Oxford: Oxford University Press, 1961) 227ff.; D. B. Redford, *Akhenaten: The Heretic King* (Princeton: Princeton University Press, 1984) ch. 15; E. Hornung, *History of Ancient Egypt: An Introduction*, trans. D. Lorton (Ithaca: Cornell University Press, 1999) 98ff.

[3] Breasted, *History of Egypt*, 399; Gardiner, *Egypt of the Pharaohs*, 229ff.; H. Kees, *Ancient Egypt: A Cultural Topography*, trans. I. F. D. Morrow (Chicago: University of Chicago Press, 1961) 295; É. Bill-De Mot, *The Age of Akhenaten*, trans. J. Lindsay (London: Evelyn, Adams, and Mackay, 1966) 129; C. Aldred, *Akhenaten, Pharaoh of Egypt: A New Study* (London: Thames and Hudson, 1968) 67; R. J. Leprohon, "The Reign of Akhenaten Seen through the Later Royal Decrees," in *Mélanges Gamal Eddin Mokhtar*, ed. P. Posener-Kriéger (Cairo: Institut Français d'Archéologie Orientale du Caire, 1985) vol. 2, 94; Hornung, *History of Ancient Egypt*, 102. Aldred recanted his opinion in *Akhenaten*,

211

in his sixth year, not to "go beyond" (*sni*) the city's boundaries.[4] They also cite the Amarna Letters, cuneiform tablets from Akhenaten's vassals and allies filled with complaints of neglect.[5] Among the correspondents, Rib-Hadda, the mayor of Byblos, is the most vociferous grumbler. He is responsible for some 70 of the 350 tablets. But various parties, including the Great Kings of Mitanni and Babylon, allege mistreatment.

Other scholars have disagreed with this opinion, however. William J. Murnane and Charles C. Van Siclen observe that if Akhenaten never left Amarna, he could not have attended the funeral of his daughter, Meketaten, which he surely did.[6] Indeed, they note that just one year before the king promised not to "go beyond" the city's boundaries, he raised the possibility of dying elsewhere, forbade certain rituals while he was away, and spoke of "going about" (*swtwt*) to found temples.[7] Murnane and Van Siclen thus conclude that his oath was not a vow of seclusion, but a pledge to limit his capital's size.[8]

As for the Amarna Letters, Mario Liverani has shown that they are not objective reports, but attempts to persuade, sometimes through deception.[9] For example, when Rib-Hadda bemoans his neglect, he is drawing on the archetype of the "righteous sufferer" in order to evoke sympathy.[10] Similarly, when the mayor accuses his neighbors of treachery,

---

King of Egypt (London: Thames and Hudson, 1988) 272.

[4] The promise is in section VI-B of the Later Proclamation, which is inscribed on boundary stelae at Amarna see W. J. Murnane and C. C. Van Siclen III, *The Boundary Stelae of Akhenaten* (London: Kegan Paul International, 1992).

[5] See W. L. Moran, *The Amarna Letters* (Baltimore: Johns Hopkins University Press, 1992).

[6] Murnane and Van Siclen, 170. Reliefs depict Akhenaten grieving at the funeral. G. T. Martin, *The Royal Tomb at El-'Amarna* (London: Egypt Exploration Society, 1974–1989) vol. 2, 43–48, pls. 63–72.

[7] Murnane and Van Siclen, *Boundary Stelae of Akhenaten*, 170.

[8] Ibid.

[9] M. Liverani, "Political Lexicon and Political Ideologies in the Amarna Letters," *Berytus* 31 (1983): 42.

[10] M. Liverani, "Rib-Addi, Righteous Sufferer," in *Myth and Politics in Ancient Near Eastern Historiography*, ed. Z. Bahrani and M. Van De Mieroop (Ithaca: Cornell University Press, 2004) 97–124.

he is using rhetoric in an attempt to acquire aid.[11] In Liverani's view, the Amarna Letters reveal more about the mechanisms of international relations than they do about Akhenaten's foreign policy or lack thereof.

If Akhenaten did not actually confine himself to Amarna, if he did not really ignore affairs of state, then it is difficult to believe that his only followers were his immediate family and intimate friends. The only remaining basis for this view is the supposition that the king's ideas were so unpalatable that they were despised in his absence. Admittedly, later rulers dismantled Akhenaten's temples and struck his name from official records, but this does not necessarily mean that his contemporaries abhorred him. Indeed, the evidence suggests that some of the leading citizens of Memphis embraced his religion.

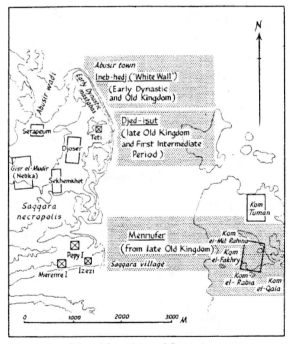

Map: Memphis and Saqqara
Courtesy of the British Museum Press

[11] Ibid., 108–11.

Memphis is located near the apex of the Nile Delta, not far south of modern Cairo. According to Herodotus (2.99) and Diodorus Siculus (1.50–51), the first king of Upper and Lower Egypt made this city his residence and fortified it.[12] Later rulers often lived in Memphis, and they invariably regarded it as a vital administrative center. Its chief god was Ptah, whose temple's name, *hwt-k3-pth*, is the origin of the word "Egypt."[13] Although Memphis' moist soil has destroyed most of the monuments, archaeologists have managed to uncover parts of the city's most important religious structures.

West of Memphis is the necropolis of Saqqara, named for the local funerary god Sokar. The cemetery is dominated by the Step Pyramid of Djoser, built in the twenty-seventh century BC, but it also includes royal and private tombs from various ages. The most significant discoveries at Saqqara are the Serapeum, a sanctuary housing the mummified remains of Apis Bulls, and the *Pyramid Texts*, or funerary spells later subsumed into the *Coffin Texts* and the *Book of the Dead*.[14]

The earliest source for Akhenaten's activities at Memphis is a fragmentary offering list from Karnak.[15] It reads:

x+1   [. . .] the Aten [up]on the offering tables of Re starting from

x+2   Memphis (*hwt-k3-pth*) and ending at Balamun.

x+3   [A diving offering] dedicated by the King of Upper and
       Lower Egypt Neferkheperure Waenre (Akhenaten), for his
       father Re, as a daily offering in Memphis.
       (*Offerings follow.*)

---

[12] Herodotus, *Histories*, trans. A. D. Godley, 4 vols. (revised ed; London/New York: W. Heinemann/Harvard University Press, 1990); Diodorus Siculus, *Library of History*, trans. C. H. Oldfather, 12 vols. (Cambridge: Harvard University Press, 1935–1967).

[13] J. K. Hoffmeier, "Egyptians," in *Peoples of the Old Testament World*, ed. A. J. Hoerth et al. (Grand Rapids: Baker, 1994) 252. Other names associated with the site include "White Wall" (*inb-hd*), "Life of the Two Lands" (*ʿnh-t3wy*), and "Established and Good is (King) Pepy (I)" (*mn-nfr-ppi*). The last is the origin of the word "Memphis."

[14] J.-P. Lauer, *Saqqara, the Royal Cemetery of Memphis: Excavations and Discoveries Since 1850* (New York: Scribner, 1976) ch. 1.

[15] B. Löhr, "Aḫanyāti in Memphis," *SAK* 2 (1975): 144–45; W. J. Murnane, *Texts from the Amarna Period in Egypt* (Atlanta: Scholars Press, 1995) 33–34.

x+12   A divine offering which His Person dedicated for his father Re-Harakhty, who rejoices on the horizon in his name of Light

x+13   which is in the Aten, as a daily offering in [the Sunshade of Re which is in Memphis.]
(*More offerings follow.*)

This list must predate Akhenaten's ninth year, for it uses the Aten's Early Didactic Name (x+12-x+13). Indeed, it must have been issued before the king's third year, for it does not place that name in cartouches. The list thus demonstrates that Akhenaten promoted Atenism in Memphis and throughout Lower Egypt at the beginning of his reign. It also reveals that he did not initially build temples, but instead co-opted Re's facilities. This policy was natural, for Re was a hypostasis of the Aten.

Another early source is a letter from Apy, the steward of Memphis, to Akhenaten.[16] This document, found in duplicate at Gurob, bears a date of "Year 5." It reports that "the temple of your father Ptah, South-of-his-Wall . . . is prosperous and flourishing" (9–10), and that "The offerings of all the gods and goddesses who are on the soil of Memphis [have been issued] in full" (12–13). The letter does not contain a single reference to the Aten, and is so formulaic and bland that Jaromir Malek has paraphrased it as "nothing is happening."[17] Evidently, although the Aten enjoyed royal patronage at Memphis, Ptah remained the city's chief god. Yet, the discovery of two copies of the document at the same site may be revealing. Murnane notes that Apy composed his letter during the year that Akhenaten changed his Great Names and transferred his residence to Amarna in order to honor his god.[18] He speculates that the steward may have reconsidered the dispatch's propriety and decided to file it away with the archival copy.

---

[16] Löhr, "Aḫanyāti in Memphis," 142–44; Murnane, *Texts from the Amarna Period in Egypt*, 50–51.

[17] J. Malek, "The Temples at Memphis: Problems Highlighted by the EES Survey," in *The Temple in Ancient Egypt: New Discoveries and Recent Research*, ed. S. Quirke (London: British Museum Press, 1997) 95.

[18] Murnane, *Texts from the Amarna Period in Egypt*, 50.

Eventually, Akhenaten did build temples in Memphis. Texts refer to four structures: the "Sunshade of Re" (*šwt-rꜥ*), the "Effective for Aten" (*ꜣḥ-n-itn*), "the Mansion of the Aten" (*tꜣ-ḥwt-pꜣ-itn*), and the "Temple of Aten" (*pr-itn*).[19] The first may have been an appropriated shrine, but the others were certainly new. Beatrix Löhr has suggested that the second was part of the fourth, proposing the full designation as the "Effective for Aten in the Temple of Aten in Memphis" (**ꜣḥ-n-itn m pr-itn m mn-nfr*).[20]

Archaeologists have found a total of seventeen limestone blocks and quartzite fragments from these structures.[21] Probably the most important block depicts four solar rays and a libation jar capped by a falcon's head (Figure 1).[22] The inscription on the jar uses the Aten's Early Didactic Name, and states that the god is "within (*ḥry-ib*) the Effective for Aten." The block thus proves that Akhenaten built at least one temple in Memphis before his ninth year.

Figure 1: A Block Depicting Solar Rays and a Libation Jar from Memphis
Courtesy of the Nicholson Museum

---

[19] Löhr, "Aḫanyāti in Memphis," 164. Despite the fact that the name "Effective for Aten" and the nomen "Akhenaten" are phoenetically identical, the former is not cartouched while the latter is. Most likely, the temple honored the Aten's "effective spirit" (*ꜣḥ*), which was manifest in the king.

[20] Ibid., 165.

[21] Malek, "Temples at Memphis," 96.

[22] Löhr, "Aḫanyāti in Memphis," 154–55.

A second block, bearing six fragmentary cartouches, sheds some light on later activities.[23] The first two cartouches on the right preserve the single word "horizon" (*3ht*), an element in the Aten's Early and Late Didactic Names. The next two each contain the word "forms" (*hprw*) and are certainly a king's prenomen and nomen. The fifth cartouche holds the seated woman determinative (Gardiner B1) and belongs to a queen. Finally, the sixth contains the phrase "Re lives" (*ʿnh rʿ*), a part of the Aten's Late Didactic Name. The third and fourth cartouches, which must be restored as "[Ankh]kheperu[re Smenkhkare Djeser]kheperu" ([*ʿnh*]-*hprw*-[*rʿ smnh-k3-rʿ dsr*]-*hprw*), are the most significant.[24] They demonstrate that Akhenaten's successor, Smenkhkare (ca. 1336–1333 BC), either built or enhanced an Aten temple at Memphis.[25]

While most of our blocks and fragments were reused as fill for the temples of Ramesses II (ca. 1279–1213 BC) in the area of the Ptah Enclosure, at least three were found at Kom el-Qala.[26] These pieces include a statue pillar inscribed with the Aten's Early Didactic Name, a block bearing the same name as well as Akhenaten's cartouches, and an unidentified statue head. Although the sample is quite small, Malek believes that it marks the location of the Temple of Aten in Memphis.[27] He notes that Kom el-Qala, like the site of the Aten temple at Karnak, is southeast of the local god's old sanctuary, beyond the limits of previous construction.

At this point, we turn to Saqqara. Over the past three decades, archaeologists have excavated a number of tombs from the fourteenth century BC in this cemetery. Most recently, they have entered the buri-

---

[23] Ibid., 157–59.

[24] P. E. Newberry, "Akhenaten's Eldest Son-in-Law 'Ankhkheperurē'," *JEA* 14 (1928): 8–9.

[25] Recently, Malek has discredited a block thought to depict Smenkhakare and Akhenaten officiating in Memphis. "The "Co-Regency Relief" of Akhenaten and Smenkhkare from Memphis," in *Studies in Honor of William Kelly Simpson*, ed. P. der Manuelian (Boston: Museum of Fine Arts, 1996) vol. 2, 553–59. Cf. Löhr, "Ahanyāti in Memphis," 155–57.

[26] Löhr, "Ahanyāti in Memphis," 148–52; Malek, "Temples at Memphis," 97.

[27] Malek, "Temples at Memphis," 99.

als of Meryneith, the "greatest of seers of the Aten" (*wr m3w n p3 itn*), and Raia, a high-ranking treasury official.[28] Unfortunately, we do not yet know much about these tombs, and so must instead focus on the recently cleared burials of Aper-El, Horemheb, and Maya.

Aper-El's tomb was cut into the escarpment of Saqqara, northeast of the Step Pyramid. Alain-Pierre Zivie entered it in 1976, an though he has not yet published an excavation report, he has published a few articles and a popular book.[29] At the same time, however, Zivie has warned against premature hypotheses.[30] In part, his anxiety stems from the fact that the name Aper-El (*ʿpr-iȝr, ʿpriȝ*) is Semitic in origin, and is the equivalent of the Biblical Abdĕel (Jeremiah 36:26) and Abdiel (1 Chronicles 5:15), which mean "Slave of God."[31] Zivie is apprehensive about speculation on the historicity of the Joseph romance (Genesis 37–50), and hopes that accurate data will discredit it.

---

[28] M. Raven, "Meryneith: High Priest of the Aten," *Minerva* 13/4 (August 2002): 31–34; A.-P. Zivie, "Mystery of the Sun God's Servant," *NG* 204/5 (November 2003): 52–59.

[29] A. P.-Zivie, "'Aper-El et ses voisins: considérations sur les tombes rupestres de la XVIIIe Dynastie à Saqqarah," in *Memphis et ses nécropoles au Nouvel Empire*, ed. A.-P. Zivie (Paris: Centre National de la Recherche Scientifique, 1978) 103–12; idem, *Découverte à Saqqarah: le vizir oublié* (Paris: Seuil, 1990); idem, "Mystery of the Sun God's Servant," *NG* 204/5 (November 2003): 52–59; idem, "Le nom du vizir 'Aper-El," *CahRB* 26 (1992): 115–23; idem, "Portrait de femme: une tête en bois stuqué récemment découverte à Saqqarah," *RdE* 39 (1988): 179–95; idem, "Recherches et découvertes récentes dans la tomb d'Aperia à Saqqarah," *CRAIBL* (April–June 1988): 490–505; idem, "Une tombe d'époque amarnienne à Saqqarah," *BSFE* 84 (1979): 21–32; idem, "Tombes rupestres de la falaise du Bubasteion à Saqqarah, campagne 1980–1981," *ASAE* 68 (1982): 63–69; idem, "Tombes rupestres de la falaise du Bubasteion à Saqqarah, IIe et IIIe campagnes (1982–1983)," *ASAE* 70 (1985): 219–32; idem, "The 'Treasury' of 'Aper-El," *EA* 1 (1991): 26–28; idem, "Le trésor funeraire du vizir 'Aper-El," *BSFE* 116 (1989): 31–34; idem, "Trois saisons à Saqqarah: les tombeaux de Bubasteion," *BSFE* 98 (1983): 40–56. Unless Zivie's articles contain significant additional information, I will only cite his book.

[30] Zivie, *Découverte à Saqqarah*, 174–75.

[31] Zivie, "Le nom du vizir 'Aper-El," passim. Cf. E. M. Yamauchi, "Slaves of God," *BETS* 9 (1966): 31–49.

Aper-El's first chamber contains evidence of Aten worship at Memphis. On the east wall, to the right of the entrance, are four panels.[32] The first three were merely painted and have faded considerably, but the fourth was carved and survives largely intact. It shows Aper-El and his wife, Taweret, receiving an ablution of water. The figures, rendered in the traditional style, were mutilated, probably during the Byzantine Period (AD 324–642) or later.[33] The inscriptions on the panels list Aper-El's most important titles, including "steward of the city" (*m-r niwt*), "vizier" (*ßty*), and "first servant of Aten" (*b3k tpy n itn*). On a band surrounding the panels, an offering formula is also visible. It reads:

> An offering which the king gives to the living Aten, lord of heaven, lord of the earth, who illuminates the Two Lands, by whose rising all men and women live; so that he may give bread, water, air . . . to the steward of the city and vizier, Aperia, justified.

Parallels to this formula, which are attributed to the vizier's son, Huy, have been found at Amarna.[34]

Aper-El's tomb consists of four levels connected by stairways and shafts. His burial chamber is on the bottom level, behind stairs leading to a dead end.[35] Within this chamber, Zivie discovered the mummies of Aper-El, Taweret, and Huy, as well as a rich collection of artifacts. Especially beautiful are the canopic jars of Aper-El and Taweret.[36] These are not capped by the familiar heads of the Sons of Horus, but by idealized busts of the owners. Yet, they also bear the names of gods like Neith, Isis, and Hapy, and thereby preserve their apotropaic function.

---

[32] Zivie, *Découverte à Saqqarah*, 54–57.

[33] Zivie, "Une tombe d'époque amarnienne à Saqqarah," n. 20.

[34] M. Sandman, *Texts from the Time of Akhenaten* (Brussels: Fondation Égyptologique Reine Élisabeth, 1938).

[35] Zivie, *Découverte à Saqqarah*, ch. 3.

[36] Ibid., 100, 102–3, 126–27, 168, 175. They are similar to canopic jars from contemporary Theban tombs. See T. M. Davis et al., *The Tomb of Iouiya and Touiyou with the Funeral Papyrus of Iouiya* (London: G. Duckworth & Co., Ltd., 2000) 24–25, pl. 17; idem et al., *The Tomb of Queen Tiyi* (San Francisco: KMT Communications, 1990) 32–34, pls. 9–21.

Interestingly, one of Aper-El's lids resembles some of Amunhotep III's (ca. 1390–1353 BC) later portraits.[37] The face is compact and fleshy, the eyes almond-shaped, the nose broad, and the lips pursed, yet full.

Aper-El's burial chamber contained a few chronological markers. An ebony strip on the lid of a wooden box bears the names of Amunhotep III and Tiye.[38] The box's knobs and a pair of green faience earring pendants also carry the former's cartouches.[39] On the other hand, some clay seal fragments bear Akhenaten's prenomen as well as the epithet "Beloved of Wenennefer (Osiris)."[40] The reference to the lord of the underworld suggests that they antedate the king's proscription of traditional gods in his ninth year. Finally, some of Huy's wine jars have "Year 10" dockets.[41] The reigning pharaoh is not named, but Akhenaten is the only reasonable possibility.

Despite this evidence, it is difficult to reconstruct the chronology of Aper-El's tomb. Huy's offering formula contains nothing overtly heretical, and could come from almost any point in Akhenaten's reign. The objects bearing Amunhotep III and Tiye's cartouches are just as likely heirlooms as they are accurate indicators. And the seal fragments stamped with Akhenaten's prenomen cannot be assigned to a specific burial. The only unambiguous markers are Huy's "Year 10" dockets, which suggest a rough date for his funeral.

It should noted that everything in Aper-El's tomb—so far as is known—is consistent with traditional Egyptian culture. In addition to the divine names on canopic jars and seal fragments, the image of the sky goddess, Nut, appears inside the sarcophagi of Taweret and Huy.[42] Excerpts from the *Book of the Dead* are carved on several items, including

---

[37] Zivie, *Découverte à Saqqarah*, 175. Cf. A. P. Kozloff et al., *Egypt's Dazzling Sun: Amenhotep III and His World* (Cleveland: Cleveland Museum of Art, 1992) ch. 5.

[38] Zivie, *Découverte à Saqqarah*, 116, 128, 163.

[39] Ibid., 160.

[40] Ibid., 128, 162.

[41] Ibid., 164–65.

[42] Ibid., 110–11, 117.

a schist scarab and a heart-shaped stone.[43] Indeed, despite his Semitic name, Aper-El seems to have been a typical Egyptian vizier. An inscription on a wooden cubit records that he was a "child of the palace nursery" (*ẖrd n k3p*), and a relief depicts him wearing the customary vizier's tunic and *m3ˁt*-pendant, rigidly holding a staff in his right hand and a scepter in his left.[44]

The traditional character of the tomb, the presence of Amunhotep III's cartouches on sentimental objects, and the reference to Akhenaten on seal fragments alone suggest that Aper-El and Taweret lived most of their adult lives under the former king. While it is a bit surprising that Huy was buried in his father's tomb, we need not presume that he died first. His offering formula, which describes Aper-El as "justified," i.e., deceased, and his "Year 10" dockets, imply the opposite.

Another factor must be considered, however. Two viziers are already known from the end of Amunhotep III's reign, a commoner named Amunhotep, and Ramose. A relief from Soleb, dating to the king's thirtieth year, depicts the viziers together, demonstrating that their terms overlapped.[45] Moreover, a scene from Ramose's tomb in Western Thebes shows him being rewarded by Akhenaten, indicating that he survived into the next reign.[46] We do not know which man oversaw Lower as opposed to Upper Egypt—presumably, Aper-El governed the north—but it is safe to say that Amunhotep III's last years were crowded with viziers. So where did Aper-El's term fall? It is possible that he served before Amunhotep III's thirtieth year, but his title "first servant of Aten" seems to push his career into Akhenaten's reign. A long co-regency between the two kings would resolve the dilemma, but scholars are divided on this issue.[47] It is also possible that Aper-El filled the position of the commoner

---

[43] Ibid., 109, 131.

[44] Ibid., 157, 60.

[45] C. Aldred, "Two Theban Notables during the Later Reign of Amenophis III," *JNES* 18/2 (April 1959): 117; A. Gordon, "Who was the Southern Vizier during the Last Part of the Reign of Amenhotep III?" *JNES* 48/1 (January 1989): 20ff., fig. 2.

[46] N. de G. Davies, *The Tomb of the Vizier Ramose* (London: Egypt Exploration Society, 1941) pls. 33, 53.

[47] Opinions on the "co-regency problem" are legion and cannot be summarized here.

Amunhotep near the time of Akhenaten's accession and occupied it for a short time. We should not forget that Apy replaced him as steward of Memphis by Akhenaten's fifth year.

However we resolve the dilemma, Aper-El's career almost certainly predates the middle of Akhenaten's reign. While the vizier may have witnessed the establishment of offerings for the Aten in Memphis, he probably did not see the construction of temples to the god. In his tomb, he employed standard reliefs and texts, invoked the customary powers, and briefly mentioned his role in the new cult. Huy, on the other hand, was more influenced by Akhenaten's ideas. He added an Atenist offering formula to the tomb, though, he did not violate any taboos in doing so.

The tomb of Horemheb differs from that of Aper-El in several respects. Most conspicuously, it sits on the Saqqara plateau itself, about 500 meters south of the Step Pyramid, and is of the "chapel" rather than the "rock cut" variety. A scientific report of the tomb's excavation, which began in 1975, has been published by Geoffrey T. Martin and Hans Diederik Schneider.[48] This report permits more certain conclusions, but also engenders an embarrassment of riches.

Horemheb's tomb was built in three stages on an east-west axis. First, a forecourt, an inner court, and a cult room with two side chapels were erected on the site of an earlier burial, which provided a substructure. Second, the original forecourt was divided into a statue room and two magazines, and a new one was constructed to the east. Finally, the new forecourt was converted into an outer court with a pylon-gateway, and a third was added. Martin believes that these modifications reflect the owner's growing power, but he admits that they could have been completed within a few months.[49]

The most recent assessment in English is F. J. Giles, *The Amarna Age: Egypt* (Warminster: Aris and Phillips, 2001) ch. 1.

[48] G. T. Martin et al., *The Memphite Tomb of Horemheb, Commander-in-Chief of Tut'ankhamūn, I: The Reliefs, Inscriptions, and Commentary* (London: Egypt Exploration Society, 1989); H. D. Schneider et al., *The Memphite Tomb of Horemheb, Commander-in-Chief of Tut'ankhamūn, II: A Catalogue of the Finds* (Leiden/London: Rijksmuseum van Oudheden/Egypt Exploration Society, 1996).

[49] Martin et al., *Memphite Tomb of Horemheb, I*, 10.

Horemheb likely began his career under Akhenaten. He may have been the same person as Paatenemheb, a military officer who began a tomb at Amarna.[50] The only difference in their names is the divine element, "Horus" (*ḥr*), as opposed to "the Aten" (*p3 itn*), and this could have been changed after Akhenaten's death.[51] Indeed, their sequential offices suggest that they were one and the same. Paatenemheb was "general" (*m-r mš˓*), "royal scribe" (*sš mš˓*), and "overseer of works at Amarna" (*m-r k3wt m 3ḫt-itn*); Horemheb was "generalissimo" (*m-r mš˓ wr*), "true royal scribe" (*sš nsw m3˓*), and "overseer of works at the mountain of stone" (*m-r k3wt m bi3t*).[52]

Many of the reliefs in Horemheb's inner court celebrate his personal achievements. A scene from the east wall, for instance, depicts the general in the field, receiving the submission of Asiatics, Libyans, and Kushites.[53] The Zizinia Block, discovered during the nineteenth century AD, bears part of its caption:

> He was sent as royal envoy as far as the Aten (*itn*) shines, returning when he had triumphed, his attack having taken place. No land stood firm against him. He overawed it instantly. His name was renowned in the land of the Hittites when he traveled northwards. Lo, His Majesty rose upon the throne of bringing tribute, (and) there was brought to him the tribute of the north and the south (x+2-9).

Although Horemheb certainly did not face Asiatics, Libyans, and Kushites in concert, the relief may commemorate the end of actual operations, for traces of the annalistic expression *ḥsbt*, "regnal year," survive nearby.[54]

---

[50] N. de G. Davies, *The Rock Tombs of El Amarna, Part V: Smaller Tombs and Boundary Stelae* (London: Egypt Exploration Society, 1908) 15.

[51] King Tutankhaten and Queen Ankhesenpaaten set the precedent, changing their names to Tutankhamun and Ankhesenamun.

[52] For a complete list of Horemheb's titles, see R. Hari, *Horemheb et la Reine Moutnedjemet* (Geneva: La Sirène, 1964) pls. 24a–c.

[53] Martin et al., *Memphite Tomb of Horemheb, I*, 78–84, pls. 78–95.

[54] Ibid., 84–86, pls. 96–98.

On the south wall, a king and queen bestow *šbyw*-collars on Horemheb, who is followed by Asiatic captives.[55] The king's name was originally Tutankhamun (ca. 1333–1326 BC), but it has been changed to Horemheb (ca. 1319–1292 BC), so that the general appears to reward himself. On the west wall, the royal pair greets Asiatic princes, whose entreaties are translated by an interpreter and relayed by Horemheb.[56] At the end of the ceremony, Egyptian troops and foreign emissaries salute a lost figure. One of the soldiers is labeled "the standard-bearer of the regiment 'Beloved of the Aten' (*mrwt p3 itn*), Minkhay."

The scenes in Horemheb's outer court are of a similar, though more symbolic, nature. A relief from the south wall, for example, shows Aegeans and Libyans standing before a Window of Appearances.[57] Perhaps the most remarkable scene depicts an official with a hooked nose, double chin, and sagging belly, receiving *šbyw*-collars from a larger man (Figure 2).[58] Normally, in this type of relief, the former figure is the tomb-owner and the latter is the reigning king. In this case, however, the official does not resemble Horemheb at all. Apparently, the larger man is the general—performing a task reserved for rulers.[59]

Figure 2: A Relief of an Official from the Tomb of Horemheb at Saqqara
Courtesy of the Egypt Exploration Society

[55] Ibid., 87–98, pls. 30, 96, 99–108.

[56] Ibid., 94–99, pls. 111–17.

[57] Ibid., 23–28, pls. 15–19.

[58] Ibid., 40–43, pls. 32, 34.

[59] Ibid., 42.

It is evident that Horemheb referred to Akhenaten's god in his tomb. His claim to have traveled "as far as the Aten shines" employs a standard expression and is fairly insignificant, but the name of Minkhay's regiment, "Beloved of the Aten," attests to the deity's continued prominence. In addition, an offering formula near the door to the south magazine reads:

> An offering which the king gives to Re-Harakhty-Atum, lord of Heliopolis. May you cause me to see your Disk (*itn*).[60]

Here, the general expresses a desire to see the Aten after death, a common wish at Amarna.[61]

The hymn carved on the de Rougé Stela, which once stood at the entrance to Horemheb's statue room, likewise evokes Akhenaten's ideas.[62] It describes the god Atum-Harakhty as "effective (*ȝḫti*) and . . . beautiful (*nfrti*), rejuvenated as the Aten (*itn*)" (1–2). It proclaims, "your beauty (*nfrw*) is in my eyes and your rays (*ȝḫw*) are upon my breast" (17). Akhenaten initially associated Re-Harakhty with the Aten and often extolled the god's splendor and radiance.[63] We should also note a seal that refers to the "Temple of Aten in [Helio]polis" (*pr-itn m [iw]nw*) and an abacus fragment that bears the title "overseer of the Temple of A[te]n" (*m-r pr-n-i[t]n*).[64]

It is important to recognize that Horemheb paid homage to many non-solar deities. The lunette of the de Rougé Stela, for instance, shows him worshipping Thoth and Maat as well as Re-Harakhty. Indeed, its hymn not only praises Atum, Harakhty, and the Aten, but also Hathor

---

[60] Ibid., 29, pl. 20.

[61] E. Hornung, *Akhenaten and the Religion of Light*, trans. D. Lorton (Ithaca: Cornell University Press, 1999) 96–99.

[62] Martin et al., *Memphite Tomb of Horemheb*, I, 29–32, pls. 21–22.

[63] J. Assmann, *Egyptian Solar Religion in the New Kingdom: Re, Amun and the Crisis of Polytheism*, trans. A. Alcock (London: Kegan Paul International, 1995) 72–79.

[64] Schneider et al., *Memphite Tomb of Horemheb*, II, 50, pl. 33; Martin et al., *Memphite Tomb of Horemheb*, I, 48, pl. 41. The *mn*-sign (Gardiner Y5) in "Amun" (*imn*) will not fit in the remaining space. The smaller *t*-sign (Gardiner X1) in "Aten" (*itn*) will, however.

(2), Ptah (12), and Sokar (25). Thus, it would be a serious mistake to equate his burial with those at Amarna.

Given the syncretism in Horemheb's tomb, a fragmentary stela from the entrance to his statue room is most intriguing.[65] It preserves the beginning of a hymn to Osiris as the nocturnal manifestation of Re. Egyptians had long associated these two gods—Spell 335 (b) of the *Coffin Texts* says they embraced in the town of Djedu[66]—but this is the earliest inscription that binds them so closely. It calls Osiris "[golden] of body" ([d^cm] h^cw) (5), "beautiful Orion ($s3h$ nfr) who crosses heaven . . . who is carried in pregnancy to the womb of Nut by day and born in profound darkness by night" (7–8). The hymn also refers to the composite god as "the $b3$ of hh and the $3h$ of dt" (7), the daily energy of the sun and the latent power of the lord of the underworld. Martin has argued that this text signals a reaction against Akhenaten's religion, which disregarded Osiris and his realm.[67] It seems more likely, however, that it reflects a compromise between the king's intense solar faith and traditional funerary beliefs.

Archaeologists found a few good chronological markers in Horemheb's tomb. Four wine jar dockets from the burial complex refer to the first year of an unnamed king and to the estate of the "nobleman ($iry-p^ct$) and royal scribe, Horemheb."[68] Reliefs in the tomb's inner court originally depicted Tutankhamun, so his first year probably antedates all of the burials in the tomb. The only good candidate for the unnamed king is Ay (1323–1319 BC), whose prenomen appears on a plaque and a small stela from the substructure. Yet another docket refers to "Year 13" of Horemheb.[69] Most likely, the two dates correspond to the funerals of the general's wives, Amunia and Mutnodjmet, whose remains were discovered in the tomb. Neither can come from Horemheb's own funeral,

---

[65] Martin et al., *Memphite Tomb of Horemheb, I*, 61–69, pls. 66–67.

[66] R. O. Faulkner, *The Ancient Egyptian Coffin Texts* (Warminster: Aris & Phillips, 2004).

[67] Martin et al., *Memphite Tomb of Horemheb, I*, 62–63.

[68] Schneider et al., *Memphite Tomb of Horemheb*, 12, pls. 2–4, 50–51.

[69] Ibid., 18–19, pls. 1, 8, 55–56.

for he eventually assumed the double crown and was ultimately buried in the Valley of the Kings.[70]

Clearly, Horemheb was one of the most powerful men of his day. The Zizinia Block proclaims his notoriety throughout the world, particularly among the Hittites, and a relief from his outer court shows him usurping the royal privilege of awarding *šbyw*-collars. Indeed, close inspection of Zizinia Block reveals that Horemheb used the cartouche determinative (Gardiner V10) when referring to his own name. After assuming the throne, the general acquired such a reputation that his assistant Paramessu, possibly the hook-nosed official depicted in the outer court, was able to succeed him as Ramesses I (ca. 1292–1290 BC).[71]

Horemheb was the only pharaoh of the later fourteenth century BC to escape the censure of subsequent generations.[72] Akhenaten, Smenkhkare, Tutankhamun, and Ay were all execrated. Yet, with the exception of Akhenaten, these kings were more or less orthodox in their piety.[73] And yet could it have been that Horemheb was responsible for their fate? He was not related to the royal house, so his legitimacy was questionable.[74] As such, he may have vilified his predecessors in order to justify his reign. At the very least, he removed Tutankhamun's name from

---

[70] See A. and A. Brack, *Das Grab des Haremheb, Theben Nr. 78* (Mainz am Rhein: Philipp von Zabern, 1980). A third wife, Atuia, is depicted in this tomb.

[71] H.-W. Helck, *Der Einfluss der Militärführer in der 18. ägyptischen Dynastie* (Hildesheim: G. Olms, 1964) 84–87; K. A. Kitchen, *Pharaoh Triumphant: The Life and Times of Ramesses II, King of Egypt* (Warminster: Aris & Phillips, 1985) 16–20.

[72] Their names were omitted from king-lists like the Tables of Abydos and Saqqara. See D. B. Redford, *Pharaonic King-Lists, Annals and Day-Books* (Mississauga: Benben, 1986) ch. 1.

[73] Judging by a graffito in western Thebes, even Smenkhkare made a bow to the traditional gods. A. H. Gardiner, "A Graffito from the Tomb of Pere," *JEA* 14 (1928): 10–11.

[74] The debate over whether Horemheb's wife, Mutnodjmet, was Nefertiti's sister is irrelevant, for Nefertiti was not of royal blood. G. T. Martin, *The Hidden Tombs of Memphis: New Discoveries from the Time of Tutankhamun and Ramesses the Great* (London: Thames and Hudson, 1991) 96. Significantly, even the commoner Ay had an association with Akhenaten's daughter, Ankhesenamun, as attested by a glass ring that joins their cartouches. N. Reeves, "The Royal Family," in *Pharaohs of the Sun: Akhenaten, Nefertiti, Tutankhamun*, ed. R. E. Freed et al. (Boston: Museum of Fine Arts, 1999) 94, fig. 5.

reliefs and appropriated his monuments, most notably his Restoration Edict.[75]

Significantly, Horemheb's tomb at Saqqara contains vestiges of Atenism. The general was inclined towards certain gods (Harakhty, Re, and the Aten), terms (*3ḥw* and *nfrw*), and hopes (seeing the sun after death). As Martin has pointed out, his reliefs even exhibit the naturalism of the Amarna artistic style.[76] Remarkably, the man who may have orchestrated the damnation of Akhenaten's family appears to have retained elements of his religion. At least one of his wives was buried with gifts from the Aten cult.

Maya's tomb, located approximately 30 meters to the north of Horemheb's, is of similar design. It features an outer court with a pylon-gateway, a statue room flanked by two magazines, an inner court with side chapels, and an elaborate substructure. Although we do not possess a complete excavation report for Maya's tomb, we do have a scientific study of its objects and skeletal remains, as well as some preliminary pieces on its contents.[77] Volumes on its architecture and decoration and on its pottery are currently in preparation.

Maya, like Horemheb, probably started out as a servant of Akhenaten. Martin, among others, has asserted that he was the same person as May, an influential courtier at Amarna.[78] The argument is not entirely convincing, however. Although Maya and May had similar names and titles,

---

[75] Murnane, *Texts from the Amarna Period in Egypt*, 212–14.

[76] Martin, *Hidden Tombs of Memphis*, 193.

[77] M. Raven et al., *The Tomb of Maya and Meryt, II, Objects and Skeletal Remains* (Leiden/London: National Museum of Antiquities/Egypt Exploration Society, 2001); G. T. Martin et al., "The Tomb of Maya and Meryt: Preliminary Report on the Saqqâra Excavations, 1987–8," *JEA* 74 (1988): 1–14; H. D. Schneider et al., "The Tomb of Maya and Meryt: Preliminary Report on the Saqqâra Excavations," *JEA* 77 (1991): 7–21; Martin, *Hidden Tombs of Memphis*, ch. 6. Again, unless the articles contain significant additional information, I will only cite the books.

[78] Martin, *Hidden Tombs of Memphis*, 191. See also Davies, *The Rock Tombs of El Amarna, Part V*, 5; J. van Dijk, "The Overseer of the Treasury Maya: A Biographical Sketch." *OMRL* 70 (1990): 26.

the former rose to an eminent bureaucratic position, while the latter was cursed in what appears to have been a fit of royal pique.[79]

A stela from Tutankhamun's eighth year records that Maya was commissioned "to tax the entire land and institute divine offerings [for] all [the gods]" (3–4).[80] It lists his titles as "treasurer" (*m-r prwy-ḥḏ*), "nobleman" (*r-pꜥt*), "count" (*ḥꜥty-ꜥ*), "fan-bearer [at the right hand of the king]" (*ṯꜣw-mḥt* [*ḥr imnty n nsw*]), and "royal scribe" (*sš nsw*) (caption). A graffito, dating to Horemheb's eighth year, also credits Maya with the restoration of Thutmose IV's (ca. 1400–1390 BC) tomb.[81] It calls him "overseer of works in the necropolis" (*m-r kꜣwt m st ḥḥ*) and "leader of the festival of Amun at Karnak" (*sšmw ḥb imn m ipt-swt*). These texts reveal not only that Maya served several kings, but also that he had a reputation for competence and integrity.

The pylon-gateway of Maya's tomb provides further information about his life. On the south jamb, the treasurer, loaded with *šbyw*-collars, and his brother, Nahuher, are greeted by his wife, Meryt, and his stepmother, Henutiunu.[82] The implication is that the men outlived the women. Above the figures is Maya's address to the living:

> . . . the governance which came into being through me, as something that was ordained for me by my God, since my youth, the presence of the King having been granted to me since I was a child. I happily reached the end [of my career], enjoying countless favors of the Lord of the Two Lands. . . . In the beginning I was good, in the end I was brilliant, one who was revered in peace in the temple of Ptah. I carried out the plans of the King of my time without neglecting anything he had commanded . . . [I

---

[79] Van Dijk's theory that Maya erased his autobiography and figures at Amarna is not convincing. Even if he wished to hide his past, he would not have execrated himself. See van Dijk, "Overseer of the Treasury Maya," 26. Cf. A. Dodson, "Death after Death in the Valley of the Kings," in *Death and Taxes in the Ancient Near East*, ed. S. E. Orel (Lewiston, NY: Mellen, 1992) 53–59.

[80] A. A. M. A. Amer, "Tutankhamun's Decree for the Chief Treasurer Maya," *RdE* 36 (1985): 17–20.

[81] H. Carter et al., *The Tomb of Thoutmôsis IV* (Westminster: Constable, 1904) xxxiii–xxxiv.

[82] Martin, *Hidden Tombs of Memphis*, 171–74.

made splendid?] the temples, fashioning the images of the gods for whom I was responsible. I entered face to face to the August Image (of Atum); it was his eldest son (Shu) who [. . .].[83]

A detailed discussion of this text must await the report on the tomb's architecture and decoration, but a few comments are in order. The address underscores Maya's influence and piety, revealing that he even had access to Atum's holy of holies. At the same time, it does not mention any of his masters by name. Martin contends that this reticence is a result of Akhenaten's execration.[84] Yet, he also notes that a devout "King of my time," probably Tutankhamun, goes unnamed as well.[85] If silence implies censure, then the text also reflects the proscription of Akhenaten's immediate successors.

Curiously, the reliefs in Maya's inner court do not resemble those in Horemheb's. Instead of commemorating the treasurer's achievements, they focus on his religiosity and his mortuary cult. One block, for instance, depicts Maya adoring the cow of Hathor.[86] It also shows him sitting with his wife, being censed and receiving offerings. The only exceptions to this rule include lists of Maya's titles, and a single representation of him supervising the registration of Asiatic prisoners and cattle.[87]

Several stela fragments were found in Maya's outer court that preserve part of a litany to the nocturnal sun previously unattested until the Ramesside Age (ca. 1292–1075 BC).[88] This litany includes the following verses:

> Hail to you, highest of the gods,
> Who illuminates the underworld with his eye.
> Hail to you, who travels in his splendor,
> Who voyages as "he who is in his Disk (*itn*)."

---

[83] For this translation, see ibid., 173.

[84] Ibid., 172.

[85] Tutankhamun's Two Ladies Name includes the epithet "who propitiates all the gods" (*shtp-ntrw-nbw*).

[86] Martin, *Hidden Tombs of Memphis*, 160–61.

[87] Ibid., 161.

[88] Martin et al., "Tomb of Maya and Meryt," 11.

Hail to you, who is greater than the gods,
Lord of the sunrise in the sky, ruler of the underworld (3–5).[89]

These lines, which describe the sun as a supreme and chthonic deity, complement a series of striking reliefs in Maya's burial complex.[90] Although these reliefs feature funerary gods like Osiris, Anubis, and Sokar, they are painted a dazzling yellow-gold, and thus presuppose the presence of the sun god.

Throughout Maya's burial complex, archaeologists discovered a great many human bones. Eugen Strouhal has carefully studied these remains and has argued that they correspond to five individuals: a male of sixty, a male of forty-five or fifty, a female of fifty or fifty-five, a female of forty, and a sub-adult of thirteen or fourteen.[91] He identifies these individuals as Maya, an unknown brother, Henutiunu, Meryt, and an unknown child (respectively). Within burial chamber H, excavators found a docket bearing a date of "Year 9."[92] The corresponding king is likely Horemheb, whose cartouches also appear on an ivory inlay fragment,[93] but he could conceivably be Tutankhamun.

Information about Maya's tomb is fairly limited, but there are a few valuable clues about its chronology. The south jamb of the pylon-gateway indicates that Meryt predeceased her husband, and the analysis of her presumed remains suggests that she was relatively young when she died. The graffito from Thutmose IV's tomb reveals that Maya was still alive in Horemheb's eighth year, and Jacobus van Dijk has assigned, with some justification, the "Year 9" (of Horemheb?) docket to his funeral.[94] Thus, the tomb's construction may have begun as early as Tutankhamun's reign, and its occupants may have been interred over a period of two decades.

---

[89] For the entire hymn, see J. Assmann, *Liturgische Lieder an den Sonnengott* (Berlin: Hessling, 1969) 77–89, 409.

[90] Martin, *Hidden Tombs of Memphis*, 178–88, pls 10–11. I had the privilege of attending a slide presentation on these reliefs at the Cincinnati Art Museum in 1995.

[91] Raven et al., *Tomb of Maya and Meryt, II*, 82–86.

[92] Ibid., 2.

[93] Ibid., 60, pls. 25, 40.

[94] Van Dijk, "Overseer of the Treasury Maya," 26.

In that case, as Maarten Raven has noted, its contents do not constitute a time capsule, but a generation's legacy.[95]

Maya's reluctance to mention former kings by name hints that the damnation of Akhenaten and his immediate successors occurred before the Ramessie Age, confirming scholars' suspicions about Horemheb. In addition, the treasurer shows little interest in the Aten cult. Were it not for his litany to the nocturnal sun and his brilliant subterranean reliefs, we might regard him as a particularly dull sort of traditionalist. But these elements attest to a vigorous solarization of the afterlife, a development which, once again, may well be related to Atenism.

Returning to Memphis itself, a final document must be considered. Papyrus Rollin 1882, which dates to the reign of Sety I (ca. 1290–1279 BC), records a delivery of wood to the Mansion of the Aten in the city (fragment a, *recto*, 4–5).[96] Curiously, the word *itn* carries the seated god determinative (Gardiner A40) rather than the sun determinative (Gardiner N5). Akhenaten represented the sun god as a being without anthropomorphic features, except for the hands in which his rays ended. Now, however, the Aten appears to have assumed a more conventional form. The change corresponds to the last phase of Atenism in Memphis. In subsequent decades, Ramesses II mined the Aten's temples for building materials, and the region's wet soil covered what little remained in place.

In view of the evidence just considered, it is extremely difficult to conclude that Akhenaten's only followers were the voluptuaries of his court, and that all of his ideas were abandoned after his death. Early on, the king advanced the Aten cult in several places, most notably in Memphis. Initially, he co-opted the altars and sunshades of Re, and, later, he built temples. Naturally, he appointed his supporters to high offices, but they were not all *novi homini*. The first servant of Aten, Aper-El, had been raised in the palace nursery, and had served Amunhotep III. After Akhenaten's demise, his temples remained open. His successor, Smenkhkare, even added to them. At the same time, however, Akhenaten's

---

[95] Raven et al., *Tomb of Maya and Meryt, II*, 3.

[96] Löhr, "Aḫanyāti in Memphis," 146–47.

revolutionary solar faith was fused with traditional funerary beliefs, and his god assumed an anthropomorphic form within the old pantheon.

Atenism's strength in Memphis was probably due to two factors. First, the city is only 25 kilometers south of Heliopolis, the ancient center of sun worship and the wellspring of Akhenaten's ideas. From Heliopolis came the Atenist title "greatest of seers," as well as the Atenist veneration of the Mnevis Bull.[97] The town boasted at least two new temples, the aforementioned Temple of Aten and the "Lifting of Re in Heliopolis of Re" (*wṯs-rꜥ m iwnw rꜥ*).[98] Second, Memphis was most likely the residence of Tutankhamun and Ay. Some Egyptologists maintain that Thebes served as their capital, but the city of Ptah is a better candidate, especially given the contemporary construction in its necropolis.[99] If Memphis hosted the royal court, then it became the home of Akhenaten's most devoted followers as well as his ateliers. The influence of the Amarna artistic style on reliefs in Horemheb's tomb may be understood in this light.

In closing, a growing problem in the study of Akhenaten's reign must be acknowledged. This essay, like many others, has supposed that the king launched a persecution of traditional gods in his ninth year. Increasingly, however, scholars like Rolf Krauss have taken issue with this view.[100] While Akhenaten certainly attacked the cults of Amun, Mut, and Khonsu in the third and fourth nomes of Upper Egypt, he does not seem to have assailed other deities throughout the Nile Valley. He preferred to ignore Osiris, and he did not attack Ptah outside of Thebes. As such, we may wonder whether moderate Atenism was the norm in Lower Egypt. Hopefully, future publication of discoveries from Memphis and Saqqara will clarify the situation.

---

[97] Redford, *Akhenaten*, 179–80; Aldred, *Akhenaten, King of Egypt*, 260.

[98] L. Habachi, "Akhenaten in Heliopolis," *BABA* 12 (1971): 35–45; "H. S. K. Bakry, "Akhenaten at Heliopolis," *CdE* 47 (1972): 55–67.

[99] See J. van Dijk and M. Eaton-Krauss, "Tutankhamun at Memphis," *MDAIK* 42 (1986): 35–41. See also J. van Dijk, "The Development of the Memphite Necropolis in the Post-Amarna Period," in *Memphis et ses nécropoles au Nouvel Empire*, ed. A.-P. Zivie (Paris: Centre National de la Recherche Scientifique, 1988) 37–46.

[100] R. Krauss, "Akhenaten: Monotheist? Polytheist?" *BACE* 11 (2000): 93–101.

Biblical Treasures
in Private Holdings
The Van Kampen Collection

Scott Carroll

❧ONE OF THE most regrettable tragedies in cultural history was the destruction of the Library at Alexandria. Hundreds of years of history literally went up in smoke in a fire that reduced to ashes hundreds of thousands of scrolls. The exact number of scrolls and the titles of the works were lost as a result of this tragedy. Scholars are painfully aware of the loss of texts and, sometimes, the willful obliteration of the Classical record. The discovery of preserved ancient archives has provided invaluable information. Texts from Ebla, Nuzi, Ugarit, Amarna, Nineva, Elephantina, Oxyrhynchus, Qumran and the Judean Desert, Nag Hammadi, Mt. St. Catherine's Monastery, the Cairo Geniza and the monasteries of Mt. Athos, to name but a few, have preserved vital information. Without these repositories any attempt to reconstruct the past would be beset by nagging problems, and any attempt to cast light on the past would, in reality, be groping in the dark.

There are, however, hidden archives that are more elusive to professional academic scholars than the sands of time. These archives are buried around the world, rich in treasures beyond imagination. They contain tens of thousands of undocumented ancient and medieval texts of immense importance and value. Hidden where pick and trowel will never penetrate, these archives are locked away in private archives, concealed by fences, guards, vaults, mystique and enormous wealth. Scholars are accustomed to scorpions, snakes, and stifling heat, but are unfamiliar with the obstacles and dangers found in the secret world of private collections.

Perhaps one reason why scholars steer clear of these repositories is because the sources often come without provenance, raising serious questions about their authenticity and rightful ownership. The antiquities market fences stolen artifacts, and has often duped collectors, museums, and well-intended scholars with forgeries. Consequently, there is justifiable caution regarding the legal status of the items in private collections. Oddly, scholars often do not have the same concerns about objects in special collection libraries and museums, which often come from the sources they denounce. Items in private collections are frequently purchased at auction from upstanding institutions like Sotheby's and Christie's. Sometimes they come through dealers who specialize in various kinds of artifacts. In either case, the items typically come with a history of the most immediate provenance at the very least, and often a more extensive history of the item's ownership.

Dealers are usually very secretive and protective of their sources. After all, such is their livelihood. This does not mean, however, that items can not be sufficiently documented. With the case of written materials, the provenance may be recovered by means of careful analysis of the object itself, the composition and nature of the material on which it is written, the orthography, and the content of the written text. It is for reasons such as these that researchers apply a less scrupulous and condemnatory attitude toward unprovenanced written items.

The owners of private archives have spent an enormous amount of money on items in their collection, and in no way want to tarnish their reputation, which is often public, or risk losing their investment along with the item they purchased. The Schøyen Collection, the largest private collection of biblical antiquities in private hands in the world, is unofficially on sale for 65 million dollars, while the Van Kampen Collection, the second largest private collection, is insured for 40 million dollars.[1] Another multimillion dollar collection of biblical manuscripts and rare printed Bibles is owned by Dr. Charles Ryrie, retired biblical scholar and commentator.[2] When collectors have invested enormous wealth to attain their collections, it is understandable that they would want to ward off any doubts or accusations regarding questions of authenticity and legal

[1] A fascinating study of the mind and passion of a book collector is Nicholas A. Basbanes, *A Gentle Madness* (New York: Holt, 1995).

[2] Valerie R. Hotchkiss, Charles C. Ryrie, and Duane Harbin, *Formatting the Word of God: The Charles Caldwell Ryrie Collection* (Dallas, TX: Bridwell Library, 1998).

ownership. This is one of the primary reasons why collectors are so secretive and protective of their collections. But being secretive should not be interpreted as a sign of guilt. The point is that while caution is advised, items in private collections are most often legally and legitimately acquired, but unknown.[3]

Scholars can be a bit duplicitous when it comes to sources. It is often the wealthy collectors who fund research, endow universities, and support museums, and all are more than happy to spend their money. Scholars can also have a short term memory. Dissertations and careers have been made on items of questionable provenance. They conveniently forget the intrigue that surrounded the discovery of the Bodmer Papyri and how they were smuggled out of Egypt in Red Cross bags. Items once part of the Dead Sea Scrolls, texts from Nag Hammadi, and leaves from the Cairo Genizah have all found their way to private collections or are presently for sale. What is to be said of Chester Beatty and the University of Michigan competing for biblical manuscripts held by a Cairo antiquities dealer? It wasn't that long ago that a Hebrew scroll was offered for sale in the *Wall Street Journal.* What should be done with Gnostic texts held by private individuals or research centers? If a highly reputed scholar from an Ivy League institution attempted to broker the sale of a significant, undocumented fragment from the Dead Sea Scrolls of a major prophet, should a reputable scholar get involved?

In the course of my work with items that came my way through the London dealer, I learned that they were being offered to a collector in the greater Chicago area. As it turned out, the collector wanted to bring definition and purpose to his collection and so I was introduced to him. I was given the opportunity to research the collection, to develop an acquisition strategy, to hire capable staff, and to research items that were virtually unknown. This invitation opened a door of immense opportunity and challenge to me. I found myself surrounded by fascinating items that spanned four millennia. It would prove to be the largest private holding of biblical antiquities and Bibles in the world in the 1990s.

---

[3] Private collections often become institutionalized like the Morgan Library and Museum, the Newberry Libarary, the Huntington Library, and the J. Paul Getty Museum, to name a few.

The collection was called the (Robert) Van Kampen Collection and the entity created around it was called The Scriptorium: Center for Christian Antiquities. Both the language training I received while studying under Dr. Yamauchi, and his steadfast support helped me in this enormous venture. Dr. Yamauchi, along with Drs. Bruce Metzger and Bastiaan Van Elderen served on my academic advisory board at the Scriptorium. What follows is a description of the holdings, particularly as they pertain to ancient and biblical studies and an analysis of the unpublished Old Testament Coptic parchment in the collection.

An Overview of the Van Kampen Collection

Cuneiform

There are well over 1,000 pieces of cuneiform dating from the Old Akkadian to the Persian period in the Van Kampen Collection (hereafter VKC).[4] Most of these were purchased in a single lot in 1995. The tablets include a number of Guti dedication cones containing important historical data, however, most of the tablets come from the Ur III period and include primarily economic and sacrificial records. Several of them are sealed with cultic imprints, one with Inanna enthroned. The cuneiform collection also includes lexical, historical, literary, and documentary tablets from the Assyrian, Neo-Babylonian, and Persian periods. The impressive cuneiform collection includes an undocumented fragment of the well-known Sennacherib Prism (see Figure 1). Three of the eight sides, or columns, have been preserved in part,[5] including a section that describes Sennacherib's confrontation with Jerusalem and the later homage of Hezekiah to his Assyrian overlord, a detail alluded to in the biblical

---

[4] This portion of the collection was studied by Erle V. Leichty, Alan Millard, and Richard Averbeck.

[5] It is a well-known practice to place fragments of duplicate historical tablets, which had been ceremonially destroyed, in the foundations of new buildings. As a result, there are a number of fragments of the Sennacherib Prism known. See for example: Jerrod S. Cooper, "A New Sennacherib Prism Fragment," *Journal of Cuneiform Studies* 26 (January 1974): 59–62 and Julian Reade, "Sources for Sennacherib: The Prisms," *Journal of Cuneiform Studies* 27 (October 1975):189–96.

text, but overshadowed by Jerusalem's miraculous deliverance from the Assyrians.[6] A nearly-intact, large royal cylindrical tablet, resembling the Cyrus Cylinder text, but dedicated to Nebuchadnezzer II, is also in the collection.

Papyri

Also in the collection are over 5,000 pieces of papyri, almost exclusively purchased in one lot in 1994 from a Jordanian family through the London dealer mentioned above. The papyri span from pharaonic times through the Byzantine period. A small portion is written in Egyptian Hieroglyphics, Hieratic and Demotic. Some of these are decorated with crude mythological and ritual vignettes. There are over 1000 complete or near complete sheets of Arabic papyri in the collection, containing both literary and documentary texts. Of great interest are several leaves of the Quran, written in a crude hand, dating to the late eighth or early ninth century, which is exceptionally early for Quranic texts. These particular papyri contain some fascinating textual variations from the accepted reading of the Qu'ran.[7] The Arabic collection of papyri itself constitutes a very large and extremely early collection of Arabic papyri for the west.

The collection also contains a variety of Greek and Coptic papyri, including a second-century-BC fragment of Herodotus which dates amongst the earliest witnesses to Herodotus, apart from a fragment from Duke[8] and from texts in a recently identified cache from Oxyrhynchus.[9] The text for Herodotus has been based on eight late manuscripts that date over a thousand years later than this particular papyrus. This papyrus and many other items from the collection described here await publication. The vast majority of the papyri date from the late Roman

---

[6] Compare the Assyrian record with 2 Kings 18:13—19:37 and Isaiah 36:1—37:38.

[7] For more on this matter see: James A. Bellamy, "Textual Criticism of the Koran", *Journal of the American Oriental Society* 121 (2001): 1–6.

[8] Herodotus, *Historiae* 4:144–45 (P. Duke. Inv. 756); Rosalia G Hatzilambrou, ed. "A Duke Papyrus of Herodotus iv, 144.2–145.1," *Bulletin of the American Society of Papyrologists* 39 (2002): 41–45.

[9] J. R. Rea, ed. *The Oxyrhynchus Papyri*, vol. 48 (London: The British Academy by the Egypt Exploration, 1981).

to the early Byzantine period. Most of the Coptic papyri were produced in monastic settings. The Greek and Coptic papyri comprised of literary, biblical, homiletic, hagiographical, and documentary texts, including a large number of Coptic letters.[10]

Miscellaneous Artifacts

Mummy wrappings on fine linen with ritualistic texts from the Egyptian Book of the Dead,[11] several ostraca with Coptic letters, slip washed writing boards, inscriptions, Roman coins, and Aramaic magic bowls round out the holdings of ancient artifacts. While these items are not germane to the collection, these miscellaneous artifacts offer examples of various writing formats, and also help to illustrate various aspects from the time the Bible was composed. The cuneiform and papyri constitute one of the largest collections of these materials in private hands in the world.

Greek Manuscripts

There are eleven Greek biblical manuscripts in the collection.[12] The earliest manuscript of this collection is a minuscule Gospel dating to the early ninth century AD, making it one of the earliest of its kind in the world. The hand is very similar to the earliest known minuscule New Testament manuscript, dating to the first half of the ninth century (see Figure 2). The earliest minuscule manuscripts represent an interesting period of transition, and carry a special weight of authority: being one step away from their lost uncial exemplars. This manuscript is unrecorded, and contains a number of early readings, including the omission of the pericope of the woman taken in adultery (John 7:53–8:11).[13] The account of the adulterer has been written in the margin by a later hand, which only exists in one other manuscript that omits the passage, vividly illustrating the interaction between reader and text over time. The transmission of

[10] These materials were examined by Leslie MacCoull and Roger Bagnall.

[11] These items were examined by James Hoffmeier.

[12] These items were examined by Bruce Metzger, Scot McKendrick and many others.

[13] Bruce M. Metzger, *Textual Commentary on the Greek New Testament*, 2d ed., (New York: The American Bible Society, 1994) 187–89.

scripture was not a static process. The manuscript includes early portraits of the Evangelists and a baptismal prayer with formulae and quotations of Scripture that seem to indicate that the prayer was in use in the second century, making it the earliest baptismal prayer known.[14]

There is also another interesting, unrecorded manuscript of the Gospels dating to 1271 in the collection, fancifully written in three colors of ink for liturgical direction to the reader, as well as for emphasis. Though late in date, it contains a number of early readings, including the omission of John 7:53—8:11. The manuscript offers an interesting solution for the ending of the Gospel of Mark, recording both the short and the long endings and claiming in colophons after both that each is the correct ending for Mark. This is an interesting variation on a theme found in some other manuscripts that clearly end Mark with the shorter ending and insert asterisks or obeli around the longer ending to signify that they considered the passage to be spurious. Luke 22:43–44 is also absent from this manuscript making it only one of seven Greek manuscripts to support this early reading.[15]

The Greek manuscripts include a tenth- and an eleventh-century Gospel, an eleventh-century Lectionary, and two manuscripts of the Acts of the Apostles and the Pauline Epistles dating to the twelfth century. One of the latter manuscripts has an extremely rare miniature depicting the conversion of Paul in an upper register, and Paul being beheaded in a lower register. While the pictures bear a similarity to several frescoes in Italy, there is no other composition like it in any manuscripts. There is also a fourteenth-century New Testament manuscript written in an uncial hand. While it is rare, a few biblical manuscripts dating to the late medieval period were written in a retro script. In addition, the collection has an illuminated manuscript of the prophets, a Psalter and a Gospel written on paper, dating from the sixteenth to the eighteenth centuries.

[14] S. T. Carroll, and Bastiaan Van Elderen, "A Recently Discovered 2nd Century Baptismal Prayer." A paper given at the annual session of the Evangelical Theological Society, 1997.

[15] Metzger, *Commentary*, 151.

Syriac Manuscripts

The VKC also has several important Syriac manuscripts of Scripture, including the so-called Yonan Codex, purported to have been the oldest Gospel in Jesus' language.[16] The manuscript toured the U. S. in the mid-1950s in a special bus, and was displayed at the Library of Congress. This had more to do with marketing and driving up the value of the manuscript than it did with biblical scholarship. The manuscript was offered for sale for one million dollars.[17] The sensationalism that surrounded it, however, was quelled by the discovery of the scrolls from the Judean desert. The manuscript was purchased by the Van Kampen's for a quarter of a million dollars prior to the establishment of the Scriptorium. Upon further investigation after the establishment of the Scriptorium, it became evident that the Yonan Codex dated somewhere between the ninth and the tenth centuries AD. While its medieval Syriac text, known as the Peshitto text, was of great interest, it in no way bore the significance ascribed to it earlier. The manuscript is best known for the fanfare and false claims made about it than for its textual significance.

The VKC also has a Peshitto Pentateuch, dating roughly to the same time as the Yonan Codex, but extremely early for the rarer Syriac Pentateuch. The manuscript includes text-critical symbols that were used to reference Origen's masterwork in textual criticism, the Hexapla. These marks are not uncommon in Syriac Old Testament manuscripts, and retain access to the Hexapla that, apart from a lone palimpsest leaf in Syriac, is no longer extent. Perhaps of greatest interest in the Syriac material is a small format Syriac Psalter, likely from the Monastery of Mt. St. Catherine, dating to the seventh century. There is one other Syriac item that will be mentioned briefly with a summary description of the Coptic parchment below.

---

[16] These items were examined by Tjitze Baarda, Rob Hiebert and others.

[17] Bruce M. Metzger, "The Saga of the Yonan," *Reminiscences of an Octogenarian* (Peabody, MA: Hendrickson, 1997) 103–16.

Coptic Manuscripts

There are a number of important Coptic manuscripts of the Bible in the collection as well. The best known is the so-called Mississippi Codex II, consisting of a portion of Jeremiah, the complete Book of Lamentations, and a portion of the Pseudepigraphical Book of Baruch (see Figure 3). It was once part of a more extensive manuscript purchased along with others by the University of Mississippi in 1955.[18] The university eventually sold the Coptic collection and split the Mississippi Codex into two parts. Mississippi Codex I,[19] which was purchased by the Schøyen Collection, is also known as the Crosby-Schøyen Codex[20]; Mississippi Codex II was acquired by VKC[21]. It is ironic that the two largest private collections would purchase portions of this important manuscript. Both are connected closely with P. Bodmer XXII at the Bibliotheca Bodmeriana in Geneva, Switzerland.[22] The manuscript, which is written in Sahidic Coptic, dates to the mid-fourth century AD. In addition, there is a Coptic papyrus fragment in the VKC of a homily that quotes from Jeremiah 5:19–20 on the verso, and the recto may refer to Jeremiah 5:26 (see Figure 4). The text dates to the last half of the sixth century and may have actually come from the library of the Bishop of the Egyptian city of Coptos. There is also a late bilingual (Coptic-Arabic) Gospel in the VKC from Wadi Natrun, the center of early monastic development in Egypt. The bilingual manuscript illustrates the Coptic Christians' loss of ability to speak and read Coptic as a result of the Arab conquerors of Egypt's ban on the language in the seventh century.

The collection presently includes around 130 parchment texts, with the exception of one written on paper.[23] The entire collection is no lon-

---

[18] *New York Times*, "Two Ancient Mss. Being Deciphered" (NYT, Feb 12, 1956. pg. 107). The University of Mississippi bought the codices for $5,000.

[19] J. E. Goehring, ed., *The Crosby-Schøyen Codex MS 193 in the Schøyen Collection* (CSCO 521; Leuven: Peeters, 1990).

[20] See: http://www.nb.no/baser/schoyen/4/4.1/413.html.

[21] See: http://www.solagroup.org/vkc/ancient.html.

[22] R. Kasser. *Papyrus Bodmer, XXII et Mississippi Coptic Codex II Jérémie XL, 3-LII, 34; Lamentations; Epître de Jérémie; Baruch I, 1–V, 5en sahidique.* Cologny-Geneva, 1964.

[23] The Coptic manuscripts were examined by Stephen Emmel, Gawdat Gabra and Leslie

ger intact. Ten manuscript leaves stayed in the possession of the dealer, several of which have been sold elsewhere. The collection originally consisted of approximately 170 leaves, but many were found to join together. None of the texts are more extensive than a bifolio leaf, although several of the bifolio leaves may have been bound together. The texts date from the fourth to tenth centuries AD. The cache of parchment was acquired through the dealer in London in 1993–94. The leaves have been given a number and letter, which are written in pencil on the leaves and on a tissue paper used to wrap the leaves. There are numerous gaps in the numbers and letters in this collection, indicating that others once existed, and have been sold. Attempts to identify some of the texts were also recorded on the tissue paper, along with an estimated date. The leaves were then put in envelopes, which were also numbered. There is no apparent correlation between the numbers on the tissues and the envelope numbers, or between the various leaves in any given folder.

The only clue regarding the manuscripts' immediate provenance was a lone letter-sized envelope holding a small fragment with the following printed as a return address: Harold H. Von Maker, Stone Eagles, Montclair, NJ. I have asked the London dealer repeatedly about where he had acquired them, but he never revealed his source. Another dealer/collector from Philadelphia claims to have seen the items prior to their purchase by the London dealer. A match for one of the leaves was found in the Coptic collection at the British Library. There are, doubtless, more to be found there and elsewhere. All of the leaves, with the exception of one, are written in Sahidic Coptic, the dialect of Upper Egypt. The lone exception is written in Bohairic, the other dominant medieval Coptic dialect.

Many of the gospel leaves resemble extant codex leaves and codices produced at the White Monastery in Upper Egypt; the monastery was founded by Pachomius (290–346), the originator of cenobitic monasticism. The VKC Coptic material includes numerous texts of Scripture from both the Old and the New Testament, and a palimpsest manuscript of the Gospel of John, based on orthographic analysis, dating to the early

MacCoull.

half of the fourth century AD. There are no less than eight manuscripts in the Coptic material that date unequivocally to the fourth century, extraordinarily early for Coptic texts. This compilation of early dated Coptic manuscripts does not include the paleographic analysis of underlying palimpsest texts yet to be studied. Most of these underlying texts are made legible by illuminating them with ultra violet light. Several manuscripts are decorated with braided headpieces, marginal decorations, rubrications, and faint traces of letters that were colored in red, yellow or green circles in the margin. In one case, a delicate drawing of two roosters crowing illustrates a passage from I Peter. There are several retrievable decorations on palimpsest manuscript leaves as well.

All of the underlying texts of the palimpsests leaves are written in Coptic, with the exception of three written in Syriac. Based on the dating of the exterior Coptic text, the Syriac manuscripts were reused in the fifth century. The Syriac text in each is written in a minuscule, elegant, Estrangela book hand—the letters measuring between .5 and 1.5 centimeters (see Figure 5). This is certainly the earliest Syriac manuscript in the collection and consequently of great interest. It appears that all three Syriac palimpsest leaves came from the same manuscript. They may have originated in Deir al-Suryani, in Wadi Natrun or ancient Scetis, one of the earliest semi-cenobitic monastic communities in Egypt.

In addition to biblical texts, the VKC Coptic parchments include unknown homiletic works, hagiographies, theological tractates, and documentary materials. The hagiographic material includes a fragment of the Martyrdom of St. Victor, a portion of the Metaphrasis of John the Apostle by his disciple Prochoros (which I worked on in 1993–94 with an undergraduate student , funded by the National Endowment for the Humanities). The collection also includes a text on Antony (AD 251–356), the founder of solitary monasticism and one-time resident of Scetis, and of Pachomius (AD 290–346), mentioned above. There is also an undocumented female martyrdom account, several texts on Colluthos, a Coptic anagyros, and a text mentioning the most prolific Coptic author of all, Shenoute (died AD 466). The collection also includes homilies, liturgical works including lectionaries, prayer books, and several undocumented apocryphal gospels. One of the apocryphal gospels is on a double-columned folio leaf containing, in first person, a dialogue between Jesus and Judas. It may be connected to the recently-published Gospel of Judas. The recto of this leaf was covered with mollified animal glue and blank papyrus. It may have had a secondary use as a paste down in the cartonage to stiffen the cover of another folio. The manuscripts also include a tract correcting Christological heresy. Two leaves appear to have some relationship to Gnosticism. One text was written against the false-possessors of so-called knowledge, and discusses their misunderstanding of the relationship between the flesh and the spirit, while another tract is attributed to a person named Mani. Over time the content of these fascinating documents will be revealed. The Old Testament documents will be discussed in greater detail at the conclusion of this chapter.

Latin Manuscripts

There are a number of important Latin manuscripts in the collection as well.[24] The earliest Latin text contains the Gospel of Matthew with the commentary of Claudius of Turin dating to AD 830. The collection also has several eleventh- to twelfth-century glossed texts of the Bible. Of particular interest is a twelfth-century glossed manuscript of the Epistles of Paul which contains a number of Vetus Latina readings. There are several thirteenth-century Paris Vulgates in the collection and several later Vulgates filled with illuminations, historated initials, marginal flourishes, headbands, and illuminated days of creation.

Perhaps of greatest interest among the Latin manuscripts is the little known Codex Wernegerodensis, dating to AD 1409 (see Figure 6). The small manuscript of the New Testament is written on paper, and is worn and soiled. While the manuscript is the least expensive Latin Manuscript in the VKC, it preserves a rich early text, important notes and translations in the vernacular: the Bohemian of the Hussite proto-reform movement. In a number of places, particularly in the Book of Acts, the manuscript has preserved readings from the *Vetus Latina* making it of great significance for textual studies. These texts are generally mixed *Vetus Latina*,

---

[24] These manuscripts were examined by Richard Marsden, Christopher de Hamel and others.

and Vulgate. Two of the Latin manuscripts omit the so-called Johannine Comma (I John 5:7). This Trinitarian passage is only found in Vulgate manuscripts after the sixth century with the exception of two extremely late and dubious Greek manuscripts.

Hebrew and Aramaic Manuscripts

A large number of late medieval and early-modern Hebrew and Aramaic manuscripts are in the VKC.[25] They include medieval Bible leaves, two leaves from Massoretic codices, one of which survived the Inquisition as a cover of a sixteenth-century Christian work, two leaves apparently from the Cairo Genizah, written on vellum dating to the thirteenth century—one of Genesis and the other of Isaiah, Aramaic Targum leaves, a complete Targum codex on paper with Palestinian pointing dating to the fifteenth century, bifolio leaves of the Samaritan Pentateuch, over fifty Hebrew Torah and Haftorah scrolls, illuminated Esther scrolls, and other scrolls of various biblical books, including a rare scroll of Isaiah. There are only three other Isaiah scrolls known in private hands. There is also a partial scroll containing Genesis from the Jewish community at Kai-Feng, China, in the collection. This particular scroll is water damaged, perhaps indicating that it was among the early scrolls from the community, and one that survived a devastating fifteenth-century flood. It is written on parchment made from antelope. There is also a Hebrew Bible codex in the collection dating to 1468, called the Seville Bible. The Massorah are embroidered in a beautiful micrographic script in an interlaced design, and framed by a woven tapestry of minuscule words. Likely the oldest scroll in the collection is a tattered Haftorah, which includes an extensive, illuminating colophon, somewhat unusual for Hebrew scrolls.

Biblical Manuscripts in Secondary Ancient Languages

In addition to manuscripts described briefly above, VKC also has several Armenian manuscripts, one beautifully illuminated, dating from the

---

[25] These manuscripts were examined by Emanuel Tov, Michael Pollack and others.

seventeenth century.[26] There are also one Georgian and two Old Church Slavonic manuscripts dating to the sixteenth century, including one with an extremely rare uncial Slavonic Gospel leaf incorporated in the inside cover dating to the eleventh century. There are also seven nineteenth- to early twentieth-century Ethiopic Bibles in the collection written in Amharic.

Other Vernacular Manuscripts and Rare Books

While outside the immediate scope of this overview, the VKC includes vernacular manuscripts in German, Bohemian, Dutch, and French, not to mention five Wycliffe Biblical manuscripts and one Lectionary, making for the largest collection of Wycliffe manuscripts outside of Europe.[27] In addition, there is a vast array of rare printed materials in the collection, including the complete text of Daniel from Gutenberg's 46-line Bible, numerous incunabula, one of the most comprehensive holdings of German Bibles, fifteenth-century Greek Bibles, polyglot Bibles, and English Bibles, including a first edition Tyndale Pentateuch and a second edition Tyndale New Testament.[28] As for American Bibles, the collection has an Eliot Indian Bible, the Saur Bible, and the Aiken Bible.

The Eberhard Nestle Collection: An Introduction

The VKC houses the library of the eminent German biblical scholar, Eberhard Nestle (1851–1913), and professor at Ulm and Maulbronn (see Figure 7).[29] Nestle published two critical editions of the Septuagint and several editions of the Psalms before he ventured into New Testament textual criticism. He is best known for his critical text of the New Testament published in 1898, known as the Stuttgart text. It was revised in 1901

---

[26] The Armenian manuscripts were examined by Sylvie Merien.

[27] The Wycliffe manuscripts were examined by Christina von Nolken.

[28] The incunabula and rare printed books were examined by Paul Saenger, David Daniell and Paul Needham.

[29] Warren Kay, "The Life and Work of Eberhard Nestle" in *The Bible As Book: The Transmission of the Greek Text* edited by Scot McKendrick and Orlaith O'Sullivan (London: The British Library & Oak Knoll, 2003).

and 1903, and was republished by the British Foreign Bible Society in 1904. The New Testament was revised by his son, Erwin, and is presently in the twenty-seventh edition.

Eberhard Nestle was both a scholar and a bibliophile. The intact library reveals the resources and interests of this prodigious scholar. One sees it as it was in Nestle's day. In the year of his death, his library was attained by his lifelong friends, the sisters Margaret Gibson and Agnes Lewis. They were scholars in their own right, involved with the discovery of the Cairo Genizah and the placement of the genizah manuscripts at Cambridge University. They also published an important palimpsest Syriac biblical manuscript they discovered at Mt. St. Catherine Monastery. The sisters' family home was given to Westminster College at Cambridge, and Nestle's library went along with the house, where it remained for nearly one hundred years. The library was stored in a dimly lit, empty room on the second floor of the main building at Westminster College, behind a locked door. It was acquired for the VKC in 1996 from Westminster College at Cambridge for roughly $145,000. It was considered a steal, literally, especially by the Institute for New Testament Textual Research at the University of Münster (Westphalia, Germany). They had a museum on the text transmission of the Greek Bible, and given their continued commitment to Nestle's life work, believed themselves to be the rightful recipients of his library. They believed that it would only be appropriate to have the library in Germany rather than in the possession of a wealthy American family and housed with, at that time, an unknown collection. But Westminster needed money, not goodwill. The Institue at Münster failed to raise the necessary funds to purchase the library and lost their opportunity to attain it.

The library contains over 4,500 books, journals, pamphlets, offprints, and Nestle's own slip-paper index made up of his own handwritten book entry, and the cost of purchase of each item. The slip-paper was written on the back of quartered letters, notes and drafts of papers, lectures, and monograph drafts. The slip-papers raise a number of unanswerable questions as well. One entry indicates that Nestle acquired the rare first edition Luther New Testament, 1522 (the September Bibel), but the entry was crossed out. There are many other entries that presently can not be accounted for in the collection, but were never crossed out on the slip-papers. One indicates that he purchased Sabatier's indispensable three volume set on the Vetus Latina text of the Bible (1751) for the staggering sum of 800 marks, 160% of the average national per capita income at the time of purchase. Nestle's career and his book acquisitions coincided with a meteoric growth in the German economy which greatly extended his buying power in the international book market. There are other hints about how he assembled his impressive collection. A postcard from one of his book dealers, that survived as a bookmark, indicates that Nestle asked the dealer whether a volume in a set he had purchased was complete. After a careful check of a duplicate found at the British Museum, the dealer confirmed Nestle's suspicion and told him that he would be given a partial refund (see Figure 8).

Many of the books are stamped on the inside of the front cover with Nestle's name. Doubtless a few books left his possession, maybe borrowed by his own students. Dr. Bruce Metzger presented a volume from Nestle's library that he had acquired from a bookshop in Europe. A sixteenth-century grammar in the library has a bookplate that tries to remedy this age-old problem. The book was originally from the Cloister of Wessobrunn. An inscription on the bookplate warns, "I am the property of the Cloister of Wessobrunn. Hey man! Return me to my rightful place!"

Nestle's Greek Bibles

At the core of Nestle's Library is an impressive array of Greek Bibles. There are nearly 200 editions, providing a near-comprehensive holdings of critical Septuagint and Greek New Testament texts. Nestle's own annotations can be found in many of the books' margins. One of his Septuagints is interleafed with paper filled with his own text-critical observations (Figure 9). The earliest printed Greek text was an edition of the Psalms published in 1524. Nestle's research began with the text-critical study of the Psalms. He owned the third (1526) and fourth (1545) editions of the Bible in Greek, which closely followed the text of the first edition published in 1518. The Sixtine Septuagint (1585/6) is one of the most celebrated sixteenth-century Greek volumes in the collection. The monumental work includes text-critical notes at the end of each chapter. He also owned the second and the fourth editions of Erasmus's (Diglot) New Testament, called the Novum Testamentum (the first edition was called the Novum Instrumentum). The second edition introduces several texts, perhaps of greatest interest was the inclusion of 1 John 5:7—the so-called Johannine Comma (see Figure 10). Erasmus' second edition was used by Luther and Melanchthon for their translation of the Greek New Testament into German (1522). Luther's personal copy of the second edition of Erasmus' Novum Testamentum came to light in 1996, copiously annotated by Luther himself. Nestle sought unsuccessfully to print the text of Erasmus's second edition in an apparatus to his own critical text of the Greek New Testament. He was extremely interested in the evolution of the text of the Greek New Testament and its influence on the translation of the New Testament into German (and English). He also owned the fourth edition of Erasmus's New Testament, which contained the Greek text, the Latin Vulgate text, and another Latin translation of the New Testament. The fact that he did not acquire Erasmus's first, third, and fifth editions because they did not represent critical transitions in the text as it relates to translations shows that Nestle was a discriminating collector who was disciplined and frugal.

In addition to Erasmus' editions, the collection has major editions by such noteworthy scholars and printers as Stephanus, Beza, Elzevir, Grabe, Fell, Mill, Bengel, Holmes and Parsons, Wettstein, Griesbach, Lachmann, Tregelles, Scrivener, Tischendorf, and Westcott and Hort, not to mention countless others. Here is a small example of identification copies in the collection. Nestle owned Tregelles' copy of Greisbach. The VKC owns an additional copy of Tregelles' copy of Elzevir, with the columns filled with text-critical notes in Tregelles' hand. The VKC also has a copy of Alford's New Testament, each page framed by larger pages, and completely covered with commentary and textual notes written in a minuscule hand. Nestle's library also includes all seven editions of Tischendorf's Septuagint. The fourth and fifth editions are heavily glossed by Nestle himself. Tischendorf died in 1874 prior to the release of the fifth edition. The last two editions of Tischendorf's monumental work were edited by Nestle (1880/87). This impressive collection of Greek Bibles, of which only a small sample has been described, is supplemented by an impressive number of classical tools for textual study, many of which though inaccessible, are still of enormous value.

Semitic Volumes

Hebrew Scriptures in Nestle's library include Bomberg's Pentateuch (1548) which includes the Megilloth, with Targumim and the Jewish commentaries of Rashi (1040–1105) and Abraham Ibn Ezra (1092–1167). He also collected a number of important later editions of the Hebrew Bible for their critical value. For instance, he owned Kennicott and de Rossi's Hebrew Bible with notes by Boothyard which was the first comprehensive attempt to provide a critical edition of the Massoretic text of the Hebrew Old Testament.

Nothing in this library is irrelevant. It includes comprehensive Aramaic and Syriac studies as well as early Hebrew works. Nestle was interested in the development of typesetting, and early attempts to replicate letters with fonts. He collected the earliest examples of printing in various languages, including a woodblock impression of the Lord's Prayer in Syriac hidden away in an otherwise small, nondescript book in the library. This was the first example of Syriac in print, albeit not in typeset. Nestle (or his agent) hunted it down and snatched it up. The collection includes the earliest Hebrew grammars, including Reuchlin's celebrated *De rudimentis hebraicus* (1506), and Syriac Grammars including Windmanstadt's *Prima elementa* (1555/6) along with the first edition of the Syriac New Testament (1556–62), also edited by Windmanstadt. There are numerous later grammars and Bibles in Hebrew and Syriac. There is also a late Quran manuscript in the library. It's marked throughout in pencil, and each marked page is indicated by a small slip of paper in the manuscript. It seems Nestle's efforts in textual criticism were not limited to the Bible. Each slip indicates pages with text variations from the official version of the Quran. In his leisure, Nestle toyed with texts. While not at work with the Bible, he collated this highly variant manuscript of the Quran.

Other Bibles of Interest

Nestle's collection also includes a number of important polyglots, a fascinating hybrid of texts in two or more languages. Nestle's polyglot collection affords one small example that illustrates his critical acquisition of books. It's a generally accepted fact that the earliest printed polyglot text of Scripture is the *Genoa Psalter* dating to 1516. But there was a slightly earlier polyglot edition of the Psalms included as the fifth volume of Erasmus' edition of the works of Jerome called the *Quadruplex Psalterium*, printed earlier in 1516. This volume has been, essentially, unobserved in the official record of polyglots, but it was not passed over by Nestle. This was not a frivolous acquisition. The volume would prove to be of great importance to him, given his interest in the text of the Psalms.

The library also contains a comprehensive collection of Latin Bibles, showing special interest with Latin Bibles not strictly-classified as Vulgate Bibles, and not sanctioned by the Church and in the Vetus Latina. There are Bibles in fifteen modern European languages, most having bearing on textual studies and modern translations. He also had a very strong interest in the evolution of the German Bible. There are a number of publications of early patristic, medieval, and incunable texts of the German Bible to compare with Luther's translation in the library. This is of immense importance, as it relates to Luther, and to Tyndale and the English Bible. The German Bible has a rich textual tradition. There were eighteen editions of the German Bible before Luther's celebrated translation.

Miscellaneous Works

Arguably, the books in this library provide the best intact example of the tools used by a distinguished biblical scholar in the nineteenth century. The library on its own is worthy of study to cast light on Nestle and his discipline. There are over 800 volumes of nineteenth-century German exegesis, philology and textual criticism, and another 400 volumes by other European scholars. Of these, the most illustrious may be the Old Testament text critical scholar Paul de Lagarde. But virtually every scholar of note, working in textual criticism, is represented in the collection. The library is a remarkable testimony to Nestle's focus and breadth.

Nestle acquired more than 1000 pamphlets and offprints. This material contains a huge body of nineteenth-century German biblical scholarship impossible to replicate today. Most of the items were collected from 1860–1912. Many of the items were presented by the authors to Nestle. The collection represents a virtual who's who of nineteenth-century German biblical scholarship. Most of the items are in German, some in Latin with others in French and English.

The pamphlets and offprints are classified and boxed by subject, with each author listed. Ten of the sixty-four boxes pertain to New Testament textual criticism, exegesis, history, and doctrine. Ten boxes contain materials about Jewish history and literature. Six boxes are filled with records of pamphlets and offprints on Church History, and six more boxes contain offprints dealing with Syriac Literature. But the collection is much more diverse than this might imply, and includes works on philology, and on the history and text of the German Bible.

There are more than 400 journals in the library, including a near complete run of the *Zeitschrift für NT Wissenschaft* (1900–1983), *Theologischer Jahresbericht, Theologische Literaturzeitung* (1876–1932), and the *Schriften des Vereins für Reformations—Geschichte*. These journals are supplemented by shorter runs of other periodicals.

A Preliminary Description of VKC Coptic Texts

There are eight unpublished Sahidic Coptic Old Testament manuscripts in the VKC. The discussion below is based upon my work on the material prior to its purchase by the Van Kampens. As mentioned above, the collection came my way with approximately 170 leaves. I spent a year and a half piecing together fragments, photographing, and identifying what turned out to be 130 composite leaves. I used the opportunity as an occasion to teach undergraduate students Coptic, early church history and codicology. They worked tirelessly making invaluable contributions to the work.[30] It is my delight to honor Dr. Yamauchi with the publication

---

[30] Five of the students went on to earn Ph.D.s and are presently teaching in universities. There have been many opportunities since to work with similar materials and to have a number of students learn firsthand about research, to attain Ph.D.s and to go on to teach

of unknown texts—as he began his own prolific career with the publication of Mandean Magic Bowls.

Extant Coptic Old Testament Manuscripts

The earliest Egyptian converts to Christianity, of which many were Jews, lived in Alexandria. Their primary language was Greek. As Christianity spread outside of Alexandria in the second century, there arose a need to translate Christian writings into the various dialects of Egyptian. The Scriptures were dispersed in the vernacular of the Christianized descendants of the pharaohs, and their language, written with a Greek script was baptized for Christian use. In the second century, portions of the Gospels were translated along with other passages that were deemed useful or important. The Gospels and Psalms were eventually translated in whole, along with Genesis. By the third century, the entire Bible was translated into Coptic. Translations were always made from the Greek Bible, never the Hebrew, and the translation tended to be very literal, thereby providing important critical evidence for the Greek Old Testament Scriptures. As with every other translation, over time it has conformed to a particular prototype. This occurred during the fifth and sixth centuries, prior to the Arab conquest of Egypt and the eventual prohibition of the Coptic language.

The two main dialects of Coptic are Sahidic (the dialect of Southern or Upper Egypt), and Bohairic (the dialect of the region around Cairo). Sahidic is the earliest documented dialect. More ancient texts are written in Sahidic than any other dialect of Coptic with the prodigious output of Coptic fathers like Shenoute, who is completely passed over in Greek and Latin patristic sources. Despite the fact that the Bible was likely translated in its entirety in both the Sahidic and Bohairic dialects, there are relatively few surviving manuscripts. The Bible was translated from Greek into these two dialects, each independent of the other. There is no evidence of a standardized version in the two dialects. Other scripture in

in higher education. I see my vocation as a scholar-teacher to be a tribute to my *Doktor-Vater*. My student/professors consider themselves to be his students as well.

other Coptic dialects seem to have been derived from either the Sahidic or Bohairic dialects.

The following will briefly describe the state of manuscript evidence for the Old Testament in both Sahidic and Bohairic in order to contextualize the VKC Old Testament manuscripts below. A summary of the New Testament manuscript evidence will not be considered. As for the Coptic manuscript evidence for the Old Testament, there is complete evidence in Bohairic for the Pentateuch. There is nearly complete manuscript evidence for Exodus, Numbers, Leviticus, and Deuteronomy in Sahidic. However, only 71% of the verses in the Pentateuch have survived in Sahidic. This tabulation includes both complete verses and ones with lacunae. Genesis is the most fragmentary book of the Sahidic Pentateuch. The lack of evidence is further compounded by the unfortunate situation that the most extensive Sahidic manuscript of Genesis has perished though not before it was published. Of the nine Sahidic Old Testament manuscript fragments discussed below, one is from an unattested portion of Genesis, and the other, from Leviticus, illustrates the chance survival of these important early documents.

It might be suggested that because the enterprise of manuscript production was completely co-opted by monks by the seventh century, monastic concerns had a direct impact on which books of the Bible were copied. With regard to the Old Testament, the Law and Poetic Books, particularly Psalms, were of greatest practical value. The Prophetic and the Historic Books may have been deemed to be less important in their spiritual and devotional content. A small number of Boharic lectionary readings have survived from Joshua, Judges, I–II Samuel, I–II Kings, and I–II Chronicles. There is no evidence whatsoever for Ruth, Judith, Tobit, Esther, Ezra, Nehemiah, and I–II Maccabees in Bohairic. There is relatively complete manuscript evidence for Joshua, Judges, Ruth, I–II Samuel, Judith, Esther, and Tobit in Sahidic. Only 16% of the verses in I Kings, 32% of the verses in II Kings, a few verses from II Chronicles and a few chapters from I Maccabees have survived in Sahidic. There is no Sahidic manuscript evidence for I Chronicles, Ezra, or Nehemiah. While not published at this time, there is a bifolio manuscript in the VKC providing an historical summary of I Kings chapters one and two which will clearly be of great interest given the fragmentary state of the evidence.

Psalms and Job are complete in Bohairic. Only Proverbs 1–14 has survived, along with a lectionary reading on the end of Proverbs (in Bohairic). The Song of Solomon, the Wisdom of Solomon, and the Wisdom of Ibn Sirach have survived in Boharaic only in lectionary readings. There is no manuscript evidence for Ecclesiastes in Bohairic. Apart from small lacunae, the Poetic Books are complete in Sahidic.

Regarding the Major Prophets: Isaiah, Jeremiah (including Lamentations, Baruch, and Epistle of Jeremiah), Ezekiel, and Daniel (including the Apocryphal sections) are complete in Bohairic. Only Isaiah, Lamentations, Baruch, and the Epistle of Jeremiah are complete in Sahidic. Calculated on the basis of the number verses in each book, only 52% of Jeremiah, 57% of Ezekiel, and 40% of Daniel (including the Apocryphal sections) have survived in Sahidic.

All twelve books of the Minor Prophets have survived in Bohairic. Only Jonah is preserved in its entirety in Sahidic. On the basis of the number of verses, what has survived of the rest is 43% of Amos, 36% of Hosea, 63% of Joel, 67% of Obadiah, 25% of Nahum, 75% of Micah, 53% of Habakkuk, 26% of Zephaniah, 63% of Haggai, and 42% of Zachariah. Sahidic Malachi did not survive in any biblical manuscript identified.

Conclusions

The items described below are unpublished. They will supplement Mississippi Codex II in the collection of Coptic Old Testament material in the VKC, as well as the unpublished Coptic papyri described briefly above. There are several other Old Testament-related manuscripts worthy of a brief description, but for sake of space they will not be published along with the others below. There is at least one leaf and two bifolio leaves which contain successive quotations from Psalms without comment, apparently used for prayer. One text attributes both the words and arrangement to David. There are at least two palimpsest leaves that have potentially retrievable texts that may be from Psalms as well. There is also a text entitled Jeremiah succeeding a brief text and followed by a slightly longer text which may prove to be ascribed to the prophet. Finally, there is a very interesting bifolio leaf that has, on one leaf, an historical account summarizing the succession of David's throne to Solomon, strictly following the narrative account in I Kings chapters one and two. It appears to be a summary of a lectionary reading, or perhaps a homily.

As for the manuscripts described below, I will follow an abbreviated format of the descriptive method outlined by Bentley Layton[31]. The method provides a consistent physical description of the manuscript including size, shape, writing materials, script, decorative features, evidence of quire and page numbers, binding and, of course, the content and its relationship to similar manuscripts. This gives the necessary data to others so they might be able to compare the manuscript with another in a collection elsewhere. As indicated by this particular collection, these items have been disseminated far and wide and are buried in museum archives and private collections. The Coptic manuscript leaves have not been catalogued in the VKC. Each fragmented leaf has a number and a letter written on it in pencil. This had been done before I saw the manuscripts for the first time. I have chosen to catalogue the manuscript with a number beginning with VKC Coptic manuscript and followed by the passage of scripture, followed in parenthesis by the number and letter written on the manuscript in pencil. This will allow for the VKC to catalogue the material as they deem fit and without confusing a future researcher hoping to access these items.

It is items like the following, lost in private collections, that illustrate the importance of access to and study of this kind of material. It is completely unknown territory. The work is hard and slow because the material is undefined. It can be, nevertheless, extremely rewarding personally and academically. In the material presented below is one of the earliest surviving Sahidic Coptic texts of Genesis, and the only extent evidence for the portion of Genesis it contains. While exact dating is difficult to determine, this manuscript certainly dates among the earliest

---

[31] Bentley Layton, *Catalogue of Coptic Literary Manuscripts in the British Library Acquired Since the Year 1906.* (London: British Library, 1987).

Coptic manuscripts known. The text of Leviticus below dates within one hundred years of the earliest known texts of this particular passage. While the manuscripts of the Psalms below date a bit later they, nevertheless, provide a voice of evidence for the life of faith and worship during Arab oppression. The text of Isaiah described below was once part of an elegant codex. The parchment is supple and the text is written in a refined book hand similar to the magnificent gospel codices produced at the White Monastery between the fifth and seventh centuries. Finally, the manuscript from Ecclesiasticus below, while Apocryphal, has been carefully copied and was also part of an elegant folio. Despite its deuterocanonical status for the Copts, it has been included because of the evidence it provides for the translation of the Septuagint into Coptic. One should keep in mind that the manuscripts discussed below date earlier than most extant Latin manuscripts of scripture, and are contemporaneous with the production of many of the important Greek uncials of the Bible. These artifacts were not to be found in the ruins of an ancient royal archive, hidden in sectarian caves, locked behind monastery walls, lost in museum archives or in national libraries. Still, private collections are the untapped repository of a wealth of unpublished texts and artifacts.

Appendix

VKC Coptic Ms
Genesis 42:34b—43:2; 43:9b–13a

A fragmentary leaf from a parchment codex. *Size*, 238 x 107 mm. *Conservation*: Encapsulated in Mylar. *Ancient pagination*, if any, wanting; modern inventory number 21[A] recorded in pencil on the H side at the foot of the leaf. *Damage*: Holes; tattered; brown spotting; deterioration; text is faded on the F side. *Collation*: No remains of signatures, quire ornaments, monograms, headlines, or catchwords. *Palimpsest*: No. *Parchment*: F and H distinguishable by color and grain; the recto (= true recto) is H. No evidence of pricking or ruling lines. *Layout*: Written area 57 x 194 mm. in 2 columns. *Script*: Upright; predominately 3-stroke M, tall Ρ ϕ and Υ with the classical non-looped Υ. *Superlineation*: Standard. *Punctuation*: Raised dot in conjunction with a space. *Contents*: Genesis 42:37b—43:2; 43:9b–13a. *There are no related texts in this collection.* *Date*: Based on the script, format and comparison with other early manuscripts it dates before the Nag Hammadi Codices and is comparable to the Mississippi Codex in the VKC placing this from between AD 320 to 360 amongst the earliest known Coptic literary texts.

(See Figure 11a)

Recto a | ΑΥΩΑΝΟΚϯΝΑ | ΕΝΤΕΜΜΟϥΕ2 | ΡΑЇϢΑΡΟΚ Ν |
ΤΟϥΧΕΠΕΧΑϥ | ΧΕΜΠΑϢΗΡΕ | ΝΗΥΑΝΕΠΕ | ϹΝΤΝΜΜΗΤΝ |
ΧΕΑΠΕϥϹΟΝ | .]ΟΥ ΑΥΩΝ | .]Ο ⳘΑΥΑΑϥ | Π]ΕΤϢΟΟΠΝΑ[Ї |
ΑΥΩΝϹ̄ϢΩΠ[Ε | Π̄ϥⲁ[Χ21[. | ΤΕ2ΙΗΤΑЇΕ[.. | ΤΝΑΒΩΚ [2 |
Ν̄2ΗΤΟ Ν̄[Τ | ΤΝ̄ΧΙΝ̄ΤΑ[. | ⳌΑΛΟ2Ν̄ΟΥ[Μ | .]Α2Μ̄2ΗΤΕΠ[. | ϹΗ[.
Τ]ΜΝ̄Τ[. | ΠΗΕΒϢΩΝΑ[Ε | ΝΕΑϥϬ[ΜϚ]Ο[Μ | Ε2ΡΑЇΕΧΜΠΚ[ⲁ
| ΑϹϢϢΠΕΔΕ | 2Ν̄ΝΕΥΝΑΟΥ | ϢΜΜ̄ΠΕϹΟ[Υ | ΠΑЇΕΝΤΑ[Υ
| ΠϥΕΒΟΛ2[Μ | ΠΚΑ2Ν̄ΚΗ[. | ΠΕΧΑϥΝΑ[| .. ΠΕΥΕΙϢ[Τ |
ΧΕΒϢΚΟΝΝ̄[Τ | ΤΝϢϢ ΠΝΑΝ[. | Ν̄2ΕΝΟΥЇΝϹΟ[Υ | Recto b | Ο
[. | Ν̄Ϛ | Χ[Ο | Ο[Υ | Α[ϥ | Ν̄[. | Χ[. | [Ν | [Ε | Τ | [. |

(See Figure 11b)

Verso a |] ΕΝ | .] ΝΟΥ |]ΑΥϢ | .].. | .].Η | .].. | Ν2 |
]Ν̄ |] . Υ | Μ]Αϥ | Verso b | ΝΟΒΕΕΡΟΚ . | ΝΕ2ΟΟΥΤΗΡϥ |
Μ̄ΠΑϢΝ2ΝϹΑ | Β . ΒΓΑΡΧΕΑΝ | ϢϹ . ΕϢΧΠΕΕ |ΑΝΚΟΤΝ̄ΜΠΜΕΗ
| ϹΕΠΕΝⲁΥ ΠΕ | ΧΑϥΔΕ ΝΑΥΝϬΙ | ΠΙϹΡⲁΗΛΑΠΟ[Υ | ΕΙϢΤ
ΧΕΕ[. | ΧΕΤΑЇΠΤΟΟ[| ΤΕΘΕⲀ[Ρ]ΙΠⲀ[. | ΧΙΕΒΟΛ2ΝΠΒ . Ρ |

ΠΟC[.]ΠΚΛ2 | ..]ΛΪ2ΝΝΕΤΜ |]ΛΛΥΝ̄...Η | .]Ν̄2ΕΝΛωΡΟΝ
| Τ̣]ΕϹΗΤΜΠΡω | .]ΠϹΟΝΤΕ | ΜΜ̄ΠΕΒΙω[Μ̣]Ν | .]ωΟΥ2Η[.]ΕΛΥ
| .]ωΤΕ[..]Λ[Κ̣]ΤΗ |]ΜΝ̄[.]ΤΕΡΕΒΙΝ |]ΘΟ[.]ΜΝ̄2ΕΝΚΛ | ΡΟΙΛ
ΛΥωΦΛΤ | Ν̄ΤΕΤΝ̄ΧΙΜΜΟϥ | 2Ν̄ΜΕΤΝϬΙΧΕϥ | ΚΗΒ Π2ΛΤΕΝ |
.]ΤΕΤΜ̣ΚΤΟΦ | .]ΝΕΤΗϬΟΟΥ | Ε]ΝΤΕΤΝ̄ΧΙΤϥ |]ΜΜΠΤΜΜΕ | .
Λ]ΚΤΛΡΟΥΟ | .]ΕϢΟΤΕΝΤΤΛϹ |]ϢωΠΕΝ̄ΤΕ |]ΤΜ̄ΧΙΜΠΕΤΝ[
| ϹΟΝΝ̄ΤΕΤΝ̄ .|

VKC Coptic Ms
Leviticus 4:22–34

A leaf from a parchment codex reused in a binding. *Size*, 280 x 220 mm.
Conservation: Encapsulated in Mylar. Modern repairs: papyrus removed
along with some of the glue obscuring the text. *Ancient pagination*: Fa
upper corner: I2̄ ; modern inventory number 23A recorded in pencil
on the H side at the right foot of the leaf. *Damage*: Torn; holes; tattered; discolored; covered by glue and papyrus; strip of leather down the
middle of the H side covering portions of the text; Ha the text is partially
obscured by glue; Hb the writing is faint in places; F the writing is partially obscured by remnants of glue. *Collation*: No remains of signatures,
quire ornaments, monograms, headlines, or catchwords. *Palimpsest*: No.
Parchment: F and H distinguishable by color and grain; the recto (= true
recto) is H. No evidence of pricking or ruling lines. *Layout*: Written area
239 x 169 mm. in 2 columns. Pinholes present along the binding. *Script*:
Upright; 4-stroke Μ, ΕΟϹ narrow/square, ΡϥΥ short, with the classical
non-looped Υ, average height 8.8 mm, single letter, serifs, style thin, no
apostophes, punctuation and one trema. Lines possible on Hb bottom.
Superlineation: Standard. *Punctuation*: Raised dot in conjunction with
a space. *Decoration*: Capitals, initials, scroll signs, extended letters, no
color, no illumination. *Contents*: Leviticus 4:22–34. No colophons, cor-

rections, marginal notes or ancient annotations. *There are no related texts in this collection. Date*: Based on the script, format, and comparison with other manuscripts, this manuscript dates to the first half of the 6c.

(See Figure 12a)

Verso b | ΠΑϨΤΝϨΑΤΕΤ | ΒΑϹΙϹΑ . ΠΕΟΥ | ΕΤΑϹΤΑΝΙΟΝ | ΝѠΤΑΕΤΗΡϤ | ΕϤΕϤΑ . ϤѠΙΑΥ | Ν̄ΘΕ . ΠѠΤ | ΕѰΑΥ . ΠΤϤΕ | ΒΟΛϨ . ΤΕΘΥ | ϹΙΑΜΠΟΥΧΑΪ | ΝΤΕΠΟΥΗΗΒ | ΤΑΛΟϤΕΧΜΠΕ | ΘΥΝΙΑϹΤΗΡΙ | ΟΠΕΥϹϯΝΟΥ | Ϥ . ΜΠΧΟΕΙϹ | ΑΥѠΕΡΕΠΟΥ | . Ν . ΤѠΒ2̄ Ε | ΧѠѰΟΕΚѠ | ΠΑΤ . . ΛΜΠΕϤ | ΝΟΒΕ Ε[Ρ .]Ѡ | ΠΕΛΕΟΥΕ[. .]ΟΥ | ΠΕΤϤΜΑ[Τ]Ϥ | ΠΛѠΡΟΝϨΑ | ΝΟΒΕ Ε . . ΕΙ | ΝΕΝ̄ΟϨ . . ΟΟΥ | ΝϹϨΪΜΕΕΜΝ̄ | ΧΒΠΙ . Ϊ . ΗΤ . | ΑΥѠΕϤΕΤΛΛΕ | ϯΟϹΤ . ΕΧΜΑ | ΠΕΜΠΕ . . .

(See Figure 12b)

Verso a | ΠΝΟΒΕ ΑΥѠΝ̄ | ϹΕΤΑΜΟϤΕΠ | ΝΟΒΕΕΝΤΑϤ | ΛΑϤΡΑΪΝϨΗΤϹ̄: | ΕϤΕΕ . . ΕΜ | ΠΕϤΛѠΡΟΝ | ΟΥ . . ΜΠΕΝ̄ | ΕϨ . . Ε Ε . [. | Π]ΕϤΝΟΒΕ . [. | . Λ]ϤΛΛϤ ΑΥѠ | Ϥ]Ε . . Λ . . Ε | Τ]ΦΕΚ ΤΑ . . | Μ̄ΠΕϤΗ . . Ε | ΝϹΕ . Ο . . . . | Ν̄ΤΒΛΛΜΠΕϨ | ΝΟΒΕϨΜΠΜΑ | ΕΤΟΥѰѠΤ | ΝϨΗΤϤΝ̄ΝΕϬ | ΛΙΛ ΑΥѠΕΡΕ | ΠΟΥΗΗΒΧΙΕ | ΒΟΛϨΜΠ[Ε . | ΝΟϤϨΜ[ΠΕ[. | ΤΜΗΗ . ΝϤΚΟ | ΑϤϨΪΧΝ̄ . ΤΑΝ | ΜΠΕ̄ ΘΥ[. .]Λ . | ΤΗΡΙΟΝΗΝΕϬ | ΛΙΛ ΑΥѠΠΕϹ | ΝΝ̄ϤΤΗΡϤΕϤ |

Recto a | ΕΝѰΘ . Ε . ΝΟ [. | ΛΑϹ ΜΙΛΛϹΗ . | ϨΝΑ . ΜΑ[ΛϹ . | ΤΑΜΟΙΕΙΠ[. | ϨΡΛΪΜ . Τ[Ν̄ | ΕϤΕΛΙ . ΡΑΪ | ΠΕϤѠΡΟΝ[| ΕΒΟΛϨΝ̄ΜΒΑ[| ΠΕΕΜΝ . . Η[Ν | ϨΗΤϤ ΑΥѠΕ[. | ΚΑΤΟΟ . ϤΕ[Χ

| ТΑΠЄΜΠΒΑ̣[. | ΗЄ . . ϢЄΥС̣[| Τ̣ . ΑΑТϥ̄2ΜṆ[. | ЄТΟΥ . . Є̣[
| Ν2ΝТϥΝΜ[. | ϬΑ1Α . ΜΠЄ[. . | ЄN . ΑX̣Є[. | ΟΥΒЄΒ . . [. |
ΑΥϢΠΟΥΗΗ̣[. | ЄṆЄΥΑΑΟ̣Є1[. | 2ΜΠṆΘ[. | ΜЄΟΛ1ΛΜ . . [| [. ϥЄ
. . . .][| ТΗΗΒЄΝϥ . . [| ΛΟϥЄX1ΠΡΠ̣[| ΝΜСΟΥЄ . [.

(See Figure 12b)

Recto b | ΝΟΒ]ЄΑ[ΥϢ | СЄТΑΜ]ΚΟ[ϥЄΝ | .]2ΑТЄ | .]СΜП̄ | .]
ЄТΗΡ1Ο̣ .Т | .]Λ.ΛΠЄϥ[. |]ЄΘΥС1Α[| .]ΟΝ ΝΘ[| Π]ΟΥXΑ[. |
.]ЄΡЄΠΟ̣Υ[|]СΟΠСЄ[| .]ЄϥΝΟΒЄ[. . | Κ]ΛΛ . . . [| .] . . ЄΡΟ̣ϥΝ[
|]X̣ΑЄΜΟΥ[| .]ΝΟΒЄЄ̣ . . [| . 2 .]ΠТΡ[| .] . . Є1ΡЄ | .]ΜЄΒΟΛ
| Ν]Ν̄ТΟΛ[Β | Ο]ΥΜX̣ .[|]ΝϢϢЄ̣ . . [|]ΝϥЄ1ΡЄΜ |

VKC Coptic Ms
Psalm 67:10–24

A folio leaf from a parchment codex. *Present Size*, 190 x 165 mm. *Conservation*: Encapsulated in Mylar. *Ancient pagination*: Trace on H side left head corner and F side right head corner П̄Є; modern inventory number 18k recorded in pencil on the H side foot. *Damage*: Torn; tattered, holes. *Palimpsest*: Perhaps retrievable. *Corrections*: One perhaps, text either smudged or crossed out by the scribe. *Marginal Apparatus*: No. *Ancient Annotations*: No. *Collation*: No remains of signatures, no quire ornaments, no monograms, headlines apparent, no catchwords or apparent verse marks. *Writing Material*: Parchment: H distinguishable by color and grain; the recto (= true recto) is H. No evidence of ruling lines. *Layout*: One column per side; writing on both sides; 95 mm per column; traces of last words centered at the foot of the colomun. *Script*: Same script both sides; orientation slight right slope; 3-stroke Μ, ЄΟС narrow, ΡϥΥ tall, with the classical non-looped Υ, average height 7 mm, superlineation for abbreviations, nonstandard; serifs, no dieresis; Coptic single period or tremas present; perhaps apostrophes. *Decoration:* None; no major initials or initials; no lectional signs or scrolls seen; an extended letter; no color; no illumination. *Contents:* Psalm 67:10–24. No colophons, perhaps one correction, no marginal notes or ancient annotations. *There are no related texts in this collection. Date:* This manuscript dates between 700–800 AD.

(See Figure 13a)

Recto | PϪNOY2ⲰYE2 | 2[K]KⲀHY.NOM..[.| ENTOKⲀENCBTⲰ
[|]NTEKNⲀOYⲰ22PⲀ[.N2. ⲀK | C]OϥTEϬMⲦ2H[.]2NTKMNT
| XPHCTOCⲦOC[Ⲡ]Ⲁ†NOYⲰⲀϪE | Ⲡ̣N]ETEYⲀⲚⲠⲉⲀⲒ2EENTϬOM
| NCⲦPPONEⲦϬOM | YⲰNCⲀEMⲦHIEMⲦⲰⲰ | ⲀⲰⲀNTETNE[. Ⲡ̣]
K | Ⲡ̣]EENKⲀYPOC[| 2]ENϬPCMⲦEEYⲀ[. . Ⲱ] EN2Ⲁ[T | .]
ⲰⲦKⲰTE E[Ⲛ]NCNⲀ2BEMⲦOY | .]TOYETEMⲦNOYϥ ⲀⲒⲀѰⲀAMⲀ
| 2MⲦT[P E]T2NEMⲦHYE ⲦⲰPϪ[| EN2N[..E] 2PⲀⲒEXⲰC CNⲀ
| OYBⲀⲰ[.]IⲦTOOYEMⲦ[.]Y[.] | ⲦTOOYETⲒ[C̣ T]OOY[ϛ̣Ⲓ]X[
.. | ⲦP]OYET[.E]T[Ⲓ̣][Ⲱ | .]TE[.]TOOY2[TϪ. | YⲰ22PⲀ[Ⲓ̣
.N]TⲦN[Ⲁ | [.ϥ] |

(See Figure 13b)

Verso |]ō̄CNⲀOYⲰ2E[.. |]ⲀPMⲀEMⲦNO[Y..OY. | ϥⲦĒ
2NⲰOONEEYPO[.. | [Ⲡ .]N2[H .]OY2NCⲒNⲀⲦϥⲦEOⲦOY | ⲀⲀ̄
BⲀBⲀAⲀ[.]ⲦXⲒCEⲀBEXMⲀ | AⲀTEYENOYEXMⲀAOCⲒAⲀ[Y†
| N2ṆTⲀⲒONⲦENPⲰME [.| ⲦNOYTENNϬOMCMⲀ | XⲒNEN2ⲰⲀEN2:
[Ⲡ . .]NOYXⲀⲒϥNⲀCO[O . | .. ⲀM .]: ⲦENNOYTEⲦEⲦNOY[. |
.]TTⲀN2OTⲀⲦ[O̅]C̅TE0OTEE[Ṃ | ⲦMOYⲦAHNⲦNOYTENⲀOYⲰⲰ[.

| ЄNTⲀⲠЄЄNNⳊⲬINⲬЄ[.] ⲀⲨⲰ | .]NTMHTЄЄNTⲀⲠЄЄN[.]OOⲰЄ
| .]NNЄⲨNOBЄⲀⲠO[C̄ . Ⲩ]KⲰ | TЄЄMⲀIOⳊЄB[. Ⲁ]NⲬЄ |
Ṇ]ⲀKTOIⳞNH[K]ЄNⲐⲀ | .]CCⲀ[. .]ЄK[. .]OⲨЄⲢ[Ⲭ | .]KⳞN[.
]ⲰN[| .]ⲰⲬⳞЄ[N .]KO[Ⲩ |]ⳞOOⲢЄB[. Ⲭ̣Ⲁ̣]ⲬЄЄT[|

VKC Ms

Psalms 88:1–29; 144:1–12; 64:1–9a

A bifolio leaf from a parchment codex. *Present Size*, 354 x 236 mm. *Conservation*: Encapsulated in Mylar. *Ancient pagination*: yes, inner right leaf head left margin; modern inventory number 22A recorded in pencil on the H side at the right foot of the leaf. *Damage*: Torn; holes; tattered. *Palimpsest*: Yes, not legible. *Marginal Apparati*: Each Psalm is numbered; Ha margin numbers *Collation*: No remains of signatures, quire ornaments, monograms, headlines, or catchwords. *Writing Material*: Parchment: F and H distinguishable by color and grain; the recto (= true recto) is H. No evidence of pricking or ruling lines. *Layout*: Written area 212.6 x 144.3 mm. page, column width n/a; lines per column 25.3. Writing on all four sides. Text rewritten where faint and is thicker and darker; stitch holes along the middle. *Script*: Orientation slight right slope; 3-stroke Ɱ, ЄOC narrow, ⲢⳊⲨ short, with the classical non-looped Ⲩ, average height 82.3 mm per 10 lines, no superlineations other than abbreviations; serifs, style thin, apostophes, logical punctuation; lines indicating break; double Coptic period; single period; no tremas. Lines possible on Hb bottom. *Decoration*: Line separates each Psalm; no color, no illumination. *Contents*: Psalms 88:1–29; 144:1–12; 64:1–9a. No colophons, corrections, marginal notes or ancient annotations. *There are no related texts in this collection*. *Date*: This manuscript dates to the last half of the 700–800 AD.

(See Figure 14a)

Recto b | ПН | †NΛ[X . . . . | XⲰMMNOYXⲰM : † [. . . . Є]Y | TΛTOⲠPC
[X .]KXЄO[. X .]CⲰTNOY | NΛⲰΛЄN2 : CЄNΛΛCOY[. . Є]2NMⲠHYЄ[
| ΛKMNЄNOYΔIΛΘH[K . .]CⲰTⲠ :[| [. I]Ç I PЄKЄΛΛΛ Ⲡ[Λ2 .]2[ΛΛ
. ЄṬNΛCO[. | TⲚⲠЄKCⲠЄPM : ΛⲰΛЄN2[.]ḲⲰTMⲠ[K | ΘPONOC
XINЄOₓXⲰMⲰΛOYXⲰMMⲠHYЄ | NΛOYⲰH2ЄBOΛNNЄKMOI2Є[Ⲡ
. Ⲅ]ΛP | TⲚⲠЄKNNЄKΛHCIΛN[.]ḲB : XЄ | NIM2NNЄKΛOOЄ
ⲠЄTN[ⲰⲰΛ]Ⲱ4OYBЄ | $\overline{ⲠOC}$ ΛYⲰNIMⲠЄTNΛ[Ⲱ]INMⲠOC 2NNⲰ
| PЄTHP[OYMⲠ]$\overline{NO}$YTЄЄTX[I 2OY]2M | ⲠⲰOX[. .]ЄTOYΛΛB :
OYNO6ⲠЄΛYⲰ[Λ TẸ | ⲠЄЄXNOYONNIMЄTMⲠЄ4KⲰTЄⲠO
$\overline{CⲠN}$[Ṭ[. | NЄN6OM : NIMⲠЄTNΛⲰЄINMMOKN[| OYXⲰⲰPЄⲠ
$\overline{OC}$ЄPЄTIMЄKⲰTЄPOKṆ[| TOKЄTONXOЄICЄXNⲠΛM2TNΘ
Λ[Λ | ΛCCΛⲠKIMNNЄC2OЄIMNTOK . [| PЄ46ⲰNTOKNTO
KΘBBIЄⲠXΛC2H[Ṭ | NΘЄNOY2ⲰTЄ4 : 2MⲠЄ6ḄOINTK6O[. |
K]XⲰⲰPЄBOΛMⲠXΛXЄ : NOYKN[M | ⲠHYЄΛYⲰⲠⲰKⲠЄⲠKΛ2NT$\overline{O}$
KⲠЄ[. | TΛMẸNÇNTẸN†KOYMṆHMNⲠЄ[C | XⲰKЄBOΛTOKNTN .
CNT . M | 2TMNΘΛΛΛCCΛ

(See Figure 14b)

Verso a | . . . . Λ . Λ]2M | Ṭ[. . . Ẹ]XBOI[M]NT6OM
| .]MΛPЄTЄ[K .]ONCXI[C]ЄN6ITЄ | KOYNΛM[. . .]YNH :
MN[Ⲡ]2ΛⲠ | ⲠЄⲠCO4[T . Ẹ .]PONOCOYNΛM[N]OY | Ṃ]Є
NЄT 2ΛTЄK2H : NΛI[ΛṬ4] | MⲠΛΛOCЄ[TC]OYNNΛOYΛΛI : $\overline{Ⲡ}$
$\overline{OC}$CЄ | NṆMOOⲰ[. . .]ⲠOYOЄINMⲠЄK2O-- | ΛYⲰ[CЄ .]T . .
ΛHΛ2MⲠЄKPΛN : MⲠẸ | 2OOY[. .]ⲰCЄNΛXICЄ2NTK | ΔIKЄ[.

. . . ⲛ]ⲧⲟⲕⲡⲉⲡϣⲁⲩϣⲟⲩⲛ | ⲧⲉϥϭⲟⲙ: ⲡⲛⲧⲉⲡⲛⲁⲭⲓⲥⲉ2ⲛⲧⲕ

| ⲁⲓⲕⲉⲟⲥⲩⲛⲏ: ⲭⲉⲡⲛⲣⲉϥϣⲟ[ⲡⲛ]ⲉⲣⲟϥ | ⲡⲉ[ⲡⲭ]ⲟ̣ⲉⲓⲥⲡⲉⲧ

ⲟⲩⲁⲁⲃⲛⲧ̣ⲡ̣ⲏ[ⲗ . ⲡ]ⲉⲛⲉ | ⲧⲟⲁⲉⲁⲕϣⲁⲭ2ⲛⲟⲩ2ⲟⲣⲁⲥⲓⲥⲙⲛ |

ⲛ]ⲕϣⲏⲣⲉⲁⲕⲭⲟⲟⲉⲭⲣⲁⲛⲕⲱⲛⲟⲩ | .]ⲟⲏⲑⲁⲉⲭⲛⲟⲩⲭϣϣⲣⲉⲁⲓⲭⲓⲥⲉ

|]ⲟⲩⲥⲓⲟⲛⲧ2ⲙⲡⲁⲗⲁⲟⲥⲁⲓⲋⲓⲛⲛⲁⲁ̄ⲁ̄ | .]ⲁ2ⲙ2ⲁⲗⲁⲓⲧⲱ

2ⲥ̣ⲉⲙⲟϥⲉⲡⲁⲛⲁ̣2 | ⲉ]ⲧⲟⲩⲁⲁⲃⲧⲁⲋⲓⲭⲧⲉⲧⲛⲁ†ⲧⲟ[. . |

ⲁ]ⲩϣⲡⲁⲋ . ⲟⲥⲛⲁ†ϭⲟⲙⲛⲁϥ: |]ⲭⲁⲭⲣⲛⲁ†2ⲏⲩⲁⲛⲛ2ⲏⲧϥⲁⲩϣ |

ⲡ]ϣⲏⲣⲉⲉⲛⲧⲁⲛⲟⲙⲓⲁⲛⲁ ⲙ | ⲕⲟⲩⲁⲛ

(See Figure 14b)

Verso b | [. . | †ⲛⲁⲣ[ϣ .]ⲏ̣ⲛⲉϥⲭ[| †ⲛⲁⲟⲩϣⲗⲉⲥⲛⲛⲉⲧⲙ[. . . .

| ⲧϣⲃⲙⲏⲡⲁⲛⲙⲙⲁⲩ[.]ϣ̣ⲡ[ⲉϥ | ⲧⲁⲡⲛⲁⲭⲓⲥⲉ[. .].ⲡⲁⲣⲁⲩ[. ⲕ̣]ⲕⲱⲛ[

| ⲧⲉ̣ϥϭⲓⲭ2ⲛⲑⲁⲗⲁⲥⲥⲁ: ⲁ[ⲩ̣ϣ]ⲧⲉⲃⲟⲩⲛ[| ⲁⲙ2ⲛⲛⲉ̣ⲉⲣⲓⲙⲟⲩ:

ⲛⲧⲟ[.]ϥⲛⲁⲙ[. | ⲧⲉⲣⲁⲓⲭⲏⲧⲙⲱⲧⲡⲟⲩⲟⲩⲧⲉⲡⲉ[ⲥ | ⲣⲉϥϣⲱⲡⲉ̄

ⲣⲟϥⲙⲡⲁⲟⲩⲭ[. .|ⲣⲉϥϣⲡⲉⲣⲟϥⲙⲡⲁⲟⲩⲭ[. .|ⲁⲉ†ⲏⲁⲕⲁⲁϥⲉⲃⲟⲛϣ[ⲉ

. . ⲙ]ⲓⲥⲉ | ⲉϥⲭⲟ̣ⲥⲉⲛⲉⲣϣⲟⲩⲧⲏⲣ[ϥϣ]ⲡⲕⲁ2 | †ⲛⲁ2ⲁⲣⲓⲍ̄

ⲛⲁϣⲙⲡⲁⲛⲁϣⲁⲉⲛ2 | ⲁⲩϣⲧⲁⲇⲓⲁⲑⲩⲕⲏⲉⲭⲟⲛ2ⲁ̣ⲧⲡⲁϥ | †ⲛⲁⲕ[. .

]ⲙⲡⲉϥⲥⲡⲉⲣⲙⲁⲧⲁ[ⲥ̣ⲛ̣]2ⲛⲉ2 | ⲁⲩϣ[ⲡ̣]ⲉϥⲑⲣⲟⲛⲟⲥⲛⲑⲛⲛⲉ2ⲟⲟⲩ[. |

ⲧⲡⲉ-- | †ⲛⲁⲭⲁⲥⲧⲕⲡⲛⲟ

ⲩⲧⲉⲡⲁⲉ2ⲣⲟ†ⲛⲁⲥⲙⲟⲩⲉⲡⲉⲕ | ⲣⲁⲛϣⲁⲉⲛ2ⲁⲩⲁ̣ⲓ̣ⲁ̣ⲓ̣ⲁ̣ⲉⲛ2ⲛⲉⲛ2†ⲛ

ⲁⲥⲙⲟⲩ: | ⲣⲟⲕⲙⲙⲏⲛⲉⲙⲙⲏⲡⲉ†ⲕⲥⲙⲟⲩⲉⲡⲓⲥⲣⲁⲛ | ϣⲁⲉⲛ2ⲛⲉⲛ2ⲟⲩ̄

ⲛⲟϭⲡⲉⲡⲟ̄ⲥ̄ⲉϥⲥⲙ . ⲁⲧ | ⲉⲙⲁⲧⲉⲁⲩⲁⲩϣⲕⲛϣⲓⲛⲧⲉϥⲙⲛⲧⲛⲟϭⲟⲩⲛ .

| .]ϣⲥⲉ . ⲭⲱⲛⲧⲕϭⲟⲙ: ⲁⲩϣ . .†ⲁⲭⲱⲩ | ⲡⲥⲁⲛⲧⲕⲙⲏⲧⲛⲟϭⲥⲉⲛⲁ

. †ⲁⲭ . ⲛⲕϣⲡⲏ | ⲣⲉ: ⲁⲩϣⲥⲉⲛ[.]ⲭⲱⲛϭⲟⲙⲛⲧⲕ2ⲟⲧⲉⲥⲉ |

ⲛⲁϣⲁⲭⲉⲉⲧ[. . ⲙ]ⲟⲧⲛⲟϭⲛϥ̣ⲉⲧ . ⲟ̣ⲧⲟ | . .]ⲟⲡⲙⲉⲉⲩⲉ

(See Figure 14a)

Recto a | .] | .]ΝΙ ⲈⲦⲈⲗ[. ⲀⲚ]ⲦⲀⲬ[! | . .]ⲦⲚϥⲚⲚⲀⲚ[.]ⲡⲉⲡⲟⲥ | ψ.
Υ]ⲚⲈⲚⲀϣⲈⲡⲈϥⲚⲀ ⲞⲨⲬⲢⲤⲡⲈ |]ⲟⲥ 2Ⲛ2[ ]ⲡⲘ ⲀⲨⲱⲚϥⲘⲚⲦϣⲈⲚ2
| Ⲧ]ⲎϥⲈⲬ[Ⲛ .]ϥ2ⲂⲎⲨⲈⲦⲎⲢⲀϥⲘⲘⲈⲚⲔ | 2]ⲂⲎⲨⲈⲦⲎ[Ⲣ .]ⲡⲟⲥⲟⲨ .
Ⲛ2ⲚⲀⲔⲈⲂⲞⲗⲀⲨⲱ | Ⲕ]ⲡⲈⲦⲞⲨⲗ[ⲁ .]ⲘⲀⲢⲞⲨⲈⲘⲞⲨⲈⲢⲞⲔ ⲥⲈⲚⲀ |
.]ⲘⲡⲈⲀϣⲚⲡⲤⲘⲚⲦⲢⲢⲞ ⲤⲈⲚⲘⲬⲀⲬⲈ | . . .Υ]ⲡⲤⲋⲞⲘ ⲦⲬⲘⲈⲚϣⲎⲨⲢⲚⲚⲚ
.Ⲣⲱ | ⲢⲱⲘ[ⲉ ..]Ⲙ: ⲀⲨⲱⲡⲈⲈⲞⲨⲚⲦⲔⲘⲚⲦⲚⲞⲋ | ⲦⲈⲔⲘ[ⲚⲦⲉ]ⲟⲧ
ⲘⲎⲦⲈⲢⲞ---ⲋⲁ-----------------------
------------------ | ⲈⲢⲈⲡⲈⲤⲘⲞⲨⲡⲢⲈⲡⲒⲚⲀⲔⲡⲚⲞⲨⲦⲈ2ⲚⲤⲒⲰⲚ | Ⲁⲩ̄
ϣⲈϥⲚⲀ†ⲚⲀⲔⲚⲚⲈⲨⲢⲎⲦ2ⲑⲒⲗⲎⲘ | ⲥ[ϣ.ⲡ]ⲀⲈⲡⲚⲞⲨⲗⲎⲗⲈⲢⲈⲞⲨⲞⲚ[Ⲛ
.ⲛ]ⲎⲨⲈ | .]Ⲥⲡ2 . ⲀⲚϣⲀⲬⲈⲚⲚⲀⲚⲞⲘⲞⲥ[ⲋ]ⲘⲋⲞⲘ | Ⲟ] ⲢⲈⲚ:
ⲀⲨⲀⲒⲚⲦⲞⲘⲈⲦⲘⲀⲔϣ . ⲞⲞⲗⲘⲎⲚ . | ϣ] Ⲙϥⲡ: ⲚⲒⲚⲘⲀⲬϥⲈⲡⲢⲱⲘⲈ
ⲈⲢⲞⲥⲦⲞⲔϣⲀϣⲨₐω: | .] ⲚⲀⲞⲨϣ22ⲚⲚⲈⲡⲀⲨⲗⲎ: ⲦⲚⲚⲀⲈⲚⲈⲂⲞⲗ |
ϥⲚⲀⲅⲀⲑⲞⲚⲘⲡ . . ⲡⲦⲞⲈⲒⲤⲈⲢⲔⲈⲞⲨⲗⲀⲂ | ⲨϣⲘⲈⲈⲡⲈ2ⲚⲀⲒⲔⲈⲟ̄
ⲤⲨⲚⲎ: ⲤϣⲦⲘⲈⲢⲞⲘ | ⲡ]ⲚⲞⲨⲦⲈⲡⲘⲤⲞⲦⲎⲢ . Ⲉⲗⲡ . ⲈⲘⲈⲔⲞϣⲞⲨ
|]ⲦⲎⲢⲞ . ⲘⲡⲔⲀ2 . ⲀⲨϣⲚⲈⲦ2ⲎⲑⲀⲗⲀⲤⲤⲀ[|]ⲦⲞⲨⲡⲀϣⲁ
ⲤⲞϥⲡⲈⲡⲦⲚⲘⲈⲚⲦⲞⲞⲨ 2ⲚⲦ[ϥ. | Ⲉ]ϥϣⲦⲢ2ⲚⲞⲨⲋⲞⲘⲡⲈⲦⲈⲨⲦⲞⲢⲦⲈⲢ
ⲁ.ⲡⲟⲥ | ϣ]ϣⲤⲚⲑⲀⲗⲀⲤⲤⲀⲦϣⲡ[2 .ⲡ]Ⲉ2ⲢⲀⲞⲨⲚⲚⲈⲥ_____ |]2ⲞⲈⲒ
. ⲤⲈⲚⲀϣⲦⲞⲢⲦⲢ[ϣ ⲋ]ⲒⲚ2ⲈⲞⲚⲞⲤ | ⲚⲤⲈⲈⲢ2ⲈⲦⲀⲚⲋⲒⲚⲈ†ⲞⲨⲎⲦ2Ⲛ[
. .Ⲟ]ϣⲞⲨ | 2ⲎⲦⲞⲨⲚⲚⲈⲔⲘⲘⲈⲒ[Ⲛ |

VKC Ms
Isaiah 57:1–3; 57:21—58:2

A folio leaf from a parchment codex. *Present Size*, 153 x 109 mm. *Conservation*: Encapsulated in Mylar. *Ancient pagination*: No; modern inventory number 5a recorded in pencil on the F side at the right foot of the leaf. *Damage*: Torn; holes; worn; dark areas caused by deterioration. *Palimpsest*: No. *Corrections*: None apparent. *Marginal Apparatus*: Perhaps on F side in the center column. *Ancient Annotations*: No. *Collation*: No remains of signatures, no quire ornaments, no monograms, headlines apparent, no catchwords; or apparent verse marks. *Writing Material*: Parchment: H distinguishable by color and grain; the recto (= true recto) is H. Evidence of ruling lines. *Layout*: Two columns per side; writing on both sides; 103 mm per column. *Script*: Same script with the possible exception of 10c F top 3–4 lines; orientation right slope; 3-stroke Μ, ЄΟⲤ wide/round, ⲢϤⲨ short, with the classical non-looped Ⲩ, average height 7 mm, superlineation for single letters, abbreviations not apparent, non-standard; serifs, dieresis; Coptic single period; no apostrophes or tremas present. *Decoration:* None; no major initials or initials; no lectional signs or scrolls seen; an extended letter; no color; no illumination. *Contents*: Isaiah 57:1–3; 57:21—58:2. No colophons, corrections, marginal notes or ancient annotations. *There are no related texts in this collection. Date*: This manuscript dates between 450–550 AD.

(See **Figure** 15a)

Recto a | . | ⲦⲞ[Ⲩ.]Є[| ⲀⲚ[Ⲁ Ⲛ]ⲦⲀ | Ⲁ̣[. ⲔⲰ]ⲞⳠ[Ⲟ. . .]
Ⲱ | ⲘⲚⲀⲀⲀⲨ[Ⲟ]ⲱⲡⲈⲢⲞϤ . | ⲡⲈϤ2ⲎⲦ ⲀⲨⲰⲤⲈϤⲓⲚ̄ | ⲓ[. .]
ⲘⲈⲚⲀⲓⲔⲀⲓⲞⳠ ⲀⲨⲰ | Ⲙ. .]ⲀⲨⲦⲚ2ⲦⲎϤ ⲀⲨⲰ | [Ⲙ. .] ⲀⲨⲦⲚ2ⲦⲎϤ
. ⲀⲨ | . [.]ⲘⲡⲀⲓⲔⲀⲓⲞⲤⲚ[.]2 | [. . ⲭ]ⲓⲚⲈⲞⲘⲞ̣ . [ⲦⲈ̣ | ⲔⲀ[.
.]ⲚⲀⲱ[.]ⲡⲉ̣ϤⲚⲞⲨ | Ⲉⲡ[.]ⲚⲎⲀⲨ[Ⲱ]ⲦϤⲚⲦⲘⲎ | ⲦⲈⲚⲦⲰⲦⲚⲀⲈ2Ⲱ[. . .]
| 2ⲞⲨⲚⲈⲡⲈ̈ⲓⲘⲀⲡⲈⳠ[. | ⲘⲀⲚⲚⲀ[Ọ . . . . . | [. . . . Ọ

SCOTT CARROLL

(See Figure 15b)

Verso a |ⲱ] | .ⲡ] | ⲁ] | ⲉ] | .] | *Verso b* | .][| .ⲉ.][ⲙⲉ][. | ϥⲓ[. .]ⲭⲓ[ⲛ . | .[ⲧ.ⲁ][.ⲱ][ⲛⲉⲩ | ϭⲟⲙⲛⲙ̄ⲧⲟⲛⲙ ⲙⲟⲟ[ⲩ | ⲙⲛ̄ ⲣⲁⲱⲉⲱⲟⲟⲡⲛⲛⲁ | ⲥⲉⲃⲏⲥⲡⲉⲭⲉⲡⲭ[. . .]ⲥ | ⲡⲛⲟⲩⲧⲉ :ⲱ[.]ⲃⲟⲗ | ⳨ⲟⲩϭⲟⲙⲛ̄ⲅⲧⲙ̄[†]ⲟ. | [ⲩ.ⳡ]ⲉⲛ̄ⲧ[ⲉ]ⲕⲥⲙⲏ[. .]ⲉ | ⲛⲟⲩⲥⲁⲗ[.]ⲓⲅⲍ̄ⲛ[. ⲭ]ⲱ | ⲙ̄ⲡⲁⲗⲗⲟⲥⲛⲛⲉⲩ[ⲛⲟ]ⲃⲉ | ⲩⲡⲏⲓ̈ⲛⲓ̈ⲁⲕⲱⲃⲛ̄ⲛⲉⲩ | .]ⲟⲙⲓⲁ ⲁⲛⲟⲕⲥⲉⲱⲓ | [. . . ⲓ̈ . ⲟⲩ. . ⲩ . |

VKC

Ecclesiasticus 2:1–6; 8–11

A folio leaf from a parchment codex. *Present Size*, 220 x 185 mm. *Conservation*: Encapsulated in Mylar. *Ancient pagination*: Trace on H side left head corner and F side right head corner ⲡⲉ̄; modern inventory number 22n recorded in pencil on the F side midway up the right margin. *Damage*: Torn; holes; worn H side; dark areas caused by deterioration. *Palimpsest*: Retrievable minuscule Syriac text. *Corrections:* None apparent. *Marginal Apparatus:* No. *Ancient Annotations:* No. *Collation:* No remains of signatures, unless a trace on the H side; no quire ornaments, no monograms, headlines apparent, no catchwords, or apparent verse marks. *Writing Material:* Parchment: H distinguishable by color and grain; the recto (= true recto) is H. Evidence of ruling lines. *Layout:* Two columns per side; writing on both sides; 77 mm per column. *Script:* Same script both sides; orientation upright; 3-stroke ⲙ, ⲉⲟⲥ wide/round, ⲣϥ tall ⲩ short, with the classical non-looped ⲩ, average height 7 mm, superlineation for single letters, abbreviations, nonstandard; serifs, dieresis; Coptic double period; no apostrophes or tremas present. *Decoration:* None; no major initials or initials; no lectional signs or scrolls seen; an extended letter; no color; no illumination. *Contents*: Ecclesiasticus 2:1–6; 8–11. No colophons, corrections, marginal notes or ancient annotations. *There are no related texts in this collection. Date*: This manuscript dates between 550–650 AD.

(See Figure 16a)

Recto a | ⲁ]2ⲁⲡⲉⲡⲕⲟ̄ ϯⲛⲁ | ⲟ]ⲩⲛⲧⲁⲃⲱⲕ | .]ⲉⲓⲱⲧ: ⲧⲁ | ⲁ]ϥ
ⲭⲉⲡⲁ | .]ⲟⲃⲉⲉ | ⲡ]ⲉⲕ | .]ϯⲙ̄ | .]ⲉⲛⲩⲟ | ⲭ]ⲉ | .] | .] | Recto
b | 2ⲁⲗⲭⲉ6ⲉⲡⲏⲁⲛⲓ | ⲛⲉⲉⲃⲟⲗⲛ̄ⲧⲉⲥϯⲟ | ⲗⲏⲉⲧⲛⲁⲛⲟⲩⲥ | ⲛ̄
ⲧⲉⲧⲛⲧⲁⲁⲥ2ⲓⲱ | ⲱϥ ⲛ̄ⲧⲉⲧⲛ̄ϯⲛ | ⲟⲩ2ⲟⲩⲣⲉⲧⲉϥ6ⲓⲭ | ⲁⲩⲱⲟⲩ̄
ⲧⲟⲟⲩⲉⲉ | ⲛⲉ[ϥ]ⲟⲩⲉⲣⲏⲧⲉ | ⲛ̄ⲧⲉⲧⲛ̄ⲙ̄ⲡⲙⲁ | ⲥⲉⲉⲧⲛⲁⲛⲁⲭ̄ⲱⲧ |
ⲛⲧⲉⲧⲛ̄ⲕⲟⲛⲥ̄ϥ | ⲛⲧⲉⲧⲛ̄ⲟⲩⲱⲙ | ⲛⲧⲉⲧⲛ̄ⲉⲩⲫⲣⲁ | .ⲁ]ϥⲱⲗⲓ2 ⲛⲉϥ
| ⲱⲡⲉⲁⲓ̈2ⲉⲉ | .]ⲁⲩⲁⲣⲭⲓⲁⲉ | ⲫ]ⲣⲁⲛⲉ ⲛⲉ | ⲛ]ⲟ6ⲁⲉⲛ̄ | ⲡ]ⲉ2ⲛ̄
ⲧ[ⲥⲱ | ⲛ]ⲏⲩⲁⲉ | .]2ⲱ[ⲛ. |][. ⲓ̈

(See Figure 16b)

Verso a | ⲡⲉⲭⲁϥⲭⲉⲡⲉⲕⲉⲟ̣ | ⲡ2ⲛⲧⲁϥⲉⲓ̈ ⲁⲡⲉⲕ | ⲉⲓ̣ⲱⲧⲱⲱⲧ |
ⲉⲣⲟϥⲙⲡⲙⲁⲥⲉ | ⲉⲧⲥⲁⲛⲁϣ̄ⲧⲭⲉ | ⲁϥ2ⲉⲉⲣⲟϥⲉϥⲟⲩ | ⲟⲭ ⲁϥⲛⲟⲩ.
ⲥⲁ2 | ⲙ̄ⲡ̄ϥⲟⲩⲉⲱ̣ⲃⲱⲕ | ⲉ2ⲟⲩⲛ ⲁⲡⲉϥⲉⲓ̈ | ⲱⲧⲉⲓⲉⲃⲟⲗⲁϥ |
ⲥⲉⲧⲥⲱⲡ̄ϥ ⲛ̄ | ⲧⲟϥⲁⲉⲁϥⲟⲩⲱ | ϣ̄ⲃⲡⲉⲭⲁϥⲙ̄[ⲡ | ⲉⲓⲱⲧⲭⲉⲉⲓⲥⲟ[
| ⲙ̣ⲏⲏϣ̣ⲉⲛ̄ⲣ[. | ϯⲟ̄ⲛ2ⲙ2ⲁⲗ[| ⲙ̣ⲡ.ⲕⲱⲛ̄ⲟ[| ⲛⲉ2ⲛ̄ⲟⲩ[ⲉ | ⲙ̣ⲓ̣ⲛⲧⲟ[.
| ⲙ̄ⲙ̄ⲙ̄ⲡ̄ⲕ [| ⲟ̣]ⲩⲙⲁ[ⲥ̣ | ⲡ̣].[ⲉⲧ][|][. | Verso a | ⲡⲙⲁⲥⲉⲉⲧ̄
ⲥⲁⲛ[| ϣ̄ⲧⲛ̄ⲧⲧⲟϥ[. | ⲭⲁϥⲛⲁϥ [ⲭ̣ | ϣⲛⲣⲉ[. | ϣⲟ[ⲟ | ⲁⲩ[| [.
| [. |

Figures

Figure 1
VKC Sennacherib Prism

Figure 2
VKC Greek Gospel—John 7–8

Figure 3
VKC Mississippi Codex II

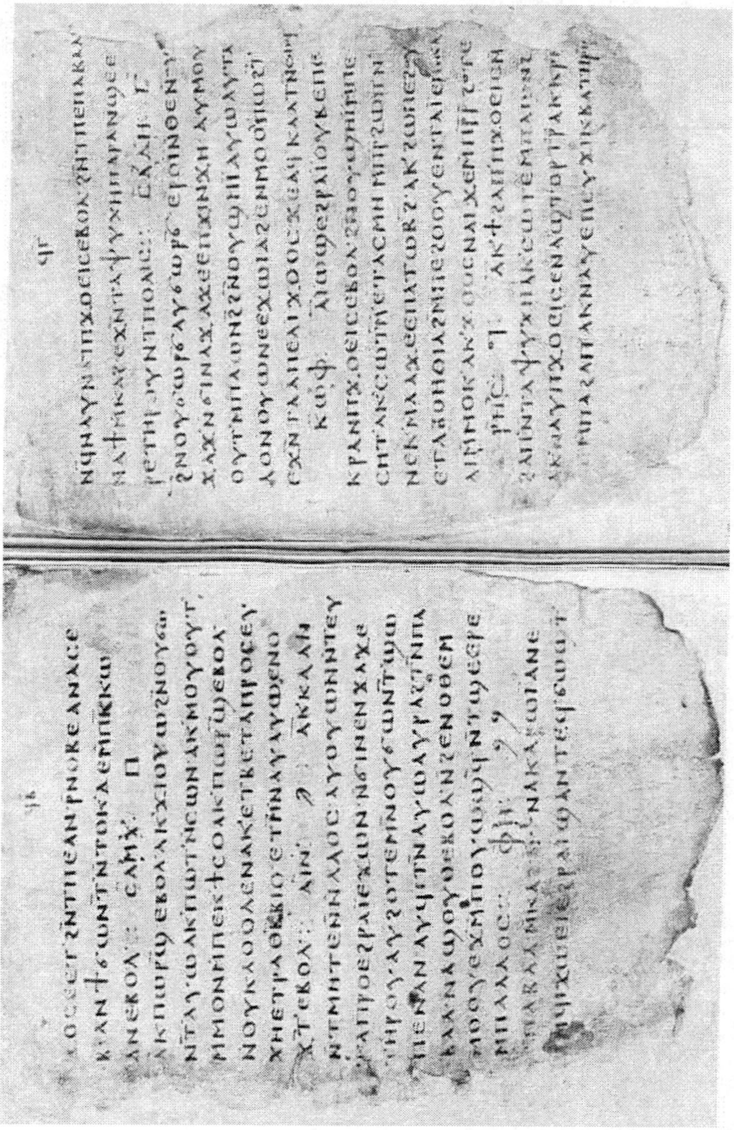

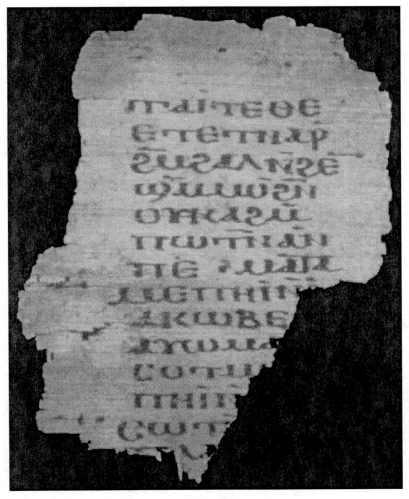

Figure 4
VKC Coptic Papyrus

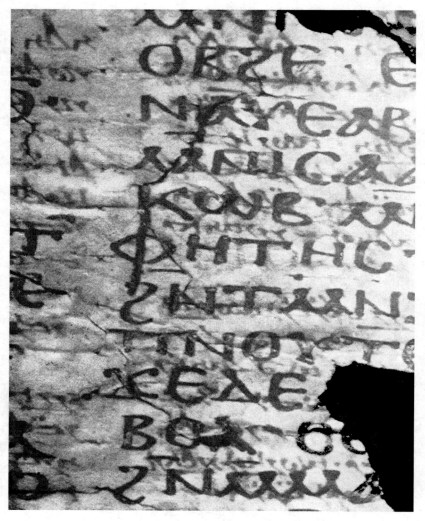

Figure 5
VKC Coptic-Syriac Palimpsest

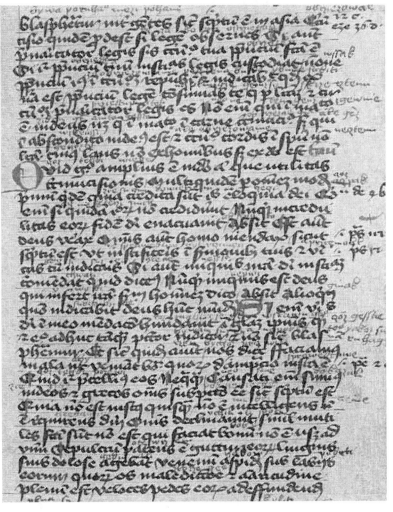

Figure 6
VKC Codex Wernegerodensis

Figure 7
Eberhard Nestle

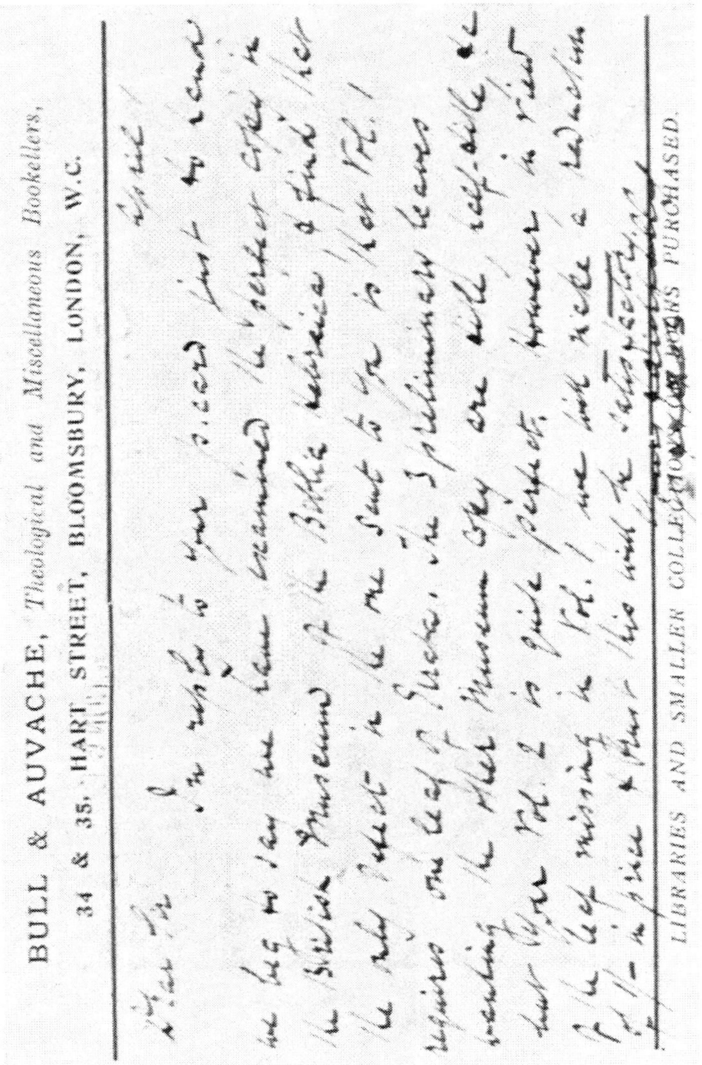
BULL & AUVACHE, *Theological and Miscellaneous Booksellers,*

34 & 35, HART STREET, BLOOMSBURY, LONDON, W.C.

LIBRARIES AND SMALLER COLLECTIONS OF BOOKS PURCHASED.

Figure 8
Book Seller's Note to Nestle

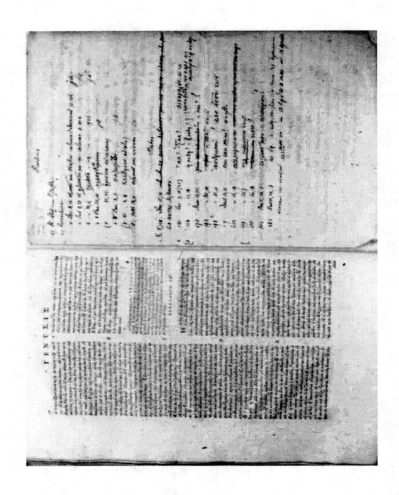

Figure 9
LXX with Nestle's Notes

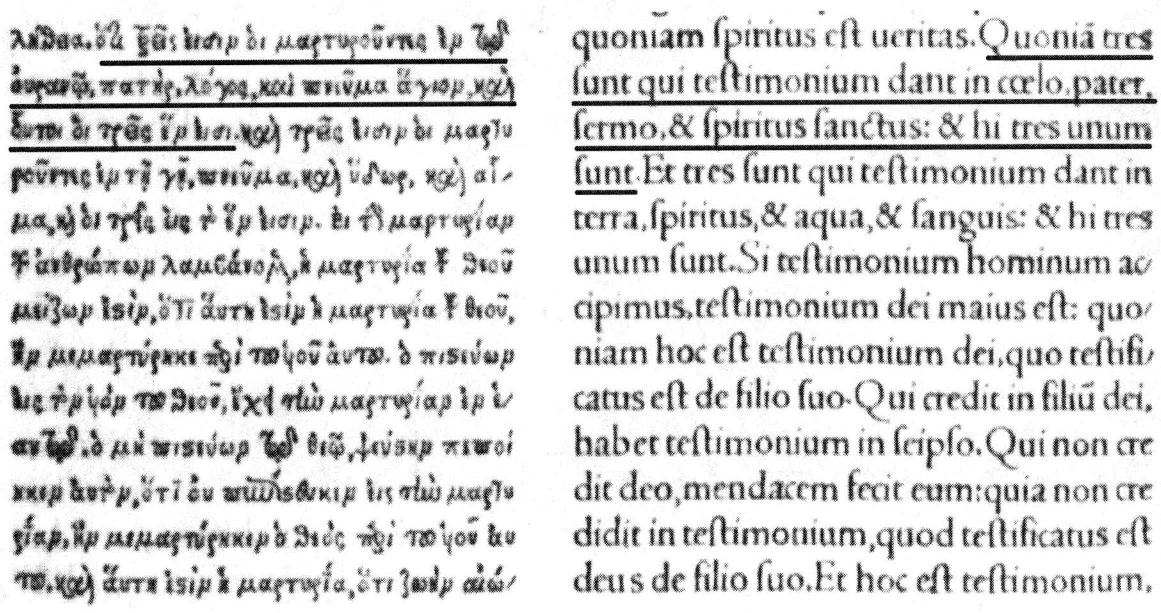
λήθεια. ὅτι τρεῖς εἰσιν οἱ μαρτυροῦντες ἐν τῷ
οὐρανῷ, πατήρ, λόγος, καὶ πνεῦμα ἅγιον, καὶ
οὗτοι οἱ τρεῖς ἕν εἰσι. καὶ τρεῖς εἰσιν οἱ μαρτυ
ροῦντες ἐν τῇ γῇ, πνεῦμα, καὶ ὕδωρ, καὶ αἷ-
μα, καὶ οἱ τρεῖς εἰς τὸ ἕν εἰσιν. εἰ τὴν μαρτυρίαν
τῶν ἀνθρώπων λαμβάνομεν, ἡ μαρτυρία τοῦ θεοῦ
μείζων ἐστίν, ὅτι αὕτη ἐστὶν ἡ μαρτυρία τοῦ θεοῦ,
ἣν μεμαρτύρηκε περὶ τοῦ υἱοῦ αὐτοῦ. ὁ πιστεύων
εἰς τὸν υἱὸν τοῦ θεοῦ, ἔχει τὴν μαρτυρίαν ἐν ἑ-
αυτῷ. ὁ μὴ πιστεύων τῷ θεῷ, ψεύστην πεποί
ηκεν αὐτόν, ὅτι οὐ πεπίστευκεν εἰς τὴν μαρτυ
ρίαν, ἣν μεμαρτύρηκεν ὁ θεὸς περὶ τοῦ υἱοῦ αὐ
τοῦ. καὶ αὕτη ἐστὶν ἡ μαρτυρία, ὅτι ζωὴν αἰώ-

quoniam ſpiritus eſt ueritas. Quoniã tres
ſunt qui teſtimonium dant in cœlo, pater,
ſermo, & ſpiritus ſanctus: & hi tres unum
ſunt. Et tres ſunt qui teſtimonium dant in
terra, ſpiritus, & aqua, & ſanguis: & hi tres
unum ſunt. Si teſtimonium hominum ac-
cipimus, teſtimonium dei maius eſt: quoniam hoc eſt teſtimonium dei, quo teſtificatus eſt de filio ſuo. Qui credit in filiũ dei,
habet teſtimonium in ſeipſo. Qui non cre
dit deo, mendacem fecit eum: quia non cre
didit in teſtimonium, quod teſtificatus eſt
deus de filio ſuo. Et hoc eſt teſtimonium,

Figure 10
Erasmus NT 2d ed.—Johannine Coma

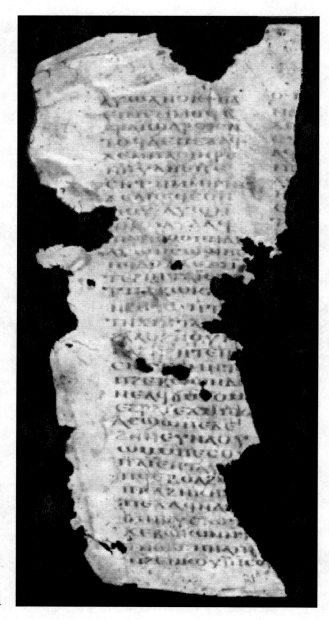

Figure 11a

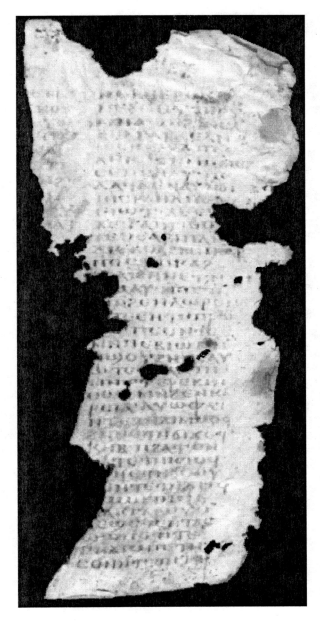

Figure 11b

Figure 12a

Figure 12b

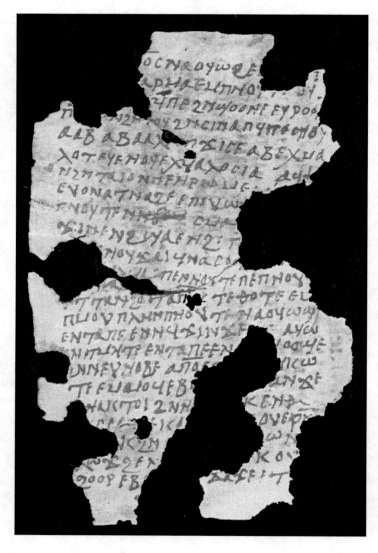

Figure 13a

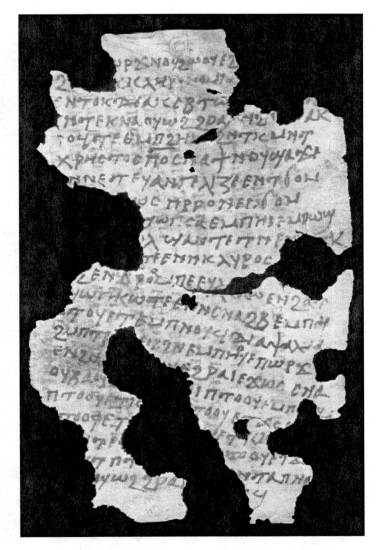

Figure 13b

Figure 14a

Figure 14b

Figure 15a

Figure 15b

Figure 16a

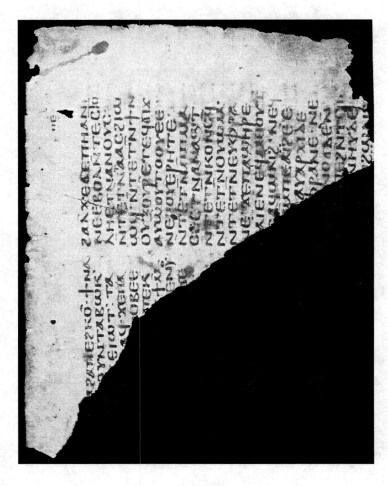

Figure 16b